Congress and Policy Change

The Contributors

David W. Brady

Edward G. Carmines

Lawrence C. Dodd

Richard F. Fenno, Jr.

John Ferejohn

Marjorie Randon Hershey

Roberta Herzberg

Leroy N. Rieselbach

Barbara Sinclair

James A. Stimson

Gerald C. Wright, Jr.

Congress and Policy Change

Edited by

Gerald C. Wright, Jr.
University of Indiana

Leroy N. Rieselbach
University of Indiana

Lawrence C. Dodd
The University of Colorado, Boulder

AGATHON PRESS, INC.
New York

Library of Congress Cataloging-in-Publication Data

Congress and policy change.

"Earlier versions of most of these papers were
delivered at the Indiana University Conference on
Congress and Policy Change in April 1983"—Acknowledge-
ments.
    Includes bibliographies and index.
    Contents: A theory of congressional cycles/Lawrence
C. Dodd—Electoral realignments in the U.S. House of
Representatives/David W. Brady—The politics and
policy of race in Congress/Edward G. Carmines and James
A. Stimson—[etc.]
    1. United States.   Congress—Congresses.
I. Wright, Gerald C., Jr.   II. Rieselbach, Leroy N.   III. Dodd,
Lawrence C.   IV. Indiana University Conference on Congress
and Policy Change (1983).
JK1061.C5857   1986   328.7   86-17429
ISBN 0-87586-076-1
ISBN 0-87586-077-X (pbk).

Contents

Preface   vii

The Contributors   xi

Part I.
A Theory of Congressional Change

1. A Theory of Congressional Cycles:
Solving the Puzzle of Change

Lawrence C. Dodd   3

Part II.
The Electoral Sources of
Policy Change in Congress

2. Electoral Realignments
in the U. S. House of Representatives

David W. Brady   47

3. The Politics and Policy of Race in Congress

Edward G. Carmines and James A. Stimson   70

4. Elections and the Potential for Policy Change
in Congress: The House of Representatives

Gerald C. Wright, Jr.   94

Part III.
From Electioneering to Policy Making:
Learning and Adjustment

5. Adjusting to the U. S. Senate

Richard F. Fenno, Jr.   123

6. Campaign Learning,
Congressional Behavior, and Policy Change

               Marjorie Randon Hershey   148

Part IV.
Leadership, Rules,
and the Congressional Policy Process

7. Party Leadership and Policy Change

                     Barbara Sinclair   175

8. Blocking Coalitions and Policy Change

                   Roberta Herzberg   201

9. Logrolling in an Institutional Context:
A Case Study of Food Stamp Legislation

                    John Ferejohn   223

Part V.
Conclusion: Pulling the Pieces Together

10. Congress and Policy Change:
Issues, Answers, and Prospects

                 Leroy N. Rieselbach   257

Index   290

Preface

Students of American politics have a particular fondness for Congress. More than the other branches of our national government, the presidency and the Supreme Court, those who study Congress have had personal contact with that institution and its members. The 535 members of Congress are necessarily more accessible than one President and his immediate staff, or the nine justices of the Court, and many congressional scholars have had experience as legislative staff or congressional fellows. The presidency and the Court, by comparison, are more remote and less accessible, and probably to some extent because of this, less thoroughly studied than the House of Representatives and Senate.

The major reason for studying Congress, however, is its constitutional role as the chief policy-making body in the country. The policy-making process in Congress is complicated greatly by our expectations that members of Congress act as representatives. They are delegates for the interests of their districts and their states and as such are necessarily in regular contact with their constituents and spokespersons for policy interests. They need to be concerned with reelection and with achieving personal, partisan, and constituent goals in Washington. As the size of government has grown, so has the policy-making role of all branches of the government, and for Congress, especially, this has entailed tremendous growth in its internal complexity, staff, and the demands placed on its members. These, like changes in the nature of elections over the last thirty years, have important and varied effects on the policies that Congress adopts.

This book is about congressional policy making, and particularly processes by which congressional policy changes—and does not change. At times in our history Congress has been a policy initiator, at others it has been the bastion of resistance to new directions of government action. It reflects the will of the citizenry at times, while at others its rules and processes have done more to serve the interests of special and minority interests.

Studying the processes of policy change in Congress and the forces that give rise to change presents interesting challeges. Congress is more than the sum of its parts. It is more than the representatives and senators that fulfill those roles at any time; more than the buildings on Capitol Hill; and more than a reflection of the wishes and interests of people the institution represents. Congress is all of these things plus its evolving norms and rules for how it makes decisions. It is a complex institution, composed of elected representatives and senators, staff, and historical traditions, all interacting with ever growing sets of interest groups, as well as the demands and constraints placed upon it by a national agenda of economic, social, and technical problems as well as other institutions of gevernment.

Congress considers thousands of bills each session and, in recent years, it enacts into law around a thousand bills each congress. Much of this is of little consequence for the country. The effects of most bills are negligible, while a few do bring about noticeable, but still incremental, policy change. Major policy change, departures that chart genuinely new directions of governmental action, or initiate government action in new areas, is rare. To achieve it requires special sets of circumstances—discussed at length in the essays here—and these must be viewed in the context of an institution better suited to protecting the status quo than to embracing bold policy actions.

The first chapter is an overview of Congress and the policy process from the perspective of the individual member of Congress. Lawrence Dodd develops a theory of congressional behavior that rests on a simple set of assumptions about the goals of individual representatives. He then builds on these in the context of Congress to lay out for us an unusually comprehensive view of the relationship among members' goals, the institution of which they are a part, and the policies they bring into being.

From this overview we then stand back from the institution in the second section and look at congressional elections and their effects on congresssional policy change. In chapter 2, David Brady provides a perspective on the nature of electoral realignments and how these influence policy change in Congress. The time perspective is shorter in the research presented by Edward Carmines and James Stimson in chapter 3. They describe the evolution of the civil rights issue in the Congress since World War II, and they explain the dynamics by which the parties took clearly opposing stands on racial issues, arguably the most important and enduring cleavage of American politics. In both of these chapters we see how elections bring about changes in Congress, and how these changes then influence the policies and consequent behavior of parties, and, through this, the voters in U.S. national politics. The final chapter in this section, by Gerald Wright, shows the potential for policy change in the current era, and then describes how the incumbency advantage in House elections, which has grown substantially in the last 30 years, has a major dampening effect on the responsiveness of Congress to electoral change.

The two essays that make up the third section, chapters 5 and 6, ask how the electoral campaigns—periodically faced by all members of Congress—influence what members do. Here, Marjorie Hershey draws on social learning theory to illuminate what members learn from their campaign experiences and how this influences the goals they adopt and the roles they set for themselves. Richard Fenno's essay draws on his close-hand observations of senators, first in the 1980 elections and then in Washington. He paints a vivid portrait of what he calls "the adjustment process," the crucial transition from a campaigner to legislator. Understanding not just that there are different arenas in which congressmen operate but the effects of one on the other informs our analysis of members' behavior in the institution and in the policy-making process.

The next section focuses on how congressional procedures and leadership combine to affect the nature and processes of coalition building in Congress. Without highly disciplined parties, policy change must necessarily be preceded by the difficult task of putting and holding together majority coalitions. In chapter 7, Barbara Sinclair discusses the resources and strategies employed by the leadership in the House of Representatives, and how the challenges of the leadership have evolved over time. Roberta Herzberg in chapter 8 lays out for us the many mechanisms used for blocking legislation and thereby highlights the challenge faced by coalitions builders in today's Congress. John Ferejohn in chapter 9 describes the interesting legislative history of the food stamp program to illustrate one important process of coalition building, the legislative logroll. Within this the party leadership in Congress must operate.

The nine chapters in the first four sections describe a good deal about Congress, and particularly about the difficult process of making and sustaining new directions in public policy. Finally, in chapter 10 Leroy Rieselbach synthesizes the elements of the various essays into an overall statement of what we know about the processes of policy change in Congress. He also offers some useful guideposts on where we go from here in future research.

Acknowledgments

Earlier versions of most of these papers were delivered at the Indiana University Conference on Congress and Policy Change in April, 1983. We would like to express our appreciation to the other participants at that conference, whose helpful and good natured comments assisted the authors significantly in revising the papers for this volume. These included Samuel Patterson, Thomas Mann, Robert Erikson, and James Kuklinski. We would like to thank Elinor Ostrom for arranging for the conference series while she was chairperson of the Department of Political Science and for obtaining initial funding. We also wish to thank the Indiana University Office of Research and Graduate Development and the Vice President for the Bloomington campus for providing those finds. Editorial and technical assistance was provided by Christine Barbour and Carolyn Cooke. We are especially grateful to Fern Bennett, who assisted through the entire project from handling all of the administration of the conference through preparation of the manuscript for Agathon Press, whom we also thank for their patience and support.

About the Contributors

David W. Brady is the Herbert Autrey Professor of Social Sciences at Rice University. He received his Ph.D. in political science from the University of Iowa in 1970. His publications include *Congressional Voting in a Partisan Era: A Study of the McKinley Houses* (1973); *Public Policy and Politics in America*, 2nd ed. (1984); *Public Policy in the Eighties* (1983); and numerous articles in professional journals. He has recently completed a Project 87-funded manuscript on critical elections in the U.S. House of Representatives.

Edward G. Carmines is Professor of Political Science at Indiana University, Bloomington. He is the coauthor of *Statistical Analysis of Social Data* (1978) and *Measurement in the Social Sciences* (1980) as well as numerous articles in professional journals. His major areas of interest are mass political behavior and quantitative methods.

Lawrence C. Dodd is Professor of Political Science at the University of Colorado, Boulder, and Director of the University's Center for the Study of American Politics. He is currently working on a general theory of legislative change, focused particularly on the U.S. Congress. Additional research interests include a comparative state study of the career patterns of professional and citizen legislators, and a crossnational study of the effect of electoral laws on the representativeness of democratic regimes. He is the author of *Coalitions in Parliamentary Government;* the coauthor, with Richard Schott, of *Congress and the Administrative State;* and the coeditor, with Bruce Oppenheimer, of *Congress Reconsidered.*

Richard F. Fenno, Jr. is Kenan Professor of Political Science at the University of Rochester. He specializes in the study of the U.S. Congress. His books on that subject include: *The Power of the Purse: Appropriations Politics in Congress; Congressmen in Committees;* and *Home Style: House Members in Their Districts.* He is currently at work on a study of the United States Senate.

John Ferejohn is Professor of Political Science at Stanford University and a Senior Research Fellow at the Hoover Institution. His research interests are centered in the study of legislative and electoral institutions, and he has written extensively on these topics. He is the author of *Pork Barrel Politics* (1974).

Marjorie Randon Hershey is Professor of Political Science at Indiana University. She studies political campaigns: what campaigners learn from campaign experiences and election results, and how their learning affects their behavior. She has published articles on political learning in a variety of journals, and is the author of *Running for Office: The Political Education of Campaigners* and *The Making of Campaign Strategy.*

xi

Roberta Herzberg is Assistant Professor of Political Science at Indiana University. Her main research interests concern the effects of institutional rules and structure of legislative choice processes. Combining the techniques of analytic choice modeling and an interest in congressional decision making, she is presently studying how rules and structural complexity relate to decision making costs.

Leroy N. Rieselbach is Professor of Political Science at Indiana University. His research focuses on Congress, and his publications include *The Roots of Isolationism* (1966); *Congressional Politics* (1973); *Congressional Reform in the Seventies*, with Joseph K. Unekis (1977); *Congressional Committee Politics* (1984); as well as a variety of journal articles and chapters contributed to books.

Barbara Sinclair is Professor of Political Science at the University of California, Riverside. Her writings on the U.S. Congress include *Congressional Realignment* (1982) and *Majority Leadership in the U.S. House* (1983). Her research centers on questions about policy change and institutional change.

James A. Stimson is Professor of Political Science at the University of Houston. He has written on Congress, the presidency, mass political behavior, and time series methods. He is completing a book (with Carmines) on the racial restructuring of American politics. He is coauthor, with Donald R. Matthews, of *Yeas and Nays: Normal Decision-Making in the U. S. House of Representatives*.

Gerald C. Wright, Jr. is Associate Professor of Political Science at Indiana University and Director of the Indiana Political Data Archive and Laboratory. He was previously Program Director for Political Science at the National Science Foundation. His research interests are in congressional and state elections and particularly on the relationship between public opinion and public policy. He is the author of *Electoral Choice in America* as well as numerous articles in professional journals.

Part

I

A Theory of
Congressional Change

1

A Theory of Congressional Cycles: Solving the Puzzle of Change

Lawrence C. Dodd

Events of the 1970s caught students of Congress by surprise. Postwar scholars had concluded that the modern Congress was a stagnant and impotent institution, incapable of rapid change or rejuvenation (Burns, 1963; Huntington, 1965). Yet in the 1970s it suddenly experienced precisely those reforms—the weakening of seniority and the Senate filibuster, the creation of a centralized budget process, the strengthening of the congressional parties—that had previously seemed impossible. These reforms, in turn, produced a dramatic resurgence in the policy activism of Congress (Sundquist, 1981).

This unexpected revitalization of Congress has presented scholars with an intriguing puzzle—the puzzle of change. Scholars can no longer hope to understand Congress fully until they can explain the processes that generate institutional change (Cooper and Brady, 1981b; Huntington, 1971; Polsby, 1975). To understand these processes, to solve the puzzle of change, scholars must construct a theory of Congress that is dynamic in character, plausible, well-grounded in existing knowledge about Congress, and susceptible to empirical test.

This chapter seeks to construct such a theory. It does so by building on empirical discoveries of the 1970s and early 1980s.[1] During this period legislative scholars sought to explain the recent congressional reforms by identifying the historical forces that gave rise to them (Cooper, 1971, 1975; Dodd, 1977, 1981; Huntington, 1981; Strom and Rundquist, 1978; Sundquist, 1981). Scholars found that the upheavals of the 1970s were not a unique occurrence to be explained by special historical circumstance. They were the product of broad and recurring cycles of change that had characterized Congress throughout its existence. These historical patterns

3

suggest that a theory of change, and thereby an explanation of the reforms and policy resurgence of the past fifteen years, lies in developing a theory of congressional cycles.[2]

These cycles of congressional change have occurred at three levels. The first level involves long-term fragmentation and short-term reform of the organizational procedures of Congress, everything from the number of committees and subcommittees to the staff allotments given to members. The second level involves the long-term rigidification of the institutional structure of Congress—the persistence of rules that imposed party government in much of the nineteenth century, for example, or committee government through much of the twentieth century—followed by intense periods of upheaval and structural transformation. The third level involves cyclical change in the policy performance of Congress. This performance declines in periods of fragmentation and rigidification and rebounds in periods of reform and structural reorganization.

The theory presented here argues that these cycles of change, and thus the reforms and policy resurgence of the 1970s, result from legislators' desire to exercise policy making power—to have an autonomous and significant impact on the nation's policy decisions. To attain their primary goal of power, legislators pursue two subsidiary goals: mastery of organizational politics within Congress, and mastery of electoral politics in their external constituencies. A legislator must realize both of these subsidiary goals to exercise policy making power.

The three cycles of change are a product of the pursuit of the two subsidiary goals. The pursuit of organizational mastery generates the cycles of organizational fragmentation and reform. The pursuit of electoral mastery generates the cycles of structural transformation. The organizational and institutional cycles together produce the cyclical changes in policy performance. The remainder of this chapter develops these arguments more extensively, starting with a discussion of the internal changes in congressional organization.

THE THEORY OF ORGANIZATIONAL CYCLES

The internal world of Congress is critical to members because it is the arena in which they acquire positions of power and influence. These positions carry with them those organizational resources—staff assistance, access to information, control over parliamentary procedure, and the like— that a member must possess if he is to have a significant personal impact on congressional policy making. Power-oriented members thus give considerable attention to the internal politics of Congress (Dodd, 1977; Schwarz and Shaw, 1976; Wolfinger and Heifetz, 1965; Jones and Woll, 1979). Their attention is focused on more, however, than the acquisition of resources. For positions of power such as committee or subcommittee chairmanships to enhance a member's policy impact he also needs the respect and support of his colleagues (Huitt, 1961, 1965; Manley, 1969; Matthews, 1960; Price, 1972). Only if they respect him and trust him will they listen to him seriously, negotiate with him, and follow his leadership. And only if his colleagues have confidence in him will they award him the additional discretionary positions and resources under their control (Peabody, 1976). The personal support of members thus is just as critical to his organizational career as is the formal acquisition of power positions and resources.

The legislator's personal impact on congressional policy making thus depends on his mastery of organizational politics, that is, on his ability to gain and use the resources and skills necessary both to attain positions of power and influence and to gain the personal trust of colleagues. The struggle to develop organizational skills while competing for the appropriate resources necessarily leads to a great deal of frustration on the part of legislators: few will ever be able to gain resources and skills as rapidly as they desire. Their frustration, or their anxiety over the slowness and tenuousness of career advancement, generates the cycles of organizational fragmentation and reform. To explain the organizational cycles we thus must first understand members' career behavior within Congress, particularly the ways they develop organizational mastery and advance their internal organizational careers.

Organizational Careers and the Stages of Mastery

Career advancement within Congress is the process by which legislators gain mastery of organizational resources and skills (Bardach, 1972; Evans and Novak, 1966; Huitt, 1961, 1965; Manley, 1969; Matthews, 1960; Muir, 1982). To become a successful powerwielder, a legislator must exercise mastery in four areas of organizational life: those that affect member's personal reelection, development of policy expertise, influence over other members, and control over organizational decision making (Dodd, 1977; Fenno, 1973; Mayhew, 1974). Only when a member masters resources and skills across all four areas can he hope to have a strong long-term impact on policy.

To gain organizational mastery, a legislator must develop a personal approach to organizational politics—an organizational style—that will allow him to interact effectively with other members (Davidson and Oleszek, 1981, pp. 98–112; Dexter, 1969). Development of such a style will earn the legislator the trust and confidence of other legislators. Their trust and confidence, in turn, will help him gain resources and skills he needs to achieve immediate policy objectives and establish a reputation as an effective legislative craftsman. His achievements and reputation will broaden and solidify his support among members, enabling him to gain more resources and skills and to further advance his career.

Each legislator's style has its own distinctive character, the result of his own unique personality and political circumstance. Yet legislators' styles also share many similarities as a result of the common problems they confront in pursuing their organizational careers. These common problems, and the natural sequential order that legislators follow in addressing them, impose a set of common stages through which members pass as they establish an organizational style and develop their mastery of organizational politics.

On entering Congress, a member's first organizational need is to ensure the electoral support of his constituents so that he can stay in office and pursue a long-term congressional career. As a result, the newly elected legislator must focus extensive attention on gaining those resources and skills in Congress, and developing the organizational style that will best nurture his security in his district (Fenno, 1978; Hershey, 1974, 1984; Jacobson, 1983; Kingdon, 1968). As the legislator acquires the organizational resources, skills, and personal style that can aid him in constituency politics, his concern necessarily turns to policy making—to advocating and presenting specific policy proposals.

Policy making is an immediate concern in part because it is so closely linked to constituent concerns—to fulfilling specific promises (Clausen, 1973; Kingdon, 1973). It is also important, however, because it provides the legislator the knowledge and experience he needs before he can address broader societal problems and before he can gain legitimacy in the eyes of the legislators he seeks to influence and lead (Manley, 1969; Price, 1972) Thus, as he approaches early midcareer, the legislator must devote considerable effort to integrating a strong policy focus into his organizational style, broadening his political identity beyond reelection concerns.

As policy expertise develops, the legislator then can concern himself with influence over other members and control of organizational decision making. Influence, the ability to persuade and bargain effectively with legislators, generally is required before a legislator has enough support from members to win a position of organizational control. Influence will come as a member gains leverage over resources—campaign funds, information, constituency appropriations—that other members want (Fenno, 1973), and as he develops an organizational style and organizational skills that facilitate his use of influence resources (Manley, 1969). Control of the organization—appointments to its committees, scheduling of bills, rulings on parliamentary conflicts, the regulation of policy debates—allows a legislator to shape the policy agenda and policy decisions of the legislature (Cooper and Brady,

1981a; Huitt, 1961; Sinclair, 1983). The acquisition of control resources and the development of the appropriate skills and organizational style are the final tasks of organizational mastery.

Congressional Parties and the Career Cycle

Legislators gain mastery of these four areas of organizational life—reelection, policy making, influence, control—primarily through membership and service in political parties (Jones, 1970; Ripley, 1969). Since the goal of each party is to govern, each seeks to use the resources and the learning opportunities that it controls to build a large group of supportive legislators who can help it gain and exercise institutional power. As a result, each party spreads its reelection and policy resources widely; each also creates numerous opportunities for members to learn reelection and policy making skills through instruction from more advanced members and through involvement in relevant party activities.

In providing extensive assistance for members' reelection and their development of policy making expertise, the party hopes to ensure members' electoral security and their satisfaction with the party. Yet precisely because a party seeks to govern, it must ensure that party leaders can coordinate the party's members and pursue the party's general interests. It seeks to ensure coordination and leadership by creating a small number of influence and control resources, and by limiting members' access to appropriate apprenticeship opportunities (Masters, 1961; Shepsle, 1978; Westefield, 1974; Nelson, 1977).

The rules and norms of legislative parties thus create a hierarchy of resources and learning opportunities that parallels and reinforces the four stages of organizational mastery that members naturally follow. These rules and norms, moreover, place much greater constraints on the availability of resources and opportunities that aid influence and control than on those that assist reelection and policy making. These constraints make it quite difficult for members to advance into the stages of influence and control. Legislators thus are unable to move through their career path, or career cycle, as rapidly as they would ideally desire (Dodd, 1977).

Legislators seek rapid career advancement for two primary reasons. First, rapid career advancement helps a legislator to create an appearance of achievement and promise, to demonstrate that his organizational reputation reflects substance as well as style. This appearance, in turn, helps him gain the continuing support of members that is essential if he is to gain additional resources, learn new organizational skills, and achieve his career objectives. Second, the vagaries of electoral politics, together with the potential success and dominance of other legislators within Congress, may

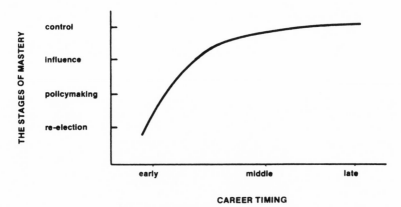

Figure 1. The desired career cycle.

deny any member the opportunity for power. This realization pressures the legislators to seek career advancement and the exercise of power as rapidly as possible.

The ambitious legislative professional thus seeks the desired career cycle illustrated in Figure 1. He wants to move rapidly through the stages of career development, spending a concentrated amount of time gaining skills and resources necessary to master each stage. The bulk of his career then can be spent in the exercise of policy making power.

In actual practice, the professional legislator spends the bulk of his career not in the exercise of mastery but in its pursuit. The rules and norms of the legislature severely limit the availability of those resources and apprentice-ship opportunities that aid influence and control. The relevant positions of power generally are possessed by senior legislators whose electoral and organizational mastery ensures their long term reelection to the legislature and to its positions of power. Young and midcareer legislators thus face a long struggle in the pursuit of influence and control.

Figure 2 illustrates the actual career path a professional legislator will experience. While the legislator may move rapidly through the reelection stage and into the policy stage, he then is caught in a midcareer stall that diverts him from influence and control; rather than a career focused on broad policies, he spends the bulk of his time concerned with narrow, middle range issues, always under the influence and control of the more advanced careerists.

The basic message of Figure 2 is that the core of a professional legislator's career will be spent in frustration, seeking to fulfill his basic organizational

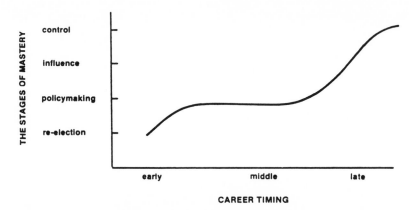

Figure 2. The actual career cycle.

needs but unable to acquire the essential resources and skills. Experiencing such frustration, younger and midcareer legislators will necessarily seek ways out of their predicament, ways to speed up their career advancement. One approach is for junior and midcareer members to unite into informal groups—ideological subcaucuses, regional caucuses, groups of members drawn from the same entering class—and plan strategies and policy initiatives as though they had positions of influence and control (Stevens, Miller, and Mann, 1974; Loomis, 1981). Such efforts help the legislators gain important skills. But informal actions such as this are not enough. Thus a second approach, the acquisition of formal influence and control resources, is also required. The most obvious and direct way to acquire these resources is to change the rules of the legislature to make the resources more available to the less senior members. The consequences of these two approaches are clearest if we examine legislators' behavior beginning with the creation or reorganization of a legislature.

Career Advancement and Organizational Fragmentation

Assume that a legislator enters a professional legislature with a large group of new professionals and at a time when the legislature is reforming. A significant aim of this organizational reform is to strengthen the governing capacity of the legislature while securing the broad career interests of its members. The reforms create numerous re-election and policy resources to serve the large junior contingent. They establish a relatively limited number of influence and control resources to meet the career needs of the senior legislators and the coordination and leadership needs of the

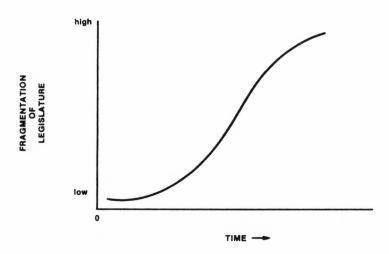

Figure 3. The pattern of legislative fragmentation.

institution. In addition, the parties establish systematic apprenticeship procedures—opportunities to learn both through observation of senior legislators and through active participation in policy making—to assist legislators in gaining necessary skills so that they can use their resources effectively.

A new legislator will have few initial quarrels with this distribution of resources, and the accompanying apprenticeship structure: it readily fulfills his reelection and policy making interests. But as the new legislator, his cohorts, and succeeding classes seek access to the stages of influence and control, they face more difficult circumstances. The career advancement of the new generation is hindered by the limited number of available resources and learning opportunities, and by the dominance of senior legislators. To end their shared frustration and gain desired resources, these junior and midcareer legislators unite, seek out new apprenticeship arrangements, and gradually introduce reforms that spread resources more widely among all members.

Over time, the legislature will experience the organizational fragmentation pictured in Figure 3. The period immediately following the creation or reorganization of the legislature will witness very little fragmentation. The new organizational arrangements and the career interests of legislators mesh fairly well. But with the aging of the new generation, the legislature will witness a steady rise in fragmentation. This fragmentation will occur in two ways. First, the effort to gain organizational skills and personal support will lead junior and midcareer members to create formal and informal groups that provide them special learning opportunities and the chance to work with colleagues who share similar career interests; in doing so the members break down the authority structure of the parties and of the Congress as a whole (Brady and Bullock, 1981; Manley, 1977; Patterson, 1977; Stevens et al., 1974), altering its internal norms and patterns of apprenticeship (Asher, 1973; Rohde, Ornstein and Peabody, 1985). Second, the junior and midcareer members will use their growing numbers and organizational savvy to challenge existing rules and disperse formal resources more widely.

The result is a breakdown in the mechanisms for coordination and leadership of the Congress. As these mechanisms collapse, the Congress increasingly loses its ability to make policy and govern. The resulting policy immobilism makes it difficult for Congress to respond to social, economic, and foreign policy crises; immobilism may even generate such crises. These crises set in motion a period of electoral upheaval during which the public attempts to find legislators who can resolve the crises (Burnham, 1970). Out of this upheaval comes a new majority party, or a new dominant majority party faction, with a mandate to pursue a new direction in public policy (for a more extensive discussion see Dodd, 1986).

Organizing to Govern

On gaining majority status, the victorious party confronts the central dilemma that undercut the former majority party: it must organize the legislature so that it can govern effectively. In approaching this task, the party inherits the fragmented legislature created by the outgoing party. This organization can cripple the new majority party just as it undermined the governing capacity of the old party. Yet the severity of the national crisis demands immediate policy changes and allows little time for organizational reforms.

The new majority party offsets legislative fragmentation initially by drawing on two distinct advantages. It possesses a relatively cohesive party organization from its days as the minority party. In addition, the new party majority contains a large number of new legislators preoccupied with reelection and policy advocacy and not yet concerned with using resources to exercise influence and control. The party thus can govern effectively despite a fragmented legislature. It can move rapidly to enact new policies (Brady, 1978) and defuse the crisis of immobilism.

These early advantages eventually disappear, however, and the new majority party faces the dilemmas of governing. The legislators elected during the realignment gain mastery of reelection and policy making resources. They increasingly pursue the numerous resources available in the fragmented legislature and use these resources to gain influence and control.

The capacity of the party to lead and coordinate its members declines and the legislature experiences renewed immobilism (Patterson, 1977).

Policy immobilism after realignment is even more difficult for the legislature to resolve than before. The new majority party is hesitant to deny its members the legislative rewards for which they worked so hard while in the minority. The party members, concerned with their personal career success, fail to connect the policy failures of the party with their pursuit of personal power. The new party thus embraces the politics of fragmentation and watches its governing mandate flounder. Seeing the legislature stiffled, even with a fresh infusion of new members and new ideas, public disenchantment with legislative decision making grows.

Legislative immobilism and the public disillusionment invite the executive to usurp the policy making power of the legislature and end the national crisis. The executive initially succeeds because the legislature is too fragmented and disorganized to oppose it effectively and because many members of the legislature and the public see executive intervention as necessary to save the republic. As the executive attempts to consolidate power, however, legislators come to realize that the institution is on the verge of permanently losing its governing power. Such a loss would make members' resources and status in the legislature worthless. The legislators' support for the strong executive thus turns to fear and opposition. They come to recognize that mastery of organizational politics enables them to have an impact on national policy making only so long as Congress itself maintains its policy making integrity.

Executive intervention demonstrates to legislators that they must strengthen the policy making capacity of Congress—both its system of internal leadership and its procedures for policy coordination—if they are to protect and nurture their own personal power. And they must do this even at the expense of some immediate personal sacrifice. They thus respond to executive intervention by reducing fragmentation and creating a more coherent decision making structure. These efforts include the disbanding of informal groups or the more effective integration of them into the formal organization of Congress. They also include efforts to provide a more coherent organization of existing resources. Once such a reformed organization is in place, the new majority party is prepared to govern until career frustrations lead its members to fragment the legislature once again.

The Organizational Cycle: An Overview

The thrust of the foregoing argument can be summarized in one sentence: professional legislatures are characterized by cycles of organizational change. During such cycles the legislature passes through six stages (see Figure 4):

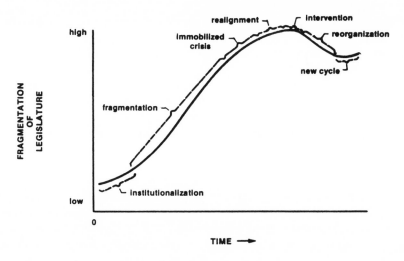

Figure 4. The organizational cycle.

Stage one: organizational stability
Stage two: fragmentation
Stage three: immobilism and crisis
Stage four: electoral upheaval and realignment
Stage five: interventionism
Stage six: reorganization and resurgence

The history of Congress after the Civil War mirrors this cyclical pattern, particularly the history of the larger, elective body, the House of Representatives. Fragmentation in the late nineteenth century, for example, centered on the committee system; the number of committees increased by approximately 50% during the two organizational cycles (1860 to the 1880s and the 1880s to 1920). From 1920 to 1946 congressional fragmentation centered on the proliferation of a variety of special committees and subcommittees, a process reversed by the 1946 Legislative Reorganization Act. And from the early 1950s to the early 1970s the committee system experienced a growth in the number and autonomy of standing subcommittees and subcommittee chairs. In each of these periods we witness roughly similar sequences of change in which fragmentation is followed by realignment (party reconstruction in the 1870s; realignment in the 1890s, 1930s, and 1960s) and then reorganization (1880s, 1910s, 1940s, and 1970s).

Microlevel career patterns likewise correspond to the general expectations of the theory. Career cycles in the House are seen in such empirical patterns as the tendency of junior and senior legislators to concentrate on different electoral strategies (Fenno, 1978; Parker, 1984) and on different types of committee and subcommittee assignments (Prindle and Franklin, 1985; Smith and Deering, 1984). The linkage between career aspirations and organizational structure is shown by the long-term tendency of the House to fragment as the proportion of careerist members grows (Huntington, 1965; Polsby, 1968; Swenson, 1982). And the linkage between career frustration and fragmentation appears in the organized efforts of disadvantaged groups such as House liberals in the 1950s to gain personal power and policy influence by pursuing decentralized reforms (Stevens, et al., 1974).

Congressional history thus provides support for the cyclical theory. It must be acknowledged, however, that the theory of organizational cycles fails to account for the substantial differences among the cycles in the extent of change they generate. The reforms of the 1880s were mild adjustments in legislative rules; those of the 1910s crippled the Speakership, made the Senate elective, created the modern revenue and appropriations committees, and instituted committee government. The reforms of the 1940s reduced the fragmentation in committee government that had developed since 1920 but left the fundamental structure and rules of Congress intact. The reforms of the 1970s, not unlike those of the 1910s, once again uprooted existing structure and process.

As these contrasts illustrate, the reform periods in the different historical eras are not equal. Some readjust the existing organizational arrangements inherent in the core structure of Congress; others transform the structure itself. The internal theory, by itself, cannot account for these differences in the extensiveness of reforms across the cycles. The theory likewise provides no explanation for differences between cycles in the magnitude of the electoral realignments, in the severity of executive intervention, or in the extensiveness of the policy changes that occur in Congress. To explain these differences in the cycles we must look beyond internal congressional politics. We must look to the impact that external politics has on congressional change.

THE THEORY OF INSTITUTIONAL CYCLES

The external world of Congress is critical to members because it is the arena in which members gain reelection. Reelection, in turn, is essential if members are to stay in Congress and pursue policy making power. Thus members devote considerable attention to their relationship with constituents (Arnold, 1979; Fiorina, 1977; Jacobson, 1983; Mann, 1978; Mayhew, 1974). But reelection is not the only dimension of constituent politics that concerns members.

Members' external relations with their constituents also influence the freedom within Congress that members possess as they pursue their career interests (Fenno, 1978). If legislators enjoy strong personal support from a broad range of constituents, they can take those actions that facilitate their acquisition of power—actions such as service on desired committees that provide no immediate particularized benefit to constituents but that aid the members' personal career. Without such freedom, reelection in itself is relatively worthless to legislators concerned with policy making power.

Seen from this perspective, the external politics of Congress centers not on members' struggle for reelection but on their quest for electoral mastery. Such mastery exists when a legislator possesses the resources and skills to obtain both the reliable votes he needs to stay in office and the personal trust from constituents he needs to pursue his career interests in Congress. The effort to obtain electoral resources and skills necessarily involves extensive feelings of insecurity on the part of the member: legislators seldom if ever possess sufficient resources and skills to fulfill personally the policy expectations that their constituents hold of them; this knowledge naturally leads them to fear the potential loss of constituent support.

Insecurity about their electoral support—and members' consequent belief that they need special rules and institutional arrangements to help them meet their constituents' expectations—generates the cyclical alteration in the structure of Congress. Thus to explain the institutional cycles of Congress, we first must understand members' behavior in their districts, particularly the processes through which they seek to gain electoral mastery.

Electoral Agendas and Constituent Mobilization

To gain electoral mastery, legislators must accomplish two tasks: they must mobilize reliable support from a winning plurality of district constituents, and they must convince these supporters that their long term personal self-interests depend on the legislators' career advancement within Congress. Since district constituents are policy-concerned individuals who vote in accord with their understanding of personal and group policy interests (Erikson and Wright, 1985; Kuklinski and West, 1981; Wright and Berkman, 1985), constituent mobilization requires legislators to commit themselves to public policies desired by a sizeable body of their constituents.

Legislators make these programmatic commitments in the policy agendas they promise to pursue in Congress. These agendas address four types of policy concerns:

1. Narrow constituent issues that effect the district and its residents in very particularistic ways, including casework service and porkbarrel programs;

2. Middle-range policies that address the particularized interests of groups such as farmers, businessmen, teachers and union members;
3. Broad national programs that involve the development of wide-ranging and highly interrelated sets of policies, such as omnibus taxing and spending programs;
4. General political world views that encompass and justify fundamental conceptions of government and society, as expressed in the legislator's personal ideology.

The legislator takes these positions to gain the support of constituent groups. This support includes vital resources that aid his campaign—money, organizational help, and ultimately votes. It also includes assistance in acquiring necessary electoral skills. This assistance comes in two ways. First, groups open themselves to him and allow him to immerse himself in their inner workings so that he can learn their problems, policy goals, and central values. Second, they provide him with key intimates and general advisers who can keep him in touch with the changing concerns and mood of district support groups. The groups thus provide the legislator with opportunities for electoral apprenticeship, opportunities that are essential to his skillful use of resources.

Groups provide the legislator with election support that he needs—both resources and apprenticeship opportunities—so long as he convincingly pursues the policies they desire. To convince constituents of his effectiveness as a representative, and thus to commit them to his career advancement, the legislator seeks to develop an electoral style—a home style—that constituents will find appealing and persuasive (Fenno, 1978). This style—this presentation of self—must help him demonstrate the authentic fit between his values, interests, and agenda commitments and those of his constituents. It must help him convince constituents that their long-term policy interests depend on his career advancement, an advancement that may even require actions at odds with short-term constituent interests. And it must help him make clear the ways that his legislative accomplishments have facilitated and will facilitate the fulfillment of their common goals. Each member's electoral style will be unique, the result of his distinctive personality and political circumstance. Yet a member's style will also share much with the styles of other members. In part, this results from a tendency of districts with similar problems and policy orientations to select legislators with similar values, personalities, and styles of communication. But similarities in electoral style also reflect the existence of a common electoral problem and common strategies for resolving the problem.

Electoral Careers and the Stages of Mastery

The overriding electoral problem that legislators face is the hesitancy of constituent groups to provide them electoral support without some clear evidence that they can deliver on their policy promises. Immediate delivery of agenda promises is virtually impossible, particularly for new legislators, both because of the breadth of policy promises candidates must make to attract support and because of the difficulty of enacting policies in Congress. For this reason, legislators follow a sequential strategy in gaining resources and skills and in developing electoral mastery.

Early in their career legislators appeal for constituent support—for access to group advice and for resources from groups—by stressing their commitment to constituent services and to policies that serve specialized groups. They do so in part because these are the issues of most immediate, particularized concern to constituents and thus the ones most likely to generate support from them. But they also do so because these are the promises they can most easily fulfill given the resources to which they have access in Congress.

As the reputation for accomplishment is established through delivery of casework and group services, legislators can widen their focus to emphasize national programmatic concerns and ideological stands. In doing so, they broaden their support base within their constituency and lessen their reliance on groups with specialized interests. They thus gain greater leeway in the specific policy actions that they must take in Congress to keep the support of constituents.

The pursuit of electoral resources and skills thus generates four stages of electoral mastery, together with four related stages in members' home style and electoral skills. Early in their careers members work to acquire district support by extensive attention to constituent service and policies that service specialized district groups, developing electoral skills and a home style that will aid their focus on constituency policies. After legislators have solidified their electoral bases (Fenno, 1978), adjusted to their insider roles as legislators (Fenno, this volume), routinized the delivery of constituent services (Fiorina, 1977), and learned to communicate their congressional accomplishments to constituent groups (Kuklinski, 1983), they are free to give greater emphasis to their national policy concerns. They thus move to the more advanced stages of electoral mastery. They seek to adjust their home styles and electoral skills to include greater emphasis on national policy debates and broad ideological controversies. They also broaden their appeal for resources to include a greater stress on individuals and groups concerned with broad-gauged policy issues.

These four stages of electoral mastery parallel the four stages of organiza-

tional mastery. Both involve progressive movement from a focus on constituent service activities to group policy issues to general programmatic
concerns and finally to broad-gauged ideological politics. Legislators pursue
electoral and organizational mastery in parallel stages because each depends
so heavily on the other: organizational mastery is required if the legislator is
to fulfill his policy promises so that he can maintain his electoral support; and
electoral mastery is required if he is to advance in his career in Congress and
exercise power.

Electoral and organizational mastery thus come together. And only
electoral and organizational mastery together can give the member the
legislative mastery that he needs to exercise power. Yet the need for parallel
advancement through the stages of organizational and electoral mastery can
create some serious problems for the members' long-term electoral success.

Two problems are paramount. The first is the slowness with which a
member acquires organizational resources and skills, particularly those
necessary for influence and control. The second is the difficulty that a
member of a large, complex, and competitive institution such as Congress
faces in using his resources and skills to gain the policy support of other
legislators. These two problems together mean that individual members will
face a difficult task in fulfilling the broad-gauged programmatic promises that
they must fulfill if they are to maintain electoral support in their district.

Policy Agendas and Congressional Structure

The problems that organizational politics causes for electoral careers
generate considerable insecurity among members—anxiety over reelection
and maintenance of constituent trust. This insecurity about electoral support
leads members to search for ways to ensure that their programmatic
promises are fulfilled. Since the legislator cannot fulfill them alone, he must
cooperate with other legislators and develop a strategy that can address the
programmatic commitments that they share in common. The need for
cooperation forces groups of legislators to agree on common policy agendas
that they can pursue collectively, and to create rules and institutional
arrangements that will help them enact these agendas.

Members are able to agree upon a common policy agenda when their
districts confront similar policy problems. Thus legislators from the same
region and state, or from districts with similar social and economic conditions, are likely to share common programmatic commitments (Froman,
1963; Clausen, 1973; Kingdon, 1973). Legislators who enter Congress at
roughly the same time, and thus build their district coalitions in response to
the same historical conditions, are likely to share a common policy agenda.
And legislators who have served together during a severe national crisis are

likely to have addressed certain common problems and thus to share certain common agenda commitments. The overlap among these various factors means that Congress is composed of a relatively small number of agenda groups.

The structure of Congress is determined, during periods of reform, by the struggle among these policy groups to impose rules and procedures that best serve their policy purposes (Lowi, 1964, 1979; Ripley and Franklin, 1980; Strom and Rundquist, 1978). Thus groups committed primarily to distributive policies will seek a decentralized structure that facilitates distributive decision making while groups that want redistributive policies will more likely seek a centralized structure capable of coordinated decisionmaking. The actual structure will be determined by the relative strength of the different groups and the skill of group members in negotiating useful compromises with other groups (Bolling, 1965, 1968; Brown, 1922; Davidson and Oleszek, 1977; Hechler, 1940; Patterson, 1977). The groups that finally dominate the creation of the congressional structure will require that the core institutional arrangements enacted by Congress—those rules and procedures which establish the type of individuals and groups that are to exercise central authority—are subject to change only by extraordinary majority votes, or by procedures of analogous difficulty. These institutional rules and procedures impose a dominant policy agenda on Congress—a tendency to facilitate certain types of policy decisions and hinder others.

The design of a congressional structure to facilitate a particular agenda, and the use of extraordinary majority procedures to protect the structure, incorporates into Congress a conservative bias, a tendency to adapt slowly to the rise of new societal problems and new policy agendas. Congress may change its *organizational rules* fairly often, as its members seek to redistribute organizational resources. But change in its *structural rules* will be slow, hindered both by the continuing commitment of legislators to the congressional agenda that underlies the structure and by the requirement of extraordinary majorities to alter core structural rules.

The eventual restructuring of Congress is linked primarily to the generational replacement of legislators (Broder, 1980; Huntington, 1981; Ornstein and Rohde, 1977; Schiff and Smith, 1983). Replacement involves change not only of the members themselves but also of the policy agenda of Congress. This agenda change occurs because new legislators, to win office, incorporate into their constituency coalitions and agendas powerful new groups and policy issues that are salient during their initial campaigns, even though absent in the agenda of the previous incumbent (Hershey, 1984). Each new generation thus follows a different agenda from the last and wants a legislative structure that facilitates the passage of the its agenda. The generations differ, however, in the ease with which they can reorganize congressional structure and impose their own agenda on Congress. These differences are tied to the stage in the organizational cycle at which a generation enters Congress.

The Formative Generation and the First Cycle

Legislators who begin service during the formation of a legislative structure—the formative generation—are committed to the institutional structure because they share the same general agenda that underlies the structure's design. They are joined in this commitment by more senior members of the legislature who have actually led the effort to redesign the institution. The relatively close congruence between these senior and junior members exists because they have lived through a period of national crisis that has forced extensive reassessment of the nation's agenda. This reassessment has created an impetus for legislators of all generations to move toward a common set of policy perspectives. This agreement on a common agenda allows them to overthrow the old structure and implement a new one. The extensive support enjoyed by the new structure ensures that it will experience considerable stability in its early years.

In the years following the creation of the structure, the primary conflict will be over the distribution of resources among members rather than the nature of the policy process itself. As the formative generation ages and confronts the limited number of resources for influence and control, it and subsequent generations push to fragment the organization. The stages of organizational immobilism and crisis come during the midcareer phase of the formative generation. The period of reorganization comes as they enter positions of control and power. They will support reorganization that increases the capacity of the existing structure to process the policy agenda for which it was created. But their own commitment to that same agenda leads them to oppose structural changes designed to foster a competing agenda.

The legislative reforms produced by the formative generation thus restore the capacity of the existing structure to facilitate its original agenda. Reorganization may include modest structural changes that prove necessary to win passage of the reforms and that enable the modified congressional structure to process new types of policies produced by societal change. These proposals will be presented by the legislators first elected in the years of fragmentation, who are more sensitive than the formative generation to the emergence of new societal problems and to the need for ameliorative reforms. More extensive structural changes, presented by the newest legislators elected during the periods of crisis and realignment preceding the reform effort, will be opposed and defeated by the congressional leaders.

The organizational cycle following the formation of the congressional

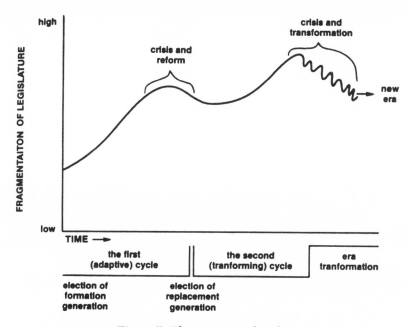

Figure 5. The institutional cycle.

structure, referred to hereafter as the "first cycle," will last roughly one legislative generation. It begins when a congressional structure is formally adopted and continues until the generation elected during the formative period gains power and reforms the Congress. The reforms of the first cycle reduce organizational fragmentation and adapt the congressional structure in modest ways to the policy agenda emerging from societal change. But the completion of the first organizational cycle leaves the fundamental structure of Congress—those institutional arrangements based on extraordinary majority rules—basically in place.

The Replacement Generation and the Second Cycle

Fundamental change of congressional structure comes in the second organizational cycle (see Figure 5). This cycle follows the same basic pattern of fragmentation, crisis, and reorganization as the first. The institutional conflicts that emerge in the second cycle, however, are more extensive in character and more wideranging in their policy impact. This growth in congressional conflict stems from the consequences that societal change and generational replacement have for the career behavior of legislators during the second cycle.

In the first cycle, most legislators generally pursue policy agendas compatible with the agenda structure of the Congress. Their ability to implement their agenda, and thus to succeed within the Congress, does not require them to redesign its structure. The second cycle begins, by contrast, with a number of legislators who support new agendas not reflected in the reformed congressional structure. These legislators, having replaced many of the formative generation during realignment and its aftermath, are the initial generation of the second cycle. These replacement legislators play the major role in shaping the internal politics of the second cycle.

The task facing this replacement generation is more daunting than the task that confronted the members of the formative generation. To succeed, the new members must not only capture organizational resources; they must alter the legislative structure itself so that the institution can process the policies contained in their new agenda. Their career goals thus operate on two levels: they seek personal acquisition of resources so that they will have policy making power; and they seek redesign of the legislature so that they can use the power they acquire to implement the policies contained in their agenda.

Career behavior in the two cycles thus responds to a very different calculus. Whereas the first cycle begins with congruence between the members' policy agenda and the legislature's structure, the second cycle begins with a fair degree of incongruence. The formative generation of the first cycle thus accepts the legislature's structure as compatible with the members' agenda and merely seeks to widen the dispersion of resources within that structure. The replacement generation of the second cycle seeks both a greater dispersion of resources and a new institutional structure appropriate to their new agenda. The differing individual calculus in the two cycles means that the second one will experience different types of change, and more extensive change, than the first cycle.

The preoccupation with a new policy agenda during the second cycle will lead the new generation to concentrate its attention not solely on organizational reforms but also on challenges to the governing structure of Congress. These challenges, while unlikely to succeed in the early years of the new cycle because of the extraordinary majorities required, can introduce extensive conflict between generations. This conflict exacerbates the policy immobilism generated by the growing organizational fragmentation. This deeper immobilism, made worse by the growing incongruence between the national policy agenda and the governing structure of Congress, produces a much broader societal crisis than in the first cycle.

The depth of the policy crisis means that the nation can move forward only by refashioning its governing institutions so that they can address the new policy problems that afflict society. This effort at institutional transformation focuses first on those political institutions most open to democratic control—participatory organizations such as political parties. To maintain public support, these institutions must realign their policy agendas and transform their organizational structures so that they can address the new societal problems. These processes take considerable time and lead to extensive intraparty conflict. As a result, the process of group realignment, particularly party realignment, will be much more extensive and lengthy during the second cycle, when it requires a transformation of the fundamental agendas of the parties, than realignment at the end of the first cycle, which requires only a change of parties.

The ultimate failure of this transforming realignment to ensure the governing effectiveness of Congress, a failure rooted in the continuing fragmentation and rigidification of Congress, leads to extensive executive intervention into congressional policy making. This intervention is much more threatening to the central power of Congress than executive intervention in the first cycle. The severity of the intervention results from the greater policy immobilism of the second cycle and from the executive's fear that his party's new coalition will fall apart without policy action of some sort, however achieved.

The congressional reforms of the second cycle that respond to this intervention are necessarily much more extensive than those in the first cycle, involving efforts to transform the structure rather than simply modify existing organizational arrangements (Polsby, 1975). Their extensiveness flows both from the depth of the policy crisis and from the severity of executive intervention. The result is a new congressional structure designed to facilitate a new agenda. The widespread conflict and policy immobilism of the second cycle thus lead to a new institutional era in which Congress is governed by a new agenda, a new structure, and a new party alignment.

As this discussion indicates, the movement from one institutional era to another is an elaborate and lengthy process, taking two political generations and two organizational cycles to complete. The two generations first fulfill policy commitments to a formative agenda and then prepare Congress to pursue a new policy agenda that addresses emerging societal problems. The resulting change is more pronounced in the second cycle, however, reflecting the presence of a new generation of legislators committed to enacting a new policy agenda and a new congressional structure.

Institutional Eras and Historical Change

Congress has experienced three institutional eras during its two hundred year history, and three transformations in its dominant agenda (Dodd, 1981; Huntington, 1974, 1981, chap. 7; Polsby, 1968). The first era, concerned with an agrarian agenda, employed an elite dominated governing structure. This structure, maintained by a small number of careerists, gave way in the Civil War and Reconstruction period to a postagrarian agenda preoccupied with the expanding economic role of government. This agenda was institutionalized in Congress through party government and a strong Speaker (Brady, 1973; Cooper and Brady, 1981a). The postagrarian era lasted for forty years, until the early 1900s. Its shorter timespan resulted from the rapid growth of careerist legislators during the period and their consequent ability to overwhelm the small group of senior careerists to impose a new structure and agenda.

The third era extended from the 1910s to the 1970s. As the first sustained period of low turnover and high careerism, this era corresponds more closely to the two-cycle theory of institutional change than the two earlier eras. The era began when progressive legislators in 1910, frustrated with the inability of party government to serve the new industrial agenda and assist their career advancement, overturned the governing rules that had dominated Congress since the Civil War (Hechler, 1940). Throughout the 1910s Congress struggled to create a new set of rules and structures—new procedures for appointing committee members and chairs, a cloture rule for the Senate, a new arrangement for the Rules Committee, a new structuring of the jurisdiction over appropriations, and the like—that would facilitate the special distributive agenda of the industrial era (Brown, 1922).

These structural arrangements, and the committee government that they created, remained intact for roughly fifty years, kept in place by complex rules and slow generational change. During this era Congress experienced two organizational cycles. The first one, the adaptive or reinforcing cycle, was from the early 1920s to the mid-1940s. It witnessed extensive fragmentation in the twenties and early thirties, followed by the realignment of the thirties, the interventionist actions of Roosevelt, and then the reforms of the mid to late 1940s. These reforms, contained in the Legislative Reorganization Act of 1946, streamlined the committee system and rejuvenated its operation while leaving the fundamental structure of committee governing in tact (Galloway, 1951).

The second cycle, the transforming cycle, began in the late 1940s and lasted until the reforms of the 1970s. The fragmentation of this cycle involved an expansion in the number and autonomy of subcommittees, a growth in the staff and personal resources of members, and a breakdown in committee jurisdictions (Davidson and Oleszek, 1981; Dodd and Schott, 1979; Fox and Hammond, 1977). This fragmentation grew not simply from the desire by midcareer members for personal resources; it also stemmed from the desire of a new generation of legislators to open up congressional decision making to the postindustrial agenda that had emerged in the postwar years (Bolling, 1965; Stevens et al., 1974), an agenda that covered new issues such as civil rights, social service delivery, economic planning, and restraints on international involvement. This fragmentation, fueled by well-organized subcaucus activity within Congress, culminated in the electoral upheavals of the mid-1960s, the interventionist efforts of Presidents Johnson and Nixon, and structural transformation in the seventies (Dodd, 1977, 1981; Sundquist, 1973, 1981).

The concern that remains is whether organizational and institutional change, illustrated by the experiences of the industrial-era Congress, produce systematic changes in the policy performance of Congress. Is the long-term decline and short-term resurgence in congressional policy making actually related to alterations in organization and structure? What dimensions of policy making are most likely to be affected, and in what ways? Does the effect differ across different types of policy? To answer these questions, we must examine more extensively the ways in which organizational and structural change can influence policy performance.

THE THEORY OF POLICY CYCLES

The institutional arrangements within Congress shape its overall policy performance, I will argue, by determining how responsive Congress is to the nation's dominant agenda (Cobb and Elder, 1972, 1981; Cooper, 1975; Huntington, 1965, 1981; Kingdon, 1984; Jones, 1977; Polsby, 1971; Rieselbach, 1978; Sundquist, 1981). When organizational and structural arrangements facilitate innovative decision making—under conditions of low fragmentation and rigidity—Congress can respond to the nation's policy problems in an effective manner. Increases in fragmentation and rigidity, by contrast, decrease the overall policy performance of Congress. These distinct patterns of change can be seen by looking at three separate dimensions of policy performance: policy making capacity, program innovation, and agenda responsiveness.

Policy Making Capacity

The policy making capacity of Congress is its ability to enact those decisions that enjoy the clear support of its members. This ability is most likely to exist when Congress is organized in a coherent manner designed to facilitate majority decision making. Such coherence results from the existence of three related conditions. First, Congress must contain the number and type of leadership positions necessary to pursue the desired policies. Too few positions will place undue demands on leaders and dissipate their energies; too many positions will encourage immobilizing conflict among competing legislators. Second, these positions must be accountable to the rank and file members. Third, the members who hold these leadership positions must possess the resources and skills they need to gain the enactment of the desired policies.

A major concern during the design or reform of Congress is the creation of a leadership system that will ensure the necessary organizational coherence. The long-term unraveling of organizational coherence comes primarily through fragmentation of the organization—that is, the division of its leadership structure into an ever larger number of positions that possess an ever more equal number of resources. Such fragmentation undermines the decision making capacity of Congress in four ways (Huntington, 1965; Kingdon, 1984; Sundquist, 1981). It deprives Congress of authoritative leaders who possess sufficient resources to bargain effectively and unite members in policy coalitions. It unravels the apprenticeship structure that underlies the existing leadership system and thereby deprives leaders of the skills they need to use effectively the resources they do possess. It breaks down the rules and procedures for coordinating the policy process. And it confuses the lines of accountability between leaders and rank and file members.

The overall decision making capacity of Congress thus varies in a cyclical fashion, declining as Congress fragments and rebounding when Congress reforms. This close linkage between the organization of Congress and its decision making capacity is broken only during periods of realignment, when the influx of a new governing majority momentarily breaks the policy deadlocks in Congress. This policy resurgence soon ends, however, when the continuing problems of organizational fragmentation engulf the new majority party. Substantial improvement in decision making will then come only through organizational reform. If this reform comes at the end of the second cycle, it also produces a change in the policy agenda that these decisions address.

This cyclical pattern of policy change is evident, in its broadest outline, in the decline in congressional policy making during the 1920s and early 1930s, and again during the 1950s and 1960s, both periods of organizational fragmentation. The first decline was halted by the Legislative Reorganization Act of 1946, the second by the reforms of the 1970s. Only the realignments of mid -thirties and mid -sixties were able to break the growth of policy immobilism, and only for a short period of time. Thus, both Roosevelt in his seond term and Johnson and Nixon in the late sixties and early seventies faced renewed problems of congressional immobilism (Patterson, 1977; Sundquist, 1981), problems that were then addressed by congressional reforms.

As Figure 6 indicates, this pattern of cyclical decline is most evident in

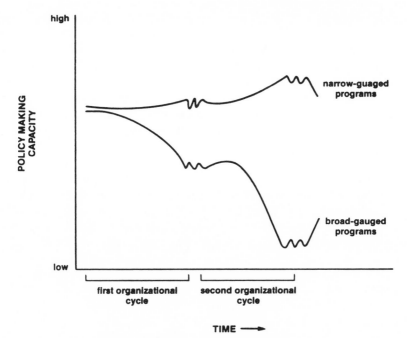

Figure 6. Change in policy-making capacity.

broad national policy making, since deliberation on national problems is likely to require procedures for leading and coordinating a vast array of legislators. The pattern is less likely to exist in the areas of narrow-gauged constituent policy making, such as casework and pork barrel politics, since these can often be handled by the individual actions of members or by norms of reciprocity among members (Fiorina, 1977; Ferejohn, 1974). In fact, constituent policy making may actually benefit from the uncoordinated spread of resources among members, increasing with fragmentation, declining when reforms impose a new organizational coherence.

These contrasting patterns make the work-a-day world of Congress difficult to decipher up close. The growth in policy making activity that results from constituent politics can give Congress the appearance of being an active policy maker. The resulting reelection of members also may give it the appearance of being responsive and popular. These effects of constituent policy making thus may deflect attention from the immobilism that characterizes broad-gauged policy questions. They can thus divert attention from the incapacity of the institution to enact new and innovative programs.

Program Innovation

Program innovation is the process by which Congress initiates and debates new types of policy proposals (Johannes, 1972; Polsby, 1984). Innovation exists even if the programs are not actually enacted into law, so long as new programs are proposed and given serious consideration. The initiation of new types of programs is most likely to come from new legislators committed to a new policy agenda at odds with the agenda of the formative generation.

The continuous replacement of the formative generation by new legislators would seem to guarantee a continuous and cumulative increase in policy innovativeness throughout an institutional era. More new legislators should produce greater innovativeness. An increase in new members fails to guarantee increased innovation, however, if the new members do not possess the resources that they need to gain serious consideration of their proposals. The effect of generational replacement on innovativeness thus depends on how fragmented the resources of Congress are and whether the new legislators have access to existing resources. It also depends on whether one examines resources linked to broad-gauged or narrow-gauged policy making.

Consider broad-gauged national policies. During the first cycle of an era, the new members who seek to develop innovative policy confront four problems. First, they are greatly outnumbered, and even more surpassed in influence, by the members who are committed to the existing congressional agenda. Second, few if any new members will have progressed in their career cycle into the influence and control positions that shape broad-gauged policy. Third, influence and control work groups may actually become more cohesive and inaccessible during organizational fragmentation, more committed to the original agenda, and thus ever greater constraints on broad-gauged innovation (Dodd, 1986). Fourth, whatever fragmentation occurs throughout the congressional organization is most likely to benefit the members of the formative generation, who are still in mid-career, and to bypass the relatively new members, who are more likely to support a new agenda.

These obstacles to the new members mean that broad-gauged policy innovation actually decreases during the first cycle. The high point for innovation will be the period immediately after the creation of the new structure; the structure facilitates the deliberation of the new ideas associated with the formative agenda. As these ideas are presented and enacted, the policy proposals of the formative generation become more routinized and less original. Yet the new emerging generation is unable to fill the void and initiate a meaningful deliberation of new broad-gauged policies. It is too small in number, too isolated from the centers that control policy making, and too overwhelmed by the growing organizational chaos.

The fate of innovative national programs is quite different in the second cycle. By the second cycle, the death and retirement of older members will have necessitated the broadening of the influence and control groups to include members of the new generation. This replacement generation includes members who entered Congress during the period of crisis, realignment, and reform that ended the first cycle, as well as the growing number of new members elected in the the second cycle. The growing size and seniority of the replacement generation enables its members to take increasing advantage of the fragmentation that occurs in the second cycle and to increasingly dominate organizational politics. As the second cycle proceeds this new generation, increasing in size and seniority, will become the dominant group in Congress and the primary beneficiary of resource fragmentation. As their access to resources increases the members of the replacement generation will be in a position to force deliberation of policies that seemed impossible in the first cycle.

The decline in policy innovation during the first cycle thus is followed by its increase during the second. Fragmentation during the first cycle of an institutional era gives power and resources to the supporters of the existing agenda, helps them win continued reelection, and thus enables them to retain power long after their innovative ideas have ended. They use this opportunity to overwhelm new members and override their new agenda commitments. Fragmentation in the second cycle, by contrast, increasingly strengthens the electoral and organizational strength of the new generation, helps them overpower the senior members who oppose the new agenda, and provides them the opportunity for serious efforts to initiate and deliberate national policy.

Fragmentation has a different effect on the innovation of constituent policy during the two cycles. Because fragmentation increases the reelection resources that all members have free access to, it gives members of the replacement generation in both cycles a growing number of resources to use to initiate new types of constituent programs. The replacement generation in the first cycle thus is free to innovate constituent policies—new types of casework or pork barrel activities, for example—as soon as the fragmentation process begins. Innovativeness in narrow-gauged constituent policies thus will grow during both cycles as the number of new members increases and as their personal reelection resources expand.

Program innovation in Congress thus follows the overall pattern outlined in Figure 7. Narrow-gauged policy experiences a cyclical rise in innovation, illustrated by the development of new casework and pork barrel projects throughout the postwar years (Fiorina, 1977). Broad-gauged policy making,

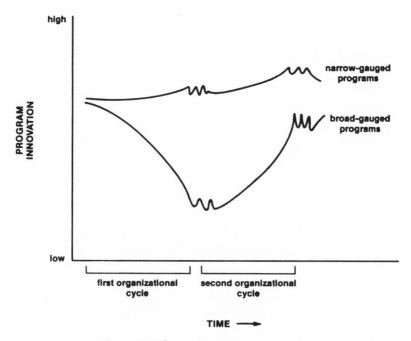

Figure 7. Change in program innovation.

by contrast, experiences an initial decline in innovation during the first cycle of an era followed by an increase of roughly equal length in the second.

We see these contrasting patterns during the twentieth century, with the interwar Congress experiencing a steady decline in the initiation of new policy proposals, according to Lawrence Chamberlain (1947), while the postwar Congress experienced a rise in policy initiation (Moe and Teel, 1970). This curvilinear pattern resulted from the interaction between generational change and cyclical fragmentation. The formative generation of the industrial era, solidifying its control of Congress during the period of interwar fragmentation, suffered a decline in new ideas and thus produced a decline in congressional innovativeness. The replacement generation, illustrated best perhaps by Hubert Humphrey, came to power during the period of postwar fragmentation; infused with a new agenda and possessing increasing resources, this generation was able to initiate a growing number of new programs.

There is, of course, an irony in this curvilinear pattern. Congress experiences its most extensive decline in innovativeness in the first cycle, illustrated here by the interwar years, when decision making capacity is still great. By contrast, Congress experiences an increase in innovative proposals in the second cycle, precisely as its decision making capacity is in the steepest period of decline. The policy performance of Congress is thus a complex and variable process. This point is reinforced when we consider how the patterns of policy making and innovation combine to shape the overall agenda responsiveness of Congress.

Agenda Responsiveness

Agenda responsiveness is the ability of Congress to produce policy decisions that are congruent with the policy agenda dominant among the nation's citizens. The struggle over the structure of Congress is in large part a battle over which groups in society Congress will respond to and how responsive Congress will be. The formative generation of an era seeks to ensure responsiveness to the groups and agenda dominant at the time of its election; it seeks to ensure responsiveness by institutionalizing the groups' agenda in a new congressional structure.

The close congruence between the congressional structure and the nation's formative agenda ensures that Congress will be a responsive policy maker during the early years following the creation of a new structure. The institutionalization of the structure ensures that Congress will become increasingly unresponsive as a new agenda arises that is less compatible with existing rules and structure.

The rise of a new agenda, and the consequent decline in public support for the formative agenda, is a natural and necessary phenomenon. It occurs in part because congressional implementation of the formative agenda removes it as a pressing public concern and in part because new societal problems emerge that require different types of policies from those advocated in the formative agenda. As this erosion occurs, responsiveness declines.

The decline in agenda responsiveness begins slowly (see Figure 8). During the early years of an era, a close congruence between the public agenda and the congressional agenda is virtually guaranteed since an extraordinary public majority must support an agenda before the legislators can reach common policy agreement and implement a new structure. The early decline that does occur in congressional responsiveness—in its ability to deliver policies that the public wants—occurs not because of emerging disagreements between Congress and the majority of the citizens, but because the initial waves of organizational fragmentation in Congress may undermine its capacity to make decisions as rapidly or as satisfactorily as the public desires.

The crisis that results from this fragmentation centers on the proper way to address the policy choices within an existing agenda, not on the

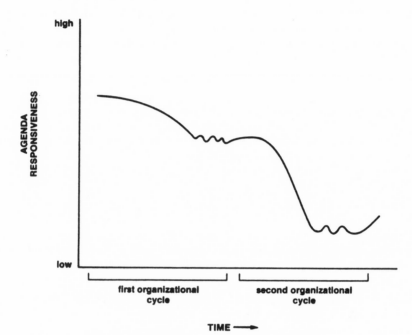

Figure 8. Change in agenda responsiveness.

appropriateness of the agenda. During the second cycle, by contrast, the public support for the formative agenda itself will have decayed and congruence between Congress and the public thus will have declined dramatically. This growing incongruence, together with the organizational fragmentation of Congress, produces a dramatic decline in its agenda responsiveness. The resulting crisis centers on the selection of a new policy agenda and the creation of a new congressional structure that can implement it.

Agenda responsiveness during the two cycles thus differs in important ways (Figure 8). The first cycle, with a close congruence between the congressional agenda and the public agenda, experiences high overall responsiveness. The crises of the first cycle may be quite severe, aggravated by events beyond the control of Congress. Thus the crisis of the interwar cycle, the first cycle of the industrial period, was the Great Depression, a worldwide phenomenon that was certainly one of the most debilitating experiences in American history. Yet the close congruence between the fundamental agenda orientation of Congress (its amenability to distributive policy making) and the broad agenda concerns of society (the need for new spending programs) meant that the crisis could be handled by a change in parties and by organizational reforms, rather than by long term struggles over the policy agenda and the structure of Congress.

The structure of Congress during the first cycle, in other words, meshes sufficiently with the type of problems society faces that it can facilitate policy responsiveness even to the most severe crisis. The second cycle of an era produces a very different situation. During this cycle, policy responsiveness declines in a very rapid and steady manner. The decline results both from the maintenance of an anachronistic structure, and from the fragmentation of the internal organizational resources. The decline culminates in societal crisis, an agenda realignment among the parties, and structural transformation.

The societal crisis of the second cycle, even if of less apparent magnitude than that of the first, may well produce a much greater challenge to the responsiveness of the institution. In the first cycle, the structure of Congress, still relatively new, facilitates the policy concerns of most of the public. The structure of Congress in the second cycle, by contrast, facilitates an agenda irrelevent to most citizens and to the critical problems of society. Crisis resolution thus will require much more extensive changes in the agenda orientation and structure of Congress and in the parties that govern Congress. The institutional and policy transformations of the 1970s are an apt illustration.

Explaining the Transformations of the Seventies

The societal crises that led to the reforms of the 1970s—the domestic problems associated with civil rights and social and economic planning, and the foreign problems associated with Vietnam and declining world dominance—lacked the sharp effect on the nation's economic and social life that the Depression had. But whereas the congressional structure of Congress in the 1930s meshed with the policy problems of the period reasonably well, the structure of the sixties and early seventies did not. The later structure, oriented for fifty years to protecting the rights of regional majorities such as whites in the South, to making distributive industrial policy, and to supporting presidential leadership of foreign policy, was unprepared to handle questions of individual liberties, redistributive planning, and the constraint of presidential war making.

The wide gap between the nation's postwar policy problems and its institutional arrangements meant that the resolution of the problems required a greater focus on institutional change than in the thirties. The struggle over party realignment thus was a fundamental change in the agenda orientation of the parties. They had to define themselves not just according to how extensively they would distribute the resources of an industrial nation but also according to how they would manage the transition to a postindustrial order (Carmines and Stimson, this volume; Collie and Brady, 1985; Sinclair, 1982).

The struggle over the policy procedures in Congress likewise involved a prolonged effort to alter the core structure of the institution. The resulting congressional changes—subcommittee government to help facilitate the creation and protection of the new social and economic policies, a new budget process to provide postindustrial planning, the weakening of the Rules Committee, seniority and the Senate filibuster to help decrease the blocking power of entrenched minorities, the War Powers Act to strengthen congressional influence over foreign policy—all of these were major alterations in policy making structure. These alterations helped ensure responsiveness of Congress to the societal agenda generated by the problems of the new era.

The institutional and policy changes of the 1970s thus can be explained as the product of a long delayed agenda change within Congress. This agenda change was delayed in part by the longevity and political skills of the formative generation of legislators who created committee government in the 1910s. Their long term dominance of Congress, combined with the extraordinary majority rules that they created, supressed the restructuring of Congress for over fifty years. This delay was fostered, moveover, by the fragmentation of organizational resources within Congress and the consequent difficulty that reformers faced in gaining support for structural changes from the many legislators who benefited from resource dispersion.

These delays ended in the sixties and early seventies with the occurrence of three critical developments. First, the last members of the formative generation of the 1910s, symbolized by Speaker Sam Rayburn, passed from power. Second, the new generation began to seek a common policy ground, pushed into this endeavor by severe domestic and foreign crises. Third, the interventionist actions of Johnson and Nixon, specifically the unconstitutional impoundments of appropriated funds and the undeclared wars in Viet Nam and Cambodia, convinced the members that their personal policy making power, whether in domestic or foreign policy, required a new congressional structure that would enable Congress to respond more adequately to the nation's policy agenda and thereby protect its policy prerogatives from presidential encroachment.

These three developments made the reforms of the 1970s possible (see also, Rieselbach, 1986). The result is a structure quite different from committee government (Smith, 1985)—a technocratic structure designed to meet the policy needs of the postindustrial era: technical experts in specific policy areas, located increasingly at the subcommittee level (Dodd and Schott, 1979; Smith and Deering, 1984), work with planning experts in the central budget committees, the party leadership and the resource agencies to create explicit budgetary agendas that reflect both the wide ranging needs of different segments of society and the general collective needs of society as a whole (Ellwood and Thurber, 1977; Schick, 1980; Sinclair, 1983). These technical experts include an increasingly large and influential body of appointed staff (Malbin, 1980). The members and staff face fewer formal hurdles to their policy proposals than did policy specialists in committee government, with Senate cloture having been modified and the Rules Committee brought under greater majority control (Oppenheimer, 1977, 1985). In addition, legislators who are concerned about the lack of policy mastery by particular committee leaders can more easily remove them from their leadership position than in the past, since the seniority norm has been weakened by rules changes (Parker, 1979).

This new technocratic structure has had a significant impact on congressional policy making. Witness the proposals for tax and spending cuts that emerged from Congress in the late seventies, the energy legislation of the mid-seventies (Oppenheimer, 1974, 1981; Sinclair, 1983), the constraints on presidential war making (Art, 1985; Kaiser, 1978), and the adaptation and institutionalization of a variety of domestic programs (Orfield, 1975; Champagne, 1986; Lyons and Taylor, 1981). Perhaps the most notable impact on the nation's governing agenda has been the passage of the 1981 budget, which reduced the annual rate of increase in social spending, expanded the rise of defense spending, and decreased taxes. These decisions would not have been made, certainly not in the extensive form they finally took, without the creation of the new budget process and related structural changes in Congress (Ferejohn and Krehbiel, 1985; Ellwood, 1985). They are a prime example of how structural change facilitates change in the policy agenda of Congress and the nation.

Looking to the future, Congress should now begin to experience renewed fragmentation of its organization and rigidification of the new structure, thereby producing a gradual decline in policy performance. We can thus expect the policy resurgence of the past decade to recede, short of extraordinary circumstances, to be replaced eventually by policy immobilism and executive dominance. The long-term ability of Congress to survive this period of decline and then to rejuvenate itself depends in part, no doubt, on whether the technocratic structure is sufficiently meshed with the nation's policy agenda to maintain a fair degree of social order and political responsiveness despite the inevitable decline in policy performance. Scholars thus must consider whether the reorganization of the 1970s sufficiently transformed Congress so that it can effectively address the postindustrial agenda (Davidson and Oleszek, 1977).

CONCLUSION

The message of this chapter should be clear: Congress is a dynamic institution characterized by recurring cycles of organizational, structural, and policy change. These cycles are an unintended consequence of the legislators' quest for power. This quest establishes a cyclical rhythm that vibrates across the entire spectrum of congressional life. This rhythm produces periodic reforms and policy resurgence, thereby explaining the institutional and policy changes of the last fifteen years. But the utility of the cyclical perspective goes far beyond the explanation of institutional reform. The cyclical variations detailed here—in the resources and skills of legislators and in the organization and structure of Congress—should help explain change in a wide variety of congressional phenomena, from electoral behavior to committee decision making to legislative-executive relations.

This broad potential significance places a great importance on empirical explorations and tests of the cyclical theory. Immediate topics for investigation range from microlevel studies of members' career cycles, career frustrations, and career agendas to macrolevel analyses of organizational fragmentation, structural rigidification, and agenda transformation. Each of these topics is relatively new to congressional research. The overall theory thus will require extensive empirical work before it can be fully assessed. Efforts to apply the theory to empirical research will also have to revise and refine its concepts and arguments before they can be applied to specific research topics.

The theory developed here, for example, is much too limited historically. Its assumptions, such as the existence of low turnover and high careerism, reflect conditions that were peculiar to the industrial era. Different patterns of turnover and careerism existed in other eras (Bullock, 1972; Fiorina, Rohde and Wissel, 1975; Polsby, 1968; Price, 1975; Swenson, 1982; Young, 1966), as a result of different social structures and policy agendas, and produced cycles of change somewhat different from those of the industrial era. Thus students of the agrarian or postagrarian period must adjust the theoretical arguments to fit the underlying empirical conditions present in these earlier periods. Students of contemporary and future politics must do likewise. They must identify the new patterns of electoral competitiveness and turnover likely to emerge during postindustrialism and determine the types of cyclical change that these new patterns of careerism are likely to produce (Dodd, 1981; Huntington, 1974; Lenchner, 1979).

Other adjustments are likewise needed to refine the theory's applicability.

The current theory ignores the bicameral nature of Congress and thus fails to indicate the different patterns of change that might characterize the two houses (Fenno, 1982; Longley and Oleszek, 1983; Carmines and Dodd, 1985; Ornstein, 1981). The theory treats the presidency as a sort of unsung antihero—always the aggressive outsider prepared to intervene in Congress—without considering the ebbs and flows of presidential activism (Barber, 1980; Lowi, 1985; Moe, 1985; Rockman, 1984; Skowronek, 1984). It likewise ignores influence from other actors such as the courts (Scigliano, 1971) and the bureaucracy (Aberbach, 1979; Arnold, 1979; Dodd and Schott, 1979; Ripley and Franklin, 1980). And the theory treats the external changes in societal structure and constituent behavior as a fairly continuous and steady process when in fact it could be, or could become, quite uneven and volitile (Huntington, 1974; Lowi, 1971). These and similar phenomena must be incorporated into the theory if it is to provide a full and accurate explanation of changes in congressional policy making.

These various refinements, however, should not alter the theory's basic argument. It sees political actors—both the legislators and their constituents—as imbued with a vital desire to shape the direction of national policy through the exercise of congressional power. Citizens exercise power by electing legislators who will deliver policies they desire; legislators exercise their power by making policy decisions.

The single-minded pursuit of personal power will foster excessively self-centered and short-sighted behavior—a preoccupation by the citizens with the election of those legislators who can most effectively provide them with immediate personal benefits through constituent services; a preoccupation by legislators with organizational resources and reelection. But such behavior ultimately will give way, in the face of crisis, to a collective realization by constituents and legislators alike that true mastery of the policy process requires the existence of a strong and vibrant Congress. Only when Congress can implement broad-gauged policy decisions can personal power in electoral and institutional decision making translate into significant power over public policy (Maass, 1983).

The cycles of congressional life thus result from a continuing struggle between the desire for personal power and the need for collective cooperation. These cycles have their tragic overtones, witnessed in the destruction of the common welfare that occurs in periods of policy immobilism (Hardin, 1968). Yet such tragedy can be offset over the long run by the capacity of legislators and citizens alike to learn from their collective experiences, adapt the structure of Congress to new societal problems, and thereby redress the public's policy grievances. It is this long term possibility of institutional transformation and rejuvenation that makes the puzzle of congressional change such a central topic in the study of American politics.

Acknowledgments. My thanks to David Brady, Edward Carmines, Joseph Cooper, Richard Fenno, John Kingdon, Gerhard Loewenberg, Thomas Mann, David Mayhew, Michael Mezey, John Padgett, John Pierce, Leroy Rieselbach, Earl Shaw, and Samuel Patterson for their advice and support at various stages during the development of this work. I am also indebted to the Hoover Institution and to the Dirksen Center for their financial support during the preparation of the essay and to the APSA Congressional Fellowship Program for providing me the first-hand experience in Congress that made the essay possible.

NOTES

1. It also builds on the vast literature on Congress (Rieselbach, 1984; Schwarz and Shaw, 1976), drawing particularly on the work of Cooper (1975, 1977), Fenno (1973), and Mayhew (1974) for the theory of organizational change, the work of Fenno (1978), Huntington (1965, 1981), Kingdon (1968, 1984), Mayhew (1974), Polsby (1968, 1975), and Sundquist (1981) for the theory of institutional change, and the work of Huntington (1965, 1981) and Sundquist (1981) for the theory of policy change. This essay also owes a special debt to Woodrow Wilson's *Congressional Government* (1885). For a more extensive discussion, see Dodd (1985, 1986).
2. The emphasis on a cyclical approach to change is also supported by the work of Blondel (1973). Surveying all contemporary legislatures he found cycles of decline and resurgence to be the single most widely shared characteristic of legislatures and thus the phenomenon around which a theory of legislative change could be most productively constructed.

REFERENCES

Aberbach, Joel D. (1979). Changes in congressional oversight. *American Behavioral Scientist* 22: 493–515.

Arnold, R. Douglas (1979). *Congress and the Bureaucracy: A Theory of Influence.* New Haven, Conn.: Yale University Press.

Art, Robert J. (1984). Congress and the Defense Budget: new procedures and old realities, 1975–1983. Unpublished manuscript, Brandeis University. See also Robert J. Art, Vincent Davis, and Samuel P. Huntington, eds. (1985). *Reorganizing America's Defense: Leadership in War and Peace.* Pergamon.

Asher, Herbert (1973). The learning of legislative norms. *American Political Science Review* 67: 499–513.

Bardach, Eugene (1972). *The Skill Factor in Politics: Repealing the Mental Commitment Laws in California.* Berkeley: University of California Press.

Blondel, Jean (1973). *Comparative Legislatures.* Englewood Cliffs, N.J.: Prentice-Hall.

Bolling, Richard (1965). *House Out of Order.* New York: Dutton.

Bolling, Richard (1968). *Power in the House.* New York: Capricorn.

Brady, David W. (1973). *Congressional Voting in a Partisan Era.* Lawrence, Kan.: University of Kansas Press.

Brady, David (1978). Critical elections, congressional parties, and clusters of policy change. *British Journal of Political Science* 8: 79–99.

Brady, David W., and Bullock, Charles (1981). Coalition politics in the House of Representatives. in Dodd and Oppenheimer *Congress Reconsidered*, 2nd ed., pp. 186–202.

Broder, David S. (1980). *Changing of the Guard: Power and Leadership In America.* New York: Simon & Schuster.

Brown, George R. (1922). *The Leadership of Congress*. Indianapolis: Bobbs-Merrill.

Bullock, Charles S. (1972). House careerists: changing patterns of longevity and attrition. *American Political Science Review* 66: 1295–1300.

Bullock, Charles S., and Burdett A. Loomis (1985). The changing congressional career. In Dodd and Oppenheimer, *Congress Reconsidered*, 3rd. ed. pp. 65–84.

Burnham, Walter Dean (1970). *Critical Elections and the Mainsprings of American Politics*. New York: Norton.

Burns, James MacGregor (1963). *The Deadlock of Democracy*. Englewood Cliffs, N. J.: Prentice-Hall.

Carmines, Edward G., and Dodd, Lawrence C. (1985). Bicameralism in Congress: The changing partnership. In Dodd and Oppenheimer, *Congress Reconsidered*, 3rd ed., pp. 414–436.

Champagne, Richard (1986). The complex evolution of U. S. civil rights policy: 1937–1984. Ph.D. dissertation, Indiana University.

Chamberlain, Lawrence H. (1947). *The President, Congress and Legislation*. New York: Columbia University Press.

Chubb, John E., and Peterson, Paul E., eds. (1985). *The New Direction in American Politics*. Washington, D.C.: The Brookings Institution.

Clausen, Aage R. (1973). *How Congressmen Decide*. New York: St Martin's Press.

Cobb, Roger W., and Charles D. Elder (1972). *Participation in America: The Dynamics of Agenda-Building*. Boston: Allyn and Bacon.

Cobb, Roger W. and Elder, Charles D. (1981). Communications and public policy. In Dan Nimmo and Keith Sanders (eds.) *Handbook of Political Communications*. Beverly Hills: Sage.

Collie, Melissa P., and Brady, David W. (1985). The decline of partisan voting coalitions in the House of Representatives. In Dodd and Oppenheimer, *Congress Reconsidered*, 3rd ed.

Cooper, Joseph (1971). *The Origins of the Standing Committees and the Development of the Modern House*. Houston: William Marsh Rice University.

Cooper, Joseph (1975). Strengthening the Congress: an organizational analysis. *Harvard Journal on Legislation* 12: 307–368.

Cooper, Joseph (1977). Congress in organizational perspective. In *Congress Reconsidered*, 1st ed.

Cooper, Joseph, and Brady, David W. (1981a). Institutional context and leadership style: The House from Cannon to Rayburn. *American Political Science Review* 75: 411–425.

Cooper, Joseph, and Brady, David W. (1981b). Toward a diachronic analysis of change. *American Political Science Review* 75: 988–1006.

Davidson, Roger H., and Oleszek, Walter J. (1977). *Congress Against Itself*. Bloomington, IN: Indiana University Press.

Davidson, Roger H., and Oleszek, Walter J. (1981). *Congress and Its Members*. Washington: D. C.: Congressional Quarterly.

Dexter, Lewis Anthony (1969). *The Sociology and Politics of Congress*. Chicago: Rand McNally.

Dodd, Lawrence C. (1977). Congress and the quest for power. In Dodd and Oppenheimer, *Congress Reconsidered*, 1st ed., pp. 269–307.

Dodd, Lawrence C. (1981). Congress, the constitution, and the crisis of legitimation. In Dodd and Oppenheimer, *Congress Reconsidered*, 2nd ed.

Dodd, Lawrence C. (1985). Woodrow Wilson and the postindustrial Congress: some lessons from *Congressional Government*. A paper prepared for delivery at the 1985 American Political Science Convention, New Orleans.

Dodd, Lawrence C. (1986). The cycles of legislative change. In Herbert Weisberg (ed.), *Political Science: the Science of Politics*, pp. 82–104. New York: Agathon Press.

Dodd, Lawrence C., and Oppenheimer, Bruce I., eds. *Congress Reconsidered*, first ed. (1977). New York: Praeger. Second ed. (1981) and third ed. (1985). Washington, D.C.: Congressional Quarterly.

Dodd, Lawrence C., and Schott, Richard L. (1979). *Congress and the Administrative State.* New York: Wiley.

Ellwood, John W., and Thurber, James A. (1977). The new congressional budget process. In Dodd and Oppenheimer, *Congress Reconsidered*, 1st ed. pp. 163–192.

Ellwood, John W. (1985). The great exception: the congressional budget process in an age of decentralization." In Dodd and Oppenheimer, *Congress Reconsidered*, 3rd ed., pp. 315–342.

Erikson, Robert S., and Wright, Gerald C. (1985). Voters, candidates, and issues in congressional elections. In Dodd and Oppenheimer, *Congress Reconsidered*, 3rd ed., pp. 87–108.

Evans, Rowland, and Novak, Robert (1966). *Lyndon B. Johnson: The Exercise of Power.* New York: New American Library.

Fenno, Richard F., Jr. (1973). *Congressmen in Committees.* Boston: Little, Brown.

Fenno, Richard F., Jr. (1978). *Home Style.* Boston: Little, Brown.

Fenno, Richard F., Jr. (1982). *The United States Senate: A Bicameral Perspective.* Washington, D. C.: American Enterprise Institute for Public Policy Research.

Ferejohn, John A. (1974). *Pork Barrel Politics.* Stanford, Calif. Stanford University Press.

Ferejohn, John A. and Krehbiel, Keith (1985). Reconciliation and the size of the budget. *Working Papers in Political Science No. P-85-2.* The Hoover Institution, Stanford University.

Fiorina, Morris P. (1977). *Congress: Keystone of the Washington Establishment.* New Haven, Conn.: Yale University Press.

Fiorina, Morris P., Rohde, David W., and Wissel, Peter (1975). Historical change in House turnover. In Norman J. Ornstein (ed.) *Congress in Change.* New York: Praeger.

Fox, Harrison W., Jr., and Hammond, Susan Webb (1977). *Congressional Staffs: The Invisible Force in American Lawmaking.* New York: Free Press.

Froman, Lewis A. (1963). *The Congressmen and Their Constituencies.* Chicago: Rand McNally.

Galloway, George B. (1951). The operation of the Legislative Reorganization Act of 1946. *American Political Science Review* 45: 41–68.

Hardin, Garrett (1968). The tragedy of the commons. *Science* 162: 1242–1248.

Hechler, Kenneth W. (1940). *Insurgency: Personalities and Politics in the Taft Era.* New York: Columbia University Press.

Hershey, Marjorie R. (1974). *The Making of Campaign Strategy.* Lexington, Mass.: Lexington Books.

Hershey, Marjorie R. (1984). *Running for Office: The Political Education of Campaigners.* Chatham N.J.: Chatham House.

Huitt, Ralph (1961). The Democratic Party leadership in the Senate. *American Political Science Review* 55: 331–344.

Huitt, Ralph (1965). The internal distribution of influence: the Senate. In Truman, *Congress and America's Future.*

Huntington, Samuel P. (1965). Congressional responses to the twentieth century. In Truman, *Congress and America's Future*, pp. 5–31.

Huntington, Samuel P. (1971). The change to change: modernization, development and politics. *Comparative Politics* 3: 283–322.

Huntington, Samuel P. (1974). Postindustrial politics: how benign will it be? *Comparative Politics* 6: 163–192.

Huntington, Samuel P. (1981). *American Politics: The Promise of Disharmony.* Cambridge, Mass.: Harvard University Press.

Jacobson, Gary C. (1983). *The Politics of Congressional Elections*. Boston: Little, Brown.

Johannes, John R. (1972). *Policy Innovation in Congress*. Morristown, N. J.: General Learning Press.

Jones, Charles O. (1970). *The Minority Party in Congress*. Boston: Little, Brown.

Jones, Charles O. (1977). How reform changes congress. In Welsh and Peters, *Legislative Reform and Public Policy*.

Jones, Rochelle, and Woll, Peter (1979). *The Private World of Congress*. New York: Free Press.

Kaiser, Fred M. (1978). Congressional change and foreign policy. In Rieselbach, *Legislative Reform*, pp. 61–72.

Kernell, Samuel (1977). Toward understanding 19th century careers, ambition, competition and rotation. *American Journal of Political Science* 21: 669–693.

Key, V. O. (1955). A theory of critical elections. *Journal of Politics* 17: 3–18.

Kingdon, John W. (1968) *Candidates for Office*. New York: Random House.

Kingdon, John W. (1973). *Congressmen's Voting Decisions*. New York: Harper & Row.

Kingdon, John W. (1984). *Agendas, Alternatives and Public Policies*. Boston: Little, Brown.

Kuklinski, James, and West, Darrell (1981). Economic expectations and mass voting in United States House and Senate elections. *American Political Science Review* 75: 436–447.

Kuklinski, James (1983). Unpublished conference talk, Indiana University.

Lenchner, Paul (1979). Postindustrialization and the new Congress. Paper presented at the annual meeting of the Southern Political Science Association, Atlanta.

Longley, Lawrence D., and Oleszek, Walter J. The three contexts of congressional conference committee politics: bicameral politics overviewed. Paper presented at the annual meeting of the American Political Science Association, Chicago.

Loomis, Burdette A. (1981). Congressional caucuses and the politics of representation. In Dodd and Oppenheimer, *Congress Reconsidered*, 2nd ed, pp. 204–220.

Lowi, Theodore (1964). American business, public policy, case studies, and political theory. *World Politics* 16: 677–715.

Lowi, Theodore (1971). *The Politics of Disorder*. New York: Basic Books.

Lowi, Theodore (1979). *The End of Liberalism*. New York: Norton.

Lowi, Theodore (1985). *The Personal President: Power Invested, Promise Unfulfilled*. Ithaca, N.Y.: Cornell University Press.

Lyons, Michael, and Taylor, Marcia Whicker (1981). Farm politics in transition: The House Agriculture Committee. *Agricultural History* 55: 128–146.

Maass, Arthur (1983). *Congress and the Common Good*. New York: Basic Books.

Malbin, Michael J. (1980). *Unelected Representatives*. New York: Basic Books.

Manley, John F. (1969). Wilbur Mills: a study in congressional influence. *American Political Science Review* LXIII: 442–464.

Manley, John F. (1977). The conservative coalition in congress. In Dodd and Oppenheimer, *Congress Reconsidered*, 2nd ed., pp. 75–95.

Mann, Thomas E. (1978). *Unsafe At Any Margin*. Washington, D. C.: American Enterprise Institute.

Masters, Nicholas (1961). Committee assignments in the House of Representatives. *American Political Science Review* 55: 345–357.

Matthews, Donald R. (1960). *U. S. Senators and Their World*. New York: Vintage Books.

Mayhew, David P. (1974). *Congress: The Electoral Connection*. New Haven, Conn.: Yale University Press.

Moe, Ronald C., and Teel, Steven C. (1970). Congress as policy-maker: a necessary reappraisal. *Political Science Quarterly* 85: 443–470.

Moe, Terry M. (1985). The politicized presidency. In Chubb and Peterson, *The New Direction in American Politics*, pp. 235–272.

Muir, William K., Jr. (1982). *Legislature: California School for Politics*. Chicago: The University of Chicago Press.

Nelson, Garrison (1977). Partisan patterns of house leadership change, 1789–1977. *American Political Science Review* 71: 918–939.

Oppenheimer, Bruce I. (1974). *Oil and the Congressional Process: The Limits of Symbolic Politics*. Lexington, Mass.: Lexington Books.

Oppenheimer, Bruce I. (1977). The Rules Committee: new arm of the leadership in a decentralized House. In Dodd and Oppenheimer, eds., *Congress Reconsidered*, 1st ed., pp. 96–116.

Oppenheimer, Bruce I. (1981). Congress and the new obstructionism: developing an energy program. In Dodd and Oppenheimer, *Congress Reconsidered*, 2nd ed.

Oppenheimer, Bruce I. (1985). Changing time constraints on Congress: historical perspectives on the use of cloture. In Dodd and Oppenheimer, *Congress Reconsidered*, 3rd ed., pp. 393–413.

Orfield, Gary (1975). *Congressional Power: Congress and Social Change*. New York: Harcourt Brace Jovanovich.

Ornstein, Norman (1981). The House and Senate in a new Congress. In Thomas Mann and Norman Ornstein (eds.), *The New Congress*. Washington, D. C.: American Enterprise Institute for Public Policy Research.

Ornstein, Norman, and Rohde, David (1977). Revolt from within: congressional change, legislative policy and the House Commerce Committee. In Welsh and Peters, *Legislative Reform and Public Policy*, pp. 54–72.

Parker, Glenn R. (1979). The selection of committee leaders in the house of representatives. *American Politics Quarterly* 7(January): 71–93.

Parker, Glenn R. (1984). Stylistic changes in the constituency orientations of U. S. senators: 1959–1980. Paper prepared for Presentation at the 1984 Midwest Political Science Convention.

Patterson, James T. (1977). *Congressional Conservatism and the New Deal*. Lexington, Ky.: University of Kentucky Press.

Patterson, Samuel C. (1978). The semi-sovereign Congress. In Anthony King, (ed.), *The New American Political System*. pp. 125–177. Washington, D. C.: American Enterprise Institute.

Peabody, Robert L. (1976). *Leadership in Congress*. Boston: Little, Brown.

Polsby, Nelson W., Gallaher, Miriam, and Rundquist, Barry S. (1968). Growth of the seniority system in the U. S. House of Representatives. *American Political Science Review* 63(Sept.): 787–807.

Polsby, Nelson W. (1968). Institutionalization of the House of Representatives. *American Political Science Review* 62: 144–68.

Polsby, Nelson W. (1971). Strengthening Congress in national policy making. In Nelson W. Polsby (ed.), *Congressional Behavior*, pp. 3–27. New York: Random House.

Polsby, Nelson W. (1975). Legislatures. In Fred I. Greenstein and Nelson W. Polsby (eds.),. *Government Institutions and Processes, Handbook of Political Science 5*, pp. 257–319. Reading, Mass.: Addison-Wesley.

Polsby, Nelson W. (1984). *Political Innovation in America*. New Haven: Yale University Press.

Price, David (1972). *Who Makes the Laws?* Cambridge, Mass.: Schenkman Publishing Co.

Price, Douglas (1975). Congress and the evolution of legislative professionalism. In Norman J. Ornstein (ed.), *Congress in Change*. New York: Praeger.

Prindle, David T., and Franklin, Daniel P. (1985). Testing two purposive theories of congressional behavior. Paper presented at the 1985 Meetings of the Western Political Science Association, Las Vegas, Nevada. March 28–30.

Rieselbach, Leroy (1978). *Legislative Reform: The Policy Impact.* Lexington, Mass.: Lexington Books.

Rieselbach, Leroy N. (1984). The forest for the trees: blazing trails for congressional research. In Ada W. Finifter (ed.), *Political Science: The State of the Discipline.* Washington, D. C.: American Political Science Association.

Rieselbach, Leroy (1986). *Congressional Reform.* Washington, D. C.: Congressional Quarterly.

Ripley, Randall B. (1969). *Majority Party Leadership in Congress.* Boston: Little, Brown.

Ripley, Randall, and Franklin, Grace A. (1980). *Congress, the Bureaucracy and Public Policy.* Homewood, Ill.: Dorsey Press.

Rockman, Bert (1984). *The Leadership Question: The Presidency and the American System.* New York: Praeger.

Rohde, David W., Ornstein, Norman J., and Peabody, Robert L. (1985). Political change and legislative norms in the U. S. Senate, 1957–1974. In Glenn R. Parker (ed.), *Studies of Congress.* pp. 147–188. Washington, D. C.: Congressional Quarterly.

Rudder, Catherine (1985). Fiscal responsibility and the revenue committees. In Dodd and Oppenheimer, *Congress Reconsidered*, 3rd ed., pp. 211–222.

Schick, Allen (1980). *Congress and Money.* Washington, D. C.: The Urban Institute.

Schiff, Steven H., and Smith, Steven S. (1983). Generational change and the allocation of staff in the U. S. Congress. *Legislative Studies Quarterly* VIII: 457–467.

Schwarz, John E. And Shaw, L. Earl (1976). *The United States Congress in Comparative Perspective.* Hinsdale, Ill.: Dryden Press.

Scigliano, Robert (1971). *The Supreme Court and the Presidency.* New York: Free Press.

Shepsle, Kenneth A. (1978). *The Giant Jigsaw Puzzle.* Chicago: University of Chicago Press.

Sinclair, Barbara (1982). *Congressional Realignment, 1925–1978.* Austin: University of Texas Press.

Sinclair, Barbara (1983). *Majority Leadership in the U.S. House.* Baltimore: Johns Hopkins Press.

Skowronek, Stephen (1984). Presidential leadership in political time. In Michael Nelson, ed., *The Presidency and the Political System.* Washington, D.C.: Congressional Quarterly.

Smith, Steven S. (1985). New patterns of decisionmaking in Congress. In Chubb and Peterson, *The New Direction in American Politics*, pp. 203–234.

Smith, Steven S., and Deering, Christopher J. (1984). *Committees in Congress.* Washington, D. C.: Congressional Quarterly.

Stevens, Arthur G., Miller, Arthur H., and Mann Thomas E. (1974). Mobilization of liberal strength in the House, 1955–1970: The Democratic Study Group. *American Political Science Review* 68: 667–681.

Strom, Gerald, and Rundquist, Barry S. (1978). On explaining legislative organization. Paper presented at the Annual Meeting of the American Political Science Association, New York.

Sundquist, James (1973). *Dynamics of the Party System: Alignment and Realignment of Political Parties in the United States.* Washington, D. C.: Brookings Institution.

Sundquist, James. (1981). *The Decline and Resurgence of Congress.* Washington, D. C.: The Brookings Institution.

Swenson, Peter (1982). The influence of recruitment on the structure of power in the U. S. House, 1870–1940. Legislative Studies Quarterly VII: 7–36.

Truman, David B., ed. (1965). *Congress and America's Future.* Englewood Cliffs, N. J.: Prentice-Hall.

Welsh, Susan, and Peters, John G., eds. (1977). *Legislative Reform and Public Policy.* New York: Praeger.

Westefield, L. P. (1974). Majority party leadership and the committee system in the House of Representatives. *American Political Science Review* 68: 1593–1604.

Wilson, Woodrow (1885). *Congressional Government.* (Reissued by the Johns Hopkins Press, Baltimore, 1985.)

Wolfinger, Raymond E., and Heifetz, Joan (1965). Safe seats, seniority and power in congress. *American Political Science Review* 59: 337–349.

Wright, Gerald C., Jr., and Berkman, Michael B. (1985). Candidates and policy in the 1982 U. S. Senate elections: a comparative state analysis. Paper presented at the 1985 Annual Meeting of the Western Political Science Association, Las Vegas, Nevada.

Young, James S. (1966). *The Washington Community, 1800–1828.* New York: Columbia University Press.

The Electoral Sources
of Policy Change in Congress

2

Electoral Realignments in the U.S. House of Representatives

David W. Brady

Public policy in the United States is normally incremental; however, there are periods where electoral change results in major policy shifts. An overview of U.S. history suggests that only certain elections have been critical in redirecting the path of public policy. "Clusters of policy change" passed by the U.S. House of Representatives during the Civil War era (1860s), the 1890s, and the New Deal (1930s) have followed "critical elections" (Brady, 1978; Brady with Stewart, 1982; Burnham, 1970; Sinclair, 1977). But, the question remains, "Why are some elections followed by significant public policy changes, but other elections are not?" It is this question that concerns us in this essay, and we begin with the hope of specifying the conditions necessary for an election to "matter" in terms of policy change.

To show how critical elections lead to House passage of major policy changes, we begin by showing why most elections do not result in changes in public policy. With this baseline established, we outline a theory of the ways critical elections change conditions so that public policy change results. We then test the theory by examining the effects of critical elections on House voting patterns.

WHY MOST ELECTIONS DON'T CHANGE THINGS

Normally, public policy changes only incrementally over time. Why is this the case? One reason lies in the structural arrangements of our governmental system—federalism, separation of powers, checks and balances, and single member plurality electoral arrangements. A second, and related, reason is that these structural factors affect the political party system—the party in the

47

electorate, the party organization, and the party as government (Sorauf, 1968). A final reason appears when we analyze how the internal structure of the House of Representatives reflects these structural and party arrangements (Cooper, 1977). In the following sections, I outline the ways that each of these reasons contributes to policy incrementalism. Only after these are made clear can we begin to understand how elections sometimes overcome the systemic incremental biases and produce significant policy change.

THE CONSTITUTIONAL CONTEXT

The first defining feature of the structure in which public policy is made is that the system of government is federal. The Articles of Confederation could not pull together the diverse state and sectional interests that existed, so the founding fathers met in Philadelphia in 1787 for the expressed purpose of amending the Articles. Their central problem was how to create a more centralized government without creating a form of government so centralized that the various sectional interests would not approve or join (Dahl, 1956). There was never any serious question of creating a unitary government. Not only would such a thought have been repugnant to many of those in attendance, but a uniform national government would have been impossible to create given the vast state and sectional differences. Delegates to the convention were selected on a state basis; voting was by states; the various governmental proposals, such as the Virginia and New Jersey plans, were proposed by and named after states; and ratification was by states. Before, during, and after the Constitutional Convention, states' interests were an accepted fact of political life.

The most obvious effect of this regionalism is that to the extent that a federal system reflects and recognizes in government organization the social, economic, and religious differences between states, it represents a "numerous and diverse population" (Dahl, 1956; *Federalist*, Nos. 10, 51). The Father of the Constitution, James Madison, argued that such a population constituted a real check on the ability to form a majority that could act hastily. From Alexander Hamilton's use of the Treasury Department to boost industrial and monied interests to the present sunbelt-snowbelt controversy, different sectional interests have pressured Congress to pass legislation viewed as beneficial to one and inimical to others. Certainly the Civil War and the 1896 realignments were highly sectional in nature. These and countless other events in American history are eloquent testimony to the effects of sectional diversity on the American system of government. As a focal point for those differences, the House has had (and continues) not only to deal with different issues in a policy sense, but also to temper sectional demands by integrating this divisiveness. And, of course, a la

Madison, such divisiveness made it difficult to form hasty majorities, i.e., majorities capable of enacting significant policy changes.

Diversity of populace as a roadblock to majorities was not sufficient for the founding fathers. Their major assumption was that the concentration of the legislative, executive, and judicial powers in the same hands would be tyranny. To prevent such tyranny, they established in the Constitution the doctrines of separation of powers and checks and balances. These doctrines have resulted in an American system of government that is characterized by "separate powers sharing functions" (Huntington, 1965). This is in contra-distinction to other western democracies where power is centralized and functions are more specific. Thus, one distinguishing feature of the U. S. House is that, unlike the British House of Commons, it shares power with the Senate, the President, the courts, and the bureaucracy. The most immediate effect of the separation of powers and checks and balances on the House is that even when it can build majorities for innovative policies, the Senate, the President, or the courts must be considered. Neustadt (1976) and others have shown that each of these institutions has different constit-uencies to please and, therefore, different policy solutions. Policy makers in the House are likely to compromise or water down proposals to enhance the possibility of final enactment (Anderson, 1979). If policy is not compromised, House members are likely to find themselves forced to water down strong policy proposals by the other branches of government.

Opponents of policy changes in the American system have access to a large number of power points where a defeat for the majority position spells defeat until the next Congress forms. In the American system having a policy majority does not readily translate into significant policy change. Thus, those who seek to preserve the status quo have decided advantages. This is in contrast to majority building in most other Western democracies.

The only popularly and directly elected body provided for in the Constitution was the U.S. House of Representatives. Each member of the House was to represent an approximately equal number of people, and, more importantly, each representative was responsible to his or her constituents. There was no national party to supervise or control nomina-tion. There was no mechanism to purge members who did not follow party principles. The electoral method of single member plurality districts has enhanced and nourished localized elections. Members elected on local issues by localized and limited constituencies owe little to House leaders, and can behave as they choose as long as their constituency is happy (Mann, 1978).

An important policy consequence of localized elections is that the intense representation of local interests pervades the House across a broad range of issues. Representatives choose committees that will enhance their reelection probabilities. Members from agricultural districts serve on committees and subcommittees that deal with policies affecting their constituents. Members from other types of districts serve on committees and subcommittees relevant to their constituencies. Thus, committees and policy outputs are dominated by local interests. This phenomenon has been called policy making or control by "little governments," "the iron triangles" of interest group liberalism, pork barrel, and policy reciprocity (Lowi, 1979; Redford, 1969). The name matters little; what counts is that the localized interests are recognized within the structure of the House's policy-making process. Forming majorities capable of enacting major policy changes against a backdrop of institutionally localized interests is a difficult task at best, and impossible at worst.

POLITICAL PARTIES IN CONTEXT

The fear of majority tyranny led the founding fathers to create a cumbersome governmental system. Federalism, separation of powers, and checks and balances were accepted as necessary to prevent majorities from tyrannizing minorities. While many of the parameters of these doctrines have changed to make the system more democratic and centralized, it is still true today that that the American system of government is fragmented and cumbersome. Shortly after the inception of the American Constitution, some of the difficulties inherent in governing within the Constitutional framework presented themselves. In response to the quest for governing, Hamilton crossed executive boundaries and led pronational factions in the Congress.

Over time, these factions developed into political parties. Essentially, American political parties were formed to fill the constitutional interstices created by the separation of powers and checks and balances. However, even though American parties were founded because without them the system was too cumbersome, the basic features of the American government also inhibited the full development of parties.

Perhaps the most distinguishing characteristic of American political parties is that the three parts—party in the electorate, party as organization, and party as government—are disjointed (Sorauf, 1968). Certainly no one claims that American parties are mass parties in the European sense of the term. Federalism, separation of powers, checks and balances, and single member plurality districts are in no small way responsible for the fragmented nature of the American party system.

The most basic effect of a federal form of government on the American party system is that rather than a two-party system we have a fifty-party system. Each state's party system has demographic, ideological, structural, and electoral peculiarities. Thus, the Democratic party in the electorate and as organization in New York has been and is distinct from the Democratic party in the electorate and as organization in Georgia. The same fact applies to the components of the Republican party in these states. The heterogeneity of the state party systems means that at the level of party as government, *unlike*-minded people wearing the same party label will come together in the House of Representatives. Put another way, the federal system brings built-in differences between states and districts to the House. While this may be useful in maintaining system equilibrium, it has most often been an extremely poor basis for building coherent congressional parties. The New Deal coalition of rural southern and agricultural interests and urban northern industrial interests is a case in point. Long after this coalition had passed its major policy changes, it served as an electoral base for the Democratic party. However, such successful electoral coalitions are often divided on major policy issues. In fact, on a number of major policy issues, such as civil rights and social welfare, the components of the New Deal coalition were (and are) poles apart. American political history abounds with examples of successful electoral coalitions that could not make major policy changes because of ideological differences. It is not difficult to surmise how such coalitions lead to status quo or incremental policy.

Separation of powers and checks and balances also enhance the fragmentary, disjointed status of American parties. Parties formed out of numerous and diverse state party systems will emphasize electoral success and minimize policy cohesion (and thus policy success). National parties formed on a sectional and coalitional basis, when given the opportunity to run for numerous offices (both appointive and elective) in the various branches, will be further fractionalized. Thus, for example, one faction of the party may be dominant in presidential politics, another in congressional politics, and since both have powers over the courts, an equal division of court appointments may result. The Democratic party from 1876 to 1976 was characterized by just such an arrangement. The northern wing dominated presidential politics and elections, the southern wing, congressional leadership posts, and both wings influenced court appointments. Such a system may enhance representation of differences, but it does little to enhance House majorities capable of legislating public policy changes.

The constitutional arrangement of single member district plurality elections also aids in fragmenting the party system. House members elected on local issues by a localized party in the electorate build local party (or personal) organizations. Once elected, and owing little to national party leaders, representatives can behave in nonpartisan ways with little personal consequence. That is, throughout most of the House's history, party leaders have only been able to persuade, not force, members to vote "correctly." Party leadership without even the threat of sanctions is likely to be unsuccessful in building consistent partisan majorities. It should not be surprising that the highest levels of party voting in the history of the House occurred at a time when the Speaker's sanctions over members was greatest (Brady and Althoff, 1974). Representatives elected by local majorities can, in turn, work for and vote those interests regardless of the national party position, and House leaders do not "persuade" from a position of power. The combination of local and state diversity being institutionalized in the American system of government allows the diversity to work its way up from party in the electorate through party organizations to congressional parties almost unchanged. Thus, at the top, as at the bottom, the American party system reflects the cumbersome and fractional nature of the American system of government. Whatever policy parties are able to enact under these conditions is bound to be incremental in nature, and changes in the status quo will be hard to come by.

Effects on House Internal Organization

Like all organizations, the House of Representatives has adapted to societal change by the creation of internal structures designed to both meet the pressures or demands from its various constituencies and to perform its policy-making function (Cooper, 1977). Given the enormous range of interests in the U.S. and the concomitant pressures generated thereby, the House responded with a division of labor. The pressures from the various regional, social, and economic interests resulted in what is today a highly complicated committee system. When the country was in its infancy and government was limited, the House formed ad hoc committees; however, by the era of Jacksonian democracy there was a standing committee system in place (Cooper, 1977). As the country grew more industrial and complicated, the House responded to these increased pressures by expanding and enlarging the committee system. The committees themselves have policy domains; thus, there were committees established early in the process of development to deal with war, post offices and roads, and ways and means to raise revenues to support the government. These committees, in Goodwin's (1970) words "little legislatures," were organized around governmental policy functions and were (and are) decentralized decision making structures. Reconstruction policy after the Civil War and Wilson's (1885) claim that "congressional government is committee government" are testimony to the power of committees at relatively early times. Decentralizing power to committees was a necessary response to pressures for government action in certain policy areas; however, to the extent that committees decided policy, party leaders were limited.

Committees were (and are) decentralized decision mechanisms dominated by members elected by and representing local interests. The fact that, within limits, members can choose on which committees to serve determines to a large extent which direction the committees' policy choices will take. The decentralized committee system, which allows members to represent local interests, has become a powerful force for policy stability. In the modern House, Huitt (1957, 1961) and others (Fenno, 1973) have shown that committees are entities unto themselves; they are stable, having little membership turnover, and new members are socialized to the committee norms which affect policy decisions. Since turnover is slow and decision norms remain stable, committee leaders were often able to prevent House majorities from enacting major policy changes. The norms of specialization and expertise as bases of power took years for new members to acquire, thus enhancing both the committee's power and policy stability. For example, even though since the late 1930s majorities of both the American people and the House favored such policies as medical aid for the aged and federal aid to schools, committee leaders were able to obstruct enactment until the 89th House (Orfield, 1975). Almost thirty years of obstructing majorities is proof both of the independence and of the power of the committee system. It is reasonable to conclude that the decentralized House committee system that nurtures local representation of interests constitutes an effective deterrent to building majorities capable of enacting major policy changes.

What the division of labor pulls apart in organizations, integrative mechanisms try to pull together. In the House, the major integrative mechanism is the majority congressional party. And, congressional parties are limited by the governmental structure established by the Constitution and by the fact that members are elected by local parties (or groups) on local issues. Members responsible to and punishable only by local electorates tend to be responsive to constituents, not parties. Under such conditions, party strength tends to be low. When party voting was at its peak in the U.S. House of Representatives, it was low compared to other western democracies. Even under ideal conditions, the congressional parties in the House have limited integrative capacity. This means that policy decisions are likely to reflect localized committee interests under normal conditions, thereby limiting the national party leaders' attempts to lead majorities toward forceful policy solutions to pressing problems. House voting patterns show different coalitions active on different policy issues (Clausen, 1973; Sinclair, 1977). Voting patterns show coalitions cutting across regional, party, social, and economic lines, making party leaders' jobs a "ceaseless maneuvering to find coalitions capable of governing" in specific policy areas (Key, 1967).

A third factor also affects the House's ability to legislate quickly: as a collegial body, the House has a limited ability to organize itself hierarchically. The American cultural emphasis on equality has affected the operation of the House. Because each member represents a separate and equal constituency, members receive the same pay and have the same rights to introduce bills, serve on committees, etc. Equality in this sense limits the House's ability to organize on a hierarchical basis, and since hierarchy is limited, the House has established elaborate procedural rules and precedents to control the passage of legislation from Speaker to committee to floor (Cooper, 1977). This procedural elaborateness emphasizes the individual member's rights to affect legislation at the various decision points in the policy process. The effect is to slow down the policy process and to encourage compromise to avoid parliamentary snafus. Both of these factors (slowness and compromise) favor incremental solutions to policy problems.

The House is then a relatively nonhierarchical body with power decentralized in committees with elaborate rules and procedures for passing legislation. The weakness of the congressional parties is partly the result of factors external to the House (local elections, cultural stress on equality, separation of powers, etc.) and partly the result of the ways the House is organized (members preference for decentralized power and the lack of leadership sanctions). In short, the facts are that "normally" committees are strong, and the parties are weak and divided. Over time, the relationship between committee power and party strength has waxed and waned, but the general rule has been that committees were strong while congressional parties have been weak. The policy choices emanating from this system have been and are normally incremental in nature. Pressures for major change are hindered by the decentralized decision making structure that has dominated in the House. The formation of the Democratic Study Group (DSG) is a case in point. The group was founded to press liberal policy alternatives in a House dominated by conservative interests. The founders of the DSG found the policy process in the House slanted toward interests (minority or otherwise) that sought to block legislation, thus preserving the status quo.

In sum, major public policy changes occur rarely in the House of Representatives for the following reasons: (1) members are normally elected by local interest on local issues; (2) once elected, members choose committee assignments (within limits) based on those local interests and issues, thus localizing rather than nationalizing policy alternatives; (3) the committee system is powerful in part because it is stable; (4) the congressional parties are normally weak and divided, thus they cannot put together coalitions that can override the localism of committee decisions; and (5) the organization, rules, and procedures of the House facilitate the interests of those who wish to preserve the status quo. It should also be mentioned that there are many historical periods where inertia or incrementalism are in accord with both the majority of the public and the majority of the House. When this is the case, the congressional system is in harmony with political pressures. However, as Burnham (1970) has argued, political systems must over time adjust to majority pressures for change. It is from this perspective that we look to elections to see how the U.S. House of Representatives has, at times, overcome these powerful biases toward incrementalism to produce significant policy changes. How do elections generate changes that allow the House to produce major policy shifts?

A THEORY OF POLICY CHANGE

It is obvious that elections do not generate changes in federalism, separation of powers, checks and balances, and single member plurality elections. These have survived many elections. The answer to the question posed above is that certain critical elections reflect partisan realignments that radically alter the standard policy making process. To understand how these realigning elections affect major public policy changes, we must begin with an understanding of the generally localized nature of congressional elections. House elections normally are determined by local factors (local interests, organization and issues), thereby assuring the dominance of localism in politics in the House. In each American realignment, however, elections are dominated by national issues. Prior to realignments, cross-cutting issues arise that do not fit within the framework of the existing two-party system. Ultimately, the parties take positions on the issues that offer clear-cut alternatives to voters. (In the case of the Civil War realignment, the Republicans replaced the Whigs before the choice was clear). When the realigning election or elections occur, the result is a new congressional majority party elected on its positions on national issues, not local issues. Moreover, historically, the new majority party has maintained uninterrupted control of the presidency and both branches of Congress for over a decade (Clubb, Flanigan and Zingale, 1980).

The effect of these elections in the House is that they reduce the major drawbacks to party voting in the House. Elections decided on a localized basis make the congressional parties amalgams of differing interests, e.g., southern rural and northern urban Democrats during the 1940s through 1970s. Under normal electoral conditions, congressional parties are not united across a whole series of issues. In recent times, Democrats disagreed over civil rights, social welfare, and Vietnam policies, among others. And, as long as elections are decided on the basis of local factors, policy differences are accommodated, and incrementalism results. During realignments, representatives are elected *on the basis of party positions on the national issues.* Thus, the majority party is united on the issues of the realignment. Local factors do not mitigate policy choices, and a *unified* majority party votes in major policy changes.

A second drawback to party voting in the Congress is the committee system. Committees have a life of their own, and the more important the committee, the more stable its membership. The stable leadership passes along committee norms and strategies to new members, and thus, policy in the committee's area does not change greatly. The influx of new members during realignments eliminates committee stability, and new leaders support the party position for major policy innovations. In sum, the influx of new members during realignments reduces the impact of localism and committee stability in the House. The result is increasing party voting, especially on the issues of the realignment.

If our notion of realignments is correct, we should be able to show that in each of the historical realignments—Civil War, 1890s, and 1930s—the following occurred:

1. The dominant parties take polar positions on the cross-cutting issues;
2. The critical election(s) is characterized by national voting;
3. There is an influx of new members;
4. The new majority party controls the presidency and the Congress for at least a decade;
5. Committee turnover is high;
6. Party voting increases;
7. Party structures voting on the realignment issues;
8. Significant policy changes occur.

Since our purpose is to show that realigning elections share these eight features, we present data from all three major realignments at the same time.

THE THEORY TESTED OVER THREE REALIGNMENTS

In the case of each of the major realignments, a principal cross-cutting issue dominated the election. The second American party system was broken up by the rise of slavery and, ultimately, the secession issues. The two dominant parties of the 1832–1856 period were the Whigs and the Democrats. Each party had northern and southern wings that ultimately could not accommodate the slavery issue. The Missouri Compromise and the Compromise of 1850 were valiant efforts to patch over differences of opinion, but the introduction of the Kansas-Nebraska Act led to the demise of the Whigs. The Republican party replaced the Whigs as the second major party in the 1856 elections, and by 1860 the Democrats were the proslavery party, while the Republicans were the antislavery party. Thus, the electorate was offered a clear-cut choice between parties and policies.

The cross-cutting issue of the 1890s realignment was the issue of "what future for America—industrial or agricultural?" The rise of industrialization in the aftermath of the Civil War generated the displacement of farmers and a change from a society of local, self-sufficient communities to a highly interrelated industrial society. The result was both the displacement of agricultural interests and the end of a way of life. The overarching issues were specifically focused on the questions of gold, silver, the protective tariff, and American expansionism. Agricultural interests favored the inflationary (since they were debtors) coinage of silver, free tariffs, and antiexpansionism. Industrial interests favored exactly the opposite. The rise of the pro-farmer Populist party is testimony for the existence of cross-cutting issues in the 1896 realignment. The Democrats, under William Jennings Bryan, adopted the Populist position while the Republicans adopted a proposition on gold, protective tariffs, and expansionism.

The cross-cutting issue during the New Deal realignment was the result of a single event—the Great Depression. The question was, Would the government adopt policies to combat the effects of the Depression? The Republican incumbent, Herbert Hoover, would not adopt policies to aid farmers, workers, cities, and the unemployed. The Democratic party had, by 1932, answered by proposing relief funds and programs to aid those most affected by the Depression. Once again, voters were offered clear-cut choices between candidates and parties. To demonstrate this point, Table 1 shows the party differences on these issues in each of the realignments. The differences are those in the party platforms as presented by Ginsberg (1972). The higher the value, the greater the disagreement.

Table 1 clearly shows that the Civil War and the 1890s realignments were characterized by deepening party differences in regard to the cross-cutting issues leading up to the critical elections. For the New Deal realignment, the pattern is somewhat different. The parties differed in 1924, but it was not until 1932 that the Democrats could convince the electorate to send a new majority party to Congress. In addition, the magnitude of these figures suggests that the parties were less polarized in the positions they took during the New Deal than they were during the Civil War and 1890s realignments (also, see Brady with Stewart, 1982). Still, statement one (above) of our theory holds: in each of the realignment eras, the major political parties took opposing positions on the issues of major concern. Thus, when voters went to the polls in the elections of 1860, 1896, and 1932, they were offered "a choice, not an echo."

Table 1. Partisan Platform Differences on Major Issues in Three Realignment
Eras[a]

Era	Slavery	Capitalism	Depression
Civil War			
1848	0		
1852	.10		
1856	.24		
1860	.71		
1890s			
1884		.08	
1888		.04	
1892		.44	
1896		.55	
New Deal			
1920			.02
1924			.30
1928			.19
1932			.26

[a]Adapted from Ginsberg (1972): 612.

NATIONAL, REGIONAL, AND LOCAL EFFECTS ON VOTING

If realigning elections are precipitated by cross-cutting national issues, the congressional election results should reveal national or regional rather than local electoral forces at work. The standard technique used to determine national rather than local factors is to calculate the variance across House election results over the relevant time period. The argument, first put forward by Butler and Stokes in *Political Change in Britain* (1969), is that when variance around the mean is low, national factors are at work; and conversely, when variance is high, local factors are predominant. Butler and Stokes used this argument to show how national factors are more important in Britain than they are in the United States. Their point was that variance around the mean swing in pairs of elections measures the uniformity of change, i.e., the extent to which national forces are at work. However, testing within a single country for change over time presents some difficulties.

The first and foremost problem is that, as Flanigan and Zingale (1974) have shown, realigning change can be either compensating or across the board. In a compensating realignment, both parties gain some votes while losing others. Of course, one party gains more than it loses and vice versa for the other party. In an across the board realignment, one party gains votes while the other party loses votes. In both cases, as one moves to the realigning election or elections, the variance around the mean is affected because vote totals in districts are shifting, and measures of variance are squared differences, thus, the direction of change is irrelevant. Determining whether a realignment is compensating or across the board is particularly important in the American case because of the regional and cultural variation across the American states (Elazar, 1972).

The strategy for analyzing electoral change in each of the three American realignments is first to show the mean swing in the vote and standard deviation for the following time periods: 1852–1876, 1884–1900 and 1924–1940. The measure of change to be used is the coefficient of variation, which is:

$$V = \frac{S}{X}$$

where S is the standard deviation and X is the mean.

We want to take into account both the mean swing for or against a party and the variance around that mean. The argument is that as the standard deviation increases relative to the mean, local variation is greater than the national trend, whereas, as the mean swing increases relative to the standard deviation, national trends eclipse local factors. In short, the lower the value of the coefficient of variation, the greater the likelihood of an election reflecting national rather than local factors.

Testing for national effects during the Civil War realignment era constitutes a problem in that the demise of the Whigs, the rise of the Republicans, the secession, and the later readmission of eleven southern states to the Union during this time period complicates analysis of electoral results. A time series testing for national effects should be run on both major parties for all points in the set (Clubb et al., 1980), but this is not possible for the 1848–1876 period. Thus, the analysis for the Civil War period focuses on the Democrats' percentage of the vote in each national election. The Democrats contested elections throughout the era including the period of secession. During the Civil War proper, the Democrats almost won control of the House in the 1861–1862 election, and they only narrowly lost the presidency in 1864. Testing for national versus local factors is possible because the Democrats were both stable and competitive over the entire time period. The analysis of electoral changes for the other two realignments is straightforward given that the Democrats and Republicans are stable in both eras. The data in Table 2 show the average swing in the vote and the average of the V coefficients for the prerealignment, realignment, and postrealignment

Table 2. Aggregate Vote Swings and V Coefficients during the Civil War, 1890s, and New Deal Realignments

	Pre-realignment	Realignment	Post-realignment	Controlling Elections
Civil War realignment	1846–1852	1854–1860	1862–1876	1860
Mean change % Dem	3.26	−5.31	2.87	−6.07
Coefficient of var (V)	8.09	−4.34	8.15	−2.81
1890s realignment	1884–1892	1894–1896	1898–1902	1896
Mean change % Dem	−1.79	−5.45	−3.13	
Coefficient of var (V)	−15.41	−3.05	6.27	
Mean change % Rep	2.62	4.39	−2.13	3.67
Coefficient of var (V)	−8.21	3.20	5.46	3.90
New Deal realignment	1924–1930	1932–1936	1938–1944	1932
Mean change % Dem	1.40	9.12	−3.79	7.2
Coefficient of var (V)	8.32	3.04	−9.64	2.14
Mean change % Rep	−1.56	−9.60	4.01	
Coefficient of var (V)	−16.60	−4.15	13.47	

periods. The realignment elections for each period are as follows: Civil War realignment, 1854–1860; 1890s realignment, 1894–1896; New Deal realignment, 1932–1936. The table also shows the mean swing and V coefficient for the single election gave the new majority party control of the presidency, the House, and Senate—1860, 1896, 1932.

During the pre-Civil War realignment (1846–1852) the average swing was 3.26, and the average V coefficient was 8.09, which indicates a relatively low swing and considerable variation in voting patterns. In contrast, the realignment period (1854–1860) has a mean swing of −5.31 away from the Democrats and an average V coefficient of −4.34, indicating national electoral factors at work. The postrealignment period (1862–1876) has a mean swing of only 2.87 and a mean V coefficient of 8.15. These data support the hypothesis of increased nationalization of electoral results during the Civil War realignment. The figures for the 1860 election are even more dramatic, with a swing vote of −6.07 away from the Democrats and a low V of −2.8.

Unlike either of the two other realignments, the Civil War era has major structural changes that affect the electoral results. The replacement of the Whig Party by the Republicans, the secession of the southern states, and their readmission are the major changes. The elections of 1853–1854 and 1855–1856 are the two decisive elections that replace the Whigs as a major party. The analysis of these elections shows a dramatic increase in the mean swing relative to the variance—scores of -2.8 and 2.9, respectively. The Republicans actually win a plurality of House seats in the 34th House.

The election of 1859–1860, which brings the Republican Party full control of the government—President, Senate, and House—also has a coefficient of variance of less than 3.0. In this election, the Democrats lose 6.07% of the vote while the standard deviation is 17.6. The only other election pair with a coefficient of variation under 3.0 is the 40th–41st (1866–1868) pair. Here, the Democrats gain 3.8% while the variance is only 8.4%. The Democratic gain is, in part, a repudiation of radical Republicanism plus the strong Democratic returns from border states. In sum, the elections with low variation coefficients correspond to the structural changes mentioned above. Or in the words of Clubb et al.: "As at the national level, electoral change during these years seems to be largely interpretable in terms of Southern secession, occupation and Reconstruction" (p. 110).

The late 1890s realignment shows a clear national trend at work. In the 1894 and 1896 elections, the Democrats lost 5.45% while the Republicans gained 4.39% and the corresponding V's were below $+$ or -3.20 in each case. This contrasts sharply with the prerealignment period (1884–1892) where the Democrats lost 1.79% swing and the Republicans lost 2.62% swing with V's of -15.41 and -8.21, respectively. The postrealignment period is characterized by smaller swing votes and V's approximately twice as high as during the realignment. The election that shows the most dramatic effect was the 1894 election. This election gave the Republicans a large majority in the House as voters swung away from the Democrats (-7.6%) and to the Republicans 5.5%). The election of 1896, normally considered the realigning election, was at the congressional level an increase for the Democrats as well as the Republicans (3.3 and 3.6% swing, respectively). The fact that both major parties gained in the 55th House elections (1896) over their totals for the 54th House is clearly the result of the Democratic merger with the Populist Party; the loss for both parties in the 53rd House reflected Populist Party gains in the 1892 election. Thus, the election pair that most clearly meets the criterion for a shift toward national electoral factors over local factors is the change between 1892 and 1894. The most likely explanation for these data lies in an analysis of vote shifts by region, and we shall turn to that analysis in a moment. However, it should be noted that these results support the assertion of Clubb et al., that "...the realignment of 1896 appears substantially less impressive than might have been expected" (p. 111).

The results for the New Deal realignment clearly point to the nationalization of electoral factors in the 1932–1936 (73rd through 75th Houses) period. The coefficient of variation is 3.0 for the Democrats and -4.2 for the Republicans. The Democrats gained 9.1% over their prerealignment vote totals while the Republicans lost 9.6% from their respective prerealignment totals. The largest portion of the Democratic gain came in the shift from 1930 to 1932 (7.2%) and the concomitant Republican loss of 8.0%. The mean swings and the V coefficients in the pre- and postrealignment periods support the nationalization hypothesis. Before the prerealignment, both parties' mean swing was less than 2.0% and the V 's were at least twice as high as during the realignment. In the postrealignment period, the mean swings for both parties were around 4%, and the V 's were between three and four times higher than during the realignment period. These results for the New Deal are so clear that the only possible explanation is that the New Deal was an across the board realignment to Roosevelt and the Democrats. The realignments of the Civil War and 1890s era present a more complicated pattern. Thus, we turn to a brief analysis of all three realignments controlling for regional effects. For brevity's sake the tables are not presented (see Brady, 1985, for results).

The results for the Civil War period show both regional variation and compensation. In a varying pattern, regions first abandoned the Whigs for the Republicans, and then the Republicans came over time to dominate the northern state elections while the South turned strongly to the Democrats. The end of the War and the readmission of the southern states brought about solid Democratic gains throughout the country such that by 1874 (44th House), the Democrats were the majority party in the U.S. House of Representatives. This pattern varied across regions and states as well as by year. Given these regional results, it is obvious why the results for the whole nation do not fit a classic across the board realignment pattern.

The national results showed 1892–1896 to be the realigning elections. The realignment of the 1890s was compensatory in that the North became more Republican while the southern and west north central states became more Democratic. The New England states swung more solidly Republican than did the northeastern and east north central states. The rise and fall of Populist Party candidates affected results in the rural east north central, west north central, and southern states. The brunt of lasting electoral change occurs in the 1892 to 1898 period with the 54th and 55th House elections benefiting Republicans, and the elections to the 56th House reversing a good portion of the Republican gains. In short, there was no clear across the board realignment to the Republicans in the 1890s.

Unlike the Civil War and 1890s realignments, the New Deal realignment fits the classic pattern. As Table 2 showed, the election pair 1930–1932 was clearly the period where the Democrats became the dominant party. The same analysis run over regions revealed some differences in the extent to which various areas shifted Democratic and to a lesser extent the times at which they shifted. However, the major finding was that across all regions there was a shift to Democratic congressional candidates in the 1932 general election, and that in four of the six regions the shift was greater than 8% and the corresponding V 's are less than 2.1. The shift was greatest in the non-New England northern states, and less in the predominantly Democratic southern and border states. Clearly, in comparison to the Civil War and 1890s realignment, the New Deal realignment meets the test of an across the board realignment.

The major point of this analysis of the three major American realignments is that at least two of the three were not the result of massive shifts of voters toward the new majority party. We do not deny that each of these were realignments, rather the point is to show that what is important about realignments is how the electoral results affect the composition of the U.S. House of Representatives. The most important effect is that in each realignment the result was undisputed control of the House of Representatives, the Senate, and the Presidency for at least 14 years. The massive shift of voters to the Democratic Party in the 1932 elections is easily translated into Democratic control of the House. The Democrats added to their solid southern and border state base a bloc of urban, northern ethnic districts (Brady, 1982). It is more difficult to understand how the less dramatic electoral shifts in the Civil War era and the 1890s resulted in Republican control for an equal period. The answer to this question entails analysis of the votes to seats ratio.

The Votes-Seats Distribution

In the American electoral system, representatives are elected through a single-member, plurality winner arrangement. This "first past the post" rule often distorts the translation of popular votes in legislative seats. For example, a party could win 50% of the votes and 70% of the seats, a 20% distortion. The argument in this section is that during the major electoral realignments in the United States, there is a high seats-votes distortion. We shall use the percentage difference between seats won and votes won as a measure of votes-seats disparity.

The hypothesis is that during realignments, the votes-seats difference will be greater than it is during other periods. I hypothesize that this is particularly the case for the Civil War and 1890s realignments because, as we have seen, there was not a major national shift of votes to Republicans during either of these realignments. In short, the hypothesis states that the long periods of Republican control brought about during the Civil War and 1890s realignments were more the results of distortions in seat-vote differences than of a massive voter shift, as in the New Deal realignment.

In the Civil War and 1890s realignments there was an overall shift of about 5% of the voters to the Republicans in the northern states. This shift caused the competitive seats to become Republican and resulted in sizable seat gains for the Republicans. In the New Deal realignment, the vote shift in the North to the Democrats should result in a significant seat-vote distortion in that region. This distortion should be masked when the solidly Democratic South is calculated into the equation.

The results for the Civil War and 1890s realignments corroborate the hypothesis. In the elections to the 34th Congress, where the Republicans became the major party in the House, they enjoyed a differential of plus 20% in seats to votes. The 1855–1856 elections were fairly even in terms of seats to votes, while in the 1857–1858 elections, the Republicans again benefited by over 20%. The major distortion in the series occurs in the presidential election of 1859 – 1860—over 25%. Thus the Republican victory in 1860 grossly increased the seats-vote difference in front of the new majority party. In the elections that followed, the Republicans retained their advantage, but by far narrower margins. In the 1894 elections in *northern* states, the seats votes difference is very high, about a 30% advantage to the Republicans. The election of 1896 in the northern states also heavily favored the Republicans, a 20% difference. Thus, in the two critical elections of 1894 and 1896, the Republicans, victories in the House can be attributed to the seats-votes advantage enjoyed in the northern states. The results for the New Deal realignment show only a slight Democratic Party seat-votes advantage, in contrast to the Civil War and 1890s realignments.

In sum, the realignment to the Republicans in the 1854–1860 and in 1894–1896 can best be understood not in terms of massive vote shifts, but rather in terms of relatively minor regional shifts in which Republicans won disproportionally large numbers of previous competitive seats. The important point is that however the House majority was created, by major vote switches or a seats to votes distortion, the result was that rare condition in American politics—unified control of government for over a decade.

Statements three, four, and five of our theory are concerned with the results of voters' choices. Here we must show that realigning elections produce (1) an increase in new members, (2) high turnover on committees, and (3) new majority control of the Congress and Presidency for at least a decade. Table 3 presents these data for each of the realignments (using Ways and Means as an example of the broader pattern of committee turnover).

Table 3 suggests that, consonant with our theory, realigning elections are characterized by higher turnover in membership and on committees and that realignment brings the new majority party into control of the government for fourteen years. Our theory also says that under electoral conditions where parties take distinct stands on national issues, the new members in

Table 3. House Member and Committee Turnover and Length of Undivided Partisan Control of Government for Three Realignments

Eras	% Member Turnover	% Turnover on Ways and Means	Years of Undivided Party Control
Pre-Civil War	49.6	38.5	2 years since 1840
Realignment	56.4	67.9	14 years (1860–1874)
Pre-1890s	38.7	26.5	2 years since 1876
Realignment	43.4	76.5	14 years (1896–1910)
Pre-New Deal	19.5	15.0	10 years since 1912
Realignment	27.8	80.0	14 years (1932–1946)

the House will vote along party lines because they have a mandate to act. Party voting in the House will increase because members are not cross-pressured by local interests differing from national party positions. Thus, we should expect to see party voting increase during the realignment relative to the period of politics preceding it. Table 4 shows the average percentage of party votes in the five Houses preceding the realignment and the percentage of party votes in the realignment Houses. Party votes are defined in two ways. First, the percentage of votes which pitted a majority of one party against a majority of the other party (50 vs. 50) is presented. Second, a more stringent criterion is used, defining party votes as those where 90% of one party opposed 90% of the other (90 vs. 90).

The results clearly indicate a rise in partisan voting during each of the realignments. While these results help to corroborate our theory, it would be better if we could show that party voting increases dramatically on the cross-cutting issues associated with the realignments. Thus, we created a set of scales for each of the following realignments and issues: Civil War—slavery, secession, and civil rights; 1890s—monetary policy; and New Deal—social welfare (for a fuller discussion, see Brady with Stewart, 1982). The hypothesis is that on each of these dimensions in the prerealignment period, party will not predict voting, whereas during the realignment era, party will be highly correlated with voting. We measure the extent of the relationship by correlating a representative's party identification (0 = Democrat, 1 = Republican) with his voting score. The higher the correlation (+1.0 = the highest) the stronger the relationship, and the greater the party structuring of the vote.

Table 5 presents the results, which support the hypothesis. In each of the realignments, the correlation between party and support for or opposition to the dominant issue dimension increases during the realignment. During the

Table 4. Percentage of Party Votes in Pre-Realignment and Realignment Eras

Era	50 vs. 50		90 vs. 90	
	Pre-	Realignment	Pre-	Realignment
Civil War	66.4	74.7	8.9	20.9
1890s	53.8	76.4	21.1	50.1
New Deal	48.7	69.4	7.9	16.4

Civil War and the 1890s realignments the Republicans became more antislavery and more progold, respectively. In the 1930s realignment, the Democrats became more pro-social welfare. In short, during each realignment, party structured voting in the House especially on the realignment issues.

Point eight asserts that during each of these realignments clusters of major policy changes occur. In one sense, this is obvious. The Civil War realignment ultimately resulted in the end of slavery, the passage of the thirteenth, fourteenth, and fifteenth amendments, and an increased governmental role in modernizing the economy. The 1890s realignment resulted in noninflationary money, protective tariffs, the annexation of Hawaii, and the Spanish-American War. In short, the 1896 realignment assured America's industrial future. The New Deal introduced the welfare state to America. Social Security, unemployment assistance, prolabor legislation, agricultural assistance, and government management of the economy are but a few of the legacies of the New Deal. Ginsberg's (1976) analysis of policy changes show this same pattern in a more sophisticated fashion. In sum, it is the case that in each of these realignments, election results were transformed into major public policy changes. Elections did matter.

CONCLUSIONS

There are two sets of findings in this chapter. The first is that there are similar linkages present in all three major American realignments. Realigning elections at the congressional level are determined more by national issues than by local factors. The electoral turnover generated by the realigning election(s) results in a congressional majority party that behaves in a partisan fashion to achieve major policy changes. The chapter shows that electoral turnover generated by the realignment results in an American form of party government. The reduction of constituent-party cross pressuring and the sense of mandate from the results creates a new majority party capable of legislating major shifts in American public policy.

Table 5. Correlation (r) between Party Voting and the Cross-Cutting Issue in Three Realignment Eras

			Civil War			
		Issue:	Slavery/secession/civil rights			
Year	1853	1855	1857	1859	1861	
Congress	33rd	34th	35th	36th	37th	
r	.51	.41	.89	.87	.88	
			1890s			
			Issue: Currency			
Year	1891	1893	1895	1897	1899	
Congress	52nd	53rd	54th	55th	56th	
r	.02	.42	.71	.96	.96	
			New Deal			
			Issue: Social welfare			
Year	1925	1927	1929	1931	1933	1935
Congress	69th	70th	71st	72nd	73rd	74th
r	0	0	0	.72	.89	.94

The second set of findings shows that at least two of the major American realignments do not meet a number of the criteria normally associated with electoral realignments. Neither the Civil War nor 1890s realignments were of the magnitude or nature of the New Deal realignment. In both these realignments, relatively minor shifts of voters to the Republicans in the North resulted in long periods of Republican dominance of government. In large part both the original electoral success and subsequent control were the result of a vote-seat distribution that favored Republicans. These seat-vote distortions especially favored the Republicans in the realigning election or elections. Thus, while there do appear to be similarities across all three realignments, it should also be clear that interpretations of American realignments that automatically ascribe policy results to massive voter shifts are facile.

This chapter, like almost all research on realignments, has focused on electoral and structural change. Very little attention has been paid to the role of congressional leadership in obtaining these policy shifts. There have been other periods in American political history where the electoral and structural shifts associated with policy change have been present (Clubb et al., 1980). The Republicans' victory in 1920 and their domination of government for a decade comes to mind, yet we know that there are no major shifts in policy associated with this period. Why some periods result in major policy changes while others do not remains an unanswered, even an unasked question. Certainly the way congressional leaders interpret election results and how they translate their perceptions into policy greatly affects policy outputs. Future research will have to focus on the role of congressional leadership in formulating and adopting policy responses to critical elections. Franklin Roosevelt is unanimously viewed as the architect of the New Deal; yet we know that Congress forced some policies, the Wagner Act for example, on a reluctant Roosevelt. Until we know how Congress itself affected the policy process during such eras, we will continue to have a view of realignments that overemphasizes the effect of both elections and Presidents. Reducing the explanatory strength of electoral and presidential variables allows us to concentrate on how electoral results change congressional structure and agendas as suggested in chapter 1 by Dodd.

REFERENCES

Anderson, James E. (1979). *Public Policy Making*. New York: Holt, Rinehart and Winston.

Butler, David, and Stokes, Donald E. (1969). *Political Change in Britain: Forces Shaping Electoral Choice*. New York: Wiley.

Brady, David, and Althoff, P. (1974). Party voting in the House of Representatives, 1890–1910: elements of a responsible party system. *Journal of Politics* 36: 753–773.

Brady, David (1978). Critical elections, congressional parties and clusters of policy changes. *British Journal of Political Science* 8: 79–99.

Brady, David (1985). A reevaluation of realignments in American politics: evidence from the House of Representatives. *American Political Science Review* 79: 28–49.

Brady, David with Stewart, J. (1982). Congressional party realignment and transformations of public policy in three realignment eras. *American Journal of Political Science* 26: 333–360.

Burnham, Walter (1970). *Critical Elections and the Mainsprings of American Politics*. New York: Norton.

Clausen, Aage (1973). *How Congressmen Decide: A Policy Focus*. New York: St. Martin's.

Clubb, J. M., Flanigan, W. H., and Zingale, N. H. (1980). *Partisan Realignment: Voters, Parties and Government in American History*. Beverley Hills, CA: Sage Publications.

Cooper, Joseph (1977). Congress in organizational perspective. In L. C. Dodd and B. I. Oppenheimer (eds.), *Congress Reconsidered* , 1st ed. New York: Praeger.

Dahl, Robert (1956). *A Preface to Democratic Theory*. Chicago: University of Chicago Press.

Elazar, Daniel (1972). *American Federalism: A View from the States*. New York: Thomas Y. Crowell.

Fenno, Richard (1973). *Congressmen In Committees*. Boston: Little, Brown.

Flanigan, W. H., and Zingale, N. H. (1974). Measures of electoral competition. *Political Methodology* 1: 31–60.

Ginsberg, Benjamin (1972). Critical elections and the substance of party conflict: 1844–1968. *Midwest Journal of Political Science* 16: 603–625.

Ginsberg, Benjamin (1976). Elections and public policy. *American Political Science Review* 70: 41–49.

Goodwin, George (1970). *The Little Legislatures: Committess of Congress*. Amherst: University of Massachusetts Press.

Huitt, Ralph (1957). The Morse Committee assignment controversy: a case study. *American Political Science Review* 51: 313 –329.

Huitt, Ralph (1961). The outsider in the Senate: an alternative role. *American Political Science Review* 55: 566–575.

Huntington, Samuel (1965). Congressional responses to the twentieth century. In D. B. Truman (ed.), *The Congress and America's Future*. Englewood Cliffs, N.J.: Prentice-Hall.

Key, V. O. (1967). *Politics, Parties and Pressure Groups*. New York: Thomas Y. Crowell.

Lowi, Theodore (1979). *The End of Liberalism*. New York: Norton.

Mann, Thomas (1978). *Unsafe At Any Margin: Interpreting Congressional Elections*. Washington, D.C.: American Enterprise Institute.

Neustadt, Richard (1976). *Presidential Power*. New York: Wiley.

Orfield, Gary (1975). *Congressional Power: Congress and Social Change*. New York: Harcourt, Brace and Jovanovich.

Redford, Emmette (1969). *Democracy and the Administrative State*. Oxford: Oxford University Press.

Sinclair, Barbara (1977). Party realignment and the transformation of the political agenda: the house of representatives 1925–38. *American Political Science Review* 71: 940–953.

Sorauf, Frank (1968). *Party Politics in America*. Boston: Little, Brown.

Wilson, Woodrow (1885). *Congressional Government*. New York.

3

The Politics and
Policy of Race in Congress

Edward G. Carmines and James A. Stimson

The U.S. Congress is sometimes a policy initiator, sometimes a forum for response to presidential initiatives. Sometimes it is in the vanguard of policy articulation, sometimes the collective voice of resistance to innovation. Sometimes it debates and does nothing; sometimes it sanctions policies with the stamp of law. In all of these roles, Congress claims a central position in issue evolution.

If Congress acts or fails to act, it lays out a public record of response to issue challenge. Its collective foot dragging through the late 1950s had a clear interpretation to racial activists, presidents, courts, and the public. The unmistakable message was that racial equality in all its forms was not the business of the United States Government. By 1964 Congress had written racial equality into law.

No presidential order or Supreme Court ruling can hope to achieve anything like the official sanction of legislation, particularly when the issue debate and the call of the roll are in the public eye. And more than any other policy in the postwar era, that has often been the case with race. Taken together, the string of congressional actions on racial issues are the most memorable acts of policy making in the post-World War II period. When civil rights legislation was offered repeatedly in the 1950s, it fell repeatedly to highly publicized filibusters in the U.S. Senate. The Senate today is a drab contrast to the confrontations of the fifties, where a small group of aging southerners used its right to debate continuously to beat back a less determined civil rights majority.

Failure, repeated painful public failure, moved racial issues to the top of the liberal agenda of the 1960s. The early—and in retrospect, small— victories for the civil rights coalition were all the more dramatic because they were so long in coming. Following the shifting tide of the 1958 Senate elections, the old struggles were reenacted, but this time fragile bipartisan majorities managed at last to overcome the southern filibusters. The drama built to a peak in the Civil Rights Act of 1964, probably the single most publicized act of Congress in our time. The exclusive business of the Senate from February to June 1964, final passage of the act came only after 124 consecutive roll-call votes. The decisive role in this public drama was left to Minority Leader Everett Dirksen who, after satisfying his concern about the hypothetical "Mrs. Murphy's Boarding House," lined up his Republican troops to finish the job.

Only slightly less dramatic was the follow-on Voting Rights Act of 1965. Amidst national turmoil over violence directed toward civil rights activists in the South, Lyndon Johnson stood in the Well of the House (before a national television audience) and with great emotion proclaimed the Voting Rights bill the solution to a national dishonor. When he concluded with "we shall overcome," he effectively incorporated the motto of the civil rights movement into national policy. A large bipartisan majority settled the issue.

Congress has addressed racial issues many times since 1964, but none of its action has achieved comparable public notice. Racial issues still arouse intense emotions, but Congressional actions on them are no longer in the spotlight of sustained public attention.

We will examine the congressional role in racial politics in this chapter. Although it would be foolish to assert that congressmen are unresponsive to constituent desires on this issue—of all policy domains it is usually the single best case of policy representation—the primary role for all institutional actors in our issue evolution scheme is to lead public opinion. Policy-making institutions, unlike the public, are confronted with specific questions that demand resolution. The public could be for or against "equal access to public accommodations" for example; Congress had to decide the question of principle and also apply it to "Mrs. Murphy's Boarding House." Policy making institutions must lead the public in the important sense of having to confront issues earlier in time. And when they act, they add both policy and political definition to the issue.

IS CONGRESSIONAL ACTION VISIBLE?

But are Congress and its voting outcomes sufficiently visible to play a leading role in issue evolution? In the present case the answer to our query is "yes, sometimes." And it is important for us that those "sometimes" include the crucial span of time in which we find the origins of a partisan issue evolution. But we shall also examine times when congressional action was below the attention threshold of all but the very most active observers.

We have two reasons for doing so. The first is the assumption on our part, evidently shared by members of Congress,[1] that patterns of behavior are fairly accurately perceived by mass publics, even when individual votes are unknown.

A second reason for close scrutiny of congressional roll calls is that the aggregated behaviors of members may be used to represent the policy stands of the national parties. Although we will look more directly at the parties through their platforms, the direct analysis of party behavior is blunted by the deliberate ambiguity for which platforms are justly famous and by the infrequency of platform utterance. The "party in Congress" is thus a surrogate indicator of "the party." It is annual, not quadrennial, and it is denied most times the escape hatch of ambiguity.

The basic data for this paper are all the roll-call votes cast by all members of both houses of Congress from 1945 through 1978. From that massive array, we selected in each year those with racial content. Sometimes manifest, as in the long series of "Civil Rights" acts, sometimes latent, as, for example, antilynching or poll tax bills, the judgments were tedious but not difficult. Where we were in doubt about the true content of a vote, we included it.

In a second stage, all roll calls selected were subjected to a principal components analysis[2] to see for each whether extraneous issue or strategic dimensions were operative. When decisions were difficult, validating information (e.g., Who sponsored? How did known proponents or opponents of civil rights vote?) was brought to bear. Votes that survived both stages of scrutiny were then recoded ("1" pro, "0" con) and summed into annual scales with implicitly equal weights for each member. Transformed into the ratio: *number of pro votes/number of votes*, the scales become indicators of racial policy liberalism.[3]

As a final check, "between Congress" correlations of the scale scores for individual members were computed for returning members. It is vivid testimony to the clarity and intensity of race that these correlations are large not only for adjacent Congresses, but also for Congresses decades apart in time. The specific content of legislative actions on racial issues has changed quite substantially over time, as we shall soon see, but these data suggest no change at all in the basic segregation/desegregation dimension.

Figure 1 displays year to year autocorrelations for the desegregation scales.[4] The autocorrelations are a first indication of the continuity of the racial dimension. The pattern of Figure 1 is high year to year autocorrelation with relatively little fluctuation. All exceptions to the pattern are produced by years where measurement reliability is constrained by a small number (minimum 2) of roll calls.

The evidence of Figure 1 does not close the case. If the meaning of an

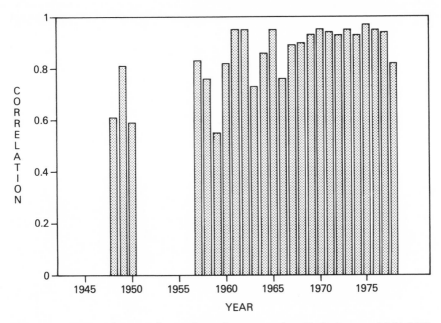

Figure 1. Autocorrelations of annual racial voting scales: U. S. Senate, 1945–1978.

issue dimension were evolving, it would be possible to observe high year to year autocorrelations and yet witness striking change from the beginning to the end of the series. For that reason we examine the correlations of each year with a base year to fix the content of the dimension. The base year chosen is 1964. In that year our measurement is reliable, because a very large number of roll calls contributed to the scales. And because every one of those roll calls involved the omnibus Civil Rights Act of 1964, we have no question that it is a valid measure of the desegregation concept.

If the meaning of the desegregation dimension were changing over time, we would expect an inverted "V" pattern around the base year. That does not occur. Only the two Carter years show some tailing off in the correlations of Figure 2. But the lowest correlation in the series is the almost adjacent 1966.[5] Very high associations occur in the Truman years and they are matched through the Ford presidency.

It is commonly believed that the nature of racial issues changed after the landmark civil rights legislation of the mid-60s, that after securing legal rights, the agenda of racial politics was redefined toward far less tractable social and economic issues. Certainly the rhetoric shifted; "segregation forever" disappeared from public speech and "black power" was born. But insofar as racial politics is reflected in roll-call votes, there is no evidence of

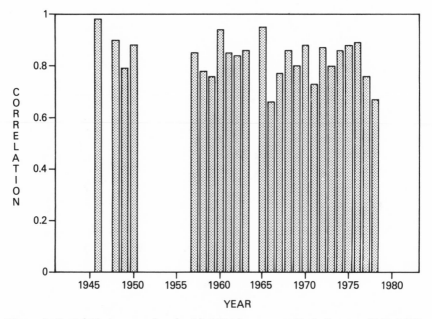

Figure 2. Racial Voting correlated with 1964 base year: U. S. Senate, 1946–1978.

the postulated change. Figure 2 shows that the continuing members from 1964 behaved as if nothing had changed.[6] Desegregation was the black/white issue of the Truman presidency. Figure 2 suggests that it was much the same under Eisenhower, Kennedy, Johnson, Nixon, Ford, and Carter. Anyone who lived through this era knows that important redefinitions of the grounds of racial politics have occurred. But our evidence, stated in its most limited sense, says that the core dimension of congressional response to questions of the racial policy of the federal government is constant.

All of this is not as anomalous as it might at first seem. Part of the explanation for congressional constancy amid environmental change is that the newer issues were fought out in different arenas. Because the issues were nonlegal, they were also nonlegislative. "Black Pride," for example, might have been quite important in the shifting racial politics of the late 1960s, but it is not the subject of any of our roll calls.

A second explanation for constancy is our own decision to exclude matters that, though relevant to racial policies, are not themselves specifically racial. Black Americans were important actors in Lyndon Johnson's "poverty" legislation, for example, as well the Nixonian counterattack in the name of "law and order." Perhaps in the popular perception only blacks were poor and only blacks were muggers, but neither of these perceptions was true, and neither written into law. In part, then, the desegregation dimension is constant over time because it is the only *specifically racial* policy almost by definition.

DESIGN OF ANALYSIS

We are now ready to confront the partisan evolution of racial issues in Congress. Our approach is two-pronged; we will raise and answer the questions, "What happened?" and "How did it happen?" The first requires a close look at the racial vote time series. That entails, among other things, description of the observed evolutionary pattern, examination of the coalitions for and against desegregation over time, a chronology of key events and issues, and, finally, a first attempt at explanation (through intervention models) of the impact of two particularly important elections.

We will then turn to the question, "How did it happened?" Our answers there will have more the flavor of systematic political science. Our concern will be to understand the mechanism of change, to apportion the observed evolution of party positions into their component pieces, among them conversion, replacement (intergenerational and interparty), shifts in the party base in the mass electorate, and the like. We will use the racial issue for leverage, ultimately, to examine the quality of representative democracy, the continuing question that haunts students of politics.

WHAT HAPPENED: THE PARTISAN EVOLUTION

Obviously not the beginning of our story, 1945 does mark a good point to begin systematic analysis of congressional response to race. The politics of race was different at the end of World War II than it had been at the end of Reconstruction, but not by much. The Republican Party marched still in the name of Lincoln. Enlightenment came naturally to its urbane Northeast heartland. It was a cheap commodity to rural Republicans across the land who saw racial segregation as a southern issue.

Congressional Democrats at the end of the war were first and foremost southern Democrats. Representatives of the decaying urban political machines of the North and Midwest were also prominent. Like the designer of the New Deal himself, the urban Democrats managed to avoid conflict between social welfare and race by ignoring race. With extremely violent race riots of the 1930s and 1940s still fresh in memory, they had no grounds for illusion about how their constituents would respond if the issue were squarely confronted.

Notably absent in this picture is the core of northern Democratic liberals which would later become so important to racial politics. The Congresses

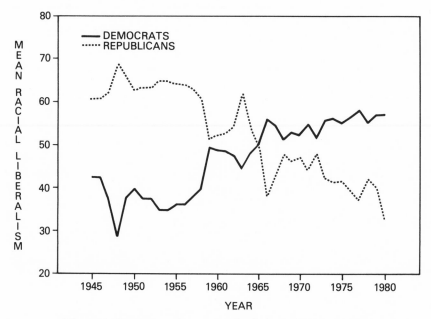

Figure 3. Senate racial voting scales by party, 1945 to 1980.

before Humphrey, Douglas, and Lehman produced no well-known civil rights advocates. When Harry Truman began to advocate racial policies closer to Eleanor Roosevelt's than to Franklin's, he had to turn mainly to the opposition party for support.

All of this has of course changed. Figures 3 and 4 lay out the basic evidence of partisan issue evolution in the House and Senate time series. Although they differ in detail, both figures demonstrate secular realignment of partisan voting patterns on race. Our ensuing task is to describe it.

A natural way to begin our narrative is to trace "the" origin of racial issues in American politics. And we have indeed pursued that question, always unsuccessfully. The problem with this strategy is that any postulated origin of the modern form of racial issues is invariably predated by an even earlier plausible origin. We have, for example, always considered the Johnson vs. Goldwater election of 1964 a critical event in the partisan evolution of racial issues. But it was preceded by almost three years of dramatic sit-ins, freedom rides, and other attention getting nonviolent protest. But the peak years of the civil rights movement were preceded by court enforced school desegregation leading to violent response (e.g., Little Rock, 1957), in turn preceded by the Brown v. Board cases in 1954 and 1955. And there were the famous bus boycotts, most notably in Montgomery, Alabama (1955 – 1956).

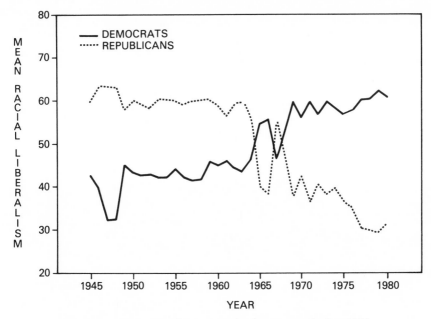

Figure 4. House racial voting scales by party, 1945 to 1980.

These seeming origins in the mid-1950s were preceded in turn by desegregation of the armed forces (1948) and by extremely violent race riots during the war years. The riots were replicas of similar events twenty years before. And all this time there was quieter agitation against "Jim Crow" laws in the South and counter agitation by the Ku Klux Klan. Jim Crow and the Klan were products of Reconstruction, which in turn was a reaction to the Civil War. Historians have filled many volumes tracing the precursors of the Civil War, abolitionism, Dred Scott, the Missouri Compromise, and so forth. Before that was the constitutional compromise that recognized a black slave as three-fifths of a person. Before that were slavery and slave trade controversies in the colonies.

The only time that seems a reasonably certain origin for racial controversy in America would be the date the first black slave was brought ashore. And if that is an historically "safe" judgment, it is also certainly a trivial one. It does, however, suggest the folly of the enterprise; we ought not to look for the origin of racial issues in American politics because racial issues predate American politics.

But we can more reasonably assess the origins of *partisan* evolution on race in the modern period. And, unlike tracing the origins of the issue, that task is tractable. The alignment of party and voting on racial issues is notably

Table 1. Intervention Scenario

Turnover	Desegregation Policy Role	
	Spurious	Causal
Small	A. No change	B. Systematic Change Possible
Large	C. Accidental Change Possible	D. Critical Change Possible

stable for the first 14 years of the Senate series (Figure 3). In every year before 1959 Republicans are in the aggregate more liberal than Democrats (and, not seen in Figure 3, about comparable to northern Democrats). The first evidence of change, the tentative origin of partisan issue evolution, is seen in the Senate series following the 1958 elections. The greater racial liberalism characteristic of the Republican Party since its origin before the Civil War vanishes in the 1959 U.S. Senate, never to reappear. Our task now is coming to terms with change.

We postulate membership replacement as the principal agent of interparty change over time. Thus replacement *mechanisms* assume a central role in explanations. That leads immediately to two conclusions:

1. Elections are the probable causal force that drives the system.
2. Where replacement mechanisms differ—as they do between House and Senate by Constitutional design—change processes also should differ.

The first conclusion leads us to look at elections as external causes of change in Congress. The second leads us to look at the two houses separately. We begin with the U.S. Senate.

Racial Policy Change in the Senate: An Intervention Analysis

Sixteen intervening elections exerted potential influence on our 34 years desegregation series. But we do not expect to see actual change associated with many of them. Two conditions influence the likelihood of election-induced interparty change for any policy. One is the magnitude of turnover. The second is whether the policy in question exerts any systematic influence on the election outcome. The two conditions provide a crude intervention scenario that is nonetheless good enough to allow us to sort out interesting possibilities, as shown in Table 1.

Two of the four contingencies can be ruled out at the beginning. Category A includes most postwar Senate elections; turnover is small and unsystematic with regard to race. These elections cannot explain change. Category D (large, causal turnover) would have been of great interest if it contained any cases, but it does not. The peak years of racial policy salience (roughly: the 1960s) produced no large turnovers in Senate membership.

The racial salience of the Goldwater presidential candidacy makes 1964 a prospect for type B, small but systematic turnover (see note 6). We know that contest produced realignment at the mass level;[7] it is reasonable to postulate similar effects in the Senate.

Very large turnovers (in a very small body) may produce substantial policy change between parties even in the absence of policy influence on the election (Type C). The 1958 Senate election appears to be a case of this kind. Propelled by Khrushchev's first sputnik and Eisenhower's second recession, Democrats scored nearly a clean sweep, effecting a large scale and long lasting turnover of Senate personnel.

We are now ready to take up the task of examining the impact of two elections on the Senate series. To be explained is the *difference* between Senate Republicans and Democrats on desegregation. The proposed explanations are the replacement effects of two elections, 1958 and 1964. The method is Box-Tiao intervention analysis.

Our goal is to test the intervention impacts of the two elections. Both are hypothesized to have sharp immediate impacts (except of course that Senators take office in the year after they are elected) that decay over time back toward the original equilibrium level of the series. Because their apparent effects are almost identical, we impose the same model on both interventions, rather than fitting them separately. The model is a first order transfer function:

$$Y_t = (1 - \delta_1 \beta)^{-1} \omega_0 I_{t-1} + \theta_0 \qquad (1)$$

where Y_t is the net difference series (Republican mean − Democratic mean); I_t is 1 for 1958 and 1964, 0 for other years; δ_1 is the rate of decay of the intervention impact; ω_0 is the initial impact; and θ_0 is the estimated mean of the series.

It describes a series in equilibrium around its mean that encounters shocks (two in the case at hand) that drive it away from equilibrium. Because the shocks are temporary, their impacts decay and, given enough time, the model projects a return to the original equilibrium.

Model (1) proves to be unsatisfactory in several regards. The parameter takes on an unacceptable (>1) value. The 1970's portion of the series is badly (and systematically) misestimated, and that in turn leads to a distortion in the estimated intervention effects. The fit of the model is not good (residual mean square = 32.6). None of these problems would have arisen if Model (1) were fit to the pre-1970 series.

The "problem" with the 1970s portion of the series is that the earlier intervention effects do not decay after 1970. We see instead a steady growth

Table 2. Senate Party Differences on Desegregation: An Intervention Model

Parameter	Value	t	Description
	Intervention 1: 1958 and 1964 Pulse		
δ_1	.95	56.3	Decay rate parameter
ω_0	23.1	10.2	Initial impact
	Intervention 2: 1970 Step Function		
δ_1	.89	11.3	Growth rate parameter
ω_0	4.4	2.6	Initial impact
	Noise Model		
θ_0	-27.5	-27.1	Mean (preintervention)
θ_1	.30	1.6	Moving average (1)
	Residual mean square $= 23.9$		

in differentiation (see Figure 3) between the parties over that period. Because this secular differentiation cannot be accounted for by the earlier interventions, we must either exclude it or model it. We choose to model it.

The form of the 1970s secular differentiation model is different from earlier interventions. Rather than an impulse with decaying impact, we model here a slow steady growth pattern. The choice of a starting point is not so obvious (nor is it as important) for these sorts of models as in the impulse decay case. We have chosen 1970 as a starting point because it is the first Senate election of the Nixon presidency. Model (2) leaves the 1958 – 1964 intervention model unchanged and adds an additional intervention for the 1970s:

$$Y_t = (1-\delta_{11}\beta)^{-1}\omega_{01}I_{1t-1} + (1-\delta_{21}\beta)^{-1}\omega_{02}I_{2t} + \theta_0 - \theta_1 a_t \qquad (2)$$

where the first intervention is as before (except for the additional subscript notation), δ_{21} is the rate of growth of intervention 2, ω_{02} is the initial impact of intervention 2, I_{2t} is zero until 1970, one thereafter, and θ_1 models a modest first order moving average noise process.

The estimated parameters for Model 2 are displayed in Table 2. The party difference series, actual and modeled, are displayed in Figure 5.

Fitting a model of the modest complexity of Model (2) is a challenge to our statistical methodology when the series in question consists of only 34 time points. That the challenge is *easily* met tells us something of importance

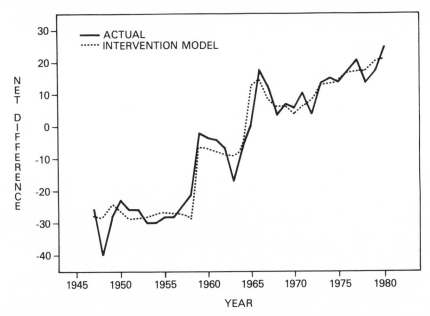

Figure 5. Senate interparty desegregation differences, actual and intervention model.

about the desegregation series; its variation is highly patterned. The net difference series of Figure 5 very clearly shows sharp impacts following the Senate elections of 1958 and 1964, each of which decays slowly back toward the preintervention mean of the series. All this is as hypothesized. Almost equally clear, but not hypothesized, is the dynamic evolution of the 1970s.[8] Figure 5 leaves little doubt that Model (2) is an adequate description of the evolving party alignments on racial issues. It does not, however, tell us why the intervention effects occurred. We take up that task now.

The "Why" of Issue Evolution in the Senate

Before we can explain why a series of Senate elections could provoke secular issue realignment, we need a picture of the world of racial politics as it existed before November, 1958. Quite probably one of the side effects of issue evolution is the development of perceptual screens that have the tendency of creating a past more like the present than it truly was. Thus, a picture of the past in its own terms is a useful starting point.

Table 3 begins our picture of the racial policy status quo of the late 1950s. There we map the composition of the liberal and conservative racial

Table 3. Racial Liberalism and Conservatism in the 85th Senate

Desegregation Voting Pattern	Republican Party		Democratic Party	
	Non-South	South and Border	Non-South	South and Border
Liberal	37	5	20	1
Conservative	4	0	5	22
	41	5	25	23
Means[a]	61.8	67.0	58.8	19.2

[a]Unrecoded 85th Senate scale.

coalitions by party and region.[9] The coalitions in Table 3 are quite different from those expected in later Senates. Most importantly, there are twice as many Republicans as Democrats (42 to 21) in the "liberal" category. Two pre-1958 factors go far to explaining this anomalous (by modern standards) situation. The more important of the two is that there were always far more northern Republicans than northern Democrats. Even if the northern Democrats had been uniformly liberal—and they were not—the Democratic Party in the Senate was half southern during this period. The Democratic Party could not become liberal in the aggregate without a massive reorientation of its electoral base from South to North.

The smaller, perhaps more interesting, phenomenon to be seen in Table 3 is that southern Republicanism—virtually all of it in the border states—was then a liberal alternative to the more traditional and conservative southern Democracy. The five border Republicans of the 85th Senate [Cooper and Morton (Ky.), Beall and Butler (Md.), and Revercomb (W.V.)] were actually more consistently liberal than the northern segments of either party.

The mean desegregation scales of Table 3 allow us to rule out composition effects as an explanation of greater Republican liberalism. The Republican senators were more liberal overall—which we already knew—and they were also more liberal than the Democrats within each region. Although the northern Republican/northern Democrat difference of means is not statistically significant, its direction clearly rules out "region" as a spurious explanation for interparty difference.

With this context established, it is now easy to understand the impact of the Democratic landslide victory in 1958. Eleven Republicans were replaced by Democrats; ten were racial liberals, each in turn replaced by a liberal Democrat. The 42 to 21 count of the liberal ranks in the 85th Senate became 32 to 31 purely by virtue of interparty electoral change. On top of the ten seats that stayed liberal but changed parties, the Democrats picked up another three seats as Alaska and Hawaii were admitted to the Union, tilting the balance even further. And while about a fourth of all liberal Republicans ended their careers in only one election, the list of their Democratic replacements reads like a "who's who" of the Democratic coalition that would dominate the Senate for two decades.[10]

The summary of the 1958 Senate elections is simple: it was a bad year for Republicans. While it would be very difficult to rule out any causal influence of racial issues on the outcome, neither do we have reason to postulate it. Racial issues were highly salient in 1958,[11] but the patterns of change do not suggest a systematic sorting process along racial lines, and we know from the later Kennedy/Nixon contest that voters perceived no interparty differences on racial desegregation. It is ironic that this first event in an unfolding issue realignment appears unrelated to the issue in question.

Whether the cause of the 1958 phenomenon was random or systematic with regard to race, the effect was certainly systematic. That single election ended the pattern of greater Republican liberalism on race, then called "civil rights." Liberal Republicans were never again the dominant force in the civil rights coalition. At the same time, the Democratic Party in the Senate developed its more modern image: the hard core of northern liberalism was sufficiently large and sufficiently liberal that it counterbalanced the traditional southern contingent. This event must have been an important precondition for the struggle for control of the Democratic Party that soon followed in the early 1960s.

Accounting for realignment on race following the 1964 Senate elections is an easier task. After the tumult of the civil rights movement, which was both on the streets and in Congress, there was clear evidence that racial issues were highly salient.[12] In that year American voters clearly perceived the Democratic party as more liberal on race issues than the Republicans.

The 1964 Senate elections contributed to further issue realignment on race in two ways. One is that the liberals of the Class of '58, who would have been expected to suffer considerable attrition because they owed their initial success to a Democratic landslide, experienced no attrition at all because they had the good fortune to seek reelection during the Goldwater debacle. It was another bad year for Republicans.

The second contribution to issue realignment was the loss of two more of the dwindling band of racially liberal Rebublicans (Beall of Maryland and Keating of New York) to be replaced by highly visible liberal Democrats (Joseph Tydings and Robert Kennedy). Republican gains were small and uniformly conservative (including J. Strom Thurmond of South Carolina, who switched parties). Few seats changed hands in 1964, but "trading" Beall and Keating for Murphy (Cal.) and Thurmond pushed the Republicans ever more rightward. This shift occurred while Tydings, Mondale (replacing

Table 4. Racial Liberalism and Conservatism in the 89th Senate

Desegregation Voting Pattern	Republican Party		Democratic Party	
	Non-South	South and Border	Non-South	South and Border
Liberal	10	0	37	8
Conservative	18	4	4	17
	28	4	41	25
Mean[a]	45.5	29.1	67.7	30.9

[a]Unrecoded 89th Senate scale.

Hubert Humphrey), and Robert Kennedy gave increasing visibility to the Democratic left.

Small but systematic realignment through replacement is difficult to document precisely because it is small. But we can say this: of the seats that changed hands, some (e.g., Keating/Kennedy) reinforced tendencies toward realignment, some (e.g., Humphrey/Mondale) had no net effect, but *none* followed the pre-1958 pattern of greater Republican liberalism. Even Barry Goldwater, who evidently played a central role in realigning race and party, was replaced by a Republican (Fannin) whose racial conservatism was more consistent than his own.[13]

Table 3 was a snapshot of racial voting alignments before the first shock of the 1958 election. Table 4 is a similar portrait taken after 1964. In the 85th Senate, two-thirds (42 of 63) of all racial liberals were Republicans; in the 89th, the comparable figure is 18% (10 of 55). Before 1958 the G.O.P. was significantly more liberal overall, and it was also more liberal in both the North and South separately. After 1964, it was more conservative within each region. All of these changes appear on both sides of the ledger. The G.O.P. not only lost seats in the Senate, it lost most of its 1957 liberal seats (roughly, 32 of 42) and *gained* conservative seats during an era when the party was faring badly at the polls. The Democratic Party meanwhile suffered minor losses to its conservative wing and made massive gains (from 21 to 45) among liberals. All of these changes proceeded more or less equally in both North and South. Two elections produced an issue realignment in Senate voting.

Secular Realignment in the 1970s

Barry Goldwater made it respectable for Republicans to oppose federal intervention to enhance desegregation. We have seen elsewhere (Carmines and Stimson, 1981) that the 1964 campaign appears to have set in motion a secular issue realignment among citizens. Both the new respectability of conservative racial positions and the assurance of mass support—particularly support in Republican primary elections—would be likely to produce a systematically more conservative crop of Republican senatorial candidates. The process is slow, in contrast to the big jolts of 1958 and 1964, and it is circular. Racially conservative candidates give the party a more conservative image, which filters the recruitment of party identifiers toward a more conservative norm, which in turn makes the nomination of the more conservative candidates yet more likely, which in turn. . . . A process of this sort is evident in the secular realignment of the 1970s.

Secular issue realignment might be manifested singly in any of a number of potent casual scenarios or multiply in weak versions of all of them. The latter appears to be the case. We give only brief illustrations here; the systematic evidence we have already seen.

The clearest manifestation of issue realignment occurs within parties. When Buckley ousted Goodell in 1970, for example, the Republican Party not only lost one of its dwindling band of liberals, but also gained a conservative. With much less drama, because the departures were usually voluntary and at advanced age, the old hard core of "segregation forever" southern Democrats has given way to racial moderates. The 1970s witnessed the departure of segregationist stalwarts such as Ellender, Ervin, Fulbright, Holland, Jordan, McClelland, and Russell. Their replacements are moderate in the aggregate; most have moderate voting records individually as well. Chiles, Stone, Gambrell, Edwards, Johnston, Nunn, Bumpers, Hodges, and Morgan, all are southern Democrats, but they are cut from a mold closer to Jimmy Carter than to the old breed. Newly elected southern (and border) Democrats are not merely different than their predecessors in style. In every year after 1972, they are more liberal in racial voting than southern Republicans; this comes as no surprise, but those elected in the last two elections of our series are even slightly more liberal than northern Republicans. Distinctive primarily for its total opposition to desegregation, the "Dixiecrat" wing of the Senate Democratic Party had died by the end of the 1970s.[14] That the old Dixiecrats could not hold on forever was to be expected. That they would be replaced only by moderates from their own party or conservatives from the opposition connotes issue evolution.

Between-party replacements have less direct effects on issue evolution. But two of the kind that matter can be seen in the 1970s. One is a long term decline in Republican control of New England. Predictably liberal on racial matters and predictably Republican in Senate voting, New England was until recently a major force for (Republican) racial liberalism in the Senate. New England's six states produced nine Republican senators prior to 1958, all racial liberals. Twenty years later the Republican delegation was still liberal, but only four in number.[15] Obviously much smaller than Republican heartland areas in the West and Midwest, New England now contributes even fewer Republican senators than the South.

The South itself is the final piece of the puzzle. Growing Republicanism has been expected since the early 1950s. That expectation has not been translated fully into Senate seats with any regularity, even through the 1970s. What has changed is the type of Republicanism now dominant in the South. Once a racially liberal alternative with electoral success primarily in the border states, Republicanism has moved into the heart of the South and it is now uniformly the conservative choice on desegregation.[16] The hard line on race is led increasingly by southern Republicans such as Helms, Thurmond, Tower, and Scott.

The Voting Rights Act of 1965 must surely have played some role in moderating at least the style, and probably the substance, of the racial positions of even old southern Democrats. The asymmetry of impact of the new participation of large numbers of black voters is simple. Blacks now constitute large proportions of eligible voters in Democratic, but not Republican, primary elections. Racism was once a free shot in southern politics; an appeal to bigotry was certain to gain votes at almost no cost. The bigots are still out there, but now the southern Democrat who openly appeals to them does so with the certain knowledge that the appeal will cost a great deal.

We have examined Senate voting at length because the U.S. Senate is a small body where trends over time can be accounted for by the comings and goings of relatively few "household" names. A briefer, more systematic look at the House of Representatives is in order.

Modeling Issue Evolution in the House

Issue evolution in the U.S. House of Representatives occurs in the same political environment as that of the U.S. Senate. The House moves to the same external forces, the tides of electoral fortune, the bias of incumbency, the realignment of issues and parties in the mass public. But the House response is different.

In an era characterized by "vanishing marginals"[17]—the phenomenon of increasing electoral security for members of both parties—the House better resists electoral boom and bust cycles. Contrary to constitutional design, the lower house is better insulated from shifting public moods. It responds just as surely to long run change as the Senate, but its response is slower, more inertial, more deliberate.

The difference between the two bodies is partly a matter of numbers. With only 33 Senate seats at stake every two years, the size and policy predisposition of each party's contingent can vary considerably from the idiosyncratic events of a few states. Or, as in the 1958 case, an electoral clock that accidently exposes a distinctive wing of the party (racially liberal Republicans that year) to a heavy electoral current in the wrong direction can spark even more dramatic change. The House, in contrast, follows baseball's mystical concept, "the odds." With all 435 seats at stake in each election, there is little room for accidental replacement patterns. With all members equally exposed, there is a large theoretical possibility for systematic replacement (as undoubtedly occurred in 1964), but very little prospect of issue evolution by the accident of local or idiosyncratic factors.

Regional composition "accidents" do occur in the House; we shall shortly see evidence of one in 1958. Before the confusion of later realignment there was a simple logic to regional composition. Seats in the South were Democratic through thick and thin. Consequently the South was the Democratic Party base. Seats in the North (except the urban machine districts) were much more marginal. During bad times for the Democratic Party, as in the early years of the Eisenhower administration, the southern base became a very large proportion of the party in the House. Good years, on the other hand, could only be good in the North for there were no seats to gain in the already "solid" South. Because race and region were closely associated, high tides for the Democratic Party produced a party more northern and liberal in composition. Bad electoral fortunes produced a more southern and conservative party. And all of this would have happened if no member changed position and no voter had racial issues in mind at the polls. It did.

Because the House faces the same external environment as the Senate, we postulate the same intervention, the 1958 and 1964 elections, as causal forces. Because House electoral mechanisms are different, we expect a difference in response. Reflecting larger numbers, the House should be more orderly.

We begin, as we did with the Senate, with a look at the longitudinal stability of racial issues. Figure 6 plots bivariate correlations between the racial issues of the 89th House [18] and all other years. As in the Senate series there is no indication of change. Votes of members who served in 1946 and were still present in 1965–1966 are correlated at .92 for the two independent issue scales. The comparable correlation between the 89th and 1977, almost the end of the series, is .88. The early 1950s, the one period that seems a bit distinct, is also a time when almost nothing was happening on race. We are quite comfortable with the assumption that the House series taps a single common dimension over time.

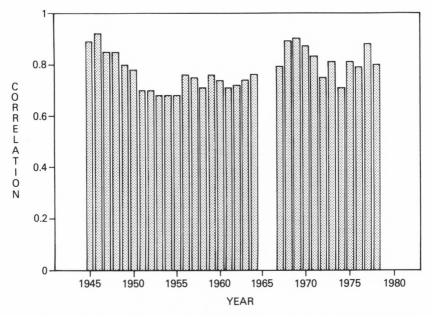

Figure 6. Racial voting correlated with 89th House: U. S. House, 1946–1978.

Racial Policy Change in the House: An Intervention Analysis

Our earlier Figure 4 leaves no question about the fact of racial issue evolution. Republicans were always more liberal than Democrats before the mid-1960s, always more conservative after. The evolutionary pattern is simpler than we saw with the Senate. A single election—and its dynamic aftermath—accounts for most of the observed shift. The 1964 election produced a large group of northern liberal Democrats in the House (unlike the Senate, where turnover was small at that critical moment), elected largely at the expense of racially liberal Republicans.

That Lyndon Johnson's landslide victory produced a large crop of liberal congressional Democrats is well known. It needs also to be appreciated that liberal Democratic victories came largely at the expense of liberal Republicanism. Of the House Republicans who did not return for the "fabulous 89th" Congress, roughly two of every three had voted in support of the strong House version of the Civil Rights Act of 1964. House Republicanism of the early 1960s was conservative on fiscal issues and proud of the heritage of Lincoln on race. The 1964 elections began the process, still underway, of purging Lincolnism from the G.O.P.

For the earlier 1958 House elections we postulate a regional composition effect. Democratic success in that year meant Democratic success in the

Table 5. House Party Differences on Desegregation: A Dual Intervention

Parameter	Value	t	Description
	Intervention 1: 1958 Step Function		
ω_0	8.86	4.7	Permanent impact
	Intervention 2: 1964 Step Function		
δ_1	.77	14.3	Growth rate parameter
ω_0	7.97	5.2	Initial impact
	Noise Model		
θ_0	−19.1	−24.2	Preintervention mean
θ_2	.78	4.5	Moving average (2)
	Residual mean square = 31.0		

North. Whether or not the emerging issue of race was on voters' minds, the northward move of the party's center of gravity would have produced a more liberal Democratic Party. But the shift could not be large for the Democratic victory in the House was much smaller than its Senate counterpart.

Our intervention model of racial issue evolution in the House (see Table 5) is technically quite different from our earlier Senate model. The 1958 intervention produces a small permanent shift, not the impulse-decay pattern of the Senate. The 1964 intervention is a dynamic evolution toward a new equilibrium. That in turn obviates the need for an additional explanation of continuing evoluton; the 1964 shift is still moving toward equilibrium through the 1970s. The differences do indeed provide evidence that constitution makers can influence the way in which institutions respond to a changing environment, but that point needs little support.

We see a good deal more similarity than difference in the two houses. A comparison of Figures 3 and 4 suggests that both evolutionary patterns were about the same, except that big changes came earlier in the Senate. Figure 7, the House interparty differences, actual and predicted, also looks much like the earlier Senate series. Two errors of prediction stand out. Both early in the series, 1947–1948, and two decades later, differences are mispredicted by a parsimonious model. The former we regard a fluke. The 1967–1968 effects are probably real; they show the compositional change of losing in 1966 all those seats so easily won in 1964. Because the shift is evidently temporary, we prefer not to model it as an additional intervention.

Getting beneath the surface of the House racial polarization series is a task of a different order than our casual approach to explaining change in the

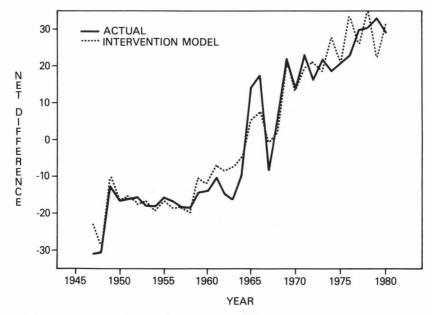

Figure 7. House interparty desegregation differences, actual and intervention model.

Senate. With few familiar names and some 1600 members serving during the period, systematic analysis requires a wholly different and considerably more complex treatment than can be taken up here.[19] We leave that for another day.

RACIAL POLICY POLARIZATION IN CONGRESS: A SUMMING UP

We came to this exploration neither as policy analysts nor congressional scholars. We are students of what we have called issue evolution, the issue based reorientation across all (partisan) aspects of American government and politics. Before the exploration we had observed the evolutionary issue response of the mass electorate. We looked to Congress (and other national political institutions) for a stimulus, an issue evolution similar to the one we had observed in a variety of indicators of mass behavior. The patterns we found in congressional votes provide that missing stimulus. They are in fact considerably stronger than the mass response that led us to this examination in the first place.[20]

In this circuitous process, which spans many years and repeated reformulations, we have produced two largely unanticipated outcomes. We have produced evidence of issue representation, but theorizing almost as evolutionary as its subject has led us to search for and find *representation in the wrong direction.* Our Congresses represent the partisan dispostions of the public; both follow similar dynamic paths. But the sort of representation that fits both theory and data leaves the public responding to the issue cues of Congress, not the other way around. Whether representation theory is more supported or battered by this exercise is an open question.

And if Congress marches to its own drummer in issue evolution, what forces can be said to produce congressional change? The primary forces are congressional elections, which bring about membership replacement, and in consequence policy change through issue evolution. Within- and between-party replacement—not individual member conversion—is the main mechanism that stimulates congressional policy change. Moreover, neither of the elections whose impacts we have examined in detail (1958 and 1964) is an obvious candidate for a classic critical election. The partisan change they produced is both less dramatic and more gradual than that implied by critical election models.[21] This suggests that major policy change is possible *without* critical realigning elections. Thus, along with the mass-to-elite direction of representation, we have had also to abandon the critical election emphasis of traditional realignment theory. Our examination of the partisan evolution of racial issues has led us to reconsider the very nature of change in American politics.

Acknowledgments. This research was supported by the National Science Foundation under grant SOC-7907543. Some of the data used in this article were originally collected by the Center for Political Studies of the University of Michigan under a grant from the National Science Foundation. We would like to thank Leroy Rieselbach for his careful editing of the manuscript.

NOTES

1. For two works that address this question see Clausen (1973) and Kingdon (1973).
2. See MacRae (1970 for a treatment of the perils of choosing appropriate correlation coefficients for principal components with roll calls. After lengthy experimentation with all options, each of which is unsatisfactory in one regard or another, we settled for phi, the simplest, which is reasonably well behaved in the absence of extreme marginals.
3. For this analysis we have standardized the annual scales to produce constant means (50) and standard deviations (25) in the aggregate for all years. Although the scales in their natural (percentage) metric do not vary greatly from these norms, variation could quite clearly occur because some Congresses face easier or tougher versions of the same legislation.
4. Years for which no autocorrelations are presented involve pairs of adjacent years at least one of which had no identifiably racial votes. In later analyses we will estimate individual scale scores for those years from earlier (if available) or later behavior.
5. The relatively low association of the 1966 votes with the earlier pattern in the Senate is

reflective of real change. That session was an important turning point in the nationalization of civil rights issues and the decay of the bipartisan desegregation coalition.

6. See Converse et al. (1965) for evidence of the racial salience of the Goldwater candidacy. Converse et al. argue (pp. 327–330) that Goldwater attempted to portray himself as a racial conservative and that he met with striking success in conveying that message to voters. An electorate that had failed to perceive much racial policy difference between Richard Nixon and John Kennedy four years earlier, consensually separated Goldwater and Johnson *and also the parties they represented.*

7. We develop the mass level evidence in Carmines and Stimson (1981); see also Pomper (1972).

8. However, see Carmines and Stimson (1981), where the same effect was hypothesized for citizen attitude alignments.

9. Members are categorized by averaging votes from 1957 and 1958 and recoding. The mean for all members (50) is the division point between "liberal" and "conservative."

10. Among them: Steven Young, Thomas Dodd, Clair Engle, Philip Hart, Vance Hartke, Frank Moss, Edmund Muskie, Eugene McCarthy, Harrison Williams, and William Proxmire (off-year).

11. Even in 1958, well before the civil rights movement, racial issues provided the single strong case of policy representation in Congress. See Miller and Stokes (1963).

12. See Converse et al. (1965) for elaboration of this point.

13. There is irony in the fact that 1964 marks a turning point in mass perceptions because, except for the purely regional voting rights issue the following year, 1964 was the last high point of Republican racial liberalism in the Senate. Only a handful of Republican Senators voted "no" on the Civil Rights Act of 1964, but the handful included the party's presidential candidate.

14. Of the warriors from the big segregation battles of the 1960s, only John Stennis and Russell Long remained at the beginning of the 1980s.

15. The Republicans have subsequently regained two seats (gaining Cohen (ME), Humphrey (NH), and Rudman (NH), losing Brooke (MA). The net shift is toward conservatism.

16. It has also remained successful in the border states, but there also (except for Maryland), it is uniformly the conservative alternative.

17. The phrase is from Mayhew (1974).

18. The two sessions of the 89th House are chosen over the 1964 baseline used in the Senate for superior measurement reliability. The Civil Rights Act of 1964 was settled in a single vote in the House.

19. The approach we take in our yet unpublished analysis is a pooled intervention analysis where cases are regions and time points. We model intervention effects with first order dynamics (as here) along with regional effects across time and region/time interactions.

20. We draw the causal connection in Carmines et al. (1984).

21. We argue that a dynamic evolutionary model fits racial policy polarization at the mass level quite well. See Carmines and Stimson (1984) for a comparison of various models of partisan change.

REFERENCES

Carmines, Edward G., and Stimson, James A. (1984). The dynamics of issue evolution: the United States. In Russell J. Dalton, Scott C. Flanagan and Paul Allen Beck (eds), *Electoral Change in Industrial Democracies.* pp. 134–158. Princeton: Princeton University Press.

Carmines, Edward G., and Stimson, James A. (1981). Issue evolution, population replacement, and normal partisan change. *American Political Science Review* 75: 107–118.

Carmines, Edward G., Renten, Steven H., and Stimson, James A. (1984). Events and alignments: the party image link. In Richard E. Niemi and Herbert F. Weisberg (eds.), *Controversies in Voting Behavior*. pp. 545–560. Washington, D.C.: Congressional Quarterly.

Clausen, Aage R. (1973). *How Congressmen Decide: A Policy Focus*. New York: St Martin's.

Converse, Philip E., Clausen, Aage R., and Miller, Warren E. (1965). Electoral myth and reality: the 1964 election. *American Political Science Review* 59: 321–334.

Kingdon, John W. (1973). *Congressmen's Voting Decisions*. New York: Harper & Row.

MacRae, Jr., Duncan (1970). *Issues and Parties in Legislative Voting*. New York: Harper & Row.

Mayhew, David R. (1974). Congressional elections: the case of the vanishing marginals. *Polity* 6: 295–317.

Miller, Warren E., and Stokes, Donald E. (1963). Constituency influence in Congress. *American Political Science Review* 57: 45–56.

Pomper, Gerald M. (1972). From confusion to clarity: issues and American voters. 1956–1968. *American Political Science Review* 66: 415–528.

4

Elections and the Potential for Policy Change in Congress: The House of Representatives

Gerald C. Wright, Jr.

Policy change in Congress is both simple to describe and difficult to explain. Policy change can be described in terms of whether a specific bill receives enough votes to pass. If a bill represents a significant departure from the status quo and, assuming it is not vetoed, it changes governmental behavior in important ways, we say that policy has changed. Explaining why these instances of policy change occur, or fail to occur, is not so simple. The passage of congressional legislation is a complex process, influenced by the rules and procedures of each chamber, the President, the strategies and effectiveness of party leaders, and the basic policy predispositions of the representatives and senators who introduce, amend, and finally vote.

The last of these influences is the subject of this paper. Member policy preferences and goals set the context within which the dynamics of the legislative process unfold. The New Deal represented major policy change, as have other realigning eras. The new legislation that defines these policy departures was passed by Congresses that had recently experienced high turnover of membership and massive changes in party labels worn by their members (Brady, 1978, 1980; Sinclair, 1977, 1982). The policy orientations of individual members of Congress appear to be quite stable over time, and such change as occurs appears to be incremental (Asher and Weisberg, 1978).

The largest and most significant source of change in policy preferences of members of Congress, therefore, appears to be through replacement (Burstein, 1980; Brady and Lynn, 1973). Old members with one set of policy attitudes are replaced by new members with different views. If of sufficient magnitude, shifts in membership can mean major changes in the context of congressional politics.

The key to changes in congressional membership lies with voters. Every two years they are given the opportunity to replace virtually the entire House and a third of the Senate. And in each biennial election we see shifts in the voters' judgments reflected in changes in the national vote; some of these are large, some small. The purpose of this paper is to determine how these vote shifts change the overall policy orientations of Congress.

THE APPROACH

Most past work on this question has only been able to view changes in congressional policy retrospectively through examination of changes in patterns of roll call behavior. However, observations of roll call change occur after, and are therefore confounded by, the influence of other factors such as the policy orientations and the effectiveness of the President, changes in committee assignments, and party leadership. We seldom have measures of members' policy orientations independent of their expression in roll calls. And even less often do we have information on nonincumbent candidates' policy views other than those inferred from party label.

This lack of data on the policy stances of incumbents and challengers has made our understanding of the ways elections influence congressional policy orientations incomplete in two respects. First, we have had little information on the policy choices voters make. Roll calls of successful challengers can be compared with those of their predecessors and with reelected incumbents, as most longitudinal studies of roll call voting have done. However, this approach cannot tell us what would have happened had voters made other choices. Do voters have much to choose between given the policy stances of competing candidates? If so, and research suggests that in general they do (Sullivan and O'Connor, 1972), does this vary in significant ways in different types of races? The point here is that measurement of the potential policy consequences of elections requires information about the policy positions of challengers as well as incumbents.

A second disadvantage of the lack of data on policy stances is that we cannot gauge with much precision the effects of incumbent defeats and retirements and the election of new members on the policy attitudes of Congress as a whole. Careful estimates of changes in congressional predispositions require comparable measures of incumbents' and their successors' policy orientations.

These measures can now be derived from the CBS-*New York Times* (CBS-NYT) polls of all congressional candidates and incumbents conducted during the 1974 and 1978 House election campaigns.[1] With these data, we can now measure candidate policy difference in House elections, and we can determine how these interact with electoral competitiveness to bring about changes in the policy predispositions of Congress.

Throughout this analysis, congressional policy stances are treated in unidimensional terms of liberalism-conservatism. The basic assumption is that the overall balance of liberals and conservatives in Congress—specifically, for this analysis, the House of Representatives—sets the broad context for congressional policy making. The strengths of the liberal and conservative groups in the House are a major factor in nature of congressional policy (Brady, Cooper, and Hurley, 1977; Brady and Lynn, 1973; Sundquist, 1968, pp. 499–505; Orfield, 1975).

For some purposes, it is very useful to consider congressional policy, and policy change, in separate issue arenas (MacRae, 1970; Clausen, 1973; Sinclair, 1977, 1982). However, it is equally reasonable to characterize policy cleavages in Congress in terms of a single liberalism-conservatism dimension. Schneider's (1979) and Shaffer's (1980) studies of congressional voting reveal a high level of ideological structure across policy arenas. Moreover, Smith's (1981) analysis indicates that the level of ideological structuring of votes across issue areas has increased substantially since the 1950s. Work on the dimensionality of interest group ratings of congressional voting records show the same single ideological continuum (Kritzer, 1978; Poole, 1981; Poole and Daniels, 1985).

The 1974 and 1978 CBS-NYT polls of congressional candidates are consistent with this unidimensional description of congressional policy cleavage. The topics included in the two surveys vary according to which issues were considered salient at the time. Principal component factor analysis reveals a clear unidimensional liberalism-conservatism structure.[2]

A number of different measurement techniques were examined in constructing measures of candidate policy liberalism-conservatism. They all yield virtually identical results.[3] Hence, I have opted for the most straightforward method of simple additive scales. (See the appendix A for a listing of the items and the scoring method used.) The scales are scored so that higher scores mean more conservative responses. "Policy conservatism" refers to scores on these CBS-NYT indices.

The correlations of these measures of candidate ideology with roll calls is evidence of their validity as measures of policy liberalism-conservatism. The measure of roll call conservatism used here combines the Americans for Constitutional Action (ACA) and Americans for Democratic Action (ADA) ratings of members of Congress. For each Congress, the measures combine ratings for both sessions, and are scored with a range of zero for strong liberals to 100 for strong conservatives.[4]

Table 1 shows the correlations among the CBS-NYT and roll call

Table 1. Correlation of Policy and Roll Call Conservatism Among Continuing
        Incumbents: 1974 and 1978[a]

	Policy Conservatism		ACA/ADA	
	1974	1978	93rd Cong.	95th Cong.
Policy 1974	1.0	.822	.890	.864
Policy 1978	.868	1.0	.886	.887
ACA/ADA, 93rd	.924	.902	1.0	.955
ACA/ADA, 95th	.920	.904	.972	1.0

[a]Correlations above the diagonal are Pearson r's based on the uncollapsed policy conservatism (CBS-NYT) and roll call measures. The figures below the diagonal are gammas from cross tabulations of the measures, each collapsed into five categories. Scores are based on the 219 incumbents who served in the 93rd through 95th Congresses and also sought reelections in 1978.

conservatism measures for those 219 representatives who were incumbents in 1974 and continued in the House to run for reelection in 1978. Overall, the correlations are very high. They suggest that all four measures tap the same ideological dimension and that the ideological positions of these incumbents over the period was very consistent.

Moreover, unless all of the incumbents are moving in a conservative or liberal direction at virtually identical rates, the high correlations between 1974 and 1978 policy and roll call conservatism suggest a great deal of consistency in policy stances and behavior. Although unidimensional scales are used in this analysis, we do not assume that the relationship between ideology and policy orientation has always held, or will always hold. For the period under study here (1974–1978), however, ideology scores are meaningful indicators of policy orientations of congressmen.

CANDIDATE POLICY DIFFERENCES

Sullivan and O'Connor (1972) used an NBC poll of candidates in the 1966 election to examine the distinctiveness of candidates' policy positions. The survey was similar in design to the CBS-NYT polls here.[5] They find rather substantial differences between pairs of candidates, with the Democratic candidates almost always more liberal than their Republican opposition. An important conclusion they reach is that the structure of electoral choice in House elections gives the public the potential for popular control of government. Voters could, by supporting Democratic candidates, elect representatives who would make Congress markedly more liberal, and by supporting Republicans they could create a Congress that would be decidedly conservative.

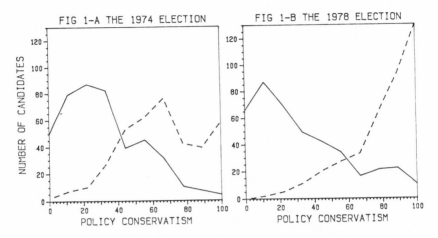

Figure 1. Distribution of candidate conservatism by party. Left panel: 1974 election. Right panel: 1978 election. *Legend.* Solid line, Democrats; dashed line, Republicans.

Overall Party Differences

Similar possibilities for major changes in the policy conservativism of Congress existed in 1974 and 1978. The policy conservatism scores of all Democratic candidates (31.4 in 1974 and 33.5 in 1978) are a good deal lower than those of Republicans (65.4 in 1974 and 78.8 in 1978). The average difference between Republicans and Democrats in districts with contested elections is 36 points in 1974 and 47 points in 1978. The ideological distinctiveness of Democratic and Republican candidates is shown in Figure 1. The solid line, which shows a distinctly leftward distribution in each panel, represents the distribution of Democratic candidates, while the dashed line shows the Republican distribution. There is some overlap, but overall the centers of gravity within the parties are quite distinct.

The simple mean differences between competing candidates, and even the overall differences in distributions of ideological positions for each of the parties, obscure a good deal of variation in the issue choices offered to voters in different districts. In a handful of districts, the candidates do not differ at all (5% in 1974 and 1% in 1978), and in some the Democrat is even more conservative than his or her Republican opposition (4% in 1974, and 5 % in 1978). In the vast majority of contests, though, the Democrat is more liberal than the Republican. The extent of this difference, or policy choice, is not at all uniform across the country: There are sizable regional differences in policy choices in congressional elections.

Table 2. Differences in Candidates' Policy Positions in House Elections by Region[a]

	East	Midwest	South	West	Total
	1974				
Mean difference, all contests[b]	26.1(117)	37.8(121)	23.6(121)	41.5(76)	31.3(435)
Mean difference, contested only	29.7(103)	384(119)	34.8(82)	44.7(71)	36.4(375)
Percent high choice[c]	24%	48%	31%	46%	
	1978				
Mean difference, all contests	37.0(117)	48.5(121)	21.5(121)	57.8(76)	39.5(435)
Mean difference, contested only	42.9(102)	51.4(114)	32.5(80)	61.19(71)	46.9(365)
Percent high choice	36%	60%	26%	67%	

[a]The definition of regions here is that used by CBS News and Congressional Quarterly. The South includes the eleven states of the Confederacy plus Tennessee and Oklahoma.
[b]This is the mean of the Republican minus Democratic policy conservatism scores. Uncontested contests are scored a zero. The second row, "Contested Only," represents contests with two major party candidates.
[c]"High Choice" refers to those contests in which a left of center Democrat was opposed to a right of center Republican. See footnote 7 for a more complete explanation.

Regional Differences

Virtually all studies of Congress discuss the North-South cleavage within the Democratic party, and many comment on the relative liberalism of eastern Republicans. If these differences occur among all candidates, and not just those who are successful, the conservatism of southern Democrats and the liberalism of eastern Republican candidates should tend to decrease the policy differences between pairs of candidates in these regions. Narrowed candidate policy differences mean that House elections in these regions would have less potential for bringing about change in Congress than elections in regions with larger policy differences between candidates.

Table 2 presents three measures of candidate distinctiveness by region. One is simply the mean differences in policy conservatism between Republican and Democratic candidates. The first version of this measure includes uncontested and contested contests, with the former given a difference score of zero; the second version of the mean difference measure is based on contested elections only. Both of these measure the ideological distance between candidates regardless of where the candidates are located on the ideological continuum. A third measure takes into account the place on the

policy spectrum where candidate differences occur. A given policy difference between opposing candidates, say 25 points, has less potential effect for
the sizes of the liberal and conservative coalitions in the House if both
candidates are on the same end of the ideological spectrum. A district where
the candidates span the center of the ideological spectrum is in a more
strategic position. Such a district influences directly the sizes of the liberal
and conservative coalitions in the House in its selection of a representative.
Thus, we are interested in the incidence of "high choice" elections, defined
as contests where a liberal Democrat opposes a conservative Republican.[6]

The regional differences are quite striking whether one examines mean
differences, or the percentage of high choice elections. The possibilities for
contributing to significant change in congressional policy orientations are
much greater in the Midwest and West than in the East or South. When
uncontested elections are included, the 1974 policy choice distances in the
Midwest and West average around 40 while those in the East and South are
in the mid-20s. Similar regional differences occur in 1978.

Differences in the incidence of high choice elections are just as dramatic,
and they are of even greater strategic significance. The 1978 pattern is
especially notable: close to two-thirds of the midwestern and western
districts had the opportunity to make significant differences in the sizes of
congressional ideological coalitions, whereas just over a third and only about
one-quarter of the eastern and southern districts respectively, had this
chance.

Incumbents, Challengers and Open Seats

We find additional interregional differences of some significance when we
look at the candidate policy differences by incumbency. Figure 2 shows, for
each region, the means in policy liberalism for Democrats and Republicans
in each of three types of elections: (1) the top (solid) line in each panel shows
the means for Democratic incumbents and their Republican challengers; (2)
the second (short dashed) line depicts the mean positions for Republican
incumbents and their Democratic challengers; and the third (dashed) line in
each region represents the mean Democratic and Republican positions for
open seat candidates. The left-hand vertical marks indicate the average
Democratic position, and the right-hand marks indicate the average Republican score. The length of the lines indicate the average ideological choice
offered to voters in contested elections in each region and type of election.

The data in Figure 2 reveal a number of things. First, they help clarify the
nature of regional differences in candidate policy distances. Notice that the
Democratic candidates in the East, Midwest, and West align at about the
same point, all clearly left of center. The attenuation of candidate differences

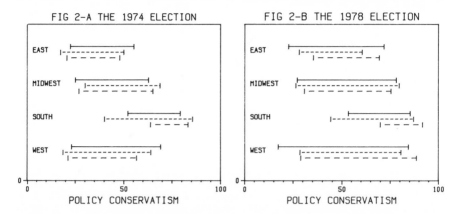

Figure 2. Candidate policy distances by incumbency and region. Left panel: 1974 election. Right panel: 1978 election. *Legend.* Solid line, Democratic incumbent—Republican challenger; short dashed line, Democratic challenger—Republican incumbent; longer dashed line, Democrat—Republican (open seat).

in the East is clearly a function of the greater liberalism of eastern Republicans who, in all types of elections, are to the left of G.O.P. aspirants in the other regions. The South's relatively anemic capacity to contribute to policy change is explained by the relative conservatism of the region's Democrats. They are a good deal more conservative than other Democrats and, moreover, all southern Democrats but those challenging Republican incumbents fall, on average, to the right of center. In addition to overall regional variation in candidates' distances, Figure 2 suggests an interesting difference between incumbent and open seat races. In most regions, the policy distances between candidates appear to be less in open seat contests than in those in which an incumbent is seeking reelection. Overall, however, these differences in candidate distances are fairly small.[7]

One incumbent versus open seat difference in Figure 2 stands out. Southern Democrats running in open-seat contests are extremely conservative while their fellow challengers who happen to be running against Republican incumbents are relatively liberal—at least by southern standards.

This pattern may have important implications for the evolution of two-party competition in the South. Those who replace incumbents determine the future character of the parties. If our 1974 and 1978 open seat Democratic candidates are typical of the new generation of southern Democrats, their election will yield a Democratic congressional party even more ideologically polarized than it is with the current incumbents. However, the election of generations of southern Democrats like those challenging Republican incumbents will result in a more moderate southern Democrat delegation, and this will yield a less polarized Democratic congressional party.

The pattern in Figure 2 suggests that policy change in the southern Democratic party congressional delegation is most likely to occur after Republicans have successfully won the loyalty of the most conservative voters, and thereby have forced Democrats to win with appeals to more moderate sentiments.[8]

ELECTORAL TURNOVER AND IDEOLOGICAL CHANGE

An underlying assumption of this research is that electoral replacement of representatives is the major source of shifts in the policy orientations of Congress. The previous section showed that voters have the option of making major alterations in the sizes of the liberal and conservative groups in Congress, and that this varies in interesting ways across regions.

This section looks at electoral turnover, or replacement, and how it brought about changes in congressional ideologies as a result of the 1974 and 1978 elections. We follow Burstein (1980) in differentiating two types of replacement. One is switches in party control of the seat, or "party replacement," either through defeat of incumbents or through an opposition party victory in open seat elections. The other is intraparty replacement, or "person replacement," which occurs in open seat districts when the retiring incumbents' party retains the seat. If we assume that incumbent ideologies are stable, then the only source of change in incumbent contests is through party replacement.[9] Open seats, by definition, will experience either person or party replacement.

This section assesses the components of ideological change in House elections, beginning with a look at the net change in 'he ideological orientations of the House that were brought about in the 1974 and 1978 elections. Replacement in incumbent elections is then compared to that occurring in open seat contests. Finally, the section compares the contribution of person and party replacement in these open seat contests.

Ideological Change in the House

The 1974 election brought about the defeat of 36 generally conservative incumbents and resulted in a net Democratic gain of 43 seats. This Watergate inspired landslide gave the Democratic Party its largest membership in the House since the famous Eighty-Ninth Congress (1965–66). The Ninety-Fourth Congress (1975–76) was noticeably more liberal than

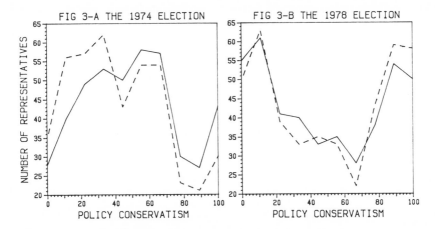

Figure 3. Before and after election distributions of congressional policy orientations. Left panel: 1974 election. Right panel: 1978 election. *Legend.* Solid line, 93rd Congress; dashed line, 94th Congress.

the Ninety-Third. This can be seen in the distributions of policy conservatism in the two Congresses shown in Figure 3. The solid lines show the policy conservatism in the old House and the dashed lines show the new House.

The shift to the liberal side is notable, if not overwhelming, in the 1974 case. The gain of Democratic seats resulted in a noticeably more liberal House. The smaller G.O.P. gains in 1978 show up as only quite marginal movement in the conservative direction (Figure 3, right panel). Both shifts are quite small compared to what was possible. But with the vast majority of incumbents being reelected, we can hardly expect really major movement in House policy orientations. Nevertheless, change in 1974 was hardly trivial, and, further, it is important to understand the processes of incremental change as well as the dramatic changes that occur in realigning elections.

Looking at the overall change in House policy orientations does not reveal much about how that change occurred. Which seats changed? How do these contribute to the net policy change in the House?

Replacement in Incumbent and Open Seat Elections

The relative contribution to changes in the ideological orientations of House members that comes from incumbent and open seats is a function of two tendencies. One is the number of possibilities for change, and here incumbent districts have a large edge. Open seats constituted only 12 and

Table 3. Changes in House Policy Conservatism Through Replacement, by Incumbency Status, 1974 and 1978

	1974			1978		
	Mean Change[a]	N of Districts	% of Overall Net Change[b]	Mean Change[a]	N of Districts	% of Overall Net Change[b]
Dem. incumb. defeated	+22.4	4	−3.6%	48.1	14	52.5%
Repub. incumb. defeated	−43.2	36	63.3	−52.9	5	−20.6
Open Seats	−19.0	52	40.3	15.1	58	68.1
Total	−27.6	92	100%	16.7	77	100%

[a]These means represent the differences between the new representatives' policy conservatism scores and those of the departing incumbents. Positive scores indicate a shift toward more conservative representation.

[b]The net change overall is the mean change for all districts with replacement times the N of these districts. The percentages of overall net change for each type of district is the product of the mean change times the number of districts in that category divided by the net change total for that year.

13% of the districts in the 1974 and 1978 elections, respectively. The second factor is the likelihood of personnel change. Here open seats are more likely to contribute to change. By definition open seat districts will have a different representative, and the probability of party replacement, which should contribute most to change, is much higher in open seat districts (Bibby, Mann, and Ornstein, 1981, pp. 2–3, 14).

Table 3 presents a decomposition of the net change in House policy conservatism for each election. Reelected incumbents are excluded. The mean change in policy conservatism is the difference between the ideologies of the new and of the old representatives.

The actual contribution of each district type to overall net change is a function of the average size of the differences between the new and old congressmen and the number of districts affected. Using these figures, it is a straightforward task to allocate to each type of district its contribution to the net ideological change. The large number of Republican incumbents defeated in the 1974 landslide make them the largest factor that year. This, together with the small number of Democratic incumbents defeated, accounted for almost 60% of the net decrease in House policy conservatism. In the 1978 election, in contrast, most of the change, which was less than in 1974, came from open seat elections. Only nineteen of the 377 incumbents running were defeated: fourteen Democrats and five Republicans. Democratic incumbent defeats thus partially offset the losses of their G.O.P. counterparts. The result is that although over 85% of the districts had incumbents running for reelection in 1978, these contests contributed less than a third of the net change in congressional ideology brought about through replacement.

The differences in our results for the 1974 and 1978 elections illustrate an important point. Without large shifts in the national partisan vote, incumbents are quite secure, and so most change is likely to come from the much smaller number of open seats where neither party has the advantage of incumbency.

Open Seat Elections

Changes in the policy conservatism of representatives that comes about in open seat districts can, as mentioned above, come about through party or person replacement. Although Figure 2 (showing mean policy differences between competing candidates) suggests that party replacement should yield significant changes in the policy views of a district's representative, we only have scattered evidence on differences in the ideologies between retiring incumbents and their successors (Burstein, 1980; Clausen, 1973).

The CBS-NYT poll included retiring incumbents as well as active candidates. This permits a systematic comparison of the potential change that can occur through person replacement by looking at all open seat districts. This comparison reveals a pattern of striking regularity. Table 4 shows the policy conservatism scores for retiring incumbents and their parties' challengers, by region. In every instance, the 1974 open seat candidates' scores are lower than those of their party's retiring incumbents. This indicates a systematic liberal shift in the challengers' policy orientations relative to their parties' retiring incumbent. Just the opposite happens in 1978. Candidates of the incumbents' party are more conservative than the departing congressmen. The differences here are not large, but they are very consistent. In each year, party successors reflect the national tides: liberal in 1974 and conservative in 1978. Across districts, these shifts among party successors could be politically significant.

That is, even intraparty replacement adds to the effects of short-term national forces. The liberalism of the House following the 1974 elections, for example, was greater than that occurring just as a result of Democrats taking seats formerly held by Republicans. For both the Democrats and Republicans, those who replaced members of their own party were more liberal than those they succeeded.

Table 4. Comparison of Policy Conservatism of Congressional Retirees and Their Parties' Nominees, 1974 and 1978

	East	Midwest	South	West	Total
1974					
Retiring Democrats	23.5	26.7	68.0	37.0	39.7
Democratic candidates[a]	18.5	20.0	63.8	16.7	31.3
(N)	(9)	(5)	(8)	(6)	(28)
Retiring Republicans	61.0	86.0	0	86.0	75.0
Republican Candidates	52.2	68.9	0	61.1	60.6
(N)	(10)	(10)	(0)	(4)	(24)
1978					
Retiring Democrats	26.5	9.3	64.5	17.6	41.9
Democratic Candidates	33.5	37.0	66.3	26.5	48.3
(N)	(9)	(3)	(19)	(8)	(39)
Retiring Republicans	59.2	65.3	85.2	82.6	70.3
Republican Candidates	75.5	78.8	97.2	94.4	83.9
(N)	(5)	(7)	(2)	(5)	(19)

[a]Candidate scores include candidates of the same party as the retiring incumbent, whether or not they won the general election.

The reasons for this pattern are not immediately obvious, but we can offer a plausible explanation. Jacobson and Kernell (1981) have argued that candidates and party elites are so sensitive to national tides that their perceptions of the political environment influence the quality of candidates who run. Stronger, more experienced, and better financed candidates emerge when the national swing is expected to be in their party's favor. If, as Jacobson and Kernell, argue, strategic politicians give careful consideration to the political environment when deciding whether to run, it makes a great deal of sense that an important component in their calculations would be a comparison of their own issue stances with their perception of political trends. More conservative candidates may sit out elections in what is expected to be a favorable year for Democrats and liberals, and vice versa. The primary system may reinforce this tendency. More liberal candidates of both parties may fare better when the tides are in a Democratic direction, while more conservative members in both parties may do better in their primary battles when the tides favor Republicans.

Such a process could operate without much voter awareness of the candidates' policy stands. It is enough if elites and candidates believe that liberals (conservatives) will do better in strong Democratic (Republican) years. In this manner, the economy and perceptions of the President could well influence the policy positions of the parties' candidates—through recruitment and greater support of candidates whose policy positions reflect shifts in the national mood—without much voter information on individual candidate policy positions. This argument is consistent with the data in Table 4, and adds a policy component to the Jacobson-Kernell thesis concerning strategic politicians.

That such a pattern occurs is interesting, but the differences between retiring incumbents and their party nominees are not terribly large. The overall mean party nominee-retiring incumbent differences (11.2 in 1974 and −8.7 in 1978) are much less than the interparty differences between all pairs of competing candidates in these elections (36 in 1974 and 47 in 1978).

How important is intraparty succession compared to changes in party control? Table 5 provides helpful information; it includes only open seat elections and shows the average change in the policy conservatism between retiring incumbents and those representing the district in the next Congress. The last two columns show the contribution of person and party replacements by party, and overall. As we would expect, party nominees diverge less from their incumbents' ideology than do winners of the opposition party. When it occurs, interparty change is much larger than intraparty change. However, two things operate to increase the relative importance of intraparty turnover in accounting for the overall net change that occurs in open seat elections.

First, person replacement is more frequent. Thirty seven of the 52 open seats were kept by the incumbent's party in 1974 as were 44 of 58 open seats in 1978. Smaller but more numerous changes add up. Second, the effects of party replacement operate in both directions. To an extent, switches that favor one party are offset by opposition gains in other open seats. This decreases the net effects of party replacement. In contrast, we have seen that the effects of person replacement are remarkably uniform.

The strong national tides of 1974 resulted in very disproportionate G.O.P. losses in open seat contests. Party replacement accounted for over two-thirds of the net change that occurred. Intraparty person replacement, however, still accounted for almost 30% of net change in open seats—an unexpectedly large amount given the landslide nature of the election.

The weaker national tides in 1978 meant that the switches in party control in open seats were more nearly equal between the parties than in 1974. As a result, the relative effects of person replacement are greater in 1978. The candidates winning in 1978 open seat contests are more conservative as a group than the incumbents they replaced, and just over one-half of this difference occurred through person replacement without changes in party control at the district level.

The relative contribution of party replacement versus person replacement

Table 5. Ideological Change in Open Seats: The Relative Contribution of Intraparty and Interparty Replacements

	Differences in Conservatism (Winner-Retiring Incumbent)	N	% of Overall Net Change	
	1974			
Person replacement				
Old *New*				
Dem. Dem.	−8.1	26	21.3%	30.3%
Repub. Repub.	−8.1	11	9.0%	
Party replacement				
Dem Repub.	22.2	2	−4.5%	69.7%
Repub. Dem.	−56.4	13	74.2%	
				100%
	1978			
Person replacement				
Dem. Dem.	4.7	31	30.8%	51.4%
Repub. Repub.	7.5	13	28.7%	
Party replacement				
Dem. Repub.	45.9	8	77.4%	48.5%
Repub. Dem.	−22.8	6	−28.9%	
				100%

to changes in the policy predispositions of House members appears to be a function of the magnitude and uniformity of national vote changes. Larger vote swings result in more switches in party control and more consistently benefit one party. Smaller vote swings presumably increase the effects of local factors, and the "localization" of House elections has increased over the last twenty years (Mann, 1978). This means a greater likelihood that party replacements will occur in both partisan directions, thus decreasing the net effects on changes in congressional ideology. What is notable here is that new party nominees were consistently responsive to national tides in both the 1974 and 1978 elections.

For open seats, person replacement was a significant factor in both

Table 6. Party Versus Person Replacement: Contributions to Net Change in Congressional Ideology by Incumbency and Winning Party

	Person Replacement (Party Retains Control)	Party Replacement (Switch Seat)	
	1974		
Democratic incumbent		−3.6%	
Republican incumbent		63.3%	
Retiring Dem. incumbents	8.6%	−1.8%	
Retiring Repub. incumbents	3.6%	29.9%	
	12.2%	87.8%	100%
	1978		
Democratic incumbent		76.3%	
Republican incumbent		−30.0%	
Retiring Dem. incumbents	16.5%	41.5%	
Retiring Repub. incumbents	11.1%	−15.5%	
	27.6%	72.3%	99.9%

elections. However, the percentages in Table 5 may overestimate the *overall importance* of person replacement for change in congressional ideology. Table 6 shows the allocation of incumbent replacement as well as open seat person and party replacement for all turnover in the two elections. With incumbent elections included in the analysis, party replacement is a much larger factor in both years. It accounts for 88% of the net change in 1974 and 72% in 1978. Given what we know about ideological differences between the parties, this is perhaps hardly surprising. On the other hand, even in 1974, with its substantial changes in party control, person replacement in open seats accounts for 12% of the net change. Person replacement accounted for 28 percent of the net change in congressional policy conservatism in the more typical election of 1978.

The analysis of change in open seats is instructive. We find that, on a seat by seat basis, switches in party control yield the largest changes in congressional ideology. However, these seat switches in party control occur in both directions, especially in elections lacking strong national tides, thus decreasing the net effects of party replacement. Person replacement, on the other hand, had effects that were surprisingly consistent with short term forces in each election. Although smaller in magnitude for each district, they add up to a meaningful contribution to changes in congressional ideology. These results point out the consistent effects of national forces on the policy orientations of new candidates. It also underlines the factor of incumbency in House elections (Erikson, 1971; Mayhew, 1974; Ferejohn, 1977; Cover and Mayhew, 1981). Incumbent safety means lower turnover and thus greater stability in congressional membership and in the policy dispositions in the House. The next section looks more closely at the policy consequences of the incumbency advantage.

INCUMBENCY AND POLICY STABILITY

The incumbency advantage in House elections was the major topic of research in congressional elections following the 1978 National Election Study.[10] It has been studied from numerous angles with various types of data. Much attention has focused on incumbents' service and advertising activities, their ability to deter strong challengers, and the effects of these as explanations of their electoral security. From this literature, we have learned a great deal about the rates and margins of House incumbents' strikingly consistent victories at the polls, and we are now approaching a new common wisdom focusing on the prerequisites of office and district service as the solution to Mayhew's (1974) "Case of the Vanishing Marginals."

Through all of this literature, however, we have not achieved a very good grasp of the policy consequences of incumbents' electoral safety. Mann (1981), for example, offers one of the few assessments of the effects of elections and incumbency on Congress. He considers effects on the balance of the parties' relative strengths, on congressional internal structure and legislative styles, and other factors. However, the effects of incumbency on policy are left largely implicit. Membership stability in Congress, however, has rather strong implications for processes of policy change through elections. Safer average electoral margins mean that fewer incumbents are defeated with any given shift in the national vote. This is readily seen in Tufte's (1973) description of the declining seats/votes ratio in House elections. One not need subscribe to Tufte's gerrymandering explanation to appreciate the decreased responsiveness of Congress (in terms of membership turnover) to shifts in the national vote.[11]

The data on the substantial policy differences between Democratic and Republican candidates certainly suggest that the incumbency effect in elections has been one of the decreasing changes in congressional policy orientations that occur as a result of electoral change at the national level. It takes larger national vote swings now than it would have twenty years ago to achieve the same shift in congressional ideology. That incumbents' large electoral margins retard changes in the policy orientations of Congress should be clear. But how large is this effect?

The approach taken here to assess policy consequences of incumbency is to ask what would have happened without the incumbents' advantage? The answer will necessarily be hypothetical, of course, but with some reasonable assumptions it should provide a useful benchmark against which to assess incumbency effects. Suppose that incumbents suddenly lost the electoral benefits they gain as House members with all the prequisites, visibility, etc., that this implies. If this advantage is taken away from their 1974 and 1978 electoral margins, we can then determine who would have won the various House contests and, more importantly for current purposes, we can determine the magnitude of policy change in House ideology that would have taken place. The difference between this hypothetical membership and the orientations of members actually elected would then indicate the policy effects of incumbency. When incumbents retire, their party usually loses some percentage of the vote relative to incumbents of the same party who did not retire (Erikson, 1971; Cover and Mayhew, 1981; Mann, 1978). To simulate an election without incumbency then, we simply subtract this "retirement slump" value from the observed percentage of the vote received by each incumbent. The retirement slump value for 1974 was 6.7% and for 1978 it was 8.9% (Cover and Mayhew, 1981, p. 70). Since there is no reason to believe the real effects of incumbency changed during the period, I assume the difference in the two values reflects to idiosyncratic factors in the two elections. Thus, to make things simpler, they are averaged so our "adjustment" for the incumbency factor in both years is 7.8%. (The analysis was repeated with the actual figures with very minor changes in the results.)

Before proceeding to the data, some problems with this procedure need to be mentioned. First, the "retirement slump" itself is an artificial concept; the actual advantage that different congressmen achieve through holding office and running as incumbents varies greatly (Mann, 1978). Thus, it is quite unrealistic to assume all margins would have magically changed by the same amount with actual retirements. However, "on average," the retirement slump is an accurate description of what occurs. We only wish to extend it to what *would* occur for heuristic purposes. Second, we assume nothing else would change if the incumbents lost their electoral advantage. This, of course, is a false assumption. Challengers would probably be stronger, and perhaps different challengers would have run against our more vulnerable incumbents. The results, therefore, are only suggestive.

The results of our hypothetical "theft" of the incumbents' electoral cushion are shown graphically in Figure 4 for 1974 and 1978. The figure is based only on contested incumbent elections since uncontested incumbents and open seats are unaffected by the incumbency advantage. The solid lines show the actual distribution of policy conservatism for the Congress previous to the election. The short dashed lines show the policy conservatism of representatives actually elected in districts in which an incumbent was

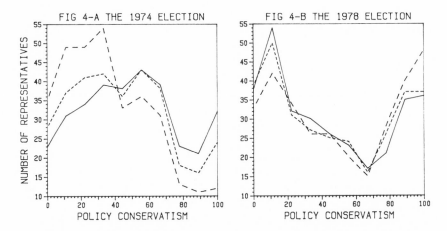

Figure 4. Policy orientations in the House: effects of the incumbency advantage. Left panel: 1974 election. Right panel: 1978 election. *Legend.* Solid line, old Congress; short dashed line, new Congress (actual); longer dashed line, estimated new Congress without incumbency.

running. The longer dashed lines show our hypothetical Congress that results from adjusting election margins for the incumbency effect.

The effects of incumbency in retarding changes in congressional ideology are readily apparent. The figures suggest that the 94th Congress would have been even more liberal than it was, and that the 96th would have had a noticeable shift to the right, with fewer liberals and more conservatives.

The Republicans suffered a net loss of 43 seats in 1974. With the incumbency advantage, 130 G.O.P. incumbents were returned to office. Without the incumbency advantage, we estimate another 49 seats would have been lost. The party balance in 1974 would have been a startling 340 Democrats to 95 Republicans. This may overestimate Republican losses, but we should note that the retirement slump in Republican districts was −11% in 1974 (Cover and Mayhew, 1981). Applying this factor to Republican incumbents rather than the combined Democratic and Republican slump of −7.9% would make our estimates of G.O.P. losses larger, not smaller. The actual change in congressional policy conservatism in 1974 was −5.6 points for all 435 districts. Without the incumbency advantage, we estimate this would have been −10.9 points. The amount of change would have been almost twice what it was.

The magnitude of incumbency effects in 1978 is less, but it is far from insignificant: 194 Democratic incumbents who faced competition were returned to the House after the election. Deprived of the incumbency advantage, only 175 of these would have been congressmen in 1979. For the whole House, the shift in policy conservatism was actually just two points when all districts are included. However, without the incumbency advantage this would have been 4.6 points. The change in policy predispositions would have been over twice as much as actually occurred. The electoral advantage of House incumbents means less turnover, and this means less change in the policy predispositions of House members. From our overview of the data, it appears that incumbency significantly retards changes in the policy predispositions of the House. The magnitude of this effect is surprisingly large. The change in policy ideology in the House would have been doubled in each year if incumbents were deprived of their advantage.

CONCLUSIONS

Policy change in Congress is said to be usually incremental, with sharp alterations in policy directions coming about only as the result of major electoral upheavals that result in large and cohesive majorities that share a vision of the right directions and policy areas for government action. This paper has examined the dynamics of change in congressional policy predispositions during a period of relative stability. The chief factor in stability appears to be high reelection rates to the House. At an elementary level, we should not be surprised that when the nation sends the same people to Congress, year after year, it gets pretty much the same types of policies, year after year. The individual congressman's perspective makes it quite rational to advocate the same types of policies over time. First, most congressmen are ideological in their attitudes and in their roll call behavior. Their public behavior in policy areas is highly constrained, politically if not logically. They are known for a set of policy positions and were elected and often reelected, representing these views. Their policy orientations are reinforced by party contacts and within the numerous informal caucuses on the Hill as well as by their personal and primary constituencies back in the district (Fenno, 1978).

Thus, this paper has argued that a major requirement for change in congressional policy orientations is membership turnover. This focuses attention on elections, which select members of Congress, and the mechanisms by which electoral forces influence, or fail to influence, changes in congressional liberalism-conservatism. Overall, Democrats stand for a set of activist-liberal policies that are quite distinct from Republicans' conservative issue positions. If the public chooses to elect Democrats, the resulting Congress would be distinctly to the left, and given the structure of congressional roll call voting, this change would influence a broad range of government policies. Similarly, the election of Republicans across the board would result, and to some extent following the 1980 election did result, in the undoing of much of the New Deal and subsequent social and civil rights legislation built up by years of Democratic dominance on the Hill. The point is simply that the possibility of change in government directions exists through the mechanism of congressional elections.

Within this, we traced a number of interesting patterns. Political change in the south and east is of less consequence generally than in the midwest or west. Opposing candidates in the latter regions tend to span the ideological spectrum, while those in the east and south tend to be different in degree rather than in kind.

How do we explain these differences between Democrats and Republicans, particularly in light of Downs' (1957) arguments concerning the wisdom of converging toward "me-too" positions? Some scholars have looked for the answer in the shape of opinion distributions within constituencies (Fiorina, 1974; Sullivan and Minns, 1976). More likely, candidate positions are influenced more by the dynamics of the recruitment process and the demands of the relatively attentive and committed voters the candidates must first please in primary elections (Wright, 1978). These party activists and supporters pull candidates from the middle of the ideological spectrum and thereby offer the much less concerned mass public the opportunity to affect the general directions of government policy. If this argument is correct, then the parties themselves, through the types of activists they attract, who then exert a strong influence on prospective nominees, provide the major force for possible change in the policy predispositions of Congress. The rather systematic variation of the parties' candidates by region suggests that constituency opinion also plays a role in determining at least the general area of political competition. And at the aggregate level, voters do a good job of picking the candidate whose ideological stance is closer to their own (Erikson and Wright, 1980, 1985).

Electoral competition, or actually the lack of it, is the major force for stability in congressional ideologies. Our data show that challengers offer a real policy choice to the voters, but numerous studies have shown that seldom is this choice made in favor of the challenger. As a result, the relatively small number of open seats in each election contribute disproportionately to the net change that elections bring about. Within this, we again see the important role of party intermediaries and candidate calculations. Change in open seats does not happen just through changes in party control. Nominees do not mimic the issue stances of their party's retiring incumbent. Rather, they run for office when the political winds are blowing in their own ideological direction. The argument here borrows heavily from that of Jacobson and Kernell, but adds a strong policy compoment to their strategic politicians' calculations.

Incumbency is the factor that does as much as anything else to diminish electoral competition. Previous work has documented the growth of the incumbency advantage and some of its consequences for different aspects of Congress. Surprisingly, however, little has been done to relate incumbency directly to policy. My effort here confirms completely the frequently implicit notion that reelecting incumbents is a force for stability in the congressional policy process. In both 1974 and 1978, if incumbents seeking reelection had been deprived of their electoral advantage, the amount of change in congressional policy liberalism-conservatism would have doubled.

Several elements must be in place for voting to bring about new directions in congressional policy making. The first, of course, is some change in patterns of voting by the electorate. If the electorate votes the same way across a series of elections, we should expect the same people to be sent to Washington and only incremental change in the policies they adopt. Indeed, something would be badly askew if Congress suddenly began entirely new policy directions with no prompting from the electorate.

But how big does the shift in voter sentiments need to be in order to register policy change in Washington? Here we find that there is no single answer. In Chapter 2, David Brady, finds that of the three widely acknowledged realignments in American electoral history, only one, the New Deal realignment, was brought about by truely widespread across the board shifts in voter sentiment. The earlier realignments, while resulting from voters' changing sentiments, were greatly facilitated by favorable seats to votes ratios for the Republican party. The key is the number of competitive seats, or more particularly for any given election, the number of marginal seats held by the party losing due to national partisan tides, as well as the uniformity of the swing across these districts.

At times just a few strategic seats can make a great deal of difference in Congress. One example is pointed out by Edward Carmines and James Stimson in Chapter 3. In the 1958 Senate elections, the strategic losses of just a few Republicans to a new crop of liberal Democrats led the move toward polarization of the parties on racial issues. More recently, the 1980 Senate elections brought the defeat of five liberal Democrats by quite meager margins, but these losses gave the Republicans control of the Senate, and this control was a major factor contributing to the tremendous policy successes of the Reagan administration in its first two years. However, such change in the current era is notable because it is so unusual.

There has been considerable stability in the membership of Congress for the last twenty years, and the increased advantages of incumbency in the House have done much to insulate current members from the vicissitudes of voter preferences for change. This lowers the seats to votes ratios, and means that perhaps even quite large changes in voter sentiments will not be reflected in new representatives. Two of our great realignments—periods of major policy innovation and change—rested on very favorable seats to votes ratios.

Patterns of voting today, with representatives connected to their constituents more by the services they provide than as representatives of party programs, diminish substantially the effects of vote swings on the ideological orientation of members of Congress. Chapter 3 by Carmines and Stimson nicely portrays the way the congressional parties led the public in giving partisan definition to the civil rights issue. And the differentiation did not stop there. Smith (1981) looked at the ideological distinctiveness of the parties across different issue areas over time and found that the parties have become systematically more ideological. The result is that by the mid-70s our data show the parties are clearly polarized on the issues of the day. The irony is that while party labels have become particularly meaningful as guides to congressional behavior, voters are picking up more on the cues of incumbency and the personal characteristics of House candidates in their voting behavior.

One effect of this is that while voters undoubtedly get better "service" from their congressmen playing an ombudsman role, there is something of a disjuncture between voters' support for or opposition to the policy directions of the President and those they send to Congress. There is nothing, of course, preventing voters from eschewing the guide of incumbency in future elections and thereby making the swing more uniform with the result of a more efficient translation of votes into seats for the victorious party. Indeed, some such phenomena will be necessary to achieve major new policy directions from the current House. In the meantime we have found that the potential for changing the ideological profile of the House is readily available in congressional elections; voters need focus only on policy to bring it about.

NOTES

1. I want to express my appreciation to Warren Mitowski and Kathleen Frankovic of the CBS News Elections and Surveys unit for kindly giving me access to these data.
2. The 1974 factor analysis actually suggested the existence of a second, but very weak, factor. In my early analysis I constructed seperate scales to measure each of these factors. However, they were highly correlated, and responded in virtually identical ways to various independent variables. There seemed to be no point in presenting almost identical sets of coefficients. Also the single index responds better to all independent variables than do variables representing two factor scores (See Erikson and Wright, 1980, for use of an earlier scale.)
3. The three measurement strategies were tried. First, factor scales were derived from the principal component factor analyses described above. Second, roll call conservatism (a

measure using ADA and ACA roll call voting) was regressed on the individual items of the CBS polls. This was done for incumbents, and then the coefficients obtained were used to make indices for all candidates. Finally, the individual items were tested for reliability. Those that correlated at .5 or higher with the sum of all other items and that showed high reliabilities were retained. Once a decision was made on item inclusion, additive indices to measure policy conservatism were created. These indices all correlate at .9 or higher among themselves. These additive indices are used here. They were rescaled (with a simple linear transformation) to achieve a range from zero to 100 so that the units would be roughly comparable to the roll call measures used in the literature and later in this paper.

4. Measures here are for the 93rd and 95th Congresses. For the 1974 election, conservatism = $((ACA1973 + ACA1974 - ADA1973 - ADA1974)/4) + 5$, and for 1978, conservatism = $((ACA1977 + ACA1978 - ADA1977 - ADA1978)/4) + 5$. Adjustments were made using only the later years when full session data were not available.

5. An important design difference is that the 1966 survey did not poll retiring incumbents. Differences between retiring incumbents (those not running in the general election for whatever reason) and the candidates who did run in the 1974 and 1978 elections are reported below.

6. Liberal and conservative are defined here as the lowest and highest 40% of scores among the incumbents who served in the 93rd through the 95th Congresses and sought reelection in 1978. In 1974 this meant Democrats with scores lower than 40 versus Republicans with scores greater than 60. In 1978, Democrats had the same cut point, but the criterion for "conservative" among Republicans was raised to 65 because of the tendency of the 1978 measure of policy conservatism to yield higher scores for the same set of conservative incumbents than the 1974 measure. Even with this higher cutoff, "high" choice appears more often in 1978, probably due more to the effect of asking somewhat different questions in the two polls than temporal differences in the distinctiveness of choices offered to voters.

7. The difference between incumbent and open contests in the average distinctiveness of candidates in contested elections is 6.3 in 1974 and just .5 in 1978, not statistically significant.

8. This theme of political change through elections in the South will be elaborated and reported elsewhere. Part of that analysis shows that the patterns in Figure 2 do not reflect other district-level partisan or demographic factors.

9. Incumbent conversion is not being considered here, although I would readily agree that individual representatives vote more or less liberally in different Congresses. Shaffer's (1980) case studies of individual representatives and senators are very instructive on this point. Such change is usually thought to be incremental and probably idiosyncratic. The impressive thing about incumbent policy behavior is its amazing stability (Asher and Weisberg, 1978). The correlation of roll call conservatism between the 93rd and 95th Congresses for incumbents who served throughout this period ($r = .955$ from Table 1) does not leave much room for individual-level ideological change. We could be missing conversion effects in the unlikely event that all congressmen moved in concert. If we had identical measures of policy conservatism for the two years we would be able to measure the effects of conversion in the same way that replacement is handled here. Unfortunately, such data are not available.

10. See Richard Beth's (1981–82) discussion for an excellent overview of many of the studies and their findings.

11. See also Collie (1981). For an unusual contrary argument concerning the electoral advantage of incumbency, see Jacobson (1985).

REFERENCES

Asher, Herbert B. and Weisberg, Herbert (1978). Voting changes in Congress: some dynamic perspectives on an evolutionary process. *American Journal of Political Science* 22: 391–425.

Beth, Richard S. (1981–1982). "Incumbency advantage" and incumbency resources: recent articles. *Congress and the Presidency* 9: 119–136.

Bibby, John F., Mann, Thomas E., and Ornstein, Norman J. (1981). Vital Statistics on Congress, 1980. Washington D.C.: Congressional Quarterly.

Brady, David (1980). Elections, Congress and public policy changes: 1886–1960. In Bruce A. Campbell and Richard J. Trilling (eds.) *Realignment in American Politics*. Austin: University of Texas Press.

Brady, David (1978). Critical elections, congressional parties and clusters of policy changes. *British Journal of Political Science* 18: 79–100.

Brady, David, Cooper, Joseph, and Hurley, Pat (1977). Legislative potential for policy changes: the House of Representatives. *Legislative Studies Quarterly* 4: 385–398.

Brady, David, and Lynn, Naomi (1973). "Switched-seat congressional districts: their effect on party voting and public policy. *American Political Science Review* 17: 528–543.

Burstein, Paul (1980). Attitudinal, demographic and electoral components of legislative change. *Sociology and Social Research* 64: 221–235.

Clausen, Aage R. (1973). *How Congressmen Decide*. New York: St. Martin's Press.

Collie, Melissa P. (1981). Incumbency, electoral safety, and electoral turnover in the House of Representatives, 1952-1976. *American Political Science Review* 75: 119–131.

Cover, Albert D., and Mayhew, David R. (1981). Congressional dynamics and the decline of competitive congressional elections. Lawrence C. Dodd and Bruce I. Oppenheimer (eds.), *Congress Reconsidered*, 2nd ed., Washington, D.C.: Congressional Quarterly Press.

Downs, Anthony (1957). *An Economic Theory of Democracy*. New York: Harper & Row.

Erikson, Robert S. (1971). The advantage of incumbency in congressional elections. *Polity* 3: 395–405.

Erikson, Robert S. (1972). Malapportionment, gerrymandering, and party fortunes in congressional elections. *American Political Science Review* 66: 1234–1255.

Erikson, Robert S. and Wright, Gerald C. (1980). Policy representation of constituency interests. *Political Behavior* 2: 91–106.

Erikson, Robert S. and Wright, Gerald C. (1985). Voters, candidates and issues in congressional elections. In Lawrence C. Dodd and Bruce I. Oppenheimer (eds.) *Congress Reconsidered*. 3rd ed. Washington, D.C.: Congressional Quarterly Press.

Fenno, Richard (1978). *Home Style*. Boston: Little, Brown. Ferejohn, John A. (1977). On the decline of competition in congressional elections. *American Political Science Review* 71: 166–176.

Ferejohn, John A. (1977). On the decline of competition in congressional elections. *American Political Science Review* 71: 166–176.

Fiorina, Morris P. (1974). *Representatives, Roll Calls and Constituencies* Lexington, MA: Lexington Books.

Jacobson, Gary C. and Kernell, Samuel (1981). *Strategy and Choice in Congressional Elections*. New Haven: Yale University Press.

Jacobson, Gary C. (1985). The marginals never vanished. Midwest Political Science Association Convention. Chicago.

Kritzer, H. M. (1978). Ideology and American political elites. *Public Opinion Quarterly* 42: 484–502.

MacRae, Duncan (1970). *Issues and Parties in Legislative Voting*. New York: Harper & Row.

Mann, Thomas (1978). *Unsafe at any Margin*. Washington, D.C.: American Enterprise Institute.

Mann, Thomas (1981). Elections and change in Congress. In Mann and Ornstein (eds.), *The New Congress*, pp. 32–54.

Mann, Thomas and Ornstein, Norman, eds. (1981). *The New Congress*. Washington, D.C.: American Enterprise Institute.

Mayhew, David R. (1974). Congressional elections: the case of the vanishing marginals. *Polity* 6: 295–317.

Orfield, Gary (1975). *Congressional Power: Congress and Social Change*. New York: Harcourt Brace Jovanovich, Inc.

Poole, Keith T. (1981). Dimensions of interest group evaluations of the U.S. Senate, 1969-1978. *American Journal of Political Science* 25: 49–67.

Poole, Keith T. and Daniels, R. Steven (1985). Ideology, party and voting in the U.S. Congress. *American Political Science Review* 79: 373–399.

Schneider, Jerrold E. (1979). *Ideological Coalitions in Congress*. Westport, Conn.: Greenwood Press.

Sinclair, Barbara (1977). Determinants of aggregate party cohesion in the U.S. House of Representatives. *Legislative Studies Quarterly* 2: 155–175.

Sinclair, Barbara (1982). *Congressional Realignment 1925-1978*. Austin: University of Texas Press.

Shaffer, William R. (1980). *Party and Ideology in the United States Congress*. Washington, D.C.: University Press of America.

Smith, Steven S. (1981). The consistency and ideological structure of U.S. Senate voting alignments, 1957-1976. *American Journal of Political Science* 25:780–795.

Sullivan, John L. and O'Connor, Robert E. (1972). Electoral choice and popular control of public policy. *American Political Science Review* 66: 1256–1268.

Sullivan, John L. and Minns, Daniel (1976). Ideological distance between candidates: an empirical examination. *American Journal of Political Science* 20: 439–468.

Sundquist, James L. (1968). *Politics and Policy*. Washington D.C.: Brookings Institution.

Tufte, Edward R. (1973). The relationship between seats and votes in two-party systems. *American Political Science Review* 67: 540–554.

Wright, Gerald C. (1978). Candidates policy positions and voting in congressional elections: the impact of the primary electorate. Midwest Political Science Association convention, Chicago.

Part

III

*From Electioneering
to Policy Making:*

Learning and Adjustment

5

Adjusting to the U.S. Senate

Richard F. Fenno, Jr.

When newly elected United States Senators move to Washington, they move from involvement in one kind of political activity to involvement in another. They move from involvement in running for office to involvement in running the country. But they do not make the transition instantaneously or without friction. A finely grained description of the campaigning-to-governing sequence would involve not two, but *three* linked and differentiable processess—campaigning, *adjusting*, and governing. This essay is about the intermediate process of adjusting. It draws upon observation over time of eleven senators, six of them newcomers, and on one-shot interviews with twenty other senators, of whom six are newcomers.

This chapter presents no theory of the adjustment process. It presents some observations, organized around three ideas. *First*, we shall think of Senators as individuals pursuing certain personal goals. Their preferences and their predispositions are the propelling and/or the guiding force in the adjustment process. How they adjust in other words, depends to an important degree on what they want. *Second*, we shall think of the adjustment process as the adjustment *from* one context *to* another context. We shall try to describe, for new senators, just what the "from" and the "to" might involve and what patterns, if any, can be observed. And we shall emphasize, in keeping with our first idea, that whatever it is newcomers adjust from and whatever it is they adjust to, it is individuals who do the adjusting. *Third*, we shall think of adjustment as a period of time, a stage, as well as a process. We assume that the length of this adjustment period will vary pretty widely among individuals, depending on what personal goals they have, and on what they are adjusting to and adjusting from. But we shall think in terms of a period that has a beginning and an end—which emerges out of campaigning at the beginning and grows, sooner or later, into governing at the end.

INDIVIDUAL GOALS

Senators are goal-seeking individuals. While they are campaigning, their goal is clear—getting elected, or reelected. But once the election returns are in, their personal choices become more complex. The electoral goal never goes away. But other goals come into play as they turn to the business of governing. And given their positioning, at the front end of a six year electoral cycle, there is a strong incentive to let up on campaign activity and to engage in some noncampaign activity. So they ask themselves: What kind of a senator do I want to be? What do I want to accomplish in the Senate? How do I want things to go for me here? Some senators bring answers to these questions with them when they come to the Senate; others work out answers once they are there (Huitt, 1961). The asking and the answering of these kinds of questions about goals are a driving ingredient of every person's adjustment process.

At the end of the 97th Congress, I asked a man who watched and worked with them every day to evaluate the 16 freshman Republican Senators of the Class of 1980. He divided them on the basis of their general attitude toward the governing process. "You have to divide them into two groups," he said:

> The first group are those who will let the process run them. They will go along with whatever happens, do what the process asks them to do. They let the system run their lives for them. You take_____ he'll never do anything here on his own. He'll go to committee, vote and send out press releases. That's all. He's a floater. The second group are those who come here and want to do something. They want to make the process work for them. No matter what it is, they want to accomplish something.

That is the overview from a man whose business is governing—some newcomers want to do it, some don't.

Of those newcomers who are passive about governing, we could say their noncampaign goal is "to get along." They will want to adjust to the Senate, surely; but their adjustment is an end in itself rather than a necessary, instrumental prelude to governing. When they must engage in governing activity—as sometimes they all must—their goal is to keep it to the barest minimum. They will remain very interested in reelection; so their ratio of campaign activity to governing activity will remain high. And they will direct nearly all their activity toward their constituencies. For senators whose goals involve more than getting along and getting reelected, their adjustment process is likely to be guided by governing related goals: making good public policy, gaining influence inside the Senate, or perhaps, running for another office—Vice President, if not President. Indeed, for those individuals who are aggressive about governing, it will be useful to think of these three—

good policy, internal influence, and higher office—as the major governing-related goals.

The attribution of goals to individual senators is a hazardous business. We shall do the best we can. But some mention of the problem is in order here. First, it is most realistic to think of senators as pursuing a mix of goals. Explanations of someone's behavior that rely on the attribution of a single, or dominant, goal are always matters of degree, matters of approximation. And these approximations are often highly dependent upon context. Second, any adequate inquiry into a senator's goals would have to encompass his or her preelection past. Following a campaign helps. But motivations sometimes reveal themselves well before that—during the decision to leave private life and enter public life, perhaps. And, that past remains hidden from our view. Third, the adjustment period may be—by its very transition nature—a time when an individual goal is unsettled. Old experiences will have yielded a mix of goals to take into the new institution. But, new experiences, in turn, may yield a new mix of goals. In any case, there is no reason to think of any individual's goals as well formed or unchangeable. Nor, finally, is there any reason to think of the early adjustment as completing an individual senator's adjustment to the Senate. That process may go on as long as he or she sits in the Senate. Our interest is in the first period of adjustment, and in the goals that affect each individual's behavior during that time.

ADJUSTMENT FROM AND ADJUSTMENT TO

The adjustment process, we have said, involves adjustment "from" and adjustment "to." And the two aspects are interconnected. What you must adjust to depends partly on what you are adjusting from. And that becomes evident in the earliest adjustment to Washington itself. One week after he was sworn in, a former governor talked about his big adjustment to a new lifestyle.

> One thing I can't get used to is waking up in the morning and not having ten people around the governor's mansion doing things for me—the state police, the housekeepers, the cook, the prison inmates. Not to have to worry about them has lifted a burden off my shoulders—and especially my wife's. We wake up in our own little house in Bethesda. I love it. It's a great freedom. We're looking forward to gearing down our life style. It will be so much more simplified. Right now it's all so new. It's like I've been in a cocoon for 4 years. The other night in the food store, they wouldn't cash my check. I said to the man beside me, "I'm learning all over again what life is like for everybody."

Of the experiences new senators have to adjust from, the two most important are their occupation-political backgrounds and their election campaigns.

Adjustment From: Occupational Background

"The Senate isn't anything like what I was used to" said a former college professor who, midway into his second year in the Senate—talked about his adjustment to and his adjustment from.

> The greatest problem I had was to adjust to the rhythm of the Senate. Every institution has a rhythm to it. Life on campus has a rhythm to it. You teach your classes, you read, you prepare your classes. You can usually plan your day. Oh, you may go to a committee meeting that runs overtime by an hour. But you aren't ever expected to be at two or three meetings at the same time. And no one expects you to teach 12 hours a day. Life in the Senate is the antithesis of academic life. There is always one more committee meeting dumping in on you, one more bill dumping in on you, one more constituency problem dumping in on you...In academic life you are expected to have leisure time. It is a condition of your employment that you have leisure time—to create, do research, write and publish. In the Senate you are not expected to have leisure time. I like to read; but there is no time to read. I can hardly keep up with the newspapers. Yet I'm supposed to be up on everything...You can't keep up and you can't plan...It took me a year to learn that the rhythm of the Senate is no rhythm. And I'm still adjusting (after a year and a half) to the lack of rhythm.

It would be hard to imagine a greater adjustment than the one he has had to make. His problems are a virtual catalogue of the basic characteristics of the Congress—the lack of time, the frantic pace, the problems of information, the short-term perspective. He is adjusting from one distinctive set of institutional routines to another set.

If there is any general distinction to be made among types of backgrounds and types of adjustment, the most apparent is that between nonlegislative and legislative experience. Like the college professor, individuals who come to the Senate without prior legislative experience dwell on the change in institutional routines. They have difficulty getting control of their work schedules and making effective use of their time. I asked a businessman if his previous experience had been helpful in adjusting to the Senate. "No, not at all. The worst thing is that you can't manage your time. You go by the clock up there calling you to vote." Another businessman-newcomer echoed. "The most disappointing thing is that you can't schedule yourself. There are so many things you have to do...I don't have any think time." I asked another senator if his background experience in a public executive position had been good training for his new job.

> It's an enormous contrast. The job here is consuming—so many things to read, so

many meetings to go to. I don't have much social life. My children are grown and my wife is pursuing her own career. So I can devote more time to the Senate than many others. We worked hard in my former job. But I had control over my time. I had a family life. Not here.

A senator with both business and public executive backgrounds commented, "I have been disappointed by the lack of efficiency in the Senate. I had no idea we would be so inefficient in the use of our time. As a businessman and a governor I made efficient use of my time." The transition from a nonlegislative job to a legislative one seems to produce a heavy emphasis on changing from a relatively controllable round of life to one that looks a good deal less controllable.

If there is a distinctiveness about legislative routines—lack of rhythm, or unpredictability, for example—then we would expect people coming from legislative backgrounds to have a different adjustment experience. And they do. Former legislators have much to say about time pressures in the Senate. But their focus is less on the new pressures that have forced them to adopt new routines than on the increased level of old pressures that have forced an alteration in old routines. "The big problem around here is time," said one in May of his first year.

> The demands are much greater than in the House. And you still have to find time for your family. In the House, I tried to do everything I was asked to do, go everywhere I was invited. The problem is: how do you learn to say no. I haven't figured that out. I'm doing 14 commencements this spring. Can you believe it?...I did one commencement in six years in the House and I've got 14 in six months in the Senate.

Other newcomers fresh from the House say simply that they work harder in the Senate. "I'm working Saturdays and Sundays just to catch up with the week's work. In the House, my desk was clean by Thursday night." From home, from the Washington community, and from the Senate the demands on their time have increased. For the former House member in the Senate, it is more of the same—a lot more. But, nonetheless, the same.

Similarly, former House members focus on the adjustment to an increase in influence that accrues to them as senators. They are used to having some influence; now, they have a lot more. When I visited a newly elected senator in his House office two weeks after his election, he sat beneath a huge painted sign "Welcome Senator." When I asked him "What's it like to be a senator?", he said,

> It's a different life style—entirely different. It's amazing. My calls get answered much more quickly now....I'm meeting with the Reagan transition team. Tomorrow I'm going to dinner with the President-elect. Everything changes—just that quickly.

In March, he returned to the same theme.

> There is definitely more power in the Senate. Who cares about a House member? When you are a Senator, the White House answers the phone, Cabinet members answer the phone. Not for a House member.

He then described how he had just obtained money to build a new wing on a building at his state university. "There is no way I could have done that in the House." When House members move from one side of the Capitol to the other, they must adjust from low levels of attention and influence to high levels of attention and influence.

It might be thought that people with legislative experience would make a quicker or easier adjustment to the Senate than those without legislative experience. But with the evidence I have, no such generalization could be supported. When the insider who evaluated the 16 Republican freshmen had worked his way to the end of the list, he concluded that "three or four" of them "are going to be good senators." Of the four he picked, one was a former legislator, three were not. And the judgments of Washington's journalistic score keepers produced a similar mix. Surely different background experiences produce different adjustment patterns. But the patterns depend on more than background—the ability to clarify, sort out, and pursue individual goals, for example.

When I asked the college professor how he learned to cope with his adjustment problems, he stressed the need to make and be guided by personal choices and personal goals.

> You need to establish a hierarchy, a set of priorities. You need to know your value system. Don't let yourself be a piece of cloth pulled at from every side. Don't let yourself unravel. The institution will pull you off in a hundred different channels if you let it. We all have different personalities and talents. Every senator can't do everything. You have to let the job become an extension of yourself. Know who you are and let the job develop out of who you are.

Yet when I asked him to be as explicit as he could about his own goals, it became clear that he was still working them out. To a large extent he was taking what the process gave him—and he was very slowly reaching out to embrace the tasks, the goals, and the choices associated with governing. "I don't know about long-term goals," he said:

> But the first near-term goal you have to deal with is your constituency operation....Those problems have to be attended to immediately. Second, of course, you have your committee assignments and that determines what you will work on....Your choice is very limited there....A third near-term goal I would like to develop is what you might call the forum role. I like to speak and I like to speak about philosophy and issues. The Senate gives you a forum—a much wider forum

than I ever had as a teacher. My talents are more related to being a spokesman than being a leader inside the Senate.

If he follows his own prescription "to let the job develop out of who you are," he will approach the governing process with an interest in its policy making rather than its inside influence aspects. And he will steer his activity to that which provides him the best opportunity to act as a public spokesman for his policy views. But, a year and a half into his tenure, his approach to the governing process remains very tentative.

It might be thought that individuals coming to the Senate with legislative experience from the House would be better equipped with a set of personal goals than the professor. But there is not a lot of supportive evidence. One ex-House member commented in May of his first year: "I don't know why I wanted to be a senator—to serve people or to fulfill my ambition or to pass legislation." And the administrative assistant of another former House member commented at the end of his senator's first year:

> He's going through a problem of role identification. He doesn't know what he wants to be. In (Elizabeth) Drew's book on John Culver, she says every senator has something he wants to accomplish...Our senator hasn't figured that out yet.

So, it is not only nonlegislators whose governing-related goals remain unsettled during their early adjustment. Most House members who run for the Senate do so after only one to three terms in the House; so they will *not* have had a great deal of experience at governing. And, even when newcomers come from the House with a well developed set of goals, they may still have some difficulty adjusting.

One former House member came to the Senate with a well developed interest in making good public policy; and he knew exactly what policies he wanted to influence. He referred repeatedly in January after his election to "my four issues" and "my policy priorities." "Cities is our number one issue," he would say, "then energy, then foreign policy, and environment is number four." And he would say "I can be good on those four issues because I'm interested in them. I'd be interested in them if I were in private life." They were the same issues that he had worked on in the House. "The only thing that makes sense is to stay with the issues you come with. Anything else is a goddamned waste of time." He made five trips to Washington between election day and early January to lobby for a spot on the most difficult of the committee assignments he wanted. He was unsuccessful but undaunted. "Eventually I'll get on that committee. The only question is when." In March, he said, "I can't imagine wanting to leave the Senate the way I wanted to leave the House. You have so much influence....It's the best place to be if you are issue-oriented." He had a well developed set of goals— much more so than the college professor. Still, his adjustment from the House was neither quick nor easy.

His problem was one of curing himself of House-grown habits of near-weekly accessibility to his constituency. The demands on him had escalated; but he was trying to meet them with his old routines. In June of his first year, on a three-day trip to his state, he commented that "when you accept appearances like this, the recognition is tremendous. So the temptation is to keep it up…politically it's fantastic, but personally it's devastating. You do it week after week after week after week and you end up not liking your job. It's insane." On the matter of scheduling his home visits, he said "I'm overscheduled." Then,

> We have principles and they all get violated. The basic principle was that we would do it every other week and accept only things that fell on those weeks. But people call and say "this is special" and the whole system breaks down. We are going to have to establish some priorities.

The general sentiment—make some choices and fix some priorities among your goals—was not different from that of the college professor.

I didn't see him to talk again about these matters till the beginning of his third year in the Senate. But, somewhere near the end of his first year, he apparently solved his adjustment problems—and was able to give top priority to his issue-related goal. Looking back, he commented,

> There was a definite period of confusion and wandering. It lasted for about a year. We didn't know what we were doing. We didn't know what issues to work on. I was running around the state like a madman. The problem was that I still thought of myself as a congressman. But I wasn't a congressman. And I had ten times the territory to cover. You need to make judgments about what you want to do here. And we began to do that. We've had nearly a year and a half of productive work.

He was fully immersed in the business of governing—and was not tentative about it. And he had, to his own satisfaction, transferred his legislative skills to the new institution. We can, perhaps, say that his adjustment from his prior occupation to that of Senator was completed more quickly than that of the college professor. But not in a fashion to support generalizations relating occupational background to ease of adjustment.

In sum, the salient features of the adjustment process differ for newcomers depending on whether they are adjusting from a nonlegislative or a legislative background experience. The switch from nonlegislative routines to legislative routines necessitates an adjustment to some fundamental but unfamiliar features of legislative life—especially the loss of control over one's time and one's schedule. The switch from one legislative body to another necessitates an adjustment to familiar features of legislative life that have taken on an increased prominence—especially the increase in demands and the increase in influence. Just what systematic impact, if any, these different adjustment problems have on the adjustment patterns of the two groups remains unanswered at this point. Each type of "adjustment from" presents difficulties. Political scientists have never had much success in relating occupational background to subsequent legislative behavior. Nor have we here. Our description of the two types of adjustment problems helps us to understand the adjustment problems of particular individuals. And it will help us to understand different features of the Senate. But generalizations about adjustment will, evidently, need to encompass more factors than a newcomer's background.

Adjustment From: The Campaign

The other major "adjustment from" factor is the individual's election campaign. Here, the general proposition, drawing from the campaign-adjusting-governing sequence, is that the dynamics of the campaign recently concluded can have a continuing effect on a newcomer's early adjustment to the Senate. Let me elaborate with a couple of examples.

One senator came fresh from a campaign in which he—a member of the House—had been charged by his opponent as having no record of accomplishment there. He was attacked, in the rhetoric of the campaign, as a person who was "all style and no substance." The description, and the attention paid to it by the media, rankled him throughout the campaign. He was upset, for example, about one reporter's approach to the campaign. "He asked me if I liked Robert Redford movies. I said, 'Yes I like Robert Redford.' He asked, 'Did you see *The Candidate*.' I said, 'Yes, I thought it was a great movie.' He said 'I hear you are patterning your campaign after Robert Redford in *The Candidate*.' I said, 'Come on now, I was campaigning long before that movie came out.' He asked me if he could take a picture of my car....I said, 'Sure, but why do you want a picture of my car? You're the one who's always complaining that politics is all style and no substance and you want to take a picture of my car? Why don't you write about the differences between us on the issues?'"

When he got to Washington he wanted to bury this kind of campaign rhetoric as soon as possible. "People here make judgments about you very quickly," he said in March. "I want to get the reputation as a substantive senator." He emphasized his work on one of the Senate's most important committees. "Ninety percent of my time has been taken up in the committee. I'm learning all the technical terms—studying a great deal. I enjoy it." In May, he commented, "It hasn't changed much. I like it....My committee dominates my time. I'm going over now to put in an amendment to try and force the committee to a decision...I'm having some fun rattling cages and learning. I'm still learning the subject." He stayed in Washington most of the time, returning home only once a month—nine days in all—from January to May.

> Yesterday I got a call from the editor of the largest paper in the state asking me why I'm keeping such a low profile in the state. They are going to write a criticism of me for not appearing at every bean supper back home. I've been studying hard, doing my home work, showing up on time. During the campaign, I had to confront the show horse-work horse argument. I've been trying to be a work horse.

His early immersion in committee work and his early inattention to his home state were heavily influenced by the circumstances of his campaign. He had been moved by his campaign to do all that he could to put the campaign behind him, to shorten his transition period, and to accelerate his adjustment to the business of governing within the new institution. Further, if we assume that getting a reputation as a substantive senator is an essential ingredient of influence inside the Senate, we can say that this senator's dominant personal goal is to achieve influence in the Senate. We can also say that he brought it with him to the Senate and that his campaign was instrumental in making it dominant.

A second newcomer, in October of his first year, had not yet shut down his campaign. And deliberately so. When I asked this former House member whether he was going home any less now that he was a senator, he answered, "I should be, but I'm not." He explained how the rhetoric of his campaign against an incumbent senator was still constraining his behavior.

> I'll bet I'm going home more than most fellas in the House. I was home all during the summer recess going to centennial celebrations. I've just been home for four weeks in a row and I'll be home the next two. Next week I'm going home to join the American Legion....I think I ought to begin to level off pretty soon. But when I ran—well, (my opponent's) problem was that he had lost touch. It was easy for me to say that in the campaign. I don't want people to start saying, "now that he's won, he doesn't think he has to come to see us anymore." I didn't want to change my pattern. That's why I rode in fifty centennial parades last summer, all over the state.

When I asked him if he wasn't still campaigning, he said "yes". The self-imposed pressure of the election campaign was still having an important impact on his behavior as a senator.

And, no great surprise, this senator was not swinging very speedily into the business of governing. The week before, I had watched him present his subcommittee's recommendation to the full committee and flounder in the face of questioning in that forum. "Wasn't that a mess," he said.

> I wasn't expecting that. They told me it would be nothing—that I would give a summary, the (full committee) Chairman would make a prepared statement and it

would go right through. Then X started grilling me. I'm afraid I wasn't prepared. And, I must say, the staff person wasn't much better prepared than I was. It came out all right. I don't know what X was trying to prove.

During the interview, he showed other signs of an uncertain adjustment to his legislative work. "I've got to keep an eye on the clock," he said. "Maybe I should be down there now on the ABC Bill. I've got a lot of things of interest to my state in this bill. And I want to talk to Senator X about my bill 1492." Or,

> My chief legislative assistant was just in here putting the heat on me on my bill 1492. He's been with me ever since I went to the House. He wants me to push the bill now. He says I've laid off it too long, and he's right. Some senators put it on hold and I didn't object. Then I wanted to put it in the LMN bill, but people asked me not to. So I backed off....I've been a little too slow....If I were in the House, I would have stayed closer to the bill all along, but there are so many things here. But this one should have had top priority and I shouldn't have let it go so long.

Then, he talked about how he regretted his decision to pass up membership on a particular committee. "Maybe I should have taken the _____ committee. That's where all the decisions were made this year." Unlike the senator who was avoiding bean suppers and immersing himself in committee work, this new senator was immersing himself in his home state and avoiding the work of the Senate. His electoral goal had not yet been replaced by governing related ones, and his adjustment period was being prolonged. But, like the first senator, the nature of the campaign he was adjusting from helps explain the nature of his adjustment to the Senate.

There is enough difference between the processes of campaigning and the processes of governing for us to make the statement that new senators (and their staff) must, to some degree, "get over" their election campaigns before they can adjust to the business of governing. They must reduce the amount of time spent at home and set aside enough in Washington to allow themselves generous periods of on the job learning in the Senate. They must become accustomed to pursuing multiple personal goals instead of the one goal they sought during the campaign. They must give up the forms of persuasion endemic to mass politics and take up forms of persuasion suitable to face-to-face coalition building. They must substitute interpersonal bases of trust for image-based sources of trust. They must operate in an arena in which they are one among equals instead of an arena in which they are indisputably the dominant force. They must cooperate to succeed instead of seeking their goals completely on their own. Issues they once simplified for public consumption must now get elaborated in adversarial argumentation. These and other habits of thought and action differ from one process to the other. And they become, therefore, part of the adjustment from the campaign to the U.S. Senate.

Adjustment To: The Senate Institution

New senators have to adjust to the Senate as an institution and to the Washington environment. Our interest lies primarily in the structure—the structural opportunities and the structural constraints—to which newcomers will adjust and through which they will shape and pursue their governing-related goals. In thinking about the structure of the Senate, nothing seems more important than its *size*. There are 100 United States senators. This fundamental fact invites observers to think of the Senate in two different ways.

First, the small size invites the idiom of the small town. Donald Matthews begins his brilliant discussion of Senate folkways by quoting an influential senator: "There is great pressure to conform in the Senate. It's just like living in a small town" (Matthews, 1960, p. 92). The 100 inhabitants of that "town" see each other a lot, talk about each other a lot, depend on each other for information, accommodate to one another, and maintain some recognizable boundaries between themselves and the outside world. They agree among themselves on some rough rules of legitimate behavior in dealing with each other. They establish mechanisms for encouraging and enforcing a rough conformity to those rules. In that town, there are always nonconformists, mavericks, or eccentrics who are allowed a good deal of behavioral latitude so long as the consensual basis of community life is not threatened (see Polsby, 1969). It is a compelling communitarian view. Sometimes it is expressed by the idea that the Senate is a club. It is an organizing view that observers would never think of imposing on the 435 member House of Representatives.

But the small number of senators also invites a second, equally compelling view—an individualistic one. Thus, Alan Ehrenhalt, one of Washington's most respected journalists, entitles his recent article, "In the Senate of the 80's, Team Spirit Has Given Way to the Rule of Individuals" (Ehrenhalt, 1982). In this idiom, the 100 Senators are prima donnas. Each senator establishes an independent identity, operates according to his own set of behavioral prescriptions, and depends only on himself for the information he lives by. He knows that the business of legislation is a collective enterprise. He knows his colleagues; he works with them; he evaluates them. But all of this is instrumental to the pursuit of a set of personal goals. He feels minimally constrained by consensual codes of behavior. The relevant distinction in his life is not between the Senate and the rest of the political world but between himself (plus his staff) and everything else. With the help of the media, he knows he can cultivate a visible national image for himself. With the help of the Senate's formal rules, he knows he can bring the collective business to a halt. He can be a force to be reckoned with whenever he wants to be. Among these prima donnas there are always leaders, people who think about the collectivity and tend to its common business. But they lead only so long as they indulge the individualism of their colleagues and obtain unanimous consent for their actions. This organizing view, too, is not one that observers would think of imposing on the 435 member House of Representatives.

The small size of the Senate as a collectivity and the small number of individual senators sustain both the communitarian and individualistic idiom. Both are Senate as opposed to House idioms. Both are exaggerations. But both will always have some validity in describing the Senate. From time to time, however, one organizing idea seems more in tune with our observations than the other and will, for that reason, lead us to better short-term explanations of senatorial behavior. In the 1950s and 1960s, the communitarian idea was the more useful analytical approximation of reality. In looking at today's adjustment process, however, what we see is closer to the prima donna than to the small town view of the Senate. The major structural characteristic of the contemporary Senate is its individualism. And it is primarily to that institutional feature that new senators must adjust.

Former House members typically find it necessary to make an emotional adjustment when they cross the Capitol—an adjustment to the atmosphere of a more individualistic institution. They come from a warm, friendly, supportive relationship with their House colleagues to what they find to be a cold, lonely, and atomistic relationship with their Senate colleagues (Baker, 1980). This may seem paradoxical, since the Senate is one quarter the size of the House. But it is precisely because the House is so large that small friendship groups form there to cope with the threat of anonymity and to form minialliances that reduce impossibly large numbers into smaller numbers for the purpose of doing business. These groups may be based on year of arrival (i.e., the Class of 1980 or 1982), on committee, subcommittee, state delegation, a policy based caucus, workouts in the gym, informal clubs, or whatever. House members who feel a part of those groups feel that they have both friends and allies in that chamber. When they become Senators, they typically find neither. Ask them about it and they say, "There's a lot less camaraderie in the Senate than in the House." Or, "On the personal side, the House is a much warmer place." Or, "It's much harder to make friends here."

When I dropped in on one Senate newcomer back home a couple of months after his election to ask "How's it going?", he immediately compared his new Senate classmates to the group with which he had come to the

House several years earlier. "I feel as close to my House class as anyone. There is no one who thinks more of that class than I do. There is no class in the Senate. Well, there's a class, but no brotherhood." "I have been to the Senate five or six times," he said, "and it's a very different atmosphere. It's more fiefdomlike than fraternitylike." Then he mused out loud about how he would adjust to the new context. "I'll be curious to see if I ever use the Senate gym. Right now I feel the need to use the House gym for emotional sustenance. If, in two years time, they never see me there, that will mean something. I have a lot of close friends in the House." Two weeks later, I tagged along with him in Washington, during his first week on the job. One afternoon, we walked over to the House gym for his regular workout. "Some day I'll have to find out where the Senate gym is," he said.

In March, he spoke of the Senate as "lonely." "There isn't the comradeship you had with the group in our (House) class. You are isolated over here. You don't get to know your colleagues well." When I went back in May he said,

> The Senate is a much stuffier place than the House. I just went over to the House to wait for the vote on the _____ bill. Everyone came up to me, rushed up.
> There's a closeness that isn't here. The Senate is more staid, more lonely. I go over to the House once a week or once every two weeks just to see my friends.

Five months into his term, he was still trying to adjust from the warm collegiality he had enjoyed in the House to the cool social atomism he had found in the Senate.

Newcomers without legislative experience have no such points of comparison; but, one way or another, they encounter and must adjust to this key structural feature. One such indiviudal picked it up via extensive preentry reading about the institution. "I don't watch television. I don't go to the movies. But I read a lot," he said. And, "Between November 4 and the day I got here, I read twenty books on the Senate, its history, its procedures, its people, biographies." Two books had impressed him particularly, Alan Drury's *Advise and Consent* ("the greatest") and Ross Baker's *Friend and Foe in the U. S. Senate* ("Baker's book is about personal relationships"). Both books are about personal relationships, and that was the structural lesson this newcomer drew from his reading.

> This is a people place. You can't do anything here if you don't know the people you're dealing with. At home you know people because you live with them. You get along with them because you know them. I didn't want to be plopped down into the middle of a strange group of people without knowing anything about them. So I read up on all my colleagues before I got here. A former district attorney for Philadelphia is going to see things much differently from a Wyoming rancher—a Specter and a Wallop. If we had the time, I could give you right now, a 5-minute

biographical summary of each of the other 99 Senators....This is not a one-man operation. It's a collective operation. . . . What I learned before I got here has been immensely helpful to me.

What he learned also eased his early adjustment to this highly personalized, highly individualistic, institution.

Another newcomer lacking in legislative background learned the same structural lesson—the hard way. Once he got to the Senate, he experienced difficulty in achieving his legislative goals. A year and a half into his first term, he said of his colleagues,

> They are a narrow-minded mean spirited, egotistical, bigoted bunch of bastards. They are only interested in themselves, their own ambitions, their own personal power. They don't deal with you unless they need you and then they make you think they are doing you a favor. They make these little deals. They can give you the most high-minded, beautiful philosophical reasons why they are doing what they are doing. But their reasons are completely selfish. It's not a matter of political ideology, it's personal ambition. They have no idea what America is all about. . . . The only way you can get their attention is when you've got the power—when you've got the votes. . . . Everyone respects power. That's the only sense in which the Senate is a club. This was a big surprise to me. I thought the Senate would be a gentlemanly, intellectual place. It isn't.

These varied introductions to the Senate show the newcomer two faces of the institution. In his need for customized, personalized dealings with 99 colleagues, he can find aspects of the small town. But in the atmosphere of atomism and conflict, he can sense the pervasiveness of individualism.

He will also find this individualism undergirded by a set of procedures that make each senator a force to be reckoned with by his colleagues, and that allow each senator a large opportunity to accomplish his or her individual goals. For those whose goals involve policy entrepreneurship, the informality and flexibility of the rules allow maximum room for maneuver. For those whose policy goals involve blocking the initiatives of others, the rules make it difficult to close off debate and render each senator capable of stopping the institution in its tracks. Senate Rule 22, the protector of the filibuster and the delineator of cloture, is the strongest formal guarantor of individual sovereignty in the body.

Again, individuals coming from the House are the quickest to see the individualistic implications of Senate rules. The adjustment from House rules to Senate rules is particularly striking for them. One emphasized the opportunity for positive individual achievement.

> In the House, I always thought it was like practicing law. You have a set of rules and they have to be followed step by step. So much of an outcome was determined by where you sat in the procedural order. Time and quickness were of the essence.

Here, everything is so informal. You can get anything you want anytime you want. And you can get things passed you never could have gotten in the House. You just talk to people. In 9 months I've gotten 15 amendments passed, most of them without a fight.

Another stressed each individual's opportunity to prevent action.

Everything that the Rules Committee does in the House, every single individual can do in the Senate. The institution is run by unanimous consent. The filibuster is the ultimate; but long before that, one senator can do almost anything he wants. I can reach over to that phone and put a hold on any bill I want, because some guy in my state hasn't been appointed Undersecretary of HUD. Every Senator is a Rules Committee.

Whether one thinks of them as formal or informal, as positive or negative, Senate rules are potent instruments for facilitating the exercise of policy influence. They are available to any individual who is eager to have an impact on the making of public policy.

Another essential bulwark of the individualistic Senate is the personal staff that is attached to each member. For it is the staff—the enterprise—that gives each senator an independent resource base with which to pursue his individual goals (Salisbury and Shepsle, 1981a,b). Next to his primary constituency at home, his staff—in Washington and at home—is the most important guarantor of his independence as an individual actor (Schick, 1983). Because the small number of senators is coupled with an institutional workload equal to that of the much larger House, a personal staff is a much more necessary life support system for a senator than for a House member. The omnipresence, the initiatives, the spokesmanship and, withal, the operating latitude of Senate staffers is one of the most immediate impressions any outsider gets of the institution. A great portion of senator-to-senator dealings are, in reality, staff-to-staff dealings—far more so than in the House. But the result of this staff activism is to empower the independent behavior of each individual senator. And the more each senator depends on the work of his own staff the more he is cut off from his colleagues, thus reenforcing individualistic patterns of behavior. Newcomers must adjust to the idea of working with a staff. The problem of turning a campaign staff into a Washington staff is but one example of a generic problem. In the words of the insider who evaluated the 1980 newcomers, "They have to adjust to the use of staff. You can't be a good senator until you learn to use staff. You can't do it all by yourself."

The Senate that must be adjusted to is an institution in which influence is very widely distributed. It is a nonhierarchical institution—even less so than the House of Representatives. Former House members recognize the difference in ways we have already discussed—particularly in the rules. But they need make only an incremental adjustment. Former executives, however, must make a quantum adjustment to this overall institutional structure and to the consensual decision-making process it encourages. Governors are accustomed to being located at the top of a pyramid-shaped decision making structure. In the Senate, they find themselves in the middle of a fairly flat decision making structure. They are used to giving orders to subordinates. Now they must negotiate with equals. No wonder they emphasize their loss of control over their time and schedules. It is a big change. "I used to ring the bell and people came," said one. "Now the bell rings and I run."

They are used to having a more direct, immediate, and measurable effect on the actions of their organization than do senators. "A governor has immediate power at his fingertips," said another during his first month in office, "power over people, jobs, patronage, programs and directions."

> But a senator's job is of a long range nature. The great frustration for me as a senator will be that you vote for a housing program, maybe three billion, and it's four years down the track before you see a housing project for the elderly in Franklin. As governor, I'd say, "I want to build a home for the elderly in Franklin"; and 18 months later, I'd go down and dedicate it.

A year later, that same former governor was still adjusting to the slowness of the operation he was so embedded in. "It's frustrating," he said "particularly frustrating for a former governor. Congress is a consensus operation." This rather special adjustment problem—to the indeterminate effects of one's actions, to the slow pace of action, and to decision making by consensus—is particularly a governor's problem. But, like all the other adjustment problems we have mentioned, it tells us something important about the institution we are studying.

Lest we forget the importance of party to institutional structure, one set of Senate newcomers was particularly sensitive to this feature in the context of the 97th Congress. They were the former Republican House members who had to make a double adjustment when they came to the Senate in 1980—from House to Senate and from minority to majority. "I think the change from minority to majority is the more important of the two," said one of them. For him, the majority status meant having to adopt, minimally at least, an interest in governing, a goal he had not much developed as a minority member of the House. He put it this way.

> I vote here the same way as I voted in the House, except on responsibility issues— issues that involve the responsibility of the majority to govern, the debt limit, for example. I never voted for a debt limit in all my years in the House. I did here. I could run against foreign aid when I was in the House; but I can't do it anymore.

That's the difference between majority and minority. You can demagogue more when you are in the minority. We have to keep these programs going.

He was adjusting to a newly felt need to help make good public policy rather than just talking about it. This adoption of a new set of governing-related goals helps explain, by the way, President Reagan's great success with his Republican Senate, while he and they were newcomers.

Adjustment To: The Media

There are many features of the Washington community to which new senators must adjust. Most of them are encompassed in those increases in attention and influence that House members find accruing to them when they become senators. And they are captured in the notion that there is more "prestige" attached to the office of senator than to any other elective position in the United States save for that of President. Everyone in Washington pays special attention to senators—Cabinet members, bureaucrats, lobbyists, socialites, the media. Newcomers have to adjust to that. Of special interest to us is the media. Their interest reveals itself first, and is nurtured by the candidate, on the campaign trail. Senators campaign in ways designed to attract free media. And media attentiveness follows them to Washington. For some, this means more attention than they have ever received before. For some, it may mean less attention than they have been accustomed to. But for virtually all of them, it means more *national* attention. And for all of them it means more national political attention.

Former House members are particularly sensitive to the phenomenon. "If we called the state press when I was in Congress, to call a press conference," said one,

> They would always ask, "What's he going to say?" Now if we call a press conference, they don't ask questions. They just come. And they report whatever we say—usually on the front page. Editorials regularly comment on my position on issues. (So) you feel like you have to stay up to date on almost everything that's going on, because the media are likely to call you for a comment on anything at anytime....You find yourself reading the morning paper formulating reactions to reactions you read there. You're preparing statements about things that haven't happened yet, to the President's State of the Union address or whatever. You get so you think that way—about national problems—because the media expects you to.

This adjustment is not always smooth and painless. Another former House member, three weeks into his Senate term, was asked to comment on his party's President's State of the Union address. He called it "dull and forgettable." He found his statement in the next day's *Washington Post*. As his aide recalls,

He had not seen the paper before he went down to meet with the President the next day. When he came back, he said he thought the President was pretty cool to him. Then he saw the *Post*. He said, "I've got to be careful now. The only paper that used to care what I said was the *Centerville Sun.*"

That adjustment experience is not likely to happen to former governors. They are used to having their every word repeated—by the statewide press. Indeed, their experience is one of adjusting to less media attention. Said one,

> I was much more in the news as governor than I am as senator. As governor I was on the news every night. On 14 TV stations and in 150 newspapers, I was the focal point of attention almost every day. In the Senate, I may make the news once a week. I'm sure my name recognition has gone down since I've been in the Senate.

Still, ex-governors have to get used to a very different kind of media attention, one that is national in scope.

All new senators, for example, must adjust to being thought of as potential presidential or vice presidential candidates by the national press. Less than two months after his victory at the polls, one senator-elect said,

> I was on a talk show this morning and the first question phoned in was, "Are you interested in running for the Presidency?" Later on, I spoke to a fifth grade class and got the same question. I just saw US *Magazine* over there on the desk and they call me "a presidential possibility." That's three references in one day. That happens to me all the time now. And I know it's nothing special about me. The same thing is happening to...the others.

Newcomers get profiled in the national press and invited to participate in postelection or presession interview programs. Present, almost always, in the background of this media attention is the possibility that the new person in town may one day be a contender for the White House. Thus we are reminded of the opportunities available to new senators to promote their candidacies for higher office—if they have the desire to do so. In every Senate, there are a sizable number who do.

While new senators are making their various adjustments, the Washington-based national press keeps score on their progress and their promise as senators. Press judgments percolate around the Washington community. Reputations are formed that become resources for senators to use in dealing with that community (Pettit, 1969). And there is feedback into the Senate itself, as new senators read about themselves and senators read about their colleagues. For some newcomers, they bring increased confidence; to others, they induce reassessment; to still others, they are deemed irrelevant. But these early media judgments, especially in the print media, have a way of sticking to the newcomer in the absence of some striking reason for reappraisal. Just what the half-life of such early evaluation is, we cannot say. But they can have some independent effect on the adjustment patterns and the adjustment success of newcomers. Since, surely, all would prefer a favorable to an unfavorable report card, the congressional score-keepers are a special element of the Washington community to which newcomers will have to adjust.

THE ADJUSTMENT PERIOD

All new senators go through an adjustment proccess—adjustment from and adjustment to. It is a process that carries them from a preoccupation with campaign activity to a concern for noncampaign activity. It is a process that, above all, takes time. It is hard to say how long this adjustment period lasts, except to say that it will vary among individuals. We have observed some of the variables that probably matter most: how quickly and how aggressively they adopt governing related goals and how much difference or reenforcement exists between what they must adjust from and what they must adjust to. There are doubtless others, for example, the relation between expectation and reality, the impact of talent and personality. We shall not attempt to devise a calculus here. If we think of each senator's six year term as divided, more or less, into three two-year segments, each one of which is a distinctive part of a six-year electoral cycle, we can postulate that the adjustment period will ordinarily end sometime during the first two years (Fenno, 1982). Instead of pinpointing a beginning and an end, we shall have to think of a band of time at either end—one band somewhere near the point where the election returns are in and the other band somewhere around the point where the individual feels pretty well adjusted to the Senate and its Washington environment. We shall think of it as a subjective matter. A new senator is adjusted when he or she feels adjusted.

Asked to describe his adjustment to the Senate, one newcomer summarized it this way:

> It was like being dropped into the jungle and having to learn to survive. Gradually, you cut out a little place for yourself, a clearing in which you can live....After a year and a half I've begun to feel comfortable. I've cleared some land; I've pitched a tent; stacked up some wood; and the bears aren't roaming through the camp anymore. I've gained a little confidence, a little experience. I've established a settlement in the jungle. It's been a very slow, very gradual, very evolutionary adjustment.

This description is pretty abstract. But, clearly, it concerns both a process and a period of time. The process posed certain problems for him; he coped with these problems in some way; and after a year and a half the period of coping is substantially behind him.

If we can extrapolate from what he says, he feels that he has adjusted to two kinds of problems—one largely emotional, the other largely organizational. On the emotional side, he has gotten to "feel comfortable" in his new surroundings. On the organizational side, he has "established a settlement" in those surroundings. He has acquired a resource base and, with it some sense of control over his own life, some confidence that he can achieve his personal goals. These ideas are vague, but important. For it is our view that every adjustment process has emotional and organizational components to it. It is also our view that a substantial degree of comfortableness coupled with a substantial degree of control are conditions that must be met before an individual's adjustment period can be said to have ended. It is not clear which condition gets satisfied earliest or easiest. They reenforce one another. When both have been satisfied, the newcomer will have that sense of *accomplishment* inside the Senate that clearly signals the end of the early adjustment period.

It is a measure of the distance newcomers move during their adjustment period that their very first adjustments are primarily physical in nature—like the former governor waking up in his own house. Observing them during those earliest days, you find them driving around and around the block trying to find out where to get in their assigned parking spot, making the wrong turn off the elevator to go to their office, coming out the wrong door to meet a waiting limousine, being bumped unceremoniously from one office suite to another. Interviews with them are punctuated with commentary on office decor.

> The first thing I'm going to do as a U.S. senator is get rid of these overhead flourescent lights. Don't they offend you?...They took the chandeliers out some years ago. So I asked where are the chandeliers' and they said 'Nobody knows. Can you imagine how beautiful a chandelier would look like in this room? As you can see, I really want to talk about chandeliers. The hell with SALT TWO.

Some newcomers do not get their permanent office suites until well into their fourth month in office. So, the process of establishing "a clearing" begins with some very elementary physical adjustments. And senators do not take control of their physical turf and their physical resources without some friction and some effort.

Physical problems of the adjustment process can be adjusted to relatively quickly. And those that cannot take on larger than physical consequences. Thus, the comment of one former House member,

> The House is a large hall, and you must shout to be heard. The Senate is a small room. The best speakers are those who speak as if they were in a living room, in a conversational tone—people who are comfortable in their surroundings. I do not feel comfortable in that room yet, and do not have a conversational tone.

In this comment, concern about physical comfortableness shades off into a concern about personal comfortableness. And a concern for control over one's physical surroundings shades off into concern for control over a reputation among colleagues. It is the two emerging concerns—which we might sum up as establishing working relationships with one's colleagues— that really take time.

A senator has absolutely nothing to do with the selection of his or her colleagues. Yet he must live and work with them. He must work with them in an organization that is highly individualistic yet can maintain itself only through a collective effort. Further, it is an organization where the norms of cooperative conduct are no longer as comprehensive, explicit, or controlling as they once were (Rohde et al. 1974; Foley, 1980; Baker, 1980). Each newcomer fashions his own working relationship, bit by bit, gaining comfortableness and control over time. One early indicator of progress in this regard comes in the form of generalized satisfaction. "I love the Senate." "I feel comfortable in the Senate." "I like it here." "I enjoy it." But an indication of more lasting success is the recitation of something tangible.

The individual who, earlier, divided the 16 freshmen Republicans of the 97th Congress into two groups—those who did not want to govern and those who did—concluded his evaluation this way:

> Of the newcomers, there are four in the first group and two more on whom the jury is still out. The other ten are in the second group. And there are three or four really good ones in that group...who are going to be good senators.

I talked with one of the two newcomers on whom "the jury is still out." And I talked with one of the "three or four really good ones." Translating these judgments into the language of adjustment, it seemed clear that the first individual had not yet completed an adjustment period while the second one clearly had.

The first individual had not held himself aloof from the legislative process. But he had not yet felt a tangible success. "I'm worried about my effectiveness for my state" he said. And he described the major legislative initiative of his first year or so, one that remained hung up between committee and the floor. He did not picture himself as a successful legislator in either arena—not, at least, in coping with his opponents.

> For six weeks, I worked and got bloodied on that (in committee). They tried to force me to back off. Even some of my supporters told me to back off. Then, when we won in committee, they talked behind my back about "that so and so." They criticized my use of proxies. Then when I offered to compromise—after I had won—they excoriated me. Some of them wouldn't speak to me. I went to one of the big ones and I said to him, "What are you doing to me? Why are you doing it to me?" That's the one thing they hate, having it out face to face. I told him, "I

don't want you for an enemy. And you don't need me as an enemy." Maybe it helped. But is he my friend? No. Will he deceive me again? Probably. We won. But we won because I had the votes. I'm going to win this year on the floor. They'll try to teach me a lesson. They'll tie my leg to a chair—figuratively. They'll say, "We'll teach this guy a little parliamentary procedure." They'll stick it in my ear. But in the fullness of time, I'll win. Not because they behave like gentlemen, not because they are willing to live and let live—oh, no, are you kidding—but because I have the votes. And that's the only reason. The only thing they understand is power.

Somehow or other, he had gotten himself locked into an unremitting legislative war and had come to view the legislative process as a matter of political hardball. His problem was not that he did not want to govern—not yet anyway. It was that he had not yet learned how—in the sense of establishing a set of working relationships with his colleagues. He was not emotionally comfortable in the Senate, nor was he yet able to manage his resources effectively in pursuit of his policy goals. "I don't know whether he will ever be a senator or not" said the insider-evaluator. "Maybe. But he'll probably float off into the wild blue yonder." The new senator echoed his ambivalence. "I don't want to be loved or be known as a braggart," he said. "I want people to have to deal with me. I want them to know that if they give it to me, I'll give it to them. But I'd rather be home doing something else." In four years, maybe he will be.

By contrast, the senator labelled as one of "the good ones," well on his way to becoming a "good senator," presented a very different adjustment pattern. "He did one hell of a job to get the _____ bill passed," said the insider-evaluator. . . . I don't think many people know what a hell of a job he did. He has the potential to mature in the process. . . . Right now he's a rough cut diamond. . . . He can become one very fine senator." Near the end of his second year, I asked this newcomer when it was that he began to feel comfortable in the Senate. He answered by talking about the major legislative accomplishment of his tenure. "I don't think I was comfortable till I'd been through a lot of the process," he said.

> When I first held hearings, I had never done that before. You don't know how a thing is going to work till you actually do it. It's a growing experience. you make mistakes, but you learn. I felt uncomfortable even at the end when I thought we might lose the bill. . . . I hadn't had enough experience to know what they would do. I was worried. . . . When I started with the bill, I knew I had to have help, so I picked _____ as cosponsor. With my latest bill, I didn't ask anybody. I didn't feel I needed anybody. I've just gone ahead with it on my own. Maybe if I started my first bill now, I could do it all by myself. You feel more comfortable once you've been all the way through the process. I don't know how you could feel comfortable in the Senate *without* having gone through the process. I'd say I probably got to feel comfortable in the summer of my second year.

Then he added "It's gradual. I don't know if you ever feel completely comfortable." Or, he might have put it "completely adjusted." For, he had interpreted comfortable to mean control as well. It is well to be reminded, again, that some adjustment will go on throughout a Senate career. But, with the passage of his major piece of legislation—a tangible success—this senator's early period of adjustment was over.

With these few examples, we have tried to indicate the conditions under which a newcomer's adjustment period will come to a close. And we have stressed legislative accomplishment as the key condition. Legislative accomplishment is at once the outward sign of an individual's ability to meet his or her governing-related goals and an inward source of confidence encouraging the individual to continue on that course.

This chapter does not purport to examine all of what it takes to govern in or through the Senate. It speaks of establishing working relationships with one's colleagues, for example, but it says little or nothing about what the scope or pattern of such relationships might be. Its major purpose is to describe a process and a period that necessarily precedes any full-blown governing process. The chapter is implicitly embedded in a notion of stages through which individual senators proceed during their careers. One of those stages is the adjusting stage. To study that stage, we must look backward to campaigning and forward to governing. We have done that, but only to help us keep our bearings on the adjustment stage. Our hope is to have shed some light on that stage. But even that effort will remain incomplete until we have examined the stages on either side of it as well.

Acknowledgment. Research for this chapter, and for the project of which it is a part, has been conducted largely under a grant from the Russell Sage Foundation. Their support is gratefully acknowledged.

References

Baker, Ross (1980). *Friend and Foe in the U.S. Senate.* New York: Free Press.
Ehrenhalt, Alan (1982). The individualist Senate. *Congressional Quarterly* 40: 2175–2182.
Fenno, Richard (1982). *The U.S. Senate: A Bicameral Perspective.* Washington, D.C.: American Enterprise Institute.
Foley, Michael (1980). *The New Senate.* New Haven, Conn.: Yale University Press.
Huitt, Ralph (1961). The outsider role in the Senate: an alternative role. *American Political Science Review* 55: 566–575.
Matthews, Donald (1960). *U.S. Senators and Their World.* New York: Norton.
Pettit, Lawrence (1969). Influence potential in the United States Senate. In Pettit, Lawrence, and Keynes, Edward (eds.), *The Legislative Process in the U.S. Senate*, pp.227–244. Chicago: Rand McNally.
Polsby, Nelson (1969). Goodbye to the Inner Club. *Washington Monthly*, 1: 30–34.
Rohde, David, Ornstein, Norman, and Peabody, Robert (1974). Political change and legislative

norms in the United States Senate. Paper prepared for American Political Science Association Meeting.

Salisbury, Robert and Shepsle, Kenneth (1981a). U.S. congressman as enterprise. *Legislative Studies Quarterly*, 6: 559–576.

Salisbury, Robert and Shepsle, Kenneth (1981b). Congressional staff turnover and the ties-that-bind. *American Political Science Review*, 75: 381–296.

Schick, Allen (1983). The staff of independence: why Congress employs more but legislates less. In James S. Young (ed.), *Problems and Prospects of Presidential Leadership in the Nineteen Eighties*, Vol. II, pp. 31–52. Washington, D.C.: University Press of America.

6

Campaign Learning, Congressional Behavior, and Policy Change

Marjorie Randon Hershey

Whatever else may be said of campaigning for public office, it is very seldom boring. Whether the experience is gratifying or terrifying (more likely, it will be both), running for office is likely to engage the candidate's undivided attention—especially if the race is one's first. Because political candidacy is so attention-riveting and ego-involving, it will probably be a time of substantial learning for a candidate. And what candidates learn while running for office—about the district, the voters, the issues, campaign techniques, even about themselves—should have major impact on their perceptions and behavior as elected officials.

Political campaigns have been a central concern of students of politics because campaigns are links in such an important chain: the process by which citizens' and groups' preferences are filtered through the men and women elected to make policy for the society. Many studies have examined the linkages between public preferences and election outcomes (Markus, 1982; Kuklinski and West, 1981; Mann and Wolfinger, 1980; Sears et al., 1980; Nie, Verba, and Petrocik, 1979). Many others have reminded readers how much might be learned by looking farther down the chain: by studying the relationships between political campaigning and the policy behavior of those candidates who win office. Donald Matthews argues, for example, that:

> It is difficult really to understand the senators, how they act and why, without considering what happens to them while they are running for office....A Senate campaign is a unique educational experience for the candidate, if for no one else. Those who have gone through the experience learn much about their future constituents, their conflicting interests, opinions, and biases, in the process (1960, pp. 68, 73).

Gary Jacobson, too, stresses the importance of asking "How are the activities of members of Congress, and the performance of Congress as an institution, connected with what goes on in elections?" (1983, p. 4).

But previous research gives us little help in answering that question. There are, of course, some bright spots. John Kingdon (1968, pp. 22–32) presents findings consistent with the expectation that candidates learn from their campaigns (he shows, for example, that winning candidates describe the voters differently than losing candidates do) in ways that could affect their activities in office. He suggests (1981, pp. 47–54) that voting behavior in the House of Representatives is influenced by House members' anticipation of the next campaign: by their expectations that they will be called on by constituents, during their term of office and in the race for reelection that follows, to explain why they voted the way they did.

David Mayhew's elegant essay *Congress: The Electoral Connection* (1974) argues that Congress members' desire for reelection has vital bearing on several aspects of their behavior in office, and on the structural arrangements of Congress as well. James H. Kuklinski (1978) has produced empirical evidence of the relationship between legislative roll-call voting and the approach of the next election. Jacobson (1983) discusses the linkages between congressional campaigns and Congress' ability to act as a representative body.

But the most important work, for our purposes, is that of Richard Fenno on Congress members' behavior in their districts. Fenno's exploration of the "home styles" of House members captures the intimate relation between campaigning and representation. He argues:

> If, therefore, we start with the congressman's perception of the people he represents, there is no way that the act of representing can be separated from the act of getting elected. If the congressman cannot win and hold the votes of some people, he cannot represent any people. Further, he cannot represent any people unless he knows, or makes an effort to know, who they are, what they think, and what they want; and it is by campaigning for electoral support among them that he finds out such things (1978, p. 233).

When Fenno turns to the Senate (1982), he observes some important differences in the relationship between campaign behavior and legislative activity. Both phases of his research shed light on these central questions: What aspects of campaigning affect a legislator's behavior when in office? What are the mechanisms through which this campaign influence occurs? Do campaign effects have a stronger pull on some kinds of legislators than on others? Are there institutional forces at work in the House and Senate that weaken the effects of the campaign on the member's legislative activity?

This chapter considers the nature of the linkage between campaign behavior and legislative activity. Its central contention is that the linkage can best be understood as a form of learning. The argument begins with a set of assumptions about campaign learning. It continues by examining the learning environments of campaigners, the systematic biases in the stimuli they receive, and the special character of the election results as a learning device—the primary means most citizens use to "teach" candidates. Next, it considers the ways in which campaign learning can affect the behavior of the winning candidates in office.

My purpose is neither to present a finished empirical study nor to offer a formal model, but to suggest a new way to look at the relationship between campaigning and congressional behavior. I will flesh out the argument with illustrations from recent campaigns, including those of six senators targeted for defeat by pro-life groups in 1980: Birch Bayh (D-IN), Frank Church (D-ID), John Culver (D-IA), Patrick Leahy (D-VT), George McGovern (D-SD) and Bob Packwood (R-OR).

CAMPAIGN LEARNING: ASSUMPTIONS

The body of theory from which this discussion derives is social-learning theory. Its assumptions and concepts and their applications to campaigning are discussed in detail elsewhere (see Bandura, 1977; Hershey, 1984). To summarize briefly: in the learning approach, attention focuses on the individual acting within a setting. That setting, or environment, consists of the many things that impinge on the individual's actions and thoughts: in a campaign, the behavior of the local media and interest groups, the opponent's actions, poll results, and so on. People's behavior is not completely at the mercy of environmental controls, nor are people's strategies of dealing with events innate, or determined only by forces within themselves. Rather, behavior is the result of a continuous interaction among the events in the environment, the individual's understanding and expectations about those events, and his or her previous experiences and current behavior. That is to say, people's behavior and strategies are *learned*.

The learning occurs through two general processes. First, people learn from their own direct experience and the results—the response consequences, reinforcements, or outcomes—that their actions produce. When people act, some of their behaviors bring positive results for them, other actions have no impact at all, and still others lead to unpleasant or unwanted consequences. As a result of this experience with actions and results, people develop expectations about strategies likely to work in a particular set of circumstances and those likely to fail.

Consider, for example, a key strategy in the 1980 Packwood campaign. Knowing that Packwood was vulnerable, his staff reasoned that his best chance to win reelection would be to discourage potentially strong opponents from running, by creating the impression that any challenger would face a very costly, tough campaign. To do so, the staff set out to raise a huge war chest by the time potential challengers would be deciding whether to run. The campaign's best hope was a letter signed by feminist Gloria Steinem, warning a carefully targeted audience of feminists and liberals that "Bob Packwood is in danger of drowning in a virtual sea of 'right-to-life' money and zealots." The mailing surpassed even the campaign's expectations; by mid-1980 it had brought in more than half a million dollars in contributions and motivated scores of campaign volunteers. No strong opponents emerged to challenge Packwood. His staff credited the widely reported "Steinem letter," and its success in raising early money, with a major role in Packwood's 1980 victory.

The beliefs that individuals develop about the effects of a strategy create expectations that enable people to anticipate the likely results of their actions and to behave accordingly. In this case, their experience in 1980 led Packwood's strategists to repeat their approach in his next race. In 1983, fully three years before he would face the voters again, another Packwood direct-mail drive began, stressing that right-to-life forces posed a renewed threat.

Learning can also take place vicariously, through seeing or hearing about other people's experiences and the results of their actions and strategies. Called observational learning or modeling (and note that this includes a lot of direct teaching), this process is a very economical means of learning, especially in the case of complex behaviors. Candidates can learn what issue appeals are effective by watching other candidates experiment with them. Consultants transmit elaborate packages of what they regard as winning strategies. Party organizations set up "campaign schools" to teach party-approved approaches to everything from fund-raising to hand-shaking. Above all, these kinds of observational learning offer information about how new strategies work, and how they can be combined with others and tailored to suit new situations.

Observational learning, then, is the learning of innovation.[1] A Senate candidate learns of a candidate in a comparable situation using an approach that seems effective in dealing with a particular problem and decides to try it. Once the success of Packwood's "Steinem letter" became known, for example, two of the other Senate campaigns targeted by pro-life groups in 1980, Culver's and McGovern's, quickly prepared similar mailings signed by Karen Mulhauser, then president of the National Abortion Rights Action League.

By examining observational learning in campaigns, we can also see how a new issue catches fire in national politics. We can see, for example, how the call for a nuclear freeze moves from church and peace group meetings to coverage by a few media outlets, from which it is learned and incorporated into the speeches of some sympathetic candidates, then reported on the network news, which makes it available for learning by other campaigners. We can see how the issue's potency is reassessed as the result of the fates of its proponents on election day. Most important, we can see how this process of observational learning affects the making of policy: how it puts some issues on the agenda for discussion by Congress and the President, and lets others fade.

So the theory directs our attention to the interaction between candidate and situation, rather than to the candidate alone. It leads us to ask what kind of learning situation a campaign can be. What are the primary forces interacting with candidates' learning? What sort of response consequence is an election result, and what does it teach? How does the nature and the adequacy of the campaign learning situation affect the policy behavior of candidates who win office?

SYSTEMATIC BIASES IN THE CAMPAIGN LEARNING ENVIRONMENT

While the qualities of individual campaign environments vary, there are some systematic biases in the campaign learning environment that affect virtually all candidates, and that help to define the nature of political campaigns as learning situations. One of the most important biases involves the sources of campaign stimuli: the information, reactions, and evaluations that campaigners receive.

It is common to think of electioneering as a time when prospective leaders listen to the voters: when candidates strive to find out what their future constituents want. It is a comforting mythology, but it has no greater resemblance to empirical reality than many other comforting myths do.

In fact, one of the most regular biases in the flow of stimuli into campaigns is that so few of the stimuli actually come directly from voters. During the race, feedback from the majority of voters is simply not available to most campaigns. Polls and canvassing—the only means through which campaigners can hear from inactive as well as politically active citizens—cost a lot. Candidates for most offices in the United States—local offices, state legislative seats, even congressional races in many areas—will not be able to afford a good professional poll, much less a series of such polls. Listen to Louis Sandy Maisel, a political scientist describing his own campaign for Congress in 1978:

> Only rarely can congressional candidates afford to expend their limited resources to commission a professional poll of their district. Consequently, most make

decisions concerning how the voters feel with only intuitive information. In some cases information gaps can be filled through reallocation of campaign resources. But in many cases the information that one would like in order to make a rational decision simply does not exist (Maisel, 1982, p. 11).

A thorough canvass is also a big investment; it requires many bodies to go door-to-door, and much staff time to supervise them. Given the size of that investment, most campaigns will be unable to canvass more than once. A one-shot poll, or a one-shot canvass, is not an optimal learning device in a campaign when many voters' reactions will change at some point prior to election day.

Other campaign tools tell even less about what the voters want. Television, radio, and newspapers are very effective means of reaching large numbers of voters, but the audiences of these media rarely get to talk back. Even the campaigners' own contact with voters does not convey much information. Most of these contacts—when the candidate shakes hands with workers at a plant gate or distributes literature at a shopping center—carry about as much information about policy preferences or other public concerns as does the conversation between two strangers who find themselves face to face in a receiving line.

Fenno puts it this way: "The more one observes members of Congress at work in their districts, the more impressed one is by the simple fact that people are hard to find. Members (and their staffs) expend incredible amounts of time and energy just trying to locate people to present themselves to" (1978, p. 234). This is true of members of Congress running for reelection—and even more true of nonincumbent candidates, whose hold on their audience is even more tenuous.

Some kinds of people are not so hard to find, however: leaders of organizations, activists, members of political groups that want something from government. Fenno continues, "There are always community elites, organization leaders, active citizens, the politically aware. The congressman need not worry about reaching them. They will reach him" (1978, pp. 235-36). Campaigners spend much or most of their time in contact with other political activists. The stimuli these activists provide are likely to be more frequent, more intense, and more explicit than those coming from most other voters. Further, they carry the kinds of information campaigners want to obtain: information about the campaign's impact, suggestions about strategy, indications of what a group would require before deciding to support the candidate.

Thus, it is the group leaders, the local elites, the organized interests that constitute most of the *actual* environment of a political campaign. The learning environment of candidates, as a result, tends systematically to amplify the voices of these activists, office holders, groups, party leaders, and media figures, and to soften the voices of other voters.

Among the most frequent and intense sources of stimuli are the candidate's strongest supporters: the people Fenno calls the candidate's primary and personal constituencies, consisting of the friends, advisers, staff members, and others whose support for the candidate is most reliable (1978, chap. 1). As Xandra Kayden suggests,

> By spending so much time together, the campaign eliminates much of an individual's private life, causing him or her to rely more heavily on the organization for the kinds of supports and rewards normally found elsewhere....Looking to each other for both professional and personal satisfactions may have added to their sense of being a group apart from others, a group engaged in a struggle (1978, p. 65).

When a campaigner considers ways to approach a new issue, or tries out a strategic innovation, not many voters will be present to respond, or interested enough to respond. Some party activists may be; some group leaders may be. But other members of the campaign organization and the candidate's closest advisers will probably be there, and will surely care enough to respond. When these colleagues are a continuing, much-valued source of reactions and there are not many other such sources available, their influence on one another's behavior increases.

The view that the voices of political elites ring out louder in the campaign environment than do the voices of other constituents is supported by research on the six senators targeted for defeat by pro-life groups in 1980 (see Hershey, 1984). Each of these six campaign organizations was led by experienced people, and each made a major effort to get information about voters' reactions. Yet even with very ample campaign budgets and the assistance of in-house and hired public opinion experts, many of the campaigns' key decisions about how to respond to the pro-life challenge were made in the absence of good data about the ways the public might react. For instance, most of these campaigns chose their response to the pro-life groups' primary campaign tool—the leafletting of churches with a single-issue brochure on abortion the Sunday before election day—by giving greatest weight to the recommendations of staff members, political allies, and other activists. In several of the races, reports from field staffers and sympathetic church leaders played a pivotal role. In others, the perceptions of the top staff members themselves were the primary influence.

In no case did the staff members of these senators believe the decision on a response to the pro-life leafletting could be derived easily and directly from poll data. Some were suspicious of the polls' track records in several Senate races during the previous election in 1978—particularly the experience of

Iowa Democrat Dick Clark, another pro-life target, who had been declared by respected poll-takers to be running ten points ahead of his opponent the weekend prior to the election, only to lose the race the following Tuesday. For a variety of reasons, even these well-funded senators, better able to afford a succession of public opinion surveys than most other candidates were, did not trust their poll results enough to base strategy decisions on them, at least with regard to this one big issue in the 1980 campaigns.

In short, while many House candidates cannot afford a series of professionally conducted polls to get fuller information about voters' preferences, many Senate candidates and their staffs incorporate poll results into their decision making only within carefully circumscribed limits. Moreover, with the polls regarded as suspect in some areas, these campaigners normally have no other direct means to get direct input from a broad range of voters— at least until election day. Even the polls qualify only in part as "direct" input from voters; the raw public responses are usually filtered through the pollster's conceptual framework, and reflect the questions regarded as important by the pollster and the campaign staff.

Other researchers confirm that the "voice of the people" is present in campaign environments only as it is sifted and reshaped by activists' understanding of politics. John Kingdon reports, for instance, that when candidates were asked about the characteristics of voters, they often responded by citing the characteristics of the people with whom they were more familiar: their volunteers, party activists, people working in interest groups. They often measured voters' interest in their campaign in terms of activist behavior: the number of volunteers coming to work at their headquarters, for example. Kingdon concludes that "to a great extent, politicians operate in an elite cognitive world, largely isolated from rank-and-file voters" (1968, p. 31; see also pp. 150–56). They hear *about* voters, but not very often *from* most voters.

For that reason, campaigning for office is usually a much better way to learn the views of those activists, and *their* interpretation of what voters want, than to learn the views of a majority of one's constituents. This would be no problem, of course, if political activists accurately reflect the interests and concerns of most other voters. But that is not very likely; by virtue of their very involvement in politics, activists have experiences and characteristics different from those of most other citizens. Activists of various kinds differ from most other people in their personal characteristics (their socio-economic level, for example), the distribution of their views on issues, and the importance they attach to various issues (see Verba and Nie, 1972, chap. 6; Jackson et al., 1982).

It could be considered rational (see Downs, 1957, pp. 88–93) for candidates' to pay greatest attention to their most vocal audiences. But the learning perspective suggests that it is also almost inevitable; in many cases, candidates have no alternative sources of stimuli from which to learn. In fact, it seems to be inevitable among other kinds of political actors as well; Tim Crouse (1972) refers to a similar phenomenon as "pack journalism"—the tendency for national political reporters to draw their cues largely from one another, and thus to develop shared interpretations of the meaning of a given set of events.

THE ELECTION RESULT AS A LEARNING DEVICE

The broader public does have one guaranteed means of providing input into campaigns, however, and that means is potentially very powerful. Remember that in social-learning theory the use of various strategies is regulated by their consequences—by experience with the results of an action, and the expectations an individual develops based on those results.

There are many kinds of response consequences that guide a candidate's behavior: approval given by people he or she values, favorable mentions in the media, financial contributions, self-respect. But perhaps the most interesting and powerful form of reinforcement is the one that is unique to campaigns: the vote on election day. In fact, if citizens are to be the main teachers of people running for elective office, then the vote must be one of the citizens' primary teaching tools. It is not the only instructional device the Constitution guarantees to members of the public; the freedoms of speech and of the press, the rights to assemble peaceably and petition the government for redress of grievances, are also means by which citizens can teach their representatives about public preferences. But the vote has naturally taken on prime importance in discussions of citizens' powers because it is almost universally available in the U.S., and because it is safer and less costly than petitioning the government or taking to the streets to demand change.

Thus, it is especially interesting that as a teaching tool, voting has some serious limitations. Ideally, the process of learning from response conse-quences is like a social contract: an expectation that if I do x, I can be reasonably sure that y will result. But when a House or Senate candidate decides whether to take a stand on a particular issue, or considers an element of his or her self-presentational style, the consequences are rarely so clear. The fate of a candidate is to take several hundreds or thousands of actions during the race—positions on various issues, types of fund-raising appeals, approaches to the media and many different kinds of groups, aspects of presentation of self—and then to receive the simple verdict of victory or defeat on election day. Which of those actions were responsible for the election result and to what degree? Do the majority of voters want a casework specialist who will also vote in favor of a strong Clean Air Act, or did they reelect the incumbent because of his or her winning smile?

The election results do not tell. To paraphrase V. O. Key, voters on election day can say only "yes" or "no" to a candidate, and observers are never really sure what was the stimulus for that response. People in the polling booth are not asked to indicate on the ballot the reasons why they have selected one candidate rather than another. An individual voter may cast a ballot for candidate A as a means of expressing concern about one particular matter—may vote for Ronald Reagan, for example, to make a statement about the need for a strong national defense. But the gesture is a silent one; the voting machine will register only "Reagan," not the reason why.

As an instrument of social choice, the vote has other drawbacks. The citizen does not set the agenda of the balloting, nor the occasion on which the election is held—both important limitations on the usefulness of the vote in conveying individuals' preferences. As Verba and Nie write (1972, chap. 7), the act of voting has less information-carrying capacity than other kinds of political acts do. Nowhere on the ballot does it say how each candidate feels about the major issues of the day. People are not permitted to write on the ballot the policy preferences they would like to see implemented. Except in the case of referenda and initiatives, voters cannot express their preferences directly at all, on any matters other than the selection among the nominees. And exit polls, which *can* provide such information, are normally used only in presidential races.

Thus, neither the winners nor the losers can be certain what the voters meant. In fact, given the great diversity of people's concerns and levels of information, it is probably safest to assume that "the voters" meant a great many things by their vote. Taken independently, then, this prime teaching tool available to citizens is very like a blunt instrument: potent, but not very specific.

In contrast, political activists are much better teachers. They have both motive and opportunity, and the rewards and punishments they can offer candidates are more varied and more explicit: endorsements, campaign contributions, expressions of approval, highly valued information. Verba and Nie (1972, p. 111) express the difference this way: "The voting situation is an uncongenial one for conveying specific citizen preferences because there is no way to cram that information into the vote, whereas one can express precise information when one contacts a leader" —in other words, when one moves toward the realm of political activism.

There are other reasons why elections are flawed as teachers of candidates. The fast pace of the action, the constant flow of stimuli, the campaigners' great personal investment in the outcome can all push participants' anxiety levels and psychological arousal well beyond the level conducive to effective learning. But the most important influence on the quality of campaign learning is the difficulty of determining the relationship between any of a campaigner's particular strategic moves during the campaign and the vote on election day. The election result, in short, is a very generalized form of reinforcement—one whose relationship to any individual campaign decision is likely to be unclear. Some campaign organizations will cope with that uncertainty more successfully than others, but none will ever be entirely free of it.

It does not necessarily follow, however, that campaigners do not learn from an election result. There may even be occasions when campaigners learn a lot about voters' preferences: for instance, the rare occasions when an election is held under the shadow of one single powerful issue, on which the candidates' stands are widely known. The election of 1860, just before the South seceded, may have been such a time. Some local elections may be justifiably interpreted as referenda on an issue that has dominated the campaign discussion. Such elections are rare.

More commonly, candidates will learn by constructing their own explanations of what the voters were trying to say. Campaigners have good reason to look for likely interpretations of the election results; if they can derive the most plausible explanation of why they won or lost, and why other candidates similarly situated won or lost, they can better understand how to increase their support in the next election.

Other political actors are also motivated to construct or find explanations of the election results. Reporters and other media people want to get or keep a reputation for political insight, and to have something more than the vote totals to report in their stories. Political consultants want to enhance their own reputations by demonstrating their expertise at analyzing election results, and to put their own campaign performance in the best possible light. Interest group and party leaders also want to puff up their own reputations for political clout as well as to gather information that can help them be more effective next time.

There are some interesting discontinuities in this process. First, what the voters are saying is not necessarily what the candidates, reporters, and other active participants are hearing. While these activists want to learn the reasons for the voters' behavior, the activists' own preconceptions will affect their ability to do so accurately. Second, the people who are directly involved in campaigning will usually have a "public" explanation for the election results—the explanation they will offer to reporters and other groups—that differs to at least some degree from their "private" explanation—the one they truly believe. The two explanations stem from their two motives: on the one hand, to put the best possible face on the current election results to make themselves seem more able and influential, and on the other hand to learn how they might compete more successfully (or hold on to their current success) next time.

Sometimes a campaigner's two explanations will merge; people do, after all, often come to believe what they say. But in the critical hours and days after the election, the public explanations take center stage. Campaigners, consultants, party and group leaders engage in quick and intense competition to get their own public explanations of the race reported as fact. Media people are the objects of this competition, for they have the means to spread and give credibility to the contending interpretations. The results of this process, described below, are a critical link in the chain connecting campaign learning to public policy.

CONSTRUCTING EXPLANATIONS FOR ELECTION RESULTS

Even before the election results are known, people connected with a candidate's organization begin to offer—sometimes to promote—their own hypotheses about the nature of the relationship between specific aspects of the campaign and the likely vote on election day. Then on election night and in the days following, one or more such explanations spread from one campaign insider to others through observational learning. Typically, one especially plausible and attractive explanation of the meaning of the election results begins to dominate. The explanation is picked up and repeated by activists close to the race: party leaders and interest group activists. It is spread by reporters covering the campaign—and that repetition makes the explanation sound even more credible. If it is not soon challenged by an alternative interpretation, it begins to take on the dignity of "established fact," even if there is little about it that seems factual.

The constructed explanation may have a great deal of empirical support, of course, reflecting the findings of careful polling and precinct analysis. To qualify as the dominant explanation, it will have to bear some relationship to the perceptions generally accepted as the "facts" of the race, but it will by no means be the only *possible* explanation of the results. Since the voters cannot explain themselves through their ballots, and since the polls, even when present, leave some room for interpretation, the accepted explanation will almost always be constructed, not just out of voting results and poll data, but out of the experience and the prior learning of political elites.

Two qualities of this process are worth stressing. One is that the explanation of a particular election result—the presumed meaning of the voting returns—is always a *constructed* explanation; the nature of elections is such that the votes do not explain themselves. The other is that because of the systematic distortions in the campaign learning environment, the explanation will most likely be offered by political elites—very often, the intuitive judgment of a trusted insider, diffusing among other activists until it becomes "common knowledge" that then appears (in news columns, textbooks, party campaign schools) to account for why so many Republicans won Senate seats in 1980 or why a particular Democrat overtook a Republican incumbent in 1982.

The congressional elections of 1982 provide an especially good example. The results seemed to have a clear meaning on the surface. The Democrats gained 26 House seats, seven governorships, and control of several state legislatures. Compared with other midterm elections in a President's first term of office, this was the largest gain for an opposition party in 60 years. Turnout was up. The cause seemed to be the declining economy and the failure of President Reagan's economic policies to reverse that decline; economic issues had dominated the campaign, media coverage, and the polls.[2]

Wasn't this a case in which the vote totals spoke for themselves? The congressional elections were a referendum on Reaganomics, they seemed to say, and the nation voted "no." Yet look again. If that explanation were accurate, then why was there no net party change in the Senate? Why, of the 29 House incumbents defeated in 1982, were so many moderate eastern Republicans—some of whom had questioned Reagan's economic policies— on the losing side, rather than conservative Republicans more closely identified with the President? And even more puzzling, if the elections were a referendum on Reaganomics, then why did a postelection poll taken by CBS and the *New York Times* find that although 41% of the respondents blamed Reagan and the Republicans for the nation's economic troubles, fully 44% blamed the *Democrats*?[3]

Evidently, even though voters seemed to be disappointed in a number of Republican officeholders, there was room for more than one explanation of the meaning of the congressional results. Starting on election night, groups of leaders began competing to get their own interpretations accepted by members of the national press corps and other political actors. House Speaker Tip O'Neill called the results a "disastrous defeat" for the Republicans, caused by the failure of Reagan's economic initiatives. U.S. Rep. Tony Coelho, head of the Democratic Congressional Campaign Committee, told reporters that "Reagan and the Republicans blew it" by following economic policies that increased unemployment among the very groups— blue-collar workers in particular—that had forsaken the Democrats in 1980 to give Reagan his victory (*Newsweek*, 1982, Nov. 15, pp. 34–37). Soon after, a group of Republican governors laid their party's losses at Reagan's doorstep, too, calling the election a "cry for help" and warning that the President and his administration had two short years to respond by adjusting its economic game plan (Broder, 1982).

The Reagan administration had reason to promote a different interpretation of the vote. On election night, Reagan's Chief of Staff James A. Baker III pointed out that the Democratic House gains were balanced by the lack of Democratic gains in the Senate, and called the results "a wash"—a phrase that came readily to the lips of Reagan aides for several weeks thereafter. Don't blame Reaganomics, they suggested; that isn't what the voters meant. If it *had* been, Republicans would also have lost seats in the Senate.

New Right leaders pressed yet another explanation. They called attention to what Evans and Novak (1982) described as "the two most fascinating campaigns of the mid-term election: Republican losses for governor of New York and Michigan." These campaigns were so fascinating, New Righters argued, because these two Republican candidates had sounded more like the Reagan of 1980 than did Reagan himself in 1982; cut taxes, they had insisted, and hew to the Right in social policy. In races they had been expected to lose badly, each of these candidates came within five or six points of winning. So the real meaning of the 1982 elections, New Right leaders contended, was that Republicans had lost ground because the administration had watered down its 1980 campaign promises. The answer, then, was to return to pure Reaganism and quit compromising.

Thus even in an election year where the trends seemed self-evident, there was still enough uncertainty about the voters' behavior and the poll results to invite efforts to "clarify" their meaning. The voters had not had the opportunity to speak directly on policy issues, or to give reasons for their choices. The voters hardly ever do. Instead, political elites fought to win the battle of the constructed explanations: to get their interpretation of the vote accepted as the definitive explanation.

Each of the competing efforts was at least in part self-serving, of course; each of these actors wanted to emerge from the race with the air of a winner. But self-serving or not, this competition to explain the election results has important effects on people's learning, and thus on their later behavior.

For example, the development of a "dominant explanation" affects public opinion. In the case of the 1982 elections, media people rapidly began to converge on a modified O'Neill-Coelho explanation: that the vote had been a Democratic success, though not of heroic proportions, for which the Reagan economic program and its lack of "fairness" bore the major responsibility. The media, in effect, were telling the voters what they had really meant. In doing so, media reports were likely to affect the weighting people assigned to various public problems (see Iyengar, 1982); reports that the election had really been about Reaganomics further supported the view that economic decline and its possible remedies ought to head the political agenda when Congress convened in 1983.

Analyses of the 1982 election results assumed that the explanation that dominated the postelection learning process *would* influence the agenda of the incoming Congress. Listen, for example, to U.S. Rep. Dan Rostenkowski in a speech the week after election day:

> It's tea leaf time in Washington....Once again politicians and the high priests of political analysis have begun to pick through last week's election returns—trying to make some sense of the new proportions in Congress—and applying their mystical conclusions to the economic and social choices ahead (Tate, 1982, p. 2835).

The explanation that voters had expressed their rejection of Reaganomics was relevant in several ways to those economic and social choices. An obvious implication was that the incoming Congress would have reason to cast a suspicious eye on the Reagan tax cuts and the heavy budget cuts in domestic programs, and would have an incentive to give top priority to bills designed to reduce the high unemployment rate. One reporter (Plattner, 1982) described the process this way: "Believing the November 2 elections gave them a mandate to do so, House Democrats plan to push a multibillion-dollar public works jobs bill and a housing stimulus measure." The word "believing" is well chosen; it was not the election results themselves, but the dominant explanation constructed for those election results that led to this policy-relevant conclusion.

The argument, in sum, is this: As mechanisms of social choice, elections provide very limited information about voters' needs and wants. Polling during the campaign is costly, and transmits individuals' views only through the filter of pollsters' questions and interpretative skills. Exit polls are common only in presidential races. And the vote on election day conveys only a choice among candidates, not the reasons for the choice.

Candidates, however, have great incentive to find some explanation of the vote totals. They turn to those sources of reactions and information that are readily available—in fact, those that are directed steadily at them: their staffs, consultants, other campaigners and activists, and especially the reporters and commentators whose job has come to include telling voters what the election meant. These are the voices that supply the meaning of the vote totals—the voices from whom candidates learn.

After the election, these activist voices compete to get their own explanation of the vote accepted by the media. Through observational learning, one or more such explanations diffuse among the activists concerned with a particular campaign. This dominant explanation (or explanations), together with those established in similar races, affects the winning candidate's behavior in office by affecting his or her expectations about the likely results of particular strategies, the strengths of various groups, the potency and impact of particular issues.

HOW CAMPAIGN LEARNING CAN AFFECT BEHAVIOR IN OFFICE

In what ways do campaign experiences influence senators' and representatives' policy actions? How do the forces coming out of campaigns enhance or limit the influence of the party leadership, the President, or other interests in bringing about policy change?

We can easily derive from the social learning framework that campaign learning affects the importance candidates place on various issues. The explanation constructed for the candidate's victory will probably include some inferences as to which issues made a difference in the race, and which approaches to those issues "worked" in gaining support. (If the constructed explanation *doesn't* include any mention of issues, that teaches campaigners a lot too: that a highly issue-oriented term in office will probably not do much for the incumbent's reelection chances.)

From that generally accepted interpretation of the vote, the new incumbent can draw some conclusions about the *salience* of various issues to the district. If an issue is thought to have made a big difference in the election outcome, there is every reason for the winning candidate to expect that it will continue to be a high priority for many or most voters after the election is over. Such an issue would be risky for an ambitious incumbent to ignore.

Similarly, the constructed explanation (and other campaign learning) can suggest the presumed *direction* of voters' views on particular issues. And it can suggest which stylistic elements in the candidate's presentation of self are important to voters, and the extent to which stylistic behavior matters, compared to position-taking on issues.

Imagine the case of a Senate challenger who beats an entrenched incumbent. Members of the challenger's staff felt that the incumbent's weakest point was his aloof style, and the feeling, widespread in the state, that he was more comfortable talking with world leaders than with commoners like his constituents. When the election results come in, the dominant explanation is that the challenger's stress on accessibility made the difference, leading voters to forgive his liberalism and his bow ties. The incumbent was also weakened, the explanation went, because he was seen as shifting position on too many issues. The acceptance of that explanation is likely to affect the challenger's self-presentational style when in office, the proportion of resources he devotes to constituent service, the frequency of his trips back to the district, his accessibility to district lobbyists and visiting constituents in Washington, and other "extrapolicy" behaviors during his first term.

If the dominant explanation of the election results in this race had been different, perhaps centering on his stands on defense issues, then we would expect some differences in his behavior as an incumbent. Fenno (1982, pp.

43–44) summarizes the expectation this way: "In general, when the campaign rhetoric emphasizes policy matters, policy concerns can be expected to have an important effect on the adjustment period. When the rhetoric of the campaign emphasizes stylistic matters, however, stylistic concerns can be expected to have an important effect on the adjustment period." The important intervening variable is the nature of the explanation constructed for the election results in that race. If a particular policy matter, though given some emphasis in the campaign, is believed to have had no effect on the election outcome, then its impact on the adjustment period is likely to be much reduced.

The 1980 Senate races provide an aggregate example of the way a constructed explanation affects the policy agenda. The headlines after election day offered a number of possible reasons for Ronald Reagan's victory and the shift of 12 Senate seats to the Republican column. The hostages in Iran, the sense that American prestige in the world community was declining, the lavish spending by national Republican committees, a "throw the bums out" mood, a national shift toward conservatism, all were mentioned by reporters and commentators in their early efforts to interpret what the voters meant.

But perhaps the greatest attention was given to economic issues, particularly the dramatic rise in inflation and record-high interest rates. Stanley Kelley, Jr. (1983, p. 190) writes that economic issues "were seen by many as important to Reagan's victory and by some as the key to it. The *Christian Science Monitor,* for example, said that the '1980 results appear uniquely tied to economic performance.' Joseph Kraft called inflation 'the big issue in the campaign,' and the *Chicago Tribune* declared that 'in simple terms, Carter's economic failures caused his defeat.' "[4] That explanation was quite predictable, according to Kelley:

> Most political reporters were probably persuaded quite early and for good reason that economic problems would have a powerful impact on the outcome of the 1980 election. The 'misery index'—a term Carter had used in 1976 to refer to the sum of the rates of inflation and unemployment—had climbed sharply since his inauguration. That fact could hardly help him, particularly when Carter's opponents were continually reminding voters of it. Reagan made inflation and joblessness the keynote of his challenge, as Senator Edward Kennedy had in his bid for the Democratic nomination (1983, pp. 190–91).

In Senate races too, even the pro-life Christian Action Council's newsletter *Action Line* stated (November 21, 1980, p. 1), "There can be no doubt that widespread anxiety about the economy and current military policy were major ingredients in the recipe which produced for Republicans their first Senate majority since 1954."

A number of groups fought to include social issues in the dominant explanation for the Republican Senate gains. The National Conservative PAC (NCPAC), a moving force in the New Right, claimed to have played a key role in the defeats of liberal Democrats Birch Bayh, Frank Church, John Culver, and George McGovern (see Keller, 1980, p. 3372). The Christian Action Council argued that in addition to economic issues, the question of abortion had made a difference in the results. The Moral Majority insisted that it had claimed some scalps, especially emphasizing the Senate races in Alabama and Oklahoma (see Keller, 1980, p. 3372). A reporter for *Congressional Quarterly* wrote:

> Before the election, the Rev. Jerry Falwell, leader of the Moral Majority, named six senators he wanted to see defeated: McGovern, Church, Culver, Bayh, Cranston, and Gaylord Nelson of Wisconsin. All but Cranston went down. While the Moral Majority cannot claim full credit for their defeats, its members did work hard at registering new voters and distributing campaign literature. (Moxley, 1980, p. 3301)

But in general, news reports deemphasized the role of social issues in Senate campaigns in favor of the importance of economic issues and broader explanations of a supposed conservative trend. One reporter wrote, "Republicans have elected a freshman class made up largely of dedicated conservatives" (ibid., p. 3300). Culver, he continued, had "refused to clip his liberal wings to adjust to the conservative wind in his state." Church "lost narrowly to an unrelenting conservative attack." Accounts of McGovern's race described it as a liberal/conservative battle (ibid., p. 3302). Most of the new Republican senators had in fact taken conservative positions on abortion, school prayer, and other social issues. But specific mentions of these issues in the explanations constructed for the 1980 Senate races were rare.

The result was that when the 97th Congress convened, its agenda was heavily weighted with economic rather than social issues. *Action Line* lamented (January 22, 1981, pp. 1–2):

> There is no question that powerful figures in the new Administration view the pro-life movement as merely one among an array of social issues which can be set aside. This message initially came in the form of an influential memorandum prepared for President Reagan by David Stockman...to argue that economics should be the Administration's exclusive concern during its first 100 days in power. 'The Moral Majority agenda,' Stockman wrote, 'should...be deferred.'

It seemed clear that a lot of senators concurred. Bob Packwood, for example, stated the same point much more approvingly (Miller et al., 1981): "Governor Reagan was elected because of foreign policy and defense spending and the economy. He would be making a tragic mistake if he were to now put abortion and school busing and prayer on the front burner....I'll be very surprised if this Adminstration makes any effort to push those issues."

And so the Senate did focus on economic measures for most of 1981, to the great chagrin of pro-lifers and other social conservatives. They were further disappointed when Reagan, in his first opportunity to appoint a Supreme Court justice, nominated Arizona judge Sandra Day O'Connor in the summer of 1981. Though O'Connor was clearly a conservative, reporters found that as a member of the Arizona state Senate she had cast several votes against pro-life measures. Pro-life groups joined with the Moral Majority and others in virulent opposition to O'Connor's nomination. But their efforts were in vain. When the Senate voted, the tally was unanimous in O'Connor's favor; every one of the new senators elected with pro-life support had voted for her nomination.

Other legislative efforts by pro-lifers and the New Right fell just as flat. Antiabortion bills, a constitutional amendment to protect unborn children, school prayer legislation, and tuition tax credits all failed to pass the Senate. These failures in part reflected the interpretation senators and presidential staff members derived from the 1980 elections. And the inability to push abortion, school prayer, and other issues onto the legislative agenda in 1981 and 1982 further cemented the belief that pro-lifers and the New Right were not as strong as they had claimed to be. In this case, then, the constructed explanation was clearly reflected in the priority given various policy questions by the newly elected senators and by the Senate more generally.

Learning from the campaign and the election result should also make a big difference in other kinds of congressional activities. When a newly elected senator decides which congressional committees to try for, what types of background and experience (on particular issues, with particular groups) to look for when hiring staff members, and what kinds of legislative or constituent service or image-building tasks to assign them, aspects of the constructed explanation are likely to figure prominently as determinants.

Finally, campaign learning affects the expectations that constituents, especially activists, hold about the new incumbent. The stands a candidate takes during the campaign, the personal qualities he or she stresses, the promises he or she makes will elicit expectations in other people. A candidate who places major stress on the nuclear freeze issue, for example, will prompt expectations, at least in the more politically aware constituents, that he or she will continue to speak out and to act legislatively on that issue. Constituents' expectations, like public opinion more generally, form a broad permissive range within which the member acts.

Activists' expectations are usually more specific and more limiting for an elected official. Many staff members and volunteers will have joined the campaign because of their attraction to one or more facets of the candidate's self-presentational style. Those issues or stylistic elements can become very much like an informal contract between candidate and active supporter. If a House candidate has declared herself in favor of a nuclear freeze, for example, she will be likely to attract "freezers" to her campaign as volunteers, contributors, and staff members. Some professional consultants, too, gravitate toward clients whose political orientations and positions on big issues resemble their own. In turn, the presence of these activists and advisers provides a continuing source of pressure for the discussion of that issue. Their expectations that the candidate will continue to support a nuclear freeze, and will vote for it when in office, produce regular incentives to deliver on that campaign promise after the election.

Those incentives will have greater force if the explanation for the candidate's victory stresses the importance of the nuclear freeze issue—a result made more likely by the ongoing presence and the preconceptions of these pro-freeze campaign insiders. After the election, if the new House member seems to be redecorating her image or changing her emphasis on issues—even if that change can be seen as a rational move to win more public or group support—she can expect an increase in communications from active supporters who want to hear the themes and see the stylistic approaches that first attracted them to the candidate's side.

The nature of the constructed explanation affects the member's behavior in other ways. If that widely accepted explanation stresses the importance of the presidential candidate's coattails in the race, then the new member will have an incentive to act and vote as a presidential loyalist on matters where the President is regarded as popular. If the explanation portrays the race as largely a party contest, or if the new member is seen as heavily indebted to the national party for campaign funds (an occurrence normally possible only among Republicans), services and visits from party heavyweights, then we can expect the incremental vote to be cast in support of the party leadership's position on issues that the leadership defines as important.

And the constructed explanation may include other forces that go beyond the winning candidate's own district. In several recent elections, the conclusion that a "Republican sweep" or a "conservative tide" has engulfed the country has become embedded in the explanations for large numbers of congressional races. In 1974, the election of 75 new House Democrats was widely interpreted not only as the result of 75 sets of local issues and conditions but as a product of broad public revulsion toward the Watergate scandals and the Republican administration responsible for them. In 1980, Republican gains in the House and Senate were similarly explained as part of a "breathtaking sweep" (Moxley, 1980, p. 3300) propelled by economic discontent, antiincumbent feeling, and Ronald Reagan's coattails.

When explanations of the election results have a strong national component, that tends to produce a sense of shared identity in the candidates elected at that time. The shared outcome increases their tendency to look to one another as models: to learn policy and stylistic innovations from one another. The result is the development of a sense of shared perspective among certain Senate or House "entering classes." The "Watergate babies" of 1974 are a good example. Their sense of shared identity, reflecting the strong national component of the explanations of their victories, has affected the legislative and stylistic behavior of the surviving members ever since.

VARIATIONS IN THE STRENGTH OF CAMPAIGN LEARNING

The impact of campaign learning on incumbents' behavior should vary in strength, however, depending on several factors: characteristics of the legislative institution, attributes of the individual, and changes in the political environment. One primary characteristic of a legislative body is the length of the term of office. Richard Fenno (1982) has emphasized the importance of the difference between the House and Senate in this regard; because of the short House term, he argues, campaign considerations can never be very far from the minds of House members, while the six-year Senate term allows more freedom from the campaign's sway.

Since the next House election is never more than two years away, and since House members can normally spend only a short time in office before their next opponent becomes known—or at least until likely opponents become the subject of avid speculation among the incumbent's staff and closest advisers—there is every reason to expect that the explanation of the most recent election result, and anticipation of the next one, will vitally affect the House member's behavior in office. The explanation can make a big difference in the incumbent's decision to emphasize some issues rather than others, his or her stands on issues, and concern with casework.

The senator's learning environment is different. The six-year term permits much more time to be spent in Washington, where the incumbent is likely to see different kinds of people and do different types of things than if he or she were back in the state several days a week. In Washington, the incumbent's environment is heavily populated by other elected officials and legislative staffers. And activity in Washington has more to do with the tasks of formulating policies than campaigning in the state does.

As Kuklinski's (1978) research shows, legislators' voting behavior more closely resembles (and so, presumably, is more sensitive to) constituent opinion during election years than during nonelection years. For House members, every other year is an election year. But the six-year Senate term gives senators the freedom to pursue issues that are not very salient at home, to take an occasional unpopular stand (especially in the first two or three years of the term), and to spend time on legislation that might, if the term were shorter, be stolen away by campaigning and constituent service. Thus the constructed explanation probably has a tighter hold on the behavior of House members than it does on senators.

Attributes of the individual officeholder also affect the impact of campaign learning. The explanation of the election result may well lead a winning candidate to seek particular committee assignments in Congress. Once made, however, those assignments will mediate the effects of that explanation on the incumbent's behavior. "One way to maintain a campaign policy interest," Fenno writes (1982, p. 42), "is to institutionalize it by obtaining membership on the committee that deals with it." He cites the case of one Senate candidate whose strongest supporters were growers of a particular farm product. During the campaign, the candidate promised these supporters that he would remain interested in agricultural issues. Once elected, though now a bit hesitant, he accepted a seat on the Agriculture Committee. "The first legislative staff person he hired was an agricultural expert. The first bill he introduced was an agricultural bill. Altogether it was a very direct, specific, and continuing influence of the campaign on this senator's subsequent legislative work."

In this case, then, the new senator's committee assignment increased and facilitated the impact of the constructed explanation on his legislative efforts. In cases where the incumbent's committee assignments are not so clearly in harmony with that explanation, then the work of those committees will compete with and limit the influence of campaign learning. If Fenno's new senator had been given a seat on Foreign Relations instead, his ability to act on his interest in agricultural issues would inevitably be affected—and with it, the impact of the constructed explanation on his behavior.

The effects of campaign learning can also be modified by changes in the political environment. Consider a Democrat first elected to the House after a campaign criticizing the Reagan administration for high unemployment rates and unfair economic policies. Two years later, unemployment has declined from over 10% to just above 7% and the economy is markedly improved. The incumbent's policy appeals—even the nature of his or her casework requests—will probably change to reflect that improvement.

The extent to which change in the environment affects a Congress member's behavior depends in part on the length of his or her incumbency (see Hershey, 1984, chap. 4). Repeated election victories build up layers of reward, layers of incentive to repeat the rewarded behaviors. This is especially likely in the case of House members, for whom six years of incumbency means three experiences with reward at the polls, compared to a senator's one victory. The building of habits can make for efficient responses—as long as the environment stays the same. But environments rarely do stay the same, and when change does occur, it will probably take a bigger, more dramatic change to alter the long-time incumbent's behavior than that of a candidate whose habits are not so firmly set. If the district is changing a little at a time—different kinds of people moving in, a potential challenger gaining support, a party organization atrophying, a staff becoming more complacent—a well-ensconced incumbent may miss the signs of change, may overlook the need for changed responses, until the situation becomes critical. The long history of reward, the surrounding cocoon of support, can buffer a long-time incumbent from an environment that is becoming, a bit at a time, increasingly hostile to his or her habitual approach.

After a long period of incumbency, then, the learning that comes from campaign stimuli and from the explanation constructed for the incumbent's victory is likely to weaken as an influence on behavior in office. So campaign learning is likely to have greatest power over the behavior of the least senior legislators.

Campaign learning, in short, does not affect all winning candidates equally. But campaign stimuli, and especially the explanation constructed for a candidate's victory, can make a significant difference in his or her behavior in office. This chapter has argued that campaign experiences can best be understood to affect public policy (and other congressional behavior) through the nature and quality of the candidate's learning.

NOTES

1. There is a great deal of literature on the diffusion of innovations (for a helpful summary, see Rogers with Shoemaker, 1971) and on the analogous process in which legislators take their cues from trusted colleagues on policy matters (see Kingdon, 1981; Matthews and Stimson, 1975). Interestingly, the findings of both sets of studies closely match those of social-learning researchers on modeling.

2. According to *Newsweek* (1982, Nov. 15, pp. 34–37), 78% of Democratic identifiers who had voted for Reagan in 1980 supported a Democrat for Congress in 1982.

3. Reported in *Newsweek* (1982, Nov. 15, pp. 34–37). An NBC poll at the same time indicated that while 36% of the respondents considered Reaganomics a failure, 49% were willing to give the President more time to prove the worth of his economic policies.

4. The quoted excerpts are from, respectively: the *Christian Science Monitor* of November 10; the *Washington Post* of November 9; and the *Chicago Tribune* of November 6.

REFERENCES

Bandura, Albert (1977). *Social Learning Theory*. Englewood Cliffs, N.J.: Prentice-Hall.

Broder, David (1982). GOP governors warn Reagan team. *Sunday Herald-Times*, November 21, p. A10.

Crouse, Timothy (1972). *The Boys on the Bus*. New York: Ballantine.

Downs, Anthony (1957). *An Economic Theory of Democracy*. New York: Harper & Row.

Evans, Rowland, and Novak, Robert (1982). Returning to 1980 theme. Bloomington *Herald-Telephone*, November 6, p. 6.

Fenno, Richard F., Jr.(1978). *Home Style: House Members in Their Districts*. Boston: Little, Brown.

Fenno, Richard F., Jr. (1982). *The United States Senate: A Bicameral Perspective*. Washington, D.C.: American Enterprise Institute.

Hershey, Marjorie Randon (1984). *Running for Office: The Political Education of Campaigners*. Chatham, N.J.: Chatham House.

Iyengar, Shanto, Peters, Mark D., and Kinder, Donald R. (1982). Experimental demonstrations of the 'not-so-minimal' consequences of television news programs. *American Political Science Review*, 76: 848–58.

Jackson, John S. III, Brown, Barbara Leavitt, and Bositis, David (1982). Herbert McClosky and friends revisited: 1980 Democratic and Republican party elites compared to the mass public. *American Politics Quarterly*, 10: 158–80.

Jacobson, Gary C. (1983). *The Politics of Congressional Elections*. Boston: Little, Brown.

Kayden, Xandra (1978). *Campaign Organization*. Boston: Little, Brown.

Keller, Bill (1980). "New Right" wants credit for Democrats' Nov. 4 losses but GOP, others don't agree. *Congressional Quarterly Weekly Report*, 38 (15 November): 3372–73.

Kelley, Stanley, Jr. (1983). *Interpreting Elections*. Princeton: Princeton University Press.

Kingdon, John W. (1968). *Candidates for Office: Beliefs and Strategies*. New York: Random House.

Kingdon, John W. (1981). *Congressmen's Voting Decisions*. 2nd ed. New York: Harper & Row.

Kuklinski, James H. (1978). Representativeness and elections: a political analysis. *American Political Science Review*, 72: 165–77.

Kuklinski, James H. and West, Darrell M. (1981). Economic expectations and voting behavior in United States House and Senate elections. *American Political Science Review*, 75: 436–47.

Maisel, Louis Sandy (1982). *From Obscurity to Oblivion: Running in the Congressional Primary*. Knoxville: University of Tennessee Press.

Mann, Thomas E. and Wolfinger, Raymond E. (1980). Candidates and parties in congressional elections. *American Political Science Review*, 74: 617–32.

Markus, Gregory B. (1982). Political attitudes during an election year: a report on the 1980 NES panel study. *American Political Science Review*, 76: 538–60.

Matthews, Donald R. (1960). *U.S. Senators and Their World*. New York: Vintage.

Mathews, Donald R, and Stimson, James A. (1975). *Yeas and Nays: Normal Decision-Making in the U.S. House of Representatives*. New York: Wiley.

Mayhew, David R. (1974). *Congress: The Electoral Connection*. New Haven: Yale University Press.

Miller, Judith et al. (1981). Enjoying its majority, G.O.P. makes plans. *New York Times*, January 18, E5.

Moxley, Warden (1980). GOP wins Senate control for first time in 28 years. *Congressional Quarterly Weekly Report*, 38 (8 November): 3300–3303.

Nie, Norman H., Verba, Sidney, and Petrocik, John R. (1979). *The Changing American Voter*, enlarged ed. Cambridge, Mass.: Harvard University Press.

Plattner, Andy (1982). Hill leaders whittle agenda for the post-election session. *Congressional Quarterly Weekly Report*, 40 (13 November): 2838.

Rogers, Everett M., and Shoemaker, F. Floyd (1971). *Communication of Innovations: A Cross-Cultural Approach*, 2nd ed. New York: Free Press.

Sears, David O., Lau, Richard R., Tyler, Tom R., and Allen, Harris M., Jr. (1980). Self-interest vs. symbolic politics in policy attitudes and presidential voting. *American Political Science Review*, 74: 670–84.

Tate, Dale (1982). Election changes raise hopes for consensus on 1984 budget. *Congressional Quarterly Weekly Report*, 40 (13 November): 2835.

Verba, Sidney, and Nie, Norman H. (1972). *Participation in America: Political Democracy and Social Equality*. New York: Harper & Row.

Leadership, Rules, and the Congressional Policy Process

7

Party Leadership and Policy Change

Barbara Sinclair

In the spring and early summer of 1984, immigration reform was the most controversial issue facing the House of Representatives. The Senate had twice passed the Simpson bill, which, its supporters claimed, offered a far-reaching solution to a major and growing societal problem. Yet Speaker of the House Tip O'Neill repeatedly postponed House floor consideration of the Simpson-Mazzoli bill. Just before the bill was to be debated in the House, both O'Neill and Majority Leader Jim Wright indicated they would not be unhappy if the rule for consideration of the bill were defeated, thus killing the legislation.

At just about the same time, the House Democratic leadership took a major role in challenging President Reagan's defense policy. During 1983 and early 1984, opposition among Democrats to the MX missile had been growing. Nevertheless, in mid-May, a leadership-supported proposal to block production of the MX was narrowly defeated in favor of a compromise proposal sponsored by Les Aspin, Democrat of Wisconsin, and supported by the Reagan administration. (*Congressional Quarterly Weekly Report,* May 19, 1984, pp. 1155–1160). Determined to win the next engagement which would come in only a few weeks, the leadership appointed a task force to coordinate the persuasion effort. Richard Gephardt, a deputy whip, directed the joint efforts of long-time MX foes and of experienced leadership tacticians. To dramatize the leadership's commitment to the effort, Majority Leader Jim Wright closed debate for the MX opponents. On a 199 to 197 vote, the majority leadership won and thereby handed Reagan a significant policy defeat (*Congressional Quarterly Weekly Report,* June 2, 1984, pp. 1291–1293).

What do these two instances tell us about the role of the congressional party leadership in policy change? Are party leaders facilitators or inhibitors of policy change in Congress? Or are they irrelevant? Does their role vary and, if so, in what way? Answering these questions requires an understanding of the role of party leadership in the Congress. In this chapter, I first develop a framework for understanding party leadership; next I apply it to both contemporary and historical House leadership. It will then be possible to assess the role of the congressional majority party leadership in policy change.

UNDERSTANDING MAJORITY PARTY LEADERSHIP: A THEORETICAL FRAMEWORK

Our framework begins with a set of assumptions about the core functions of party leadership. As satisfying the expectations of followers and of other significant actors is central to successful leadership, our assumptions about leadership functions can derive from such expectations. House leaders must at least minimally satisfy the expectations of their membership simply to keep their positions as leaders. To be considered successful, House leaders must also satisfy the expectations of various significant political actors outside the chamber; especially important are major groups aligned with the party and, certainly during the twentieth century, the President if he is a fellow partisan. Both the membership and these outside actors have expectations concerning legislative outputs; consequently, a primary function of majority party leadership is building winning coalitions on legislation so as to satisfy these expectations. "Keeping peace in the family," as the current leaders themselves express it, is an equally important function. "Party maintenance," as this function will also be called, requires that leaders aid members in satisfying their expectations about their individual roles in the chamber, that they mitigate intraparty conflicts and foster cooperative patterns of behavior among party members. In the contemporary House, for example, members expect to participate fully in the legislative process; party maintenance dictates that the leadership facilitate such broad participation by rank-and-file members. The Democratic party, which has controlled the House continuously since 1955, is heterogeneous in membership and thus prone to intraparty splits. Leaders must keep internecine fights from starting if possible and, if not, prevent them from becoming bitter irreconcilable divisions.

These two primary party leadership functions are related in a complex fashion. The need to "keep peace in the family" places limits on the coalition building strategies that can be used. Winning coalitions must be built repeatedly; consequently, tactics that might succeed in the short run are nevertheless counterproductive if they exacerbate intraparty conflicts or produce generalized dissatisfaction among the members. Because members and significant outside actors expect legislative outputs, the peace-keeping function cannot be allowed to lead to immobilism. Yet, unless a policy consensus exists, the necessity of passing legislation which is controversial within the party will strain party harmony. For example, the Simpson-Mazzoli immigration bill badly split the Democratic party, with labor strongly supporting the measure and minority groups, particularly Hispanics, inalterably opposed. No matter what the leadership did, some members and their allied interest groups would be dissatisfied. In the end, the leaders decided that "sitting on their hands" would do the least damage to intraparty harmony. There is, thus, a tension between the two functions. Yet successful performance of one can increase the leadership's chances of success at the other. To the extent leaders succeed at "keeping peace in the family," their probability of future success in building winning coalitions is increased; to the extent leaders are successful at building winning coalitions on bills that satisfy their members' expectations about legislative outputs, they contribute to party maintenance.

Majority party members benefit collectively when their leadership builds winning coalitions and keeps peace in the family. The party's legislative record depends on successful coalition building; such success also contributes to the maintenance of the power of the House in the governmental system. A minimum level of party coherence is necessary for the party to organize the House, and organizing the House provides great benefits to members in the form of chairmanships of committees and subcommittees. Intraparty harmony also contributes to coalition building success and makes the members' job easier and more pleasant.

Members' collective interest in leadership success does not necessarily lead to individual behavior conducive to that outcome. Members also have individual goals, and behavior that furthers the attainment of those individual goals may work against leadership success. Leadership success is a collective good and any member's actions will have only a small impact on its realization. Consequently, when there is a conflict, an individual member is likely to behave in ways that further his individual goals at the expense of leadership success. A member may, for example, vote against foreign aid even though he knows it is important to U.S. foreign policy. A nay vote will be popular with his constituents and, after all, his is only one vote. Thus the leadership cannot assume that its members will freely act to further coalition building success or intraparty harmony.

Leaders' potential to influence their members' behavior depends on the impact leaders can have on member goal achievement. The more leaders can help or hurt members in attaining their individual goals, the greater the leaders' potential influence. The leaders' actual influence depends, in addition, both on their willingness to use whatever resources they have and

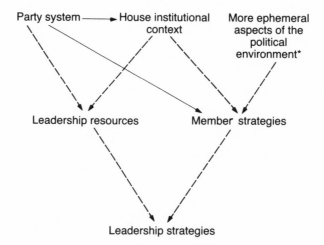

Figure 1. Schematic model of leadership strategies. (*Especially character of the salient issues.)

on their skill in doing so. The leaders' success at building winning coalitions and at keeping peace in the family is not a function of their influence alone. It also depends on whether members in pursuing their own goals act in accordance with leadership wishes. For example, if their goal pursuit leads most members to support the leadership's position on major legislation, leaders will succeed at building winning coalitions without needing to wield influence.

While the goals of House members are undoubtedly multiple and diverse, building a framework for analysis requires some simplifying assumptions. Following Fenno (1973) and Kingdon (1973, 1977), I assume that reelection, intra-Washington influence, and good public policy are the primary goals of House members. Although the relative weight placed on the three goals varies from member to member and may also vary across time, I assume these have been the primary goals of House members throughout the period under study.

How then do we account for systematic variations in leadership strategies over time? Figure 1 presents the model in schematic form. Leadership strategies for performing the two principal functions are posited to reflect both the influence resources the leadership has available and members' strategies for attaining their individual goals. Leadership resources are a function of the party system and of the House institutional context. The strategies that members develop for attaining their individual goals are a function of the party system, the House institutional context, and more ephemeral aspects of the political environment, most especially the character of the issues at the center of controversy.

This is a contextual model. It assumes that context or environment is a much more powerful determinant of leadership strategies than personal characteristics of the leaders themselves (see Jones, 1981, pp. 118–120). Within this model, understanding party leadership strategies at a given time requires an analysis of leadership resources and member strategies as a function of the basic context variables.

LEADERSHIP STRATEGIES IN THE POSTREFORM ERA

During the 1970s, new leadership strategies became necessary because members' behavioral strategies for attaining their individual goals changed. The modal member strategy came to be based on early, broad, and relatively unrestrained participation in the House political process. A change in the House institutional context made this new strategy possible: House rules were altered to allow, and norms changed to encourage, high rates of participation (see Sinclair, 1983, pp. 3–19).

The first set of rules changes were contained in the 1970 Reorganization Act. It included a variety of sunshine provisions: it encouraged open committee proceedings and required that all committee roll calls be made public. Other provisions were aimed at safeguarding the rights of minorities (for example, minority members were guaranteed the right to call witnesses at committee hearings) and at enabling members to obtain information on measures before they reached the floor (conference reports were required to be available for three days before a House vote could be taken, and debate on a conference report was to be evenly divided between the majority and the minority). One of the most important changes was the institution of recorded teller votes in the Committee of the Whole House, where bills are amended; prior to the 1970 act, no recorded votes were taken at this crucial stage.

Beginning in 1971 the Democratic Caucus passed a series of rules changes the effect of which was to distribute positions of influence more widely among members and to shift power from full committee chairs to subcommittee chairs. Each member was limited to chairing only one subcommittee, and each subcommittee chair was empowered to hire one professional staff member. The Subcommittee Bill of Rights, passed in 1973, contained provisions to circumscribe the power of the full committee chairs: it removed from full committee chairs the power to select subcommittee chairs and gave it to the Democratic caucus of the committee, which consists of all Democratic members of the committee; it required subcommittees to have fixed jurisdiction and adequate budget and staff; and it mandated that legislation be referred to subcommittee within a fixed time. As a result of a series of rules changes instituted in 1971 and 1973, full committee chairs and the chairmen of Appropriations subcommittees have to be approved by secret ballot in the Democratic Caucus.

The 1970s also saw an immense growth in the staff resources available to members of the House. In 1967 personal staff totaled 4,055; in 1979 that figure stood at 7,067. The number of employees of House committees increased from 702 in 1970 to 1,959 in 1979 (Bibby, Mann, and Ornstein, 1980, pp. 69–70). The most junior member is now entitled to hire a staff of at least eighteen.

High membership turnover in the 1970s had a strong influence on the actual effects of the rules changes. By and large, the new members were young; their formative political experiences had taken place in the turbulent 1960s, and they entered the House during a period of challenge to the power structure. Furthermore, many of the large 1974 Democratic freshmen class were elected from previously Republican districts.

These members were not inclined, nor could they afford politically, to wait before attempting to make their mark in the House. Norms of apprenticeship and of deference to senior members, already weakened during the 1960s, received a final blow. New members actively participated in committee and on the floor, feeling no need to refrain from speaking and offering amendments even during their first months in office.

As a result of these changes, the majority party leadership team of O'Neill and Wright which took over in 1977 faced performing the coalition building and party maintenance functions within a highly unpredictable environment. The transformation of the House institutional structure multiplied both the number of significant actors and the number of significant arenas; and the party-fragmenting issues at the center of controversy exacerbated the resulting uncertainty. Some of the rules changes of the 1970s, however, augmented the resources of the party leadership. Leaders gained greater influence over committee assignments, over bill referral and, through their control of the Rules Committee, over legislative scheduling and the conditions of floor consideration.

According to our model, changes in leadership resources and in member strategies should result in change in leadership strategies. Understanding those new strategies requires a more detailed analysis of current member strategies for attaining their individual goals and of the extent to which leaders can influence members' goal achievement.

The Reelection Goal

What patterns of behavior does the reelection goal entail? The member, recent research indicates, must establish and maintain high favorable name recognition (Jacobson, 1983, pp. 86–120), and that requires a high rate of district-related activity. Frequent local appearances, effective casework and projects are all important. In addition, members believe they must keep their overall voting record in line with constituency sentiment and that, on issues highly salient to the constituency, voting the constituency is by far the safest course (Fenno, 1978; Kingdon, 1973).

Most of the time, leaders cannot significantly affect their members' reelection chances. For example, although leaders can help members with campaign funds, incumbents generally can raise as much money as they need without such help. While the leadership can help a member obtain a committee assignment useful to his district, the competition for many constituency-service committees is not intense. The leaders can sometimes help a member get projects or grants for his district by using their influence with the administration. They can also help a member to secure passage of minor but locally important legislation. Such assistance can be important, but it will seldom make the difference between victory and defeat.

The leadership's ability to influence the reelection chances of its members, thus, is usually marginal. Furthermore, the leaders are severely constrained in withholding the help they can give. Success at building winning coalitions is, in part, a function of the size of the majority party. Since leaders have absolutely no control over nominations, withholding help, if it had any effect, would only increase the chances of the Republican challenger. The need to "keep peace in the family" also limits the leadership. A systematic withholding of all favors from members who only erratically support the leadership would be perceived as unfair and would strain party harmony. Most members believe they are only doing what they must to insure reelection.

The party leadership's marginal influence over the reelection chances of its members is not new to the postreform era. The situation faced by members as they seek reelection has, however, changed. Members now command much greater resources for serving the district. Staffs, office budgets, access to sophisticated technology like computers, and the number of paid trips home have all greatly increased. As party organizations have declined, the local elites on whom the congressman depends for support are less likely to be party-based. It seems likely that, as a result, current members see their reelection as even more dependent on their own efforts and less so on the party's record than members in the 1950s and 1960s did. The importunings members get from non-party based local elites are less likely to reinforce party regularity. Consequently, reelection-directed behavior is more likely than previously to conflict with leadership-desired behavior.

Furthermore, because participation is so little restrained in the postreform House, "grandstanding" has become a viable reelection strategy. Junior members, particularly those from marginal districts, are not loath to gain publicity at the expense of their party colleagues or the institution. Members have, for example, undertaken personal crusades on matters such as ethics or congressional pay raises. Such behavior strains intraparty harmony and makes the leadership's party maintenance function more difficult. New House rules and altered norms have also provided the minority with opportunities for complicating the majority leadership's coalition building. Republicans—and dissident Democrats—have become very adept at fashioning amendments, opposition to which is difficult to explain back home: for example, amendments written so that a clever election opponent can represent a "nay" vote as favoring federal legal aid for homosexuals or supporting experimentation on live fetuses. Since only 25 members can force a recorded vote, this tactic can be used by small groups of members and often by individuals for reelection-related benefits.

The Influence Goal

In the pre-reform House, a member's routes to intra-Washington influence were through attaining institutional leadership positions on a committee or in the party hierarchy. Seniority determined the first; party leaders, to a large extent, controlled the second. Committee-based influence is still important, but rules changes, by increasing the importance of subcommittee chairmanships, have multiplied the number of influential positions. Changes in the House have also made the outsider role viable for members; it is now possible for a member to become influential within the Washington community as a spokesman for a national policy coalition—as, for example, Bella Abzug did.

Party leaders can provide important though seldom decisive help to those members who choose traditional routes to influence. The leadership has more influence over committee assignments than it did in the pre-reform days; since competition for assignments to the most influential committees is intense, the leadership's support or opposition can be decisive. The number of such desirable positions is, however, limited and once a member gets on a committee he is considered entitled to remain. Over the distribution of committee and subcommittee chairmanships, the leadership has little real control. Although committee chairmen are now nominated by the Steering and Policy Committee and approved by the full caucus, only under very special circumstances is seniority not followed. The new procedure does give the leadership leverage it did not have previously; chairmen are aware they must be responsive to the Democratic membership. Subcommittee chairmen are chosen by the Democratic caucus of the committee, a process in which the leadership has no official role. The leaders appoint deputy and at large whips and some members of the Steering and Policy Committee. These positions give some influence to their holders and so provide a resource to the leadership.

To a considerable extent, the influence of committee or subcommittee chairmen depends on their ability to pass legislation intact. With that, the leadership can provide important aid. The leadership can help a committee leader get a rule, can schedule the legislation on a favorable day, can provide a whip check, can engage in persuasion. With the increase in the number of amendments offered, the floor has become a much more important decision making arena; consequently, the help the leadership can provide has also become more important. The limitation of one subcommittee chairmanship per member combined with high membership turnover has resulted in a number of junior, and thus inexperienced, subcommittee chairmen. Such members are especially likely to need leadership help when managing legislation on the floor.

Those members who seek intra-Washington influence through an outsider strategy are largely beyond the leadership's control. There is little the leaders' can do to affect their probability of attaining that goal. The vast majority of House members, however, still seek influence by more traditional routes and, for their goal attainment, the leadership's resources are relevant.

The leadership's use of its resources to influence members' behavior is, however, constrained by a variety of considerations. In the making of assignments to the choice committees, norms concerning regional balance and fair representation of various segments of the party act as constraints. A single-minded attempt to use such assignments to ensure loyalty would be perceived as unfair, would probably fail, and would certainly strain party harmony. Such norms also limit the leadership's discretion in the appointment of whips and Steering and Policy Committee members. Furthermore, including members with ties to all sections of the party is important for successful coalition building. The leaders have very considerable resources to help or hinder legislation at the floor stage; yet, since building majority coalitions to pass major legislation is necessary to satisfy the output expectations of members and other significant actors, leaders cannot withhold their help from a committee or subcommittee chairman just because he is often uncooperative. On lesser legislation, the leaders do have more leeway, but the desire to help or teach a lesson to a chairman is only one of many factors they must consider in deciding how much to become involved.

The altered House institutional context has changed member behavior in pursuit of the power goal. Because rules changes give subcommittees very considerable autonomy from their parent committees, subcommittee chairmanships provide a real basis for attaining influence within the Washington community. Because members may now chair only one subcommittee, they can concentrate on its activities. Because members are chosen as subcommittee chairs by their fellow partisans on the committee, they must be active to justify their reelection as subcommittee chairs. As a result, there is more subcommittee activity than in the past. For the majority party leadership, this high activity rate by a multitude of subcommittees creates an information problem. There are many more bases to be touched, and it is more difficult to be sure one has touched all that are necessary. Furthermore, rules and norms now allow even those members too junior to have attained a subcommittee chairmanship to seek influence by participating actively in committee or on the floor. This again increases the uncertainty involved in coalition building.

The Policy Goal

For those members who want to participate in the making of good public policy, the right committee assignment is important. So, too, is attaining an institutional position of influence on the committee. The leadership can help the member get a desired committee assignment but, as discussed earlier, the leverage this gives the leadership is limited. The leaders have no formal role in the allotment of subcommittee chairmenships. Policy-oriented members are interested not only in having an impact in committee, but also in seeing their policy preferences translated into law. Consequently, leadership aid at the postcommittee stage is important for such members' goal attainment. The greater importance of the floor as a decision making arena has increased the value of the resources the leadership possesses for influencing floor activity. Active leadership support greatly increases a controversial bill's probability of passage. If the leaders agree with a policy-oriented member on what is good (and politically feasible) public policy, the leaders, in the course of doing their job, contribute significantly to the member's goal attainment. If there is substantial disagreement, the leadership, in doing its job, frustrates the member's goals.

The transformed House environment gives rank-and-file members very considerable opportunities to pursue their policy goals, even in opposition to the leadership of their own party. In the battle over MX procurement, for example, opposition to the leadership position was led by Les Aspin, a middle-ranking Democratic member of the Armed Services Committee with a liberal voting record. Aspin had for several years and with considerable success pursued his own policy preference of approving some MX production but tying it to the resumption of arms control negotiations. Committee chairmen, however, are much less able than they used to be to oppose the leadership if it is supported by a party majority. A series of rules changes curbed the power of committee chairmen over the decisions of their committees. Because chairmen must now be approved by secret ballot in the Democratic caucus, they must be responsive to majority sentiment.

Thus, changes in House rules and norms during the 1970s have made possible new reelection, power, and policy-directed strategies. All members can now participate actively in the legislative process and use that participation to facilitate their goal achievement. Although leadership resources were augmented during the 1970s, the leadership's ability to affect members' goal achievement is nevertheless peripheral or sporadic rather than central and continuous. For most members most of the time, leadership help is not critical for reelection or power. Furthermore, the leaders are constrained in using negative sanctions and even in withholding favors; the costs of so doing often outweigh the benefits.

The goal toward which the leadership can make the most significant contribution is good public policy. If a core consensus on policy exists within the party, the leaders can aid members to achieve their policy goals. Furthermore, if the consensus has its origins in the members' constituencies, if the members are receiving strong and congruent policy signals from their districts, the leaders, by facilitating the passage of responsive legislation, also contribute to their members' reelection. When such a constituency-based consensus exists, the leadership not only can affect members' goal achievement and consequently their behavior, but member behavior uninfluenced by the leadership is likely to be consonant with leadership preferences.

A constituency-based consensus of both strength and breadth such as existed during the New Deal and the 89th Congress is rare. More typically, a substantial proportion of majority party members agree on some core tenets but disagree on many issues. During the late 1970s and early 1980s, the Democrats' core of agreement was shrinking under the impact of seemingly intractable economic problems. In performing their leadership functions, the current leaders are faced with a far from united party as well as limited resources and a highly unpredictable institutional environment.

In their attempts to cope with these problems, the current leaders have developed a three-pronged strategy: they are heavily engaged in providing services to members; they make use of their formal powers and influence to structure choice situations; and they attempt to involve as many Democrats as possible in the coalition building process.

By providing services to members collectively and individually, the leaders help them play the role they desire in the chamber and facilitate their goal achievement. Leadership information dissemination helps members play an active role in the House. Legislative scheduling that is sensitive to member needs conserves members' limited time and can contribute to the attainment of reelection, policy, and power goals. The many favors leaders do for individual members also furthers those members' goal attainment.

The leadership expects the collective services it provides to contribute to party maintenance and to produce a favorable climate for coalition building. Favors for individuals are expected to have the same effect; no direct quid pro quo is involved. Furthermore, the leadership will seldom withhold favors as a punishment. Speaker O'Neill strongly believes that the carrot is more effective than the stick. Some House Democrats believe the Speaker does not make enough use of negative sanctions. The problem O'Neill faces, however, is that the stick is not much of a threat; he does not possess sufficient resources to affect decisively members' probability of goal attainment. Consequently, using the stick is likely to have a negative impact on keeping peace in the family without significantly increasing coalition building success. To a large extent, this is the situation which all Speakers since Cannon have faced, and most have been heavily engaged in doing favors for individual members. The present leadership is much more involved in providing services to its membership collectively than its predecessors were. Because of new rules and norms, almost any member can cause problems for the leadership. Rank-and-file satisfaction or dissatisfaction is more important than it was in the pre-reform House.

Lacking resources sufficient to affect decisively members' goal attainment, the leadership cannot base its coalition building efforts on the employment of direct rewards and punishments. Structuring the choice situation is not a new leadership strategy, but the reforms of the 1970s have augmented leadership resources for doing so effectively. The Panama Canal Treaty implementation legislation of 1979 exemplifies the usefulness of the new multiple referral rules; using those rules, the Speaker referred that legislation to four committees. By so doing, the Speaker brought into the process committees friendly to the administration position to counter the basically hostile Merchant Marine Committee and, by using a reporting deadline, he forced Merchant Marine to report the bill out in timely fashion. Both the Panama bill and synfuels legislation, also passed in 1979, illustrate how significant a resource control over the floor schedule is. Such control allowed the leadership to postpone the Panama legislation until the votes to pass it were in hand. Consideration of synthetic fuels legislation was moved up so that a possible opposition tactic of attempting to delay a vote until after the recess would stand little chance of success. The Speaker's control of the Rules Committee provides an immensely important resource because it makes possible the use of carefully constructed rules to structure floor choices. The 1980 reconciliation bill was considered under a closed rule;

thus the choice members faced was whether to vote for or against savings; if amendments had been allowed, the choice would have been whether to vote for or against cutting a number of popular programs.

Structuring choices is a means of coercing members collectively. The strategy is limited by the requirement of overt or tacit member approval. When the strategy is skillfully used, members will acquiesce because what they gain is greater than what they lose by having their choices constrained. If, for example, members' policy goals dictate a proleadership vote but their reelection needs a contrary vote, structuring the choice situation so that the key roll call occurs on a procedural motion may allow members to vote their policy preferences. Members may, for instance, be willing to vote for a rule barring amendments requiring a balanced budget or prohibiting school busing, even though, were the amendments offered, they would feel constrained to vote for them.

From the leadership's point of view, the need for member acquiescence is both a disadvantage and an advantage. It limits the use of the strategy of constraining choice. Yet coercion to which one has consented tends not to be perceived as unreasonable. Because of the uncertain environment, leaders do not always know what their members will consider acceptable. Misjudgment may lead to a legislative defeat; members may, for example, vote down a rule. But for the leadership, losing almost any particular legislative battle is preferable to creating serious dissatisfaction among the membership. Few legislative battles are worth winning at the price of a severe reduction in the probability of future coalition building success.

The attempt to involve as many Democrats as possible in the coalition building process is the third element of the current leadership's strategy. As rule and norm changes dispersed influence more widely in the chamber, more extensive vote mobilization efforts became necessary. The high rate of activity in a multitude of arenas also made more formalized information gathering essential. In response, the leadership expanded and used formal leadership structures. The whip system has been greatly expanded by the addition of deputy and at large whips appointed by the leadership (see Dodd, 1979). The elected regional whips, whose support of the leadership position is often problematical, are now expected only to collect and disseminate information; the appointed whips are involved in persuasion. The membership of the Steering and Policy Committee is also a mix of regionally elected and leadership-appointed members. The Committee is involved in coalition building formally by virtue of its role of endorsing legislation and informally by providing a forum for working out intraparty disputes. The Rules Committee has lost its independence of the Speaker but, in recompense, committee Democrats who so desire have become members of the leadership (see Oppenheimer, 1981).

The leadership also involves other members in specific coalition building efforts. On certain bills that are highly important to the party, the Speaker appoints a task force and charges the members with passing the legislation. Membership will include Democrats from the committee of origin and also others who are simply interested in the legislation for policy or reelection reasons. Often when no task force is appointed, such interested members are nevertheless included in the coalition building effort in an informal way.

The 1984 battle over MX production, for example, involved members who had established themselves as leading MX opponents such as Nicholas Mavroules, a junior member of the Armed Services Committee, and Tom Downey, who does not serve on the committee; members with skill and experience at coalition building such as Richard Gephardt, a deputy whip, and Tony Coelho, Democratic Congressional Campaign Committee Chairman; Charles Bennett, a sympathetic senior member of the Armed Services Committee; and certain other members—like Mike Synar, a three termer from Oklahoma who serves on no defense-related committee—who were simply interested in the issue and willing to work.

The campaign to pass the first budget resolution in 1983 saw the leadership attempting to involve the entire Democratic membership. After two years of failing to pass the Democratic budget resolution, the leadership was determined to prevail. Before the Budget Committee drafted its resolution, all Democrats were sent a questionnaire that simulated the tough choices the Budget Committee majority would have to make. The Speaker pressured members to fill it out and over 200 did so. The results provided the Budget Committee majority with some guidance about sentiments within the party and gave rank-and-file Democrats some influence on the Budget Committee's resolution. Members' perception that they had had some influence and their increased understanding of the difficult trade-offs involved in writing a budget made leadership appeals for floor support more effective, and the resolution passed handily.

The current leaders' use of task forces and of less formal ad hoc groups to work on specific legislation and their use of the expanded whip system, the Steering and Policy Committee, and the Rules Committee are all elements of the strategy of inclusion. Leaders' regular interactions with members of the extended leadership circle provide information vital to successful coalition building in the unpredictable postreform House. By enlisting a large number and broad variety of Democrats in leadership efforts, the leaders get the help they so badly need. The large number involved makes one-on-one persuasion with a large proportion of the membership possible. The broad variety ensures that the group as a whole will have ties to all sections of the party. The strategy of inclusion, thus, contributes to coalition building success.

The leaders believe that the strategy of inclusion also contributes to party maintenance. In the postreform House, rules allow and norms dictate high rank-and-file participation. Involvement in the extended leadership circle and in specific coalition building efforts gives a large number of members the opportunity to participate actively, but in a way that helps rather than hurts the leadership.

LEADERSHIP STRATEGIES IN HISTORICAL PERSPECTIVE

During the latter part of the nineteenth century an extremely powerful speakership developed. The power to appoint committees had long been vested in the Speaker (see Follett, 1974, pp. 217–218). In the 1880s and 1890s, the Speaker gained control over the flow of business to and on the House floor. The Rules Committee, which the Speaker chaired, began to report special orders (e.g., rules) providing for the consideration of a particular bill and, according to Hinds, this procedure "since 1890 has been in favor as an efficient means of bringing up for consideration bills difficult to reach in the regular order" (IV Hinds' Precedents S3152). Through a series of rulings and rules changes, most notably the "Reed rules," the Speaker severely curtailed the minority's ability to delay and obstruct and enhanced the presiding officer's control over the flow of business on the floor. What circumstances made the development of such a powerful speakership possible? Why were House member willing to vest such immense powers in the Speaker?

The development of the strong speakership is most associated with the name of Thomas Brackett Reed. When Reed became Speaker in 1889, use of the disappearing quorum and of dilatory motions made it possible for minorities to delay severely the business of the House. Determined to prevent such obstruction, Reed ruled that a vote is valid if a quorum is physically present even though a quorum does not vote and that the Speaker need not entertain dilatory motions (Follett, 1974, p. 194). Later during the Congress, the "Reed rules," which consisted of these and several other changes intended to expedite business, were adopted by the House (Robinson, 1930, pp. 223–227).

The proximate reasons for Republican members' support of these changes, which they themselves acknowledged greatly increased the Speaker's powers, lies in the immediate political situation. The Republican majority in the 51st Congress was extremely narrow; thus the disappearing quorum was a serious threat. As Republicans would often be unable to produce a quorum from their own ranks, Democrats could prevent the House from taking action by simply refusing to vote. Given the narrowness of the margin, Republicans were eager to "settle" (in favor of the majority party as was typical of the time) a number of contested elections and thereby increase their margin sufficiently to insure Republican control throughout the Congress. Furthermore, the 1888 election gave the Republicans control of the presidency, the Senate, and the House for the first time since 1875, and Republicans believed they had a mandate to legislate (Robinson, 1930, p. 235). The only way in which the leadership could satisfy members expectations concerning legislative outputs was to change the House rules. Republican members, realizing that, supported their leadership in the rules battle.

Although Reed's counting of a quorum was the single most spectacular event in the development of the strong speakership, that office had been increasing in power since the Civil War (Follett, 1974, pp. 120–121). Furthermore, the majority Democrats, who went back to the old rules in the 52nd Congress, adopted the Reed rules in the 53rd. As the business of the House increased, the old rules made it more and more difficult for a majority to legislate, and Speakers, as majority party leaders, attempted to respond to their members' expectations of legislative outputs by altering House procedures.

Restoring the ability of a House majority to legislate required some rules changes but did not necessitate the creation of such a powerful speakership. Members acquiesced in that development because, within the context of the strong party system that existed during this period, member goal achievement depended on party success. Party fortunes rather than individual efforts determined a member's electoral fate. Power in the chamber was attained through the party; the Speaker appointed all members and chairmen of committees. The policy goal was most likely to be attained through the party: the committees that wrote legislation were formed by the Speaker, the Speaker determined which bills would reach the floor, and floor voting was heavily partisan (Brady, Cooper, and Hurley, 1979, pp. 384–85). Because goal attainment depended on party success, majority members were willing to vest in the Speaker, as leader of the majority party, powers that would increase the probability of party success.

The strong party system made possible a House institutional structure that centralized immense power in the speakership. The party system and the House institutional context in combination produced member behavioral strategies that, to a large extent, were consonant rather than in conflict with leadership-desired behavior. For Republicans, the issues at the center of controversy during the 1890s were not divisive; consequently, the immediate political environment also contributed to members' behavior agreeing with what the leadership wanted.

The resulting leadership strategies were characterized by centralization, including the melding of committee and party systems, by full exploitation of the resources available and by reliance on partisan majorities. Since the

Speaker appointed the committees, the chairmen of the major committees were party leaders. Typically, during this period, the inner circle consisted of the chairmen of Ways and Means and Appropriations and the majority members of Rules. The chairman of Ways and Means also acted as majority floor leader. Quite frequently centralization was taken to the point that the chairmen of these two major committees also served as the majority members of Rules. During this period, Speakers were expected to use their power over committee assignments to build a supportive coalition; especially during their first speakership, they were little constrained by seniority (Polsby, Gallaher, and Rundquist, 1969). Building a supportive coalition often meant appointing the Speaker's chief intraparty rivals to inner circle positions. In the 51st Congress, for example, William McKinley and Joseph Cannon were runners-up to Reed in the contest for the speakership. Reed made the former chairman of Ways and Means and the latter chairman of Appropriations; both received appointments to Rules (Robinson, 1930, pp. 198–200; for other Speakers' committee appointments, see Robinson, pp. 81–82, 102–103, 274).

Building a supportive coalition through the cooptation of rivals worked for Speakers of this period because the norms a strong party system fosters ensured loyalty on the part of the former rivals. The Speaker's power to remove chairmen, of course, served to reinforce the norms. The one example I have found of an inner circle member acting independently of and contrary to the wishes of the Speaker actually illustrates the strength of the norms. In 1898, President McKinley asked Cannon, as chairman of the Appropriations Committee, to sponsor a special defense appropriations bill. The money was necessary, McKinley argued, to prepare for a war with Spain that he feared could not be avoided. Reed was well known to be contemptuous of the jingoists and of those politicians who caved in to them. Cannon's biographer has Cannon describe what happened:

> There was more unanimity, more harmony and more real enthusiasm on the floor that afternoon when I reported the bill than I ever saw before or since. There was no division of sentiment. Everybody was for the appropriation. As I was leaving the Capitol that Monday evening after introducing the bill, I met Speaker Reed. We walked to the street car together and he asked, "Joe, why did you do it?" "Because it was necessary," I replied. "I suppose I should have consulted you, but you had left the Appropriation Committee to my direction, and after considering the whole situation I felt that this was the only way to get ready for the war that is sure to come. We can't prevent it. If I had consulted you and you did not approve I would have introduced the bill anyway without your approval, and that would given you cause for feeling that I had not been quite sincere in seeking your advice."

> "Perhaps you are right. Perhaps you are right," the Speaker commented and we never discussed the matter afterward. (Busbey, 1927, pp. 191–192).

Asked to introduce the bill by a president of his party as an emergency national security measure, supported overwhelmingly by his fellow partisans and by members of the other party, Cannon nevertheless felt a considerable need to justify going against the Speaker.

Given strong party loyalty norms, the cooptation strategy contributed to both party maintenance and coalition building success. Clearly, so long as they were loyal, having members with a power base of their own as part of the inner circle was an asset.

The centralization that the rules and norms allowed contributed greatly to legislative success: it was truly possible for the party leadership to run the House. Reed described his inner circle and the need for and consequence of such centralization:

> I appointed the Committee on Rules in the last Congress, to consist of four men, two of whom were the chairmen of the Committee on Ways and Means and Appropriations...the chairmen of these committees are practically the advisers of the Speaker. They know the great legislation which is to come before the House, and they are in a better position to pass on the order of business than are chairmen or members of other committees. Despite the great outcry which was raised against us in the last Congress, there must be a "steering" committee to arrange the order of business and decide how and in what way certain measures shall be considered (Robinson, 1930, p. 274).

The rules conferred immense powers on the Speaker and norms placed only minor restrictions on their use. As Polsby et al.(1969) have shown, Speakers did not violate seniority capriciously, but they had wide discretion, especially at the beginning of their speakership, and they used it. Speakers could employ the carrot of committee assignments to insure good behavior later during their tenure as well. During the special session that began March 15, 1897, for example, Reed appointed only the Ways and Means Committee. Members might well infer that their committee assignments would depend on how they voted on the Dingley tariff bill (Robinson, 1930, pp. 151–153). The lack of functioning committees also prevented the consideration of some Senate measures that Reed opposed (ibid., p. 357).

Finally, Speakers relied on partisan majorities; their task was more frequently mobilization than piecemeal persuasion and bargaining (Cooper and Brady, 1981, p. 420). A strong party system is likely to result in the election of strongly partisan legislators. In addition to genuine policy agreement within the Republican party, the widespread belief in party government encouraged party loyalty in voting behavior. During the rules fight in the 51st Congress, Reed argued:

Are elections a farce, and is government by the people a juggle? Do we marshal our tens of millions to the polls for sport? If there be anything in popular government it means that whenever the people have elected one party to take control of the House or the Senate that party shall have both the power and the responsibility. If this is not the effect, what is the use of the election? (Robinson, 1930, p. 223)

This equation of party government with popular government is typical of the time. Of course, the immense powers vested in the Speaker were also conducive to party voting. Members were undoubtedly aware that opposing the Speaker could be costly and the Speaker could, if necessary, use his ample resources directly to induce members to support the party position.

For the majority leadership during this period, certainly when it was Republican, coalition building and party maintenance were easy to reconcile. Because of the strong party system, the highly centralized House power structure, and the lack of divisive issues, member strategies in pursuit of their goals, by and large, contributed to both coalition building and party maintenance. The Speaker's great resources, which allowed him to do many valuable favors for members and, by the same token, withhold such favors, could be used to induce such behavior when member self-interest might have otherwise dictated behavior detrimental to leadership success. But because member goal achievement dependend on party success, members' behavior tended to futher both party maintenance and coalition building.

The leadership strategies of Speaker Joseph Cannon did not differ significantly from those of his predecessors of the strong speakership era. In fact, early in his speakership, Cannon made less expansive use of his committee assignment powers than most of his predecessors had (Polsby et al., 1969, p. 799). Why then the great outcry against Cannon and the revolt that stripped the speakership of much of its powers?

The proximate cause was the ideological split between regulars and progressives within the Republican party that developed in the first decade of the twentieth century. The split began to be felt in the House in the 60th Congress (1907–9), Cannon's third as Speaker. In that and in the succeeding Congress, Cannon did use his immense powers against the insurgents. Insurgents lost committee chairmanships and other desirable committee positions (Polsby et al., 1969, p. 799–801; Bolles, 1951, p. 195). Cannon made sure that their legislation did not receive floor consideration. In 1910, insurgent Republicans responded by combining with the minority Democrats to remove the Speaker from the Rules Committee. In the next Congress, the Speaker lost the power to make committee assignments.

Clearly, Cannon had failed disastrously at keeping peace in the family. Strategies that had worked for his predecessors and for him during the early part of his speakership were no longer effective. In order to satisfy the legislative output expectations (which were mostly negative) of the great bulk of his members who were regulars, Cannon had to prevent the insurgents from achieving their policy goals. Concessions of any magnitude to the insurgents would also have been detrimental to peace-keeping among the regulars, who believed that party loyalty should be rewarded and dissidence punished. Yet, by meeting the expectations of the regulars, he frustrated the insurgents' goal achievement. By depriving them of good committee positions and blocking their legislation from reaching the floor, Cannon thwarted the insurgents' achievement of influence and of good public policy. Because insurgents believed their constituents demanded reform legislation, Cannon's actions also endangered their reelection goal.

The party system was changing, and the insurgents were, in part, a result of that change. The direct primary was spreading and insurgents were much more likely than regulars to have won their nomination in a primary (Hasbrouck, 1927, pp. 178–183). The direct primary changed members' reelection calculus. Insurgents, who had often defeated regular Republicans in the primary, believed that their reelection depended more on personal than on party efforts. One of the insurgents' major complaints was that the Speaker prevented them from representing their constituents (Gwinn, 1957, p. 171).

For the insurgents, individual goal achievement no longer depended on party success; on the contrary, behavior conducive to the achievement of the insurgents' goals conflicted with that requisite to party success. Yet the House institutional structure rewarded behavior that contributed to party success and thus, for the insurgents, punished behavior conducive to the achievement of their individual goals. For the insurgents, the group most affected by the changing party system, no behavioral strategies for attaining their goals existed within the strong speakership system. Consequently, the insurgents were willing to combine with the minority Democrats to destroy the strong speakership.

The revolt did not instantly transform the House. Democrats won control in the 1910 elections and were to maintain a majority until the 1918 elections. In the 62nd Congress, their first in the majority, Democrats took the power to make committee assignments away from the Speaker. Although formally that power was transferred to the House as a whole, Democrats actually vested it in their Ways and Means members. Since Oscar Underwood, chair of the Ways and Means Committee, was also majority leader and the real leader of the House Democrats, this vital resource remained in the hands of the party leadership (Brown, 1922, p. 175). As Polsby et al. have shown, seniority was not yet the only criterion for the choice of committee chairmen; in the 1911–1919 period, the party leadership continued to exercise discretion (Polsby et al., 1969, p. 800.)

During the 62nd Congress and then during the Wilson presidency, the Democratic leadership employed the binding caucus as a primary leadership tool. Underwood used the caucus both to obtain broad consensus and to bind members on specific measures. The caucus was also employed to control the committees; a 62nd Congress caucus resolution, for example, directed committees concerning the subjects on which they were to report legislation (Ripley, 1969, pp. 61–62, 142–144).

The Democratic party's unusual policy consensus made such highly centralized leadership possible. In the 62nd Congress, Democrats controlled the House for the first time in 16 years; most had run on a progressive platform and believed they had a legislative mandate. The 1912 elections, which saw Democrats make additional substantial gains in the House and win control of the presidency and the Senate, further intensified members' belief in their mandate. For most Democrats, pursuit of their reelection and policy goals contributed to the success of the party legislative program.

Because the caucus system depended on a strong action-oriented intraparty policy consensus, which is rare in American politics, it could not last. The party system continued to weaken. The realignment of 1896 had produced many one-party areas. The lack of interparty competition encouraged the adoption of the direct primary and the atrophy of party organization. The number of House members who depended on the party organization for their seats continued to decline. The large number of noncompetitive seats made a House career a viable option for many members, and the average length of service increased (Polsby, 1968, pp. 146–7).

A highly centralized party-controlled structure did not serve the needs of such members. For them, individual goal achievement and party success were no longer synonymous. Consequently, a party leadership with resources sufficient to affect significantly members' goal achievement was a threat. The already weakened party leadership could not resist the hardening of the seniority rule. Once seniority became the sole criterion for selection, chairmanships, especially those of the major committees, became positions of power independent of the party leadership.

Decentralization and the separation of the committee and the party systems characterized the House after about 1920. Committee chairmen wielded very considerable power over their committees and were largely independent of the party leadership. "The Insurgents wanted to beat the Czar," a Democrat involved in the revolt against Cannon said in the 1930s. "And what did they do but immediately pave the way for eighteen Czars instead of one" (Hechler, 1940, p. 81). The Speaker's resources were limited, and norms further constrained their use. The progressives' creed that representatives should follow their own conscience and be answerable only to their constituents had won out over older notions of party regularity. Within such a context, party leaders had to rely on the carrot rather than the stick; Speakers could do numerous small favors for members and thereby accumulate a favorable credit balance with members. In building winning coalitions, party leaders had to bargain and persuade much more than their predecessors during the strong speakership era.

From 1931 on, Democrats controlled the House almost continuously. The Depression made the Democrats the nation's majority party, and the large Democratic majorities of the New Deal period believed themselves mandated to respond to the crisis. The result was high cohesion in support of Roosevelt's program. By the late 1930s, however, many members perceived the emergency to be over and the party began to split (Sinclair, 1982, pp. 37–89). The party that Sam Rayburn led was, after World War II, divided fairly evenly between a conservative southern bloc and a liberal northern contingent.

As a result of the committee reorganization of 1946 and the elections of the same year in which large numbers of northern Democrats were defeated, southern Democrats dominated and, by virtue of seniority, would continue throughout the 1950s to dominate most of the committees. The decrease in the number of committees and the long tenure of committee leaders resulted in a highly stable, even rigid system. A small number of committee chairmen wielded tremendous influence. A chairman had almost total control over the organization, staffing, and agenda of his committee. There was little opportunity for rank-and-file members to participate meaningfully either in committee or on the floor.

Sam Rayburn, Speaker during this period, used a highly personalized leadership style. He made little use of formal leadership structures. An informal network of colleagues served as his primary source of information. In coalition building, he relied on personal negotiation with a few key actors. Norms of apprenticeship and deference to senior members contributed to keeping peace in the family. So too, Rayburn believed, did his highly informal and personalized style by providing as few forums as possible for antagonistic elements in the party to confront each other directly. In addition, Rayburn was heavily engaged in doing favors for members, again on a very personal and informal basis.

Liberal Democrats were dissatisfied throughout the 1950s. Conservative southern Democrats, who chaired most of the major committees, frequently blocked legislation the more liberal northern Democrats desired; many also ran their committees autocratically and denied junior members the opportunity for meaningful participation. During most of the decade, the liberals were not sufficiently numerous to do much about their dissatisfaction. But after the 1958 election swelled their numbers, they organized the Democratic Study Group that later spearheaded the reforms. When John Kennedy was elected president they prevailed on Speaker Rayburn to take on the Rules Committee. That critical committee was controlled by a bipartisan conservative coalition and frequently blocked liberal legislation. Rayburn realized that, were nothing done, the Rules Committee would prevent him from satisfying the legislative output expectations of the new Democratic President, of major groups allied with the party, and of the now numerically preponderant liberal segment of his membership. Breaking the conservative grip on the Rules Committee was a prerequisite to coalition building success. Rayburn chose to do so by enlarging the committee because he believed that to be the option least detrimental to party maintenance.

During the 1960s and 1970s, the composition of the Democratic House membership continued to change, with northerners becoming increasingly predominant. Many of these new members came from areas in which party organizations were of minor importance; a number were elected from districts that had previously been Republican. Around the country, party organizations continued to decay, and House members increasingly came to believe that their reelection depended much more on their own efforts than on the party record.

The existing House institutional structure, in which influence was distributed in a decentralized but highly unequal fashion, frustrated these members' goal attainment. The concentration of power in the hands of generally conservative and often arbitrary committee chairmen thwarted liberal members' policy and power goals. A system in which rank-and-file members' participation was severely circumscribed was increasingly perceived by junior members as detrimental to their reelection goal.

House members reacted as they had in 1910. When behavioral strategies for attaining their individual goals are not feasible within the House's institutional structure, members will eventually change that structure. The reforms of the 1970s were aimed at the committee chairmen; both the party leadership and rank-and-file members gained at their expense. But, because most members believed that to attain their individual goals they needed greater autonomy and greater opportunities to participate in the legislative process, the major thrust of the reforms was to expand the opportunities of the rank-and-file.

MAJORITY PARTY LEADERSHIP AND POLICY CHANGE

House majority party leaders, owing their leadership positions to their members, over whose selection they have no control—must concentrate their efforts on satisfying the expectations of their membership and of other significant political actors. Leaders may have policy goals of their own, and these may affect what they do at the margins, but member expectations are the primary determinant of the leaders' policy-relevant behavior. The policy expectations of the membership, of the President if he is a fellow partisan, and of groups allied with the party largely determine which legislative battles the leadership will be involved in and the depth of that participation. The leaders have neither the time nor the resources to engage in significant coalition building efforts purely to satisfy personal policy preference.

Thus, when the party leadership builds coalitions for policy change, it does so as an agent of its membership. When it acts to block policy change, either the membership opposes policy change or is badly divided. The leadership is charged with party maintenance as well as with coalition building; when the party is split, building a coalition for policy change advocated by one segment may be too expensive in terms of party maintenance.

When an intraparty consensus for policy change exists, and especially if the consensus is the result of members receiving strong, clear prochange signals from their constituencies, the Congress will respond with policy change (see Sinclair, 1982). Under such circumstances, the leaders' task is relatively easy. Because members basically agree, successful coalition building requires neither extensive resources nor unusual skill. Because members believe their constituents demand policy change, they perceive coalition building success as contributing significantly to their reelections and, therefore, such success contributes to party maintenance.

The twentieth century has seen three instances of major concentrated policy change: the New Freedom, the New Deal, and the Great Society. The House majority party leadership during Woodrow Wilson's first term was, by all accounts, extraordinarily skillful; but neither of the other two leaderships can be so characterized (see Ripley, 1969, pp. 70–71). During the New Deal and the Great Society, the President assumed the leadership role. Majority party members of the House were willing to let the President do so because the resulting legislative success contributed to their reelection and policy goals. Clearly policy change of this magnitude does not depend on the quality of the congressional majority party leadership.

Such periods of nonincremental policy change are rare because a prochange consensus of both breadth and depth is rare. Under more normal circumstances, a substantial proportion of majority party members agree on some core tenets but disagree on many issues. Such a majority will not pass major nonincremental legislation, but it can produce a credible legislative record or it can be stalemated. The character of the majority party leadership does affect the legislative productivity of such a majority. If the party leadership has extensive resources and the skill to use them, it can get maximum legislative advantage out of whatever intraparty agreement exists. The leadership will, of course, build on such intraparty agreement but, because it possesses resources that it can use for side-payments, it need not rely purely on the extent of agreement among party members. In contrast, a leadership with few resources is largely dependent on the existence of an intraparty consensus. At the extreme, the leadership no longer builds coalitions; winning coalitions are a function purely of the extent of agreement among members and, thus, they exist or do not exist.

It is, thus, during times of normal politics that the strength of the party leadership has a significant impact on policy. The party leadership, whether its resources are ample or meager, works at the margins; it cannot build a coalition from scratch; a core of policy agreement must exist. But, within that constraint, the leadership's resources are an important determinant of coalition building success.

That the leadership's impact is at the margins does not mean it is unimportant. On controversial measures the difference between winning and losing is often only a few votes. Post-1910 leaderships are less likely than their predecessors of the strong speakership era to win such votes. Ironically, as the United States entered the twentieth century, the House "reformed" itself in such a way as to make it less capable of dealing with the complex problems the modern world would bring.

The root cause of the destruction of the strong speakership system, I have argued, was a change in the party system. A major strengthening of the leadership is improbable unless the party system strengthens—an unlikely development. Members over time mold the institution to make it serve their individual goals. So long as the behavior requisite to members' attainment of reelection, policy, and power frequently conflicts with party success, members will not vest in their leadership a significant fraction of the immense power Reed or Cannon had. The current leadership has developed strategies that maximize the effectiveness of its limited resources. Nevertheless, those resources are severely limited when compared to those wielded by majority party leaders during the strong speakership era. As a result, leadership coalition building is more difficult and will be less frequently successful. A larger proportion of leadership resources have to be devoted to party maintenance.

The U. S. government with its division of powers has a strong status quo bias; opponents of change are advantaged and proponents disadvantaged. Political parties are a potential mechanism for overcoming this bias. To be sure, American parties have often been unsuccessful at mobilizing coherent majorities. But no other mechanism has developed for combining and compromising the disparate interests of a majority in the legislature and in the country into broadly acceptable policy. Consequently, when parties are weak, problems must often reach crisis proportion, before a winning coalition for decisive action can be constructed.

REFERENCES

Bibby, John F., Mann, Thomas, and Ornstein, Norman (1980). *Vital Statistics on Congress.* Washington, D.C.: American Enterprise Institute.

Bolles, Blair (1951). *Tyrant from Illinois.* New York: Norton.

Brady, David, Cooper, Joseph, and Hurley, Patricia (1979). The decline of party in the U.S. House of Represntatives, 1887–1968. *Legislative Studies Quarterly* 4: 384–385.

Brown, George Rothwell (1922). *The Leadership of Congress.* Indianapolis: Bobbs-Merrill.

Busbey, L. White (1927). *Uncle Joe Cannon.* New York: Henry Holt.

Cooper, Joseph, and Brady, David W. (1981). Institutional context and leadership style: the House from Cannon to Rayburn. *American Political Science Review* 75: 411–425.

Dodd, Lawrence C. (1979). The expanded roles of the House Democratic Whip system: the 93rd and 94th Congress. *Congressional Studies* 7: 27–56.

Fenno, Richard (1973). *Congressmen in Committees.* Boston: Little, Brown.

Fenno, Richard (1978). *Home Style.* Boston: Little, Brown.

Follett, Mary Parker (1974). *The Speaker of the House of Representatives.* New York: Bert Franklin Reprints. (Originally published in 1896.)

Gwinn, William Rea (1957). *Uncle Joe Cannon: Archfoe of Insurgency.* Bookman Associates.

Hasbrouck, Paul Dewitt (1927). *Party Government in the House of Representatives.* New York: Macmillan.

Hechler, Kenneth (1940). *Insurgency.* New York: Columbia University Press.

Jacobson, Gary C. (1983). *The Politics of Congressional Elections.* Boston: Little, Brown.

Jones, Charles O. (1981). House leadership in an age of reform. In Frank H. MacKaman (ed.), *Understanding Congressional Leadership.* Washington, D.C.: Congressional Quarterly Press.

Kingdon, John (1977). Models of legislative voting. *Journal of Politics* 39: 563–595.

Kingdon, John (1973). *Congressmen's Voting Decisions.* New York: Harper & Row.

Oppenheimer, Bruce I. (1981). The changing relationship between House leadership and the Committee on Rules. In Frank H. MacKaman (ed.), *Understanding Congressional Leadership.* Washington, D.C.: Congressional Quarterly Press.

Polsby, Nelson W. (1968). The institutionalization of the U.S. House of Representatives. *American Political Science Review* 6: 144–168.

Polsby, Nelson W., Gallaher, Miriam, and Rundquist, Barry S. (1969). The growth of the seniority system in the U.S. House of Representatives. *American Political Science Review* 63: 787–807.

Ripley, Randall B. (1969). *Majority Party Leadership in Congress.* Boston: Little, Brown.

Robinson, William A. (1930). *Thomas B. Reed, Parliamentarian.* New York: Dodd, Mead.

Sinclair, Barbara (1982). *Congressional Realignment 1925–1978.* Austin: University of Texas Press.

Sinclair, Barbara (1983). *Majority Leadership in the U.S. House.* Baltimore: Johns Hopkins University Press.

8

Blocking Coalitions
and Policy Change

Roberta Herzberg

> A United States congressman has two principal functions: to make laws and
> to keep laws from being made. The first of these he and his colleagues
> perform only with sweat, patience and a remarkable skill in the handling of
> creaking machinery; but the second they perform daily, with ease and
> infinite variety. Indeed, if that government is best that governs least, then
> Congress is one of the most perfect instruments of government.
>
> Robert Bendiner (1964, p. 15).

For the student of Congress, the underlying tension between legislating
and acting to prevent legislation from being enacted is a familiar one. A
number of institutional features structure Congress and allow minorities to
block majority action. Rules that structure voting and an extensive committee system contribute to the potential for blocking. Every complex and large
political system will need mechanisms to sort out and distinguish among
decisions. The specific form of such rules, however, has clear implications
for policy outcomes. In this chapter, I outline the negative powers in
Congress today, how they have evolved, and their effect on policy making in
Congress.

Although Congress was established in the Constitution as a legislature that
makes decisions by simple majority rule, its decision making process today
is quite complex so that legislation faces a number of potential veto points in
each chamber. A bill might be defeated in the substantive subcommittee(s)
in either chamber; in the substantive committee(s) in either chamber;
through a failure to schedule (by the Rules Committee in the House or by
the Majority Leader in the Senate); or on the floor of either chamber, using
any one of a number of different methods (i.e., power to recommit, defeat of
a rule, defeat of the bill itself). Once legislation has passed through these

many stages in each chamber, it must be considered in conference committee and then reconsidered for final vote by each chamber. Through the adoption of both formal and informal rules, members have made it relatively easy for minorities to protect and promote their interests and to achieve their goals. Members at each stage are able to block undesirable policy alternatives from subsequent consideration. The power to decide what will not be law is common to each.

This chapter focuses on the use of such negative powers, emphasizing their policy implications. Some of the policy effects of extensive reliance on negative decision power are straightforward. Veto powers distributed among the membership make change difficult. Since any of the involved committees or actors can enforce retention of the status quo, the decision process favors existing policy. Policy change, therefore, is slow and incremental. The difficulty in achieving recent budgetary cuts is just one example of the bias towards existing policy. Any administration seeking dramatic changes in existing policy will find Congress a reluctant policy partner, as minorities use their positions in the policy process to protect present policies. Other policy effects of obstructionist behavior are less obvious. The movement to more extensive use of the suspension calendar, omnibus bills, and entitlements are just a few of the recent trends in legislative decision making that may be traced to the cumbersome nature of the decision process.

This chapter first defines negative power, distinguishing between defeating powers and delaying powers. It then discusses those negative powers most prominent in the modern Congressional decision process. Consideration of the evolution of these negative powers is also included. Next, I consider some methods developed to circumvent the obstructionist efforts of minorities. Then I analyze the policy implications of this cumbersome decision process and consider examples of recent legislative struggles.

DEFINING CONGRESSIONAL BLOCKING POWERS

The study of legislative decision making usually focuses on the legislation passed and the politics involved in those decisions. What is not passed is rarely considered systematically. One important reason for this is the difficulty in separating obstruction from simple inaction. There is insufficient time and resources to consider and pass every piece of legislation introduced each year. Some proposals will have to be eliminated simply because of a lack of resources. It is not easy to separate the decisions excluded for a lack of time from those eliminated because of minority blocking power. Although this presents some difficulty, it should not foreclose considering the importance of negative powers in shaping legislation. In this study, I suggest broadly those rules and procedures that can be used to block, and I use recent legislative battles to consider the potential of such decision power. To understand these actions requires a better specification of negative decision power and the ways it manifests itself in the Congress.

Negative power differs from positive decision power in scope and intention. If a coalition of members possesses *positive decision power*, it may impose a favored decision on the entire legislature. If a decisive coalition prefers a particular alternative, that alternative is the outcome regardless of the preference of other members. In a simple majority rule situation, a coalition of 50% plus one would be decisive and could control the outcome without regard to the actions of other players. In the Congress, decisiveness requires more than a simple majority and must include majority coalitions from each of the involved committees and leaders in the process.

Negative power prevents an alternative from being selected and, thus, it limits the available alternatives. Those with negative powers are not able to ensure themselves of any alternative they favor. Rather, they must rely on their ability to prevent acceptance of any alternative they do not prefer, therefore ensuring at least the status quo. Members using negative power may prevent changes that make them worse off but, *on their own*, are unable to bring the policy outcome closer to one they would like. For example, in most cases the House Agriculture Committee can prevent a specific change in the farm price support policy by refusing to report out any proposal for full House consideration. They cannot, however, force the full Congress to accept a policy proposal against majority opposition.

In the Congress, a number of coalitions have the potential to exercise negative power. I define these coalitions as *blocking coalitions*. Members manipulating floor rules, a committee or subcommittee that refuses to report out a piece of legislation, or a Rules Committee chair who fails to schedule hearings may each be considered within the broad category of blocking coalitions. Each can prevent change in the status quo that would result in policy they consider inferior to that status quo. Although each blocking coalition relies on its ability to prevent adoption of inferior policy, they do so through two distinct forms of negative power. The first form is defined here as *defeating power* because it prevents the consideration of inferior alternatives at future stages in the decision process. A committee charged with holding hearings and reporting a legislative proposal can prevent the adoption of that proposal by simply failing to report the proposal. Thus, an agenda committee often relies on its defeating power to block inferior proposals. The second form is defined as *delaying power* because it relies on the power to delay the legislative process to exact concessions, and thereby prevents passage of the exact measure.

Defeating powers in the modern Congress are often located in the committee structure, while delaying powers are primarily used at the floor stage of legislative consideration. Despite the greater finality of the defeating powers, use of such powers usually faces less opposition than the delaying powers. Committees defeat proposals daily without controversy or fanfare. Delaying tactics such as the Senate filibuster often attract considerable attention, as cries of obstruction prevail. Part of the difference in reaction can be attributed to the place in the process where each takes place. Defeating actions take place in committee chambers before the proposal is considered in the more public arena of the floor. Delaying actions rely on the members' ability to use floor procedures and rules to stall consideration of a given proposal. Recent reforms intended to open up the committee process have modified the ability of committees to block policy action without outside attention. Despite these changes, committee members remain better able to block proposals quietly than are those members relying on floor action. Thus, reaction would indicate that delaying tactics are most troublesome, but in fact, in terms of policy, the defeating actions of substantive committees have a greater impact on decisions made.

Two major distinctions between delaying and defeating power suggest greater reliance on the defeating power—first, the latter's greater finality, and second, the amount of effort required to use the defeating tactic relative to the delaying form. Negative committee or subcommittee decisions are rarely overturned, and therefore a defeat at this stage usually kills the proposal. Dilatory tactics, on the other hand, are just that; they delay proposals but do not necessarily defeat them. Since committees of the modern Congress operate with a reciprocity norm, the power they use to defeat a proposal is rarely questioned.[1] Furthermore, defeat requires less effort than does delay. The success of a delaying action is a function of the parliamentary skill of those involved, whereas a defeating bloc usually requires simple inaction or a negative vote in committee. Whenever possible, members rely on defeating power to block action.

Two factors may work to offset sole reliance on defeating power to block. First, the right to participate in defeating legislation through the committee system depends on position in the process. Only those committees with jurisdictional control over a policy area can block selection or consideration of a policy proposal. Members not on the appropriate committee or subcommittee may find that floor tactics such as a filibuster or other delays present the best opportunity to prevent action in that policy area. Thus, delaying power is generally available to a larger group while defeating power is distributed to specific members. Second, floor tactics become increasingly effective as the pressure of limited time increases. Time restrictions tend to increase the effectiveness of delaying tactics, which may in turn make them a more attractive strategy for members to pursue (Oppenheimer, 1985). Thus, the simple threat to delay may be sufficient to insure members of the concessions they seek. At the end of every legislative session, time becomes increasingly scarce, and the threat of even a small delay can result in major changes in policy proposals.

Delaying and defeating powers have not always been used as they are in the modern Congress. As the institutional rules have changed so has dependence on, and use of, one form or another of blocking power. For example, during the era of party government in the late nineteenth century House, defeating power was lodged in the Speakership. Minority interests relied primarily on informal delaying tactics, such as the disappearing quorum, because they had little or no access to other legislative controls. These dilatory tactics were particularly effective as powerful parties organized and maintained obstructionist activity. As the strong Speaker's powers were reduced, defeating powers were distributed more broadly, first to committees and their strong chairs, and later more widely to subcommittees and younger members. As greater numbers acquired access to defeating controls, fewer members had to rely on delaying tactics for an effective voice in the legislative process. Thus, in the modern Congress blocking activity can best be understood through the activity of the committee system.

In the Senate, delaying tactics have also had a privileged position in the decision making process, as the rule allowing unlimited debate gave rise to the filibuster. Although cloture restrictions and reforms intended to reduce use of the postcloture filibuster have constrained this delaying tactic somewhat, senators still have extensive defeating and delaying powers.

With this general understanding of the tactics used in blocking policy change, I examine those mechanisms most commonly used in the modern Congress. Congressional government is first and foremost committee government, so the analysis of the modern congressional blocking logically begins with negative powers in a decentralized committee structure. Although every committee has the potential to block certain proposals, the House Rules Committee has played a special role in blocking activity in Congress and deserves special attention. Next, I consider the policy effects of the Rules Committee defeating power. A third way to organize policy making in Congress relies on partisan organization. Although party organizations have not always been strong in Congress, a cohesive minority party can effectively slow and even stop the majority's legislative program. Moreover, the majority leaders are the primary impetus behind reform efforts to stop obstructionist activity. Delaying tactics on the floor have been effective at various times to create pressure for compromise and are considered as the fourth major form of congressional blocking power.

THE BLOCKING COALITION IN THE MODERN CONGRESS

A number of defeating and delaying mechanisms exist in the contemporary Congress. In this section, the major features of each type of congressional blocking mechanism are examined to determine the form that blocking behavior takes and the ways it responds to members' interests.

Obstruction in a Decentralized Arena

The serial nature of decision making in the Congress has led to nothing short of frustration for many policy makers. Blocking within the committee system in the Congress requires consideration of the continuing effort to transfer legislative control to smaller and smaller subsets of the membership. Division of labor implies that committees, subcommittees, and their chairmen have primary control over legislation within their jurisdictional domains. Committees may amend, add to, subtract from, report unaltered, or not report at all legislation referred to them.

The general method adopted to coordinate the activities of these independent units is a system of "reciprocity." Although the reforms of the early seventies modified committee powers somewhat, most committee members avoid interfering with the work of other members. There is a strong tendency for members to accept the work and expertise of the other committees while expecting the same consideration for themselves. Certain limits on committee members' powers to block do exist. The Speaker's power to use multiple referrals to split up a single bill or package has altered somewhat the committees' ability to claim exclusive control over an entire jurisdiction (Dodd and Schott, 1979, p. 144). Moreover, methods are available to members to discharge a bill from committee or to recommit legislation that the chamber does not find satisfactory. In addition, increased control of the committee assignment and chairmen appointment processes has increased party leaders' control over committee action and limited committee independence somewhat. Members and leaders are usually reluctant, however, to exercise their prerogatives to bypass the committees for fear of upsetting others who might use these same tactics against them at a future date (Fenno, 1973). For the most part, committees have active control over legislation in their area.

Accompanying the norm of reciprocity is the self-selecting mechanism by which committee assignments are made. Biases are inherent in a committee assignment process that seeks to match members with committees that might best serve their constituency or electoral interests (Shepsle, 1978). Those most interested in drafting new or blocking proposed legislation in a particular policy area seek an assignment on the committee whose jurisdiction includes that legislation. With only the most interested members aware of and in control of what does or does not get through the committee system, the biases may kill many bills that a majority of the Congress, if given an opportunity to decide, might deem in the country's best interests.

Committees have a number of ways to block legislation. First, they may delay referring the bill to a subcommittee for consideration. Second, they can refuse to schedule hearings on the bill once it is reported back from subcommittee. Finally, they can simply refuse to report the legislation (Oleszek, 1984). Given the large number of bills introduced and assigned to committee for consideration, many will not be reported out for lack of time. Evidence of blocking action in committees is difficult to gather because the motives of members are hard to determine. In certain cases, the blocking by committees is so extensive that there is little question. One such case is the Judiciary Committee's action with respect to civil rights policy in the 1970s and 1980s. Time and again, the committee has refused to report out antibusing proposals and other conservative civil rights legislation. Progress made by conservative forces has required exceptional efforts to circumvent the committee, such as discharge petitions and legislative riders. Protecting the liberal status quo established in the 1960s civil rights movement presents the best option for a committee faced with a more conservative majority (Herzberg and Champagne, 1985). If committees were representative of the full body, the proposals prevented from consideration by Judiciary might be proposed and passed into law.

Before the reforms of the early seventies, the power to decide which of the bills would be sacrificed fell mainly to the committee chair. Agenda control in the hands of the relatively conservative chairmen led to a number of frustrations. By controlling the flow of legislation, hiring staff, dominating the paperwork, determining the work load of subcommittees and controlling subcommittees' chairmanships, a determined chairman could prevent legislation from receiving full House consideration. Reformers believed that strict adherence to the seniority norm led to an increasingly conservative cohort of chairmen, unresponsive to the demands of the growing liberal constituency in the congressional Democratic Party. Conservative committee chairs became major and visible blocking forces. The Democratic Study Group and the Democratic Caucus sought control over the appointment of chairmen. Although the seniority norm remains the guideline for selecting leadership, it is no longer a hard and fast rule.

Requiring approval of committee chairmen by the Democratic Caucus did much to reduce the obstructionist power of committee chairmen. An accompanying reform, also intended to curtail the powers of the chairmen, served to disperse rather than eliminate the potential use of blocking powers the chairmen once controlled. The advent of subcommittee government divided the powers to block among numerous less senior leaders with mixed effects.

On the one hand, the reforms increased the number of individuals in positions of power and thus increased the number of people who possess blocking ability. On the other hand, the reforms, by dispersing power and placing control of subcommittee chairmen and jurisdictions in the hands of the whole committee caucus, did make these units more accountable to a majority of the committee. These reforms may have served as an incentive to avoid obstructionist behavior. But with the reform, subcommittees have gained independent power beyond that possessed by the full committees (Deering and Smith, 1985). As power devolves to the subcommittee, veto power is controlled by increasingly smaller groups of interested members, increasing the possibility for blocking. In the civil rights example considered above, the increase in subcommittee control has increased the potential for blocking as civil rights proposals are now considered by a House Judiciary subcommittee with a majority membership even more liberal than the full committee.

Reforms of the Senate committee structure have paralleled House changes, but the effects on blocking coalitions have been somewhat different. Senate reductions in the number of power positions available to any single member have dispersed power to junior members. Moreover, efforts to make the full committee chairmen accountable to the party have been undertaken. In 1977, rules were passed that limited to three the number of committee and subcommittee chairmanships any senator might hold. Full committee chairmen would be subject to selection by secret ballot in party caucus. Although similar to House reforms the effects of Senate changes were less dramatic. In part, these changes simply reinforced the existing distribution of power within the Senate. The nonhierarchical nature of the Senate establishes a different starting point for reform. While House members rely on their positions within the committee structure to determine their policy effectiveness, Senators have always had independent sources of control and thus have been less concerned with the formal rules and structure.

The decentralized Congressional structure has made the potential for blocking coalitions a fundamental problem. The division of labor has required that small minorities weed out a great deal of legislation before it reaches a majority decision stage. In part, the increase in staff resources available to members has tempered the ability of committees and subcommittees to make policy and to block other legislation. However, this increase in information through staff has had the opposite effect as well. Now, informed members use delaying and blocking techniques to obstruct legislation on the floor of either chamber. Bills that once might have been accepted as a plausible compromise out of committee are being confronted and blocked. Clearly increased staff resources have led to an increase in the amount of legislation proposed, but may also have increased the potential of members to use negative powers and thereby reduce the amount enacted.

The Blocking Committee: House Rules

Legislation reported by committee must be scheduled for floor consideration. In the House, this in most cases requires a decision by the Rules Committee and then the Speaker. The Rules Committee has attained its power and prestige through its ability to obstruct and defeat substantive legislation. The blocking power of the Rules Committee is most effective because its jurisdictional domain is far broader than other committees. Almost all legislation must pass through this committee, not merely legislation in any particular policy area. It takes little imagination to determine the effect of a strong committee chair, such as "Judge" Howard Smith, rising to the top during a time of relative committee freedom.

The strength of the seniority norm, and the belief that violations in one committee might create a domino effect, allowed the Rules Committee to act in its own interest within fairly broad constraints. Under Smith, the committee managed to hold up legislation without regard to the interests of the majority coalition. "The Rules Committee could simply refuse to schedule key legislation and thus, kill it" (Dodd and Schott, 1979, p. 76). By continually frustrating members of the majority party, including its leadership, Smith exceeded the tolerable limits of his power (passing the point at which members are willing to risk action to gain control over these excesses). As chair of this legislative filter, Smith relied on a wide variety of powers available to him, using overt actions as well as more subtle means to influence the substance of legislation.

The complexity of the House rules affords the Rules Committee great latitude to set the terms of debate. This power permits the committee to influence the fate of any piece of legislation. With its power to grant or refuse a rule, it serves as a legislative "traffic cop." The Rules Committee's power to obstruct has allowed it influence across a far broader jurisdiction than any standing committee in a substantive policy area. The potential for use and abuse of negative powers is therefore greater.

The members of the House have long recognized the need for a scheduling mechanism and have, thus, been willing to tolerate a certain amount of the frustration under these procedures. The revolt against Smith's excesses demonstrates, however, the limits to which the blocking power of any single unit in Congress may be carried without reprisal. In 1961, the committee was enlarged from 12 to 15 members, adding two new liberals favored by the leadership to offset the conservative edge. After enlargement, Smith had to operate under a new threat of restraint. Although many of the chairman's powers were not formally curtailed, Smith was quite aware of his new limitations. In 1963, the enlargement was made permanent. Smith's powers were curtailed but by no means destroyed. With the increase in membership, the majority now held a slim 8–7 margin. Smith's power as chairman and his parliamentary skills allowed him to continue as a power to be reckoned with. The slim majority was simply not enough to guarantee compliance with the majority. In this environment, the House passed the 21-day rule.[2] The 21-day rule acted as a warning to the committee that they might be by-passed if necessary.

In the last ten years the committee has passed into a period of subordination to the majority leadership. Reforms which gave the Speaker the power to appoint all Rules Committee members quite possibly ended the period of Rules Committee obstruction forever. In fact, the committee has become so noncontroversial that it has recently had trouble attracting new members. In 1983, for the first time since its enlargement in the early sixties, the size of the committee was reduced to 13 members. Although the Rules Committee was once a powerful independent blocking force, any blocking done by recent Rules Committees can be assumed to have leadership sanction.

Leadership

Throughout the history of the Congress, leaders have played a crucial role in the success of the blocking action. Minority party blocking often depends on the effectiveness of its leaders and the tactics they select. Alternatively, majority party leaders can be the most important factor in preventing effective blocking action. When strong majority leaders are in control, blocking is more difficult and limited.

Given the powers available to the majority leadership in each body, to block legislation is as possible as to counteract blocking by minorities. In the House, leaders may use the power of referral to split up a bill and refer it to committees they believe will act in ways they approve, or will sit on the legislation and kill it. In the Senate, leaders may use their powers of scheduling to delay consideration of a bill or to block it completely.

Although the majority leadership may use any of its powers to obstruct legislation, the rationale behind increasing majority leadership powers was to enable it to play a positive role in guiding the majority's program through the maze of obstructionist behavior. We would expect the majority leadership to try to minimize blocking behavior. However, as long as the leadership's powers exist, the potential exists to use those powers to obstruct.

The minority party leadership, in contrast, has a greater interest in blocking activity. The classic goal of the minority party has been to thwart the majority's legislative plans. The degree to which the minority leadership will pursue a strategy of blocking at the expense of other activity depends on the degree of party cohesion, the strength of the minority leadership, and the degree to which the goal of changing their minority status to a majority position is feasible.

The legislative task of the minority leadership is less clearly defined than that of the majority leaders. The minority leaders can act on the majority program in a number of different ways. They may simply seek to block proposals of the majority, without offering alternatives, or they may oppose by offering their own alternatives. They may promote bipartisan compromise in one of two ways—either offering compromise alternatives or simply accepting the majority program without change (Ripley, 1967, p. 189).

Minority party members are interested in gaining majority status, and the strategy of minority leadership depends in part on their assessment of attaining that goal. When the minority party believes the prospects of gaining majority status at the next election are good, the leadership may pursue a unified party blocking position to prevent the majority program from passage. When the minority has held a minority status for some time, however, members of the party may no longer perceive their interests tied to the party's goal of attaining majority status (Jones, 1970, pp. 22–24). In this latter case, members recognize that the benefits of positive action will be available to them only if they work with the majority party.

The minority leaders' ability to pursue any of these strategies depends on the ability to maintain party cohesiveness. Moreover, being in the minority position for a long time makes it harder to convince members to sacrifice present payoffs from compromises with the majority for some risky possibility of majority status in the future. The Republican leadership in recent years has been unwilling to separate themselves entirely from the majority to pursue a pure strategy of blocking on the floor. The strategy of working from within for policy change has not been well received by a handful of conservative mavericks, headed by Rep. Newt Gingrich (Ga.). The philosophy of this new branch of the party is that the only way to achieve majority status is to separate themselves completely from the opposition party and to pursue every tactic to obstruct that majority program. Caught between these conflicting interests, minority leadership has sought to maintain a balance between having some legislative impact and blocking the legislative program.

One Man Blocs

> The worst cliques are those that consist of one man.
>
> George Bernard Shaw

Possibly the most frustrating blocking behavior in the modern Congress is that conducted by one or two members, using the rules to delay legislation a clear majority supports. The Senate filibuster is perhaps the starkest example of a single member tying Congress in knots. The use of parliamentary techniques to delay legislation is a time-honored and fiercely protected tradition and a rash of filibusters at session's end is a familiar staple of Senate history. Operating under a rule of unlimited debate, minorities have rarely found themselves without some opportunity to participate. The filibuster is the use of extended debate or dilatory tactics to delay business to defeat or exact major amendments to legislation, or to force unwilling adoption as a price for time to consider other important measures. In 1917, the Senate adopted Rule 22 which limited debate to 100 hours on the vote of two-thirds of the membership. In 1975, the necessary vote was reduced from two-thirds present and voting to 60 Senators, thereby tightening the constraint on minority blocking.

The filibuster of recent years differs somewhat from its earlier counterpart. Historically, an outvoted minority used filibusters to defend threatened interests or to obtain concessions from the majority. More and more, however, this tactic is becoming the tool of one or two senators opposed to a particular bill.

The most powerful weapon used by the militant minority in the Senate is the postcloture filibuster as refined by James Allen (Ala.) in 1976. The major factor restricting filibusters is Senate custom, which limited senators to occasional use of the disruptive tactic. Custom also dictated, prior to Allen's Senate career, that once cloture was invoked, a filibuster was ended. Prior to 1976, no amendment could be considered after cloture was invoked unless it had been formally read or considered read before the cloture vote was taken. In 1976, the cloture rule was reformed to allow consideration of amendments introduced but not read prior to cloture. Allen used this change to extend debate beyond the 100 hours. The ability to introduce amendments after cloture, accompanied by the exclusion of voting time from the 100 hour limit, weakened the cloture rule's potential to stop debate. In the Senate of the last six years, the filibuster threat is fast becoming the most popular way to fight legislation. The more militant members, some liberal Democrats as well as conservative Republicans, have made it clear that cloture alone will not stop filibusters.

The increase in delaying tactics and the abuse of the postcloture filibuster have stimulated efforts to reform the rules governing Senate debate and scheduling. In 1979, Majority Leader Byrd took a hard line in confronting a noncomplying Senate with rules changes. In the reforms, debate after cloture was limited to 100 hours, including votes and any other delaying tactics. Moreover, any sixty senators might limit debate to as little as twenty hours. Byrd used a clause in the rules regarding organizational changes at the beginning of the session to elicit a time agreement on the modified rules changes. Ruling with an iron fist, Byrd was finally able to tighten controls over the delays of the filibuster.

Filibusters in the House?

The tradition of the filibuster as a legitimate and protected legislative tool has historically been limited to the Senate. The rules of the House guarantee a far greater degree of routine and structure; they do not allow for unlimited debate. Recently, the delaying tactics of a few maverick Republicans in the House resemble the Senate more than the House. In an apparent return to the dilatory tactics of the pre-Reed period, the legislative stalemate has grown proportionately with the willingness of a few recalcitrant members to frustrate their colleagues. These new tactics work on the floor rather than in committee or subcommittee sessions where compromises are usually worked out. The tools available to these representatives are far more limited than those of their Senate counterparts, but they have been used exceedingly well.

The tactics most often used in the "House filibuster" are to call for vote after vote on minor matters, to force readings of lengthy sections of a bill, and simply to argue for hours with biting sarcasm and persistence. These tactics are in many ways similar to those used in the postcloture filibuster of the Senate. The conservative mavericks, presently led by Gingrich, have served notice that they are less interested in achieving policy goals than they are in stopping the policy program of the Democratic majority. Given the limits on time, such tactics could prove effective in assuring that many proposals are never heard due to a lack of time.

SANCTIONS ON BLOCKING COALITIONS: LIMITING NEGATIVE POWER

Given the need to pass some legislation, members have created mechanisms to deal with most negative powers. Congress cannot afford to be tied up in knots, and thus alternative methods to pass legislation were adopted and refined as new problems arose. Of the rules to be condsidered here, three are shortcuts around Rules Committee stalling, three can be used to release a blocked bill from any substantive committee, and the last set are directed at delaying tactics on the floor of the House and the Senate. In this section, I examine the asymmetry in the legislative process that has led to the use of legislative shortcuts.

Of those mechanisms meant to circumvent the Rules Committee, the suspension calendar has been dominant in recent years. Other mechanisms designed to deal with the Rules Committee are Calendar Wednesday and the unanimous consent calendar. Each of these calendars allow members to circumvent the normal requirement that a rule be attached before a bill is reported. The consent calendar allows noncontroversial bills to be considered immediately unless a single member objects when the bill is first called or three members object when the bill is called a second time. If more than three objections are heard the second time, the bill is dropped from the consent calendar and returned to the union or House calendar. Each party assigns official objectors to police this calendar. Given the restrictive nature of the consent calendar, little abuse has taken place. However, the possibility does exist in any of these procedures, as we will see with respect to the suspension calendar, to alter the initial intentions of the mechanism.

Calendar Wednesday is an additional mechanism to circumvent Rules; it is rarely used because it is so susceptible to dilatory action by opponents of the legislation it is meant to facilitate. According to House rules, committees may be called alphabetically for the purpose of bringing up any of their bills without further delay. The procedure requires that any action be completed on the same legislative day, and thus, any delay often kills the measure. Since it is rarely successful, few committees care to use it and it is usually dispensed with by unanimous consent.

Under suspension, the House rules are suspended and the bill is considered, with a two-thirds majority required for passage. Debate is limited to forty minutes on each bill and no amendments are permitted. If a bill fails under suspension, it may be considered later under the regular rules of procedure. The major growth in the use of the suspension calendar has led many members to worry about the type of legislation considered under suspension. The major objections stem from increased use of the calendar to consider bills critics feel should be subjected to full debate and amendment. Although the informal norms suggest only noncontroversial bills be considered, the lack of formal restrictions led to serious problems in the late 1970s. Major complaints focused on large authorization bills placed on the calendar, such as a $1.9 billion health centers reauthorization and a $1.49 billion health planning bill. In 1979, the Democratic Caucus established informal guidelines that instruct the Speaker to schedule no authorization of more than $100 million on the suspension calendar unless the Steering and Policy Committee approve.

A number of factors create difficulties with reliance on the suspension calendar. First, debate is limited to forty minutes, all bills are taken up at once, and votes are postponed until the end of debate on all the measures. The result is that most members are not present during what debate does occur and are, therefore, relatively uninformed about any controversy that does exist. Second, and related, the sheer number of bills raised makes it almost impossible for members to be informed on each one. Thus, members who are prone to vote against any bill they believe to be controversial may not be able to catch all of them, even with the information sources available through staff or caucuses. Finally, legislation tends to be relatively complex, composed of many component parts, and consideration of complex legislation under suspension of the rules does not allow a member who supports the bill in general to question or alter sections of the bill through amendment. Many committee chairmen use the supsension calendar to protect sections of bills the committee does not want altered; it is, in effect, attaching a closed rule to a generally acceptable bill to protect particular sections. This is a difficult problem when the issue is something the members cannot afford to oppose openly (Drew, 1978).

The fundamental reason behind growth in the suspension calendar has been the rise of legislative obstructionism in a time of increasing workloads. Most members recognize the need for some method to speed up the legislative system, but many are not convinced the suspension calendar is adequate. Members and leaders are interested in speeding up the legislative process, to eliminate the frustrating delaying tactics so common in recent Congresses.

Most reforms directed at defeating powers focus on the actions of the Rules Committee, the major exception is the discharge petition, the purpose of which is to release a blocked proposal from any House committee, including the Rules Committee. The procedure stipulates that any standing committee may be discharged of further consideration of any bill if a majority insists. The modern rule, first adopted in 1910 and revised in 1935, requires a number of complicated parliamentary steps. Any public bill referred to a committee for at least thirty days or any committee approved bill before the Rules Committee for seven days is eligible for a discharge motion. A petition may be filed with the clerk; if 218 members sign, the legislation is placed on the discharge calendar. After seven days on the calendar, a grace period designed to allow the standing committee to act before discharge, any signer may move that the committee be discharged. If the motion carries, the bill is considered immediately or placed on the House or Union calendars.

Given the difficulty of the discharge process, it is not surprising that it is rarely used to prevent blocks. The threat of a discharge may be enough to spur a committee to action on a bill, but it is doubtful if a method successfully used only a handful of times each decade will pose much of a threat. The discharge petition has been primarily used to release legislation on only the most controversial issues such as civil rights. Members are reluctant to use these exceptional methods to challenge the decisions of the assigned committee except under the most intense of political battles.

Two further methods exist to release a blocked bill from any standing committee, but they are used even more rarely than the discharge petitition. Both methods require working through the Rules Committee. Rules can extract a bill by reporting a rule for a bill that has not been reported by the substantive committee. Used only a handful of times since it was first put in place, the threat of extraction can be enough to prevent some of the worst obstruction. Similarly, a discharge petition can be directed towards the

Rules Committee to call up a bill blocked in another substantive committee. A frustrated member can introduce a rule and then discharge that rule and the initial bill after a period of only seven days. The advantage over the more direct discharge of the standing committee is that it requires only seven and not 30 days to take effect (Oleszak, 1984).

These rules aim at the primary defeating powers in Congress, but recently several methods have been adopted to deal with the delaying tactics prevalent in the Senate and becoming more common in the House. In the Senate, most legislation is brought up under unanimous consent, and therefore, it is simple for any senator to block it. The recent "abuses" of the filibuster have resulted in a number of attempts at reform. The new 1979 cloture rule requires that a final vote must be taken within 100 hours, unless debate is extended by a three-fifths majority vote. Also, a provision prohibits any senator from calling up more than two amendments until every senator has a chance to call up one. It permits waiver of reading of any postcloture amendment if it is available in print for 24 hours, and limits the time at which postcloture amendments may be submitted to be eligible.

In the House, the major reforms have sought to speed up floor action. They include the rules that, first, only one vote may be taken on approval of the previous day's journal; second, a recorded vote on amendment following a recorded quorum call is limited to five minutes; and third, the Speaker should defer or 'cluster' roll call votes on final passage or adoption of the rules, delaying all until the first thing next legislative day. The first vote in the cluster would be granted 15 minutes, and all subsequent votes would be limited to five minutes each. This is the same procedure used for suspension calendar action, and it appears to have limited attendance at much of the debate. It remains to be seen if controversial legislation, open to amendment, will produce similar results. The motivation for these reforms is to eliminate some of the frustrations associated with the delaying tactics the conservatives have used in recent years.

In both the House and the Senate, reforms intended to curb blocking behavior have focused on the more visible dilatory tactics, on the floor and in the Rules Committee. There appears little interest in changing the more extensive blocking activity in the committees except to extend these powers even further. To understand this requires a full understanding of the blocking behavior in the committee system in general. Negative powers are intricately tied to the positive actions in committees. Most committees use their ability to report legislation to prevent introduction of undesirable legislation. To reduce veto control would necessitate removing positive control over legislation from committee members. Taking away committee power to not introduce, or block, legislation must necessarily alter the power to introduce favored legislation. The wave of reforms and the growth in the use of the suspension calendar seem to indicate a recognition that obstructionist behavior is problematic and needs to be curbed. The question remains, however, whether frustration is sufficient to threaten change in the positive policy making powers Congressmen enjoy.

THE POLICY IMPLICATIONS OF NEGATIVE POWERS

These obstructionist behaviors, most widely used in the Congress, generate three major policy effects. The first impact is the status quo bias implied by such a cumbersome decision process. Blocking makes change more difficult and, thus, the policy outcome is more likely to reflect past policy. The second policy effects stem from the problem of restrictive time constraints. Policy analysis and debate take time that is often unavailable, particularly at the end of a legislative session. When deliberation is rushed, unexpected policy consequences are more likely. Wanting to get a policy program in place, members may accept vague legislation because the time to work out the specifics does not exist. To the extent that blocking uses valuable time, it increases these time-related policy problems. Finally, the presence of blocking powers has led to different packaging of legislation for consideration. In structuring legislation, members use the status quo bias available through blocking efforts. Increased reliance on entitlements that place the burden of action on opponents of the policy makes reducing federal spending more difficult. Recognition of the fragmentation in policy has forced an increase in the use of the omnibus bill. If each individual program is considered separately, the blocking powers of committees can be used to protect special policy interests. If packaged as a single large bill, the specifics are more difficult to protect and blocking is minimized. Members are forced to consider the full package. A block in this instance prevents desired policy change as well as the undesirable aspects. I consider each of these effects in order.

Status Quo Bias

The conservative bias in a system that requires agreement by a number of procedural minorities cannot be minimized. To change policy, proponents must convince those members in control of blocking power. If members are assigned to committees on the basis of their own interest in a policy area, we might expect those committees to hold more extreme positions on the policy than a majority of the full Congress. Blocking power in the hands of such interested actors may enforce bias for an extended period of time. Once committee members have achieved a favored position, changing that position will be virtually impossible. To demonstrate the status quo bias that can be maintained by negative tactics, I consider an example where blocking is the rule of policy making and not the exception.

Change in civil rights policy has been rare. A stable policy limiting the rights of minorities was enforced by the negative power of the conservative coalition on the Rules Committee for the entire period from 1937 to 1963. At every opportunity it had to vote on a civil rights issue, the full House passed the bill. But opportunities to vote on civil rights legislation were limited by the obstructionist tactics of the Rules Committee. Of the eight civil rights bills passed from 1937 to 1956, all were brought to the floor by circumventing the Rules Committee using one of the onerous methods outlined in the previous section (Robinson, 1963). The Rules Committee did its best to prevent any change in policy and for several years they were successful. With the expansion of the committee and more regular use of the 21-day rule, the blocking powers of the Rules Committee were limited, and major new civil rights legislation was passed.

The blocking tactics outlined here are available to protect any status quo policies and not simply conservative positions. The House Judiciary Committee, for example, has used similar blocking powers to protect favored civil rights policy almost as successfully as the Rules Committee did earlier. In this case, however, the status quo policy they protect is the liberal civil rights decisions of the 1960s. The late seventies and eighties are marked by a rise in proposals intended to limit civil rights legislation. The Democrtaic majority on the Judiciary Committee has prevented consideration of all but a few of these proposals, and no major change has been achieved by the conservative majority favoring limitations (Herzberg and Champagne, 1985). The important point is that the status quo is the operative policy. Whether conservative or liberal, blocking allows interested members to protect preferred existing policy. The implication of a status quo bias is clear. If policy makers wish to reduce the size of government, they must convince the most interested members to go along. Now the burden of change falls on many of the same conservative forces that perfected these blocking tactics in earlier battles.

Blocking and Time Constraints

Possibly one of the most costly policy effects of obstructionist behavior is that it uses valuable deliberation time in an era of increasing time and work load pressures. As blocking increases it uses a larger part of the limited time now available for legislating. The result is that more policy is made without full consideration of possible consequences. The chances of policy failure increase as members rush to put something in place before the end of the session. Limited time also implies that more of the specifics of the decision processs may be delegated to bureaucrats, often with policy failure the result (Lowi, 1979).

Oppenheimer (1985) notes three points in the session when time is most important: (1) late in the Congress; (2) late in a session or close to a major recess; and (3) when a major legislative issue is pending. At each of these points, policy making is vulnerable to any obstructionist activity, and members are most likely to take action in response to obstruction. One explanation of the increased use of cloture is not that the filibuster is being used more than in earlier Congresses, but rather, that its use is more costly and, thus, it is less likely to be tolerated.

Without time for full consideration, members may find the need to rely on the specialists from committees even more than they do presently. As noted in the discussion of the suspension calendar, legislation rushed through using short cut methods may be even more biased towards the interests represented on the committees and subcommittees charged with consideration.

As time constraints become more onerous with increasing work loads, blocking can be more effective, and members may turn to such tactics with even greater frequency as is evidenced by increasing use of the filibuster (Oppenheimer, 1985). Limited time implies that some legislation will not be considered at all. In the Senate, where delay is so easy, a few members can prevent any action on bills considered late in the session. In this circumstance policy making in effect requires almost unanimous consent, thereby increasing the bias towards existing policy.

Scheduling

The final policy consequence implied by an increase in blocking tactics is found in the packaging of legislation. Two different forms of legislation can be related to the obstructionist nature of congressional policy making. The first is the use of entitlements to fund desired programs such as social security. The second trend in packaging legislation seeks to circumvent special interest blocking through an increased reliance on omnibus legislation.

An entitlement sets up a program on the basis of specific eligibility criteria and not on set funding amounts. As long as a citizen meets the eligibility criteria he or she is entitled to the benefits of the program. Funding levels, thus, depend on economic conditions and not specific congressional decisions. To limit such programs, opponents must change the eligibility criteria. Cutting the program, therefore, requires positive action, while simple inaction maintains the policy. Policy supporters can benefit from the difficulty in positive action by structuring their program as an entitlement. Once in place, these appropriations can be reduced only by positive action that program supporters readily block. Blocking and recent budgetary reforms make initial passage of such programs difficult, but once in place they benefit from the decentralized process.

A second form of legislative packaging, the omnibus bill, has evolved in an effort to minimize the effects of obstructionist activity. Pulling many small program changes into a large budgetary package allows a compromise coalition to form. A compromise bill that calls for cuts in every program is preferred by a majority. Each individual cut is preferred weakly by a majority, but is opposed by an intense policy interest often with blocking power to prevent the reduction. Members are unwilling to give in on their own programs for fear that others will not follow along and their sacrifice will do little to ease the deficit. When policy is packaged as an omnibus bill, members know their sacrifices will only occur if all other changes are also made. The risk of policy change is minimized and members can consider the more general budgetary issues.

President Reagan has found how effective the blocking tactics of Congress can be as he has pursued his policy of reduced government spending. To avoid some of the worst of these problems, successful budgets in recent years have been packaged as single omnibus bills. The 1985 battle over the Senate Budget resolution indicates that support obtained for a general piece of legislation begins to unravel as it is disaggregated and considered by the blocking forces most interested in the specifics of the program. Given the effectiveness of these specialized policy interests, major change may occur only if the debate and decision can be structured broadly.

The cost of relying on entitlements and omnibus legislation is reduced control over the specifics of a policy program. Members cannot make small changes or fine tune the policy. In the area of entitlements there is no control over how much is spent and Congress loses control over budgetary totals. In the area of omnibus legislation, members cannot consider the specifics of programs within the larger package. Any attempt to separate out specifics could make the entire program support coalition unravel.

CONCLUSIONS

Blocking powers are a central part of the congressional decision process. Members use a number of different institutional arrangements and floor rules to prevent undesirable policy, usually without controversy. From committee control over policy proposals to the stalling tactics of a postcloture filibuster, blocking powers are available to all members in a variety of forms. Reformers have extended the number of potential blocking powers even further as congressional operations have become more decentralized.

The consequences for policy change are many. First, policy made today is likely to reflect existing and past policy decisions as members protect favored aspects of the status quo. Second, as time pressures become more acute with increased work loads and more complex policy problems, blocking actions become more effective as tactics for minorities to exact concessions. If the majority wishes to accomplish anything, it must take the interests of every involved party into account. Policy change requires consensus approaching unanimity, particularly at the end of the session. On major issues such consensus may be impossible to obtain. Large problems, such as the deficit, which cannot be managed as a result of repeated blocking behavior, will only be solved if cohesive coalitions can be maintained or the structure that allows such blocking is changed. Finally, time pressure and packaging required to circumvent the many blocking powers in place can produce even greater confusion regarding the details of policy programs. Incomplete deliberation and specification necessary to achieve agreement among broad coalitions create even greater relaince on the bureaucracy to sort out vague policy guidelines and contradictory objectives.

NOTES

1. The reforms of the 1970s challenged committee autonomy so that committee members are aware of limits on blocking behavior opposed by a strong majority of the full body. Committees, however, continue to use their control over policy to sort legislation as to priority. Although they are now more constrained than was once the case, committees retain primary discretion in their respective jurisdictional domains.
2. The 21-day rule allowed any committee-approved bill before the Rules Committee for more than 21 days to be called up on the floor automatically. This device was one of the primary reforms used to limit the obstructionist tactics of the Rules Committee under "Judge" Smith. This rule has not always been available and was only implemented when the leadership could not control the actions of the committee. When it was available, however, its use, or the threat of use, was very effective in taming the obstructive powers of the Rules Committee.

REFERENCES

Bendiner, Robert (1964). *Obstacle Course on Capitol Hill.* New York: McGraw-Hill.

Deering, Christopher, and Smith, Steven (1985). Subcommittees in Congress. In Dodd and Oppenheimer, *Congress Reconsidered,* 3rd ed.

Dodd, Lawrence C., and Oppenheimer, Bruce I., eds. (1985). *Congress Reconsidered,* 3rd. ed. Washington, D.C.: Congressional Quarterly Press.

Dodd, Lawrence C., and Schott, Richard L. (1979). *Congress and the Administrative State.* New York: Wiley.

Drew, Elizabeth (1978). A reporter at large: a tendency to legislate. *The New Yorker,* vol. 54, no. 19.

Fenno, Richard (1973). *Congressmen in Committees.* Boston: Little, Brown.

Herzberg, Roberta, and Champagne, Richard (1985). A comparative study of committee blocking power: the case of civil rights. Paper presented at the Midwest Political Science Association Meetings, April.

Jones, Charles O. (1970). *The Minority Party To Congress.* Boston: Little, Brown.

Lowi, Theodore (1979). *The End of Liberalism.* New York: Norton.

Oleszek, Walter J. (1984). *Congressional Procedures and the Policy Process.* 2nd ed. Washington, D.C.: Congressional Quarterly Press.

Oppenheimer, Bruce I. (1985). Changing time constraints on Congress: historical perspectives on the use of cloture. In Dodd and Oppenheimer, *Congress Reconsidered,* 3rd ed.

Ripley, Randall B. (1967). *Party Leaders in the House of Representatives.* Washington, D.C.: Brookings Institute.

Robinson, James A. (1963). *House Rules Committee.* Indianapolis: Bobbs-Merrill.

Shepsle, Kenneth A. (1978). *The Giant Jigsaw Puzzle: Democratic Committee Assignments in the Modern House.* Chicago: University of Chicago Press.

9

Logrolling in an Institutional Context: A Case Study of Food Stamp Legislation

John Ferejohn

The food stamps program is often cited as an example of logrolling between proponents of two unconnected policies. Allegedly, representatives of agricultural districts, facing increasing difficulties getting their commodities programs enacted, saw food stamps as an opportunity to obtain support by advancing a program that would serve urban districts. On their side, urban congressmen, who were having difficulty getting welfare programs through the conservatively led Congress of the late 1950s, agreed to support farm legislation in exchange for a food stamps program.

As we will see there is abundant anecdotal evidence for this account. Congressmen of all descriptions seem to agree that "deals" were struck at various critical points of the legislative process and, indeed, that the political foundation for the two programs rests squarely on an explicit alliance between urban and rural Democrats. Thus, the logrolling hypothesis appears not only as a plausible theory but also as a true account.

Recent advances in the theory of collective choice[1] appear to cast some doubt on the adequacy of this account of the foundations of the food stamps program. Logrolling relationships are inherently unstable: if a logroll is required to enact some set of bills, then there can be no package of bills that could win a majority against every other package. Thus, while a logrolling arrangement may, because of the procedural rules of the chamber, allow some package of bills to pass in a given session, there will always be other packages of bills preferred to it by a majority. Thus, to say of some particular piece of legislation that "it passed because of a logroll" is no explanation at all. Many alternative outcomes must have been equally possible, and the logrolling hypothesis cannot explain why none of these occurred.

The logic of this argument can be illustrated with a simple example. Suppose we divide Congress into three groups, any two of which can form a majority: northern (or urban) Democrats, southern (or rural) Democrats, and Republicans. Suppose further that the most preferred outcome for the northern Democrats is the enactment of a welfare program and the defeat of farm subsidies (call this alternative A). After that, they would rate passage of both programs (B), then passage of neither (C) and, finally, passage of subsidies and the defeat of the welfare program (D). For southerners the preference ordering is as follows: D is best, B is second best, C is third, and A fourth. Republicans would rank the alternatives in the following order: C is best, A and D are tied for second place, and B is worst.

It is easy to see that this example contains no "majority rule equilibrium." While it is true that alternative B, the passage of both programs, would defeat alternative C, the passage of neither, it could then be beaten by either A or D. In turn, each of these alternatives could be beaten by C. If Democrats seek to create a party-based alliance that would enact B, the Republicans would offer to make a better deal with either the southern or northern Democrats in order to secure their second best alternative (A or D) in place of their worst one.

Evidently, the political support for food stamps and the commodities programs cannot be explained by appeal to the logrolling hypothesis. A logroll is inherently vulnerable to tactical counter-offers by those who are excluded from it. In this case, the Republicans necessarily have both the motivation and opportunity to offer a better deal to either farm or city Democrats. We shall see several examples of this phenomenon when we turn to an explicit consideration of the case.

If there is a sense in which an exchange of votes accounts for the continued existence of these programs, this exchange must be different from the one proposed above. In particular, the exchange, once made, must have the property that none of the agents involved in it can be induced to defect from it. In fact, when fuller account is taken of the institutional setting within Congress, such an exchange may be located.

LOGROLLING IN AN INSTITUTIONAL SETTING

Just how might an institutionally modified logrolling hypothesis work? Students of Congress, working in the tradition of the theory of collective choice, have suggested an answer (Shepsle, 1979; Shepsle and Weingast, 1981; Ferejohn, 1974). While Congress employs majority voting as one method to resolve disagreements, it also contains a complex structure of internal decision making institutions to which it has delegated substantial authority. Choices made in these institutions constrain the influence of chamber majorities by prohibiting the comparison of some alternatives and facilitating the comparison of others. Principal among these internal institutions is the committee system.

Congressional committees, it is argued, have a monopoly right to initiate legislation within their own jurisdictions. Moreover, at least in the House, rules of germaneness require that amendments brought against such proposals are confined to the subject matter of the proposal. When legislation is reported by committees, legislative consideration is managed by committee leaders and is governed by rules of amendment that require that, in the end, the bill as amended be voted up or down. Finally, in the event that legislation produced by the chambers is not identical, the committees may choose representatives to attend a conference to try to resolve the differences. Chamber rules then protect the resulting conference report from amendment.

The power of congressional committees in the legislative process provides opportunities for exchanges of support that span different stages of congressional action. In the case of food stamps legislation, rural Democrats on the committees may exchange their support for food stamps in the committees for urban support for commodity programs on the floors of the two chambers. This exchange of support should not be understood as a symmetric logroll organized in the Congress as a whole. Rather the agriculture committees bundle the two programs, one popular in committee and the other on the floor, into a single legislative package which is popular enough to survive the whole process.

The critical aspect of committee power is found in control over the packaging of the conference report and in the restrictive rules governing consideration of legislation at this stage. If we assume that congressional preferences are the same as in the example given above and that the committees collectively prefer D (subsidies) to B (subsidies and food stamps) to C (neither program) to A (food stamps), the committees would ensure that the conference report contained both programs (B), and it would pass in both chambers. Though D is preferred to B in the committees, D would fail in a floor vote. Moreover, even if congressional preferences are altered in such a way that A beats B, which beats C, which beats D,[2] the conference report would still be B, and it would pass. In this case, A would pass if it emerged from conference but, given the preferences of committee members, it cannot.

The sequential nature of the process guarantees that an equilibrium exists and that it corresponds to the outcome at which the committees obtain their most favorable outcome among those that can be enacted in Congress. In the present case, we argue that the legislated outcome is achieved by packaging congressionally favored food stamps legislation with less popular commodities programs.

Conservative opponents of the two programs might wish to entice either urban or rural Democrats to defect from the alliance, but they lack credible means to do so. They cannot help food stamp supporters get their legislation out of committee or protect it once it reaches conference. From the standpoint of farm state Democrats, while conservatives might promise to support commodities legislation on the floor, farm Democrats must recognize that they would have a strong temptation to break this agreement during chamber consideration. If the committees were to decide not to report food stamps legislation, commodity program supporters would surrender their capacity to persuade Congress to pass commodities legislation.

INSTITUTIONAL DYNAMICS

The theory of committee-based logrolling takes the institutional structure of Congress as essentially exogenous. Any particular distribution of authority among internal congressional institutions facilitates some exchanges and inhibits others. But the structure of Congress is not fixed: the composition and jurisdictions of committees, the powers of chairmen relative to members, and the autonomy of committee processes have undergone substantial shifts in the past quarter century. While many of these changes may be attributed to the impacts of external events, the institutional theory suggests that some of them might be deliberately chosen for political or programmatic advantage.

Specifically, if the institutional account of legislative exchange is correct, we should expect committees to try to claim jurisdiction over popular programs. To the extent that they are successful in this quest, they should try to combine programs that are popular in Congress with others that are desired by committee members but that do not enjoy widespread support. If a committee is able to use its procedural advantages, it gains an ability to build support for desired programs without greatly compromising their appeal. In turn, this ability to build support for programs of interest to members can be expected to increase the relative attractiveness of the committee.

On this account, we might expect a legislative exchange to exhibit a particular "natural history." Initially, a logroll may be conceived outside the framework of committees but, because of the instability of such arrangements, it will require the regular intervention of party leaders to consummate. Such bargains should be expected to be unstable and to be plagued by defections, misunderstandings, and even double-crosses. As leaders of the committee, whose program gains support through the logroll, come to recognize its value, they can be expected to press for an expansion of jurisdiction to accommodate both programs. In this period, we would expect to see disagreements among committee members as to the wisdom of the new course and the terms of the trade. Finally, as jurisdictional matters are settled, we expect to see a tendency to package formally the trade in omnibus legislation. During this phase, the committees will be able to use their full advantages within the structure of congressional procedures and the programs should become quite insulated from external forces.

The history of the food stamps program offers an excellent opportunity to examine the various aspects of the theory of committee based logrolling and its associated institutional dynamics. Enough information is available in the public record to permit a fairly detailed reconstruction of the various legislative exchanges that occurred between supporters of food stamps and supporters of farm legislation. Specifically, we should be able to tell if the structure of congressional preferences was sufficient for the formation of a stable institutional logroll.

Moreover, the length of the historical record will also allow an examination of the hypotheses concerning institutional dynamics. We shall be able to determine if the relationship between farm and food stamps programs begins as an ad hoc exchange that relies on the good offices of party leaders and evolves into a stable set of institutional relationships in which the two programs are merged legislatively so that explicit renegotiation of the terms of trade is unnecessary.[3]

THE EVOLUTION OF FOOD STAMP LEGISLATION

How Food Stamps Became an Agricultural Program

Many observers find it hard to understand why the food stamps program is located in the Department of Agriculture and is supervised by the agricultural committees. The primary purpose of the program is to enhance the diets of the poor, a purpose that seems far removed from the traditional mission of the agriculture department. But, viewed from the perspective of the New Deal legacy, many Democrats envisioned a natural alliance between small farmers and the urban poor. More conservative farmers saw a need to stabilize their markets and dispose of excess production without upsetting prices. In any event, the basic farm legislation provided a sufficiently flexible framework that allowed experimentation with food stamps during the late 1930s.

A number of food stamps programs operated between 1939 and 1943 at a time of high unemployment and farm surpluses. Those programs were initiated by the Department of Agriculture under the authority conferred by Section 32 of the 1935 Agriculture act, which gave the Secretary of Agriculture authority to use customs revenues to dispose of surplus commodities. During the war, as surpluses disappeared and unemployment abated, the programs were allowed to lapse.

Following the war, Congress passed legislation enabling the Agriculture Department to run programs to distribute surplus commodities directly to counties requesting aid. Subsequent legislation allowed surplus commodities to be shipped overseas. But the growth of commodity price support programs, also authorized in the 1935 act, provided a continuing stimulus for farmers to generate surpluses and, as a result, there was continuing congressional interest in finding ways to eliminate surpluses.

Though members of the agriculture committees occasionally proposed food stamp plans during the middle 1950s, the aim of these proposals was to permit the more efficient elimination of farm surpluses. Whatever nutritional benefits might come from such programs were considered to be of secondary importance. In the view of most committee members, the business of the agriculture committees was to support the production of food by American farmers, not to deliver nutritional services to the needy.

During the same period, liberal members were repeatedly frustrated in their attempts to enlarge the nation's welfare system. The main obstacles to these efforts were found in the conservative domination of the three House committees with jurisdiction in the area: the Education and Labor Committee (chaired by Graham Barden, Dem., S.C.), the Rules Committee (led by Howard Smith, Dem., Va.), and the Ways and Means Committee. While Democratic majorities were secure in both chambers, they met with little legislative success in getting their legislative proposals to the floor.

In this light, it is not surprising that initiatives for more broadly aimed food programs came from outside the committees. The agriculture committees wanted to pass farm legislation and needed the support of nonfarm members to do so. On the surface at least, it appeared that urban Democrats might persuade farm Democrats to embrace a program that would deliver benfits to the poor in exchange for urban support for farm legislation. Indeed, throughout the 1950s urban members introduced proposals aimed at using the agricultural surpluses to alleviate nutritional problems in the cities.

While some of these ideas attracted attention in the committees, farm members remained cool to the idea. They were unsure whether they really needed to enter into any such arrangement to secure urban support on farm bills. Perhaps they could continue to rely on the appeals of the leadership for urban support of New Deal farm programs without having to make any specific concessions. Besides, it was not obvious that a nutritional program would be popular enough to secure urban votes for farm bills. Finally, committee members worried that the price of a nutritional program would somehow be "charged against" the farmer, reducing the level of subsidies that could be enacted in Congress. For these reasons, serious legislative action on nutritional programs awaited the appearance of a political entrepreneur who could convince the agriculture committees that it was in their interests to expand their scope.

That person turned out to be a freshman Democrat from Missouri who arrived in Congress during the Republican tide in 1952. Leonor Sullivan (Dem., Mo.) began introducing food stamps proposals during her first term. She represented a St. Louis district, and her interest in food stamps stemmed from exposure to the nutritional problems of her constituents. In the early 1950s, Missouri was one of the few states that did not take part in federally subsidized programs to distribute surplus commodities, and Mrs. Sullivan saw an opportunity to develop a program that might be attractive to the states and popular in city districts.

She tried first to interest her own committee, the Banking and Currency Committee, in a food stamps plan on the argument that stamps were a "currency". When that attempt failed, she approached the agriculture committee with her plans. The House Agriculture Committee held hearings on food stamp proposals during the 83rd and 84th Congresses, but reported no legislation. Though some were attracted by the possibility that a food stamps program might permit efficient disposal of surpluses, most committee members worried that it was a welfare program and that it did not belong in the Department of Agriculture.

In 1957, impatient with the lack of progress in the committee, Mrs. Sullivan offered a floor amendment, authorizing a food stamps program, to a bill extending the PL 480 program. While that attempt failed, hearings were held the next year and the Committee reported out her proposals. Predictably, the bill was bottled up in the conservative Rules Committee and failed to receive a rule allowing floor consideration. Lacking a rule, Mrs. Sullivan brought the bill up under a suspension of the rules (which requires a two thirds vote for passage and permits no amendments), and obtained a majority, though not the required two-thirds, of the House on a roll call vote.

By 1959, it was clear that food stamps were a popular idea in Congress. Not only had a majority of the House expressed interest in the idea, a number of senators were pushing proposals of their own. More important, the chairman of the House Agriculture Committee (Harold Cooley, Dem., N.C.) was attracted to the idea. Aside from the attraction of a program that promised to distribute benefits to a large number of constituencies, organized labor and a number of farm groups supported the concept of linking farm and urban interests through nutritional programs. Of course, there were powerful opponents as well: the Chamber of Commerce, the American Farm Bureau, and the Eisenhower administration were all philosophically opposed to the extension of federal activities into the nutritional domain. Within the Agriculture Committee, most of the Republicans and many of the southern Democrats remained skeptical of extending the committee's jurisdiction outside its traditional agricultural bailiwick.

The 86th Congress was a propitious occasion to launch a food stamp program. The nation was in recession, unemployment was high, and the nation's farms were plagued with large surpluses in many of the basic commodities. Moreover, the Democrats had scored substantial gains in the 1958 elections. Farmers were faced with a substantial problem of surplus disposal, and there was every reason to believe that the food stamps idea would enjoy an unusually warm legislative reception in the heavily Democratic Congress.

The House Committee reported a pilot food stamp plan, on a partisan vote, on August 15, 1959. As in the previous year, there did not seem to be much prospect of obtaining a rule for floor consideration. Thus, five days later, with the support of Chairman Cooley, Mrs. Sullivan moved to tack the food stamps bill on to the proposed PL 480 extension. The amendment carried easily, with Democrats dividing 210 to 28 in favor (nearly all the opposition was from the South). Having survived this crucial legislative test, the House bill emerged substantially unscathed through the remainder of the legislative process.

Though the President signed the bill, the administration took advantage of permissive language in the legislation and refused to set up the program. Even if the program was not implemented in 1959, important steps had been taken. The agriculture committees had embraced the jurisdiction of a nutritional program without any dispute from other committees. Just as important, Chairman Cooley had recognized his need to court urban members with policy benefits. It had become clear that nutritional programs were attractive to northern members and could be useful in this regard. Last, Mrs. Sullivan had assumed an important role in "brokering" arrangements between the Agriculture Committee and urban Democrats.

Things remained in this state until President Kennedy took office in 1961. Soon after his inauguration, he directed the Secretary of Agriculture to institute a pilot food stamps program. Secretary Freeman immediately proceeded to set up pilot programs in eight states. The important features of the Kennedy administration's plan were these. First, stamps were to be usable for any food, not just those in surplus. Second, participant families in the program were required to pay for stamps an amount determined to be equal to what they would have paid for food without the stamps. Moreover, participants were required to purchase their whole allotment. Determination of eligibility was by local welfare agencies, subject to income-based guidelines the Secretary set.

The crucial difference between the Kennedy administration's food stamps program and the earlier proposals was that the provision of stamps to recipients was severed from existence of surplus commodities. In fact, the remaining linkage between food stamps and surpluses was to be statistical and based on studies linking food purchases by participating families to demand for food. Nevertheless, in his defense of the program, Secretary Freeman continued to argue that the program was an efficient way to distribute surplus commodities.

Explicit Vote Trading: 1964–1968

It was in this setting that the Kennedy administration sought to establish the program on a permanent basis. In 1963, Kennedy requested Congress to authorize the food stamps program on a nationwide basis. House hearings were held in June of 1963, but Senate hearings were not held until after President Johnson had assumed office. It soon became clear that the extension of the program would face serious difficulties in the House Agriculture Committee.

Several objections to the President's proposal surfaced in the committee hearings. First, representatives of agricultural districts questioned whether a food stamp plan that was not restricted to surplus commodities could alleviate surplus problems in the basic commodities (wheat and feed grains). Second, the purchase requirement seemed to have the effect of severely reducing the number of people who were qualified to receive aid. In the St. Louis pilot experiment, the number of recipients dropped from somewhat over 60,000 in the direct food distribution program to around 11,000 with the food stamp program. Some of this reduction might have reflected to an improved economy, more accurate determination of eligibility, or unfamiliarity with a new program, but the size of the reduction was large enough to cause concern. Third, and perhaps most substantial, there was a general concern that the Agriculture Department was undertaking a new and broader mission with a new clientele and that this might deflect it from its traditional concern for agricultural producers. Finally, there was some concern that the administration was choosing sites for the pilot program in a partisan fashion.

Following spirited consideration, the committee tabled the food stamps bill on a vote in which five Democrats allied with all 14 Republicans. Liberal members retaliated by persuading members of the Rules Committee to hold up a tobacco research bill that was important not only to Chairman Cooley (who was after all a supporter of the program) but also to Watkins Abbitt (Dem., Va.), the committee member who offered the tabling motion. Within a month, the committee reversed itself and reported a bill (with only three

Democratic defections) that embodied most of the administration's proposals. But it also contained a cost-sharing provision introduced by Albert Quie (Rep., Minn.) that would have reduced the appeal of the program to the states.

Randall Ripley (1969) argues that the Democratic leadership believed that the bill would clear the House, though they were not sure that they had the votes to remove the Quie amendment. While the food stamps program seemed likely to pass in one form or another, the fate of the farm bill remained uncertain. Though a cotton program had been successfully negotiated in both chambers, wheat price supports were still unsettled. The House farm bill had omitted a wheat section because no settlement had been reached, and the Senate had added its own wheat program to the farm bill without House participation. In any event, the whole package promised to be quite controversial when it reached the House floor. The leadership recognized that it probably did not have the votes to pass the farm bill without the support of urban Democrats.

Democratic leaders decided to schedule the two bills together, with the food stamp bill coming up first and the farm bill immediately afterward. According to Ripley (1969, p. 300), the exact terms of the trade were never made formal among either rural or urban Democrats. Rather, it was a matter of creating an appropriate "psychological climate" in which members were made aware of the existence of an agreement and of the ways they were expected to behave. In the event, whether agricultural and urban members explicitly agreed to the matter was probably less important than the fact that President Johnson and the House leadership devoted substantial effort to the task of convincing urban Democrats that the food stamps bill would receive substantial support from rural Democrats and that they were then expected to vote for the cotton-wheat bill.

Republicans attempted several tactical ploys designed to upset the arrangement. First, the Quie amendment was aimed at restricting the number of states and counties that could participate in the plan and would therefore diminish the attractiveness of the food stamps bill to the urban Democrats. This amendment was removed in a critical teller vote. Second, the minority report argued that the bill had substantial civil rights implications that would prohibit states practicing segregation from participating in the plan. Clearly, this argument was directed at southerners, but it failed largely on the realization that the Civil Rights Act itself (which was pending in the Senate) would supersede this section of the bill. Third, Mark Andrews (Rep., N.D.) attempted to shift the program out of the Agriculture Department and into HEW; this motion failed on a teller vote. Had the Andrews proposal succeeded, the institutional basis for coordination between the farm bills and food stamps would have been undermined. Finally, a number of delaying actions were successfully forestalled by the Democratic leadership.

In the end, the bill passed 229 to 189, with Republicans providing only thirteen votes for enactment and the southern Democrats splitting 75–24 in favor of the bill. On the Committee, all the Republicans and three of the southern Democrats opposed the bill on final passage. Subsequent to this vote, the farm bill was considered under a closed rule, which was aimed at prohibiting House alteration of the Senate's wheat plan. The bill passed 211 to 203, with Republicans lining up solidly against it and with Democratic lines holding firm. As might be expected, southern Democratic support for the farm bill was stronger and northern Democratic support was weaker than they had been on the food stamps vote. But, all told, only forty Democrats failed to vote the same way on both bills and of these fourteen were from the South.

The Senate passed the food stamps bill by a voice vote with only minor changes. The House subsequently acceded to the Senate amendments and the President signed it. As enacted, the bill authorized the program to spend a total of $400 million for three years beginning in fiscal 1965. The Secretary of Agriculture was directed to set up programs as requested by localities subject to the availability of authorized funds.

The passage of the 1964 act was the first occasion on which food stamps legislation was part of a logroll. Our reconstruction of the legislative events suggests that the food stamps program was "used" by the Agriculture Committee and the Democratic leadership to secure votes for a controversial farm program. Had it come up for a vote by itself, it would have passed anyway without any special need to court the votes of farm state Democrats. But the program did provide crucial support for a shaky farm bill, and committee leaders emerged from the battle with a new weapon that would assist them in finding urban support for farm legislation. In any case, the food stamps program was to come up for renewal in 1967, without major farm legislation on the legislative calendar.

The food stamps program was up for reauthorization in the 90th Congress, and there were forecasts that it would have a difficult time, with the chief problem centered in the House and its Agriculture Committee. The new Chairman of the Agriculture Committee, W. R. Poage (Dem., Tex.), was decidedly less enthusiastic about the program than Cooley had been.

On the other hand, the program was popular in those districts in which it operated, and members with food stamps programs in their districts might be expected to support it. Indeed, the Secretary of Agriculture had managed to set up programs in more than half of the Republican districts. In her testimony before the Agriculture Committee, Mrs. Sullivan emphasized the constituency benefits: "Every Member of Congress who has had food stamp projects operating for any length of time in his district can tell heart warming stories about the change the food stamp plan has brought to elderly couples on social security, families on relief, and large families...." (House Committee on Agriculture, 1967, p. 77).

Committee hearings in the House revealed deep misgivings about the program. Committee members were not accustomed to dealing with recipients of welfare programs or their representatives and were put off by their insistence on increasing benefit levels. Members were also troubled by reports of administrative irregularities and allegations of abuses of congressional intent. In the end, the House Committee recommended only a one year authorization for $195 million and required that the states pay 20% of the program costs. The committee vote was 19 to 14, with opposition concentrated among Republicans and southern Democrats. On the other hand, four of the six Republicans who had or were scheduled to have food stamps projects operating in their districts supported the majority.

During floor consideration, the cost sharing provision was dropped, but the House defeated an attempt to extend the authorization to three years. The critical vote was on a recommittal motion that would have restored the committee's cost sharing provision. The vote was 173 to 191, with the Republicans providing only 27 votes against recommittal and the southern Democrats splitting 47–32. On the final passage vote, 39% of the Republicans with food stamp projects in their districts supported the program, as opposed to only 19% of those without district projects.

The Senate bill, again without significant opposition, recommended a three year extension at a funding level of $675 million. Because the House conferees were determined to grant a shorter recommended authorization, the conference lasted into the fall. While the bills lingered in conference, frustrated supporters of the program led an attack on a House Agriculture Committee proposal for sale or leasing of acreage allotments for peanuts. The bill was favored by Maston O'Neal (Dem., Ga.) and Page Belcher (Rep., Okla.), both of whom had opposed the passage of the food stamps bill. When it came up under a suspension of the rules (requiring two thirds majority for passage) northern Democrats voted 32 to 87 and the bill failed (208 to 146).

Finally, on September 19, the conferees returned to their chambers, reporting that they had been unable to agree on a compromise. Then, with the conferees having refused to come to an agreement, the Senate unilaterally passed, by voice vote, a compromise bill that extended the program for two years at a level of $425 million. The House then voted 196 to 154 in favor of the Senate proposal. On this vote the Republicans provided 45 votes in favor of the two-year extension while the southern Democrats split evenly.

The 1967 extension of the food stamps program indicated two things.

First, supporters of the program did not need to link food stamps bills to farm bills to gain favorable action on the House floor. Food stamps would pass on the floor without much additional southern support. While members from agricultural districts needed urban votes on the floor in order to pass farm legislation, food stamps had become sufficiently popular in the constituencies of Republican and southern Democratic members that principled opposition to the program had attenuated.

Second, for all the popularity of the legislation on the House floor, the Agriculture Committee still did not support expansion of the program or increases in its autonomy. From the point of view of program supporters, the reason for linking the program to general farm legislation was to get favorable treatment from the committee. If they were to reduce the ability of the Agriculture Committee to affect the program, their need for linkage would be reduced. From the standpoint of rural members, the value of linkage was to obtain support for farm legislation on the House floor, and this purpose would not be served if the program were granted more autonomy. The ability of Agriculture Committee members to get their subsidy programs through Congress depended on maintaining close control over food stamps. The clarity of these calculations was illustrated again in 1968.

In a message to Congress in February 1968, President Johnson asked that the fiscal 1969 authorization be increased from $225 million to $245 million. The Senate acted within a month to approve Johnson's request. Meanwhile, Mrs. Sullivan introduced the administration's bill in the House along with one of her own that provided a four-year open-ended authorization for food stamps. In addition, because she had learned the lessons of the previous session well, she also took some precautionary actions prior to Agriculture Committee consideration of this legislation. On May 8, prior to committee hearings, she wrote letters to the liberal members of the rules committee asking for their help in delaying consideration of a bill extending the 1965 commodities bill. And on May 21 the Rules Committee defeated a motion to send the farm bill to the House floor for debate.

When Mrs. Sullivan appeared to testify before the House Agricultural Committee in 1968 in favor of putting the food stamp program under an open-ended authorization, she took a much less deferential tack than she had in previous testimony:

> a vast number of the members of the House of Representatives believe, with me, that this program must be allowed to expand and not just a little bit but a lot....I asked last year for an open end authorization, as I did also in 1964. Both times you tried instead to kill the program, then reluctantly let it continue on a short string....If we have to have another fight, let's have it. But let's make it clear now what the issue is going to be: If you won't let us use this method to assure adequate diets for all needy Americans, wherever they live, then many from urban

areas are simply going to withhold our votes on farm legislation until we again make another "deal" as we had to do in 1964 (House Committee on Agriculture, 1968, p. 13).

Whatever their intended purpose, the effect of these words on the committee was inflammatory. There were several heated exchanges during which members deplored the practices of logrolling and expressed resentment at being threatened by urban members. Republican members, eager to assist their Democratic colleagues, suggested that perhaps the real problem was that food stamps was a welfare program and that it properly belongs in the HEW under the jurisdiction of the Education and Labor Committee. The hearings also reflected an increasing testiness on the part of committee members directed at the "ungratefulness" of recipients and an increasing concern over the uses to which food stamps were being put.

In the event, the committee reported a bill providing a one-year authorization of the program at a level of $245 million and rejected Mrs. Sullivan's proposal (moved by John Dow, Dem., N.Y.) by a 4 to 26 vote. The committee also added provisions to exclude college students and strikers from receiving food stamp benefits.

Mrs. Sullivan was once again required to wage her battle on the floor of the House. She had already persuaded liberals on the Rules Committee to hold up a rule for a proposed one-year extension of the 1965 farm bill so that it would come to the floor immediately after the food stamps bill. When the food stamps bill reached the floor, she offered an amendment to provide a four-year open-ended authorization for the program, arguing that "we have had to fight constantly with the Committee on Agriculture to get any bill at all out of that committee. When a bill does come out it usually comes out crippled and we have to correct it on the floor...we should not have to go back to that committee every single year to plead with them to let this program survive" (*Congressional Record*, July 30, 1968, p. 22–24).

After the House added a provision to her amendment prohibiting the distribution of food stamps to strikers and college students, it accepted the Sullivan amendment by a 227 to 172 vote. The vote breakdown was similar to those in previous congresses: northern Democrats voted 144–2, southern Democrats 51–32, and Republicans 32–138. But the important fact was that the fate of Sullivan's language was in the hands of the conferees, and they were to be appointed from the agriculture committees of the two chambers.

For a month, the House was unable to agree to a conference. Once assembled, however, the conferees rapidly forged an agreement. They agreed to extend the authorization of the Food Stamp program to the end of calendar 1970 (when the authorization of the general farm legislation was to expire); they increased the authorization for fiscal 1969 to $315 million, and provided $340 million for fiscal 1970 and $170 million for the first half of fiscal 1971. The conferees also dropped the House provisions prohibiting strikers and college students. The conference report also contained a minority dissent from Republicans who were interested in retaining this last provision and, when it was reported to the House, was subjected to a motion to recommit prior to final approval. The recommittal motion failed 159–187, with Republicans providing all but 43 of the positive votes. The conference report then passed easily.

The events of 1967 and 1968 revealed a structural weakness in the vote trading system that had evolved. As program opponents forced the parties to more and more floor votes, the bargain began to seem more and more precarious. There was an increasing sense among the parties to the trade that the other side was not keeping its part of the bargain. As a result, there was a tendency on each side to try to hold one program hostage to the other. Threats and ultimatums were typical of this period because the logroll required the parties to withstand powerful temptations during floor votes. By the time Congress had completed action on the 1968 reauthorization, members of the House committee had begun to see the advantages of consolidating both programs into a single bill in order to take fuller advantage of the power of committees to hold their bills together during legislative consideration.

By 1969, it was clear that House Agriculture Chairman Poage was attracted to the idea of considering food stamps and farm legislation within the same bill: he opened the 1969 hearings by introducing a bill that would provide permanent open-ended authorizations for both programs. By linking the programs, the committee would have the best chance to obtain urban votes for its farm programs. Moreover, unless the two programs were packaged in the committee, Poage would have to go to the leadership or to the Rules Committee if he needed to have the programs considered together on the floor. Finally, by linking the programs inside the committee, the committee majority would obtain the greatest leverage over the contents of both bills.

Neither the Senate nor the administration seemed to share Poage's enthusiasm for linkage. Liberal dominance in the Senate permitted passage of food stamps bills that were far more generous than any that would emerge from the House. Program supporters in the Senate had already demonstrated that they would not tolerate any efforts by rural members to hold the program hostage to their interests.[4] If such a ploy were attempted, they would simply ignore the committee proposals on the floor.

President Nixon, for his part, preferred to coordinate the food stamps program with his own welfare proposals and, ultimately, to place the program in HEW. Any linkage between the programs would ultimately stand in the way of rationalizing the nation's welfare system in the ways to which Nixon was committed.

In the event, the House committee did not report a food stamps bill until August, 1970, almost a year after the Senate had passed authorizing legislation. Surprisingly, in light of the events of the previous year, the food stamp authorization was kept separate from the general farm bill (which had been reported out of committee a couple of weeks earlier). As reported, the bill extended the authorization of the program through fiscal 1973, permitted the establishment of uniform eligibility standards, and lowered the minimum purchase requirements. Unlike the Senate bill and the President's request, however, the committee did not permit provision of free stamps to the poorest recipients. Moreover, the committee bill imposed a work requirement on those who received food stamps and also required the states to pay a portion of the costs.

Following a minor skirmish in which food stamps supporters on the committee attempted further liberalization of the program, the committee bill was enacted substantially as written. The provisions of the conference report were close to those in the Senate bill. The work requirement was weakened, state cost-sharing was omitted, and free stamps were provided for the poorest income group. The conference report was accepted by voice vote in each chamber. Once again it was clear that food stamps were sufficiently popular in the Congress as a whole that extension of the program did not require an explicit bargain with farm Democrats.

Between 1970 and 1973, congressional action on food stamps took place on two fronts. First, President Nixon's proposed welfare reforms, which were sent to Congress in 1971, would have had severe consequences for the food stamps program. While those proposals were not enacted, revisions in the social security system had the effect of "cashing out" food stamps benefits for beneficiaries of old age or disability insurance.

Second, congressional efforts centered on Agriculture Department appropriations legislation. The expenditure level of the program grew steadily to $2.5 billion in fiscal 1973. As had happened earlier, occasional amendments were proposed to the House appropriations bill that would restrict the provision of food stamps to strikers. These attempts were beaten back by the leadership in concert with the appropriations committee.

During the same period, amendments to restrict the maximum payment under the commodity programs were also being moved on the appropriations bill (such amendments had passed the House in 1968 and 1969, but had been omitted in conference). These amendments passed the House in both 1971 and 1973; in this last year, the conference accepted the subsidy limitation (though it permitted leasing and sale of acreage allotments, which largely nullified the effect of the limitation).

Omnibus Legislation: 1973-1981

By 1973, when both food stamps and the farm program required reauthorization, both agriculture committees agreed on the wisdom of combining the programs. The bitter disagreements and recriminations that regularly occurred when the programs were based on "expectations" of reciprocity were seen as avoidable if the legislation was considered in one piece. The experiments with the unification seemed satisfactory and both committees were ready to take this final step in the alliance of the programs.

In 1973, the program was again up for reauthorization, and there was renewed attention to the issue of providing stamps to strikers and other "nonneedy" recipients. The Supreme Court had just struck down a provision of the previous authorization that restricted the provision of stamps to households containing unrelated individuals on the grounds that it was too broad and violated due process (*USDA v. Moreno*). These concerns dominated the committee hearings. Not only did conservative committee members repeatedly express their concerns over what they saw as abuses, but a number of business groups appeared to complain that the provision of benefits to strikers discouraged the early settlement of strikes. It was clear, early on, that conservatives would make an effort to impose new restrictions on the program.

In May, the Senate reported a unified bill to extend the authorization of the commodities programs and the food stamps program for four years. The food stamps authorization was for about $2 billion per year, down somewhat from previous levels.[5] The farm bill restricted subsidies to a level that was adequate to get farmers to "target price" levels; this amounted to a reduction of subsidy payments relative to the previous program.

The Senate bill passed easily, but passage in the House required clearing two familiar hurdles. First, conservatives were determined to impose restrictions on the provision of food stamps to strikers, and Republicans (led by Findley and Conte) would try, once again, to put a maximum on payments under the commodity programs. Each of these motions was likely to command majorities on the floor and, if either passed, the enactment of the overall bill was no longer assured.

In order to forestall these efforts, urban Democrats (led by Foley and Bob Bergland, Dem., Minn.) agreed to oppose the subsidy limitation in exchange for southern support in defeating the limitation on food stamps for strikers. When the bill reached the floor, Bergland successfully moved that the cotton sections of the bill be dropped (which would make a subsidy limitation nongermane). The Senate bill, of course, had a cotton section, and so it could be added into the conference report. While the vote was close, there were enough urban Democratic votes to complete this first part of the transaction.

But three days later, when William Dickinson (Rep., Ala.), moved to prohibit the distribution of food stamps to strikers, the coalition failed to hold. After a complicated series of maneuvers, Dickinson's motion passed in several votes by very close margins (the closest being 208 to 207). At this point, Conte asked to reconsider the Bergland amendment, which had passed a few days earlier, and this time it failed on a voice vote. The agreement had completely unraveled, and what was left of the bill was unattractive to both wings of the Democratic party. There was hope, however, that what was done could be undone in the conference.

The conferees were able to reconcile all but one of the differences between the two bills: the antistriker provision. The conference report retained the subsidy limitation but with the provision that acreage allotments could be sold or leased. It also provided for an open-ended authorization for both programs for four years. Poage, more concerned with getting an agriculture bill than with retaining the House's position on the antistriker amendment, moved to accept the Senate version of the conference report.

The rules of debate on conference motions permitted just one amendment (normally a motion to recommit), and so Poage himself, to forestall a recommittal motion, moved that farmers be urged to produce as much as possible. Faced with the choice of accepting Poage's motion or having no bill, the House passed it by a vote of 252 to 151, with a large majority of southern Democrats supporting their party's position.

Thus, by taking advantage of relatively restrictive House rules for considering a conference report, the two programs survived intact. But it was clear that such maneuvering depended not only on restrictive rules but also on Democratic control of both the Senate and the House Agriculture Committees. Moreover, unless House consideration of the programs was linked either in the committee or by the leadership, Democratic majorities in both chambers might be thwarted if Republicans were able to induce coalition partners to defect on separate votes. If any of these conditions changed, the quality of the two programs could shift substantially.

Once again, legislative treatment of food stamps reverted to the appropriations process. But the political climate had shifted in several ways that proved relevant to congressional treatment of the program. First, President Nixon had raised congressional resentment with his efforts to withhold funding from various authorized programs. There were concerns among program supporters that the food stamps program was among those suffering from presidential attention. Second, the recession of 1974 and 1975 led to vastly increased enrollments in the program: the number of participants increased by seven million as unemployment figures rose and program costs increased apace. Third, Congress had shifted in a much more Democratic direction as a result of the 1974 midterm elections: there were now more than 290 Democrats in the House, and the new members were not inclined to be deferential to the President or to committee leaders. In fact, in the Democratic caucus vote, Poage failed to retain his chairmanship and was replaced by Tom Foley. Finally, by the time the budgetary implications of the program expansion had become clear, a new and more conservative president was sitting in the White House.

While the sources of these changes were largely extraneous to the program, they were bound to affect its consideration. The effects were felt over the next several years. House Republicans continued to try to place restrictions on eligibility for the programs (aiming still at strikers and students). And in strategically related actions, they continued to press against subsidies to Democratic farm interests. Thus, Silvio Conte conducted a campaign against funding for Cotton, Inc. (an organization charged with conducting cotton-related research), and Conte and Findley both continued to push for restrictions on maximum payments.

Outside of the appropriations process, the most significant congressional event was triggered by President Ford's attempt, in November 1974, to impose regulations to increase the price that recipients would have to pay for stamps. In its first legislative measure, the 94th Congress overturned the proposed regulations by a vote of 374 to 38 in the House and 76 to 8 in the Senate. The vote margin, coming soon after the onset of the recession, indicated the general popularity of the program at a time when it served nearly 20 million people. On the other hand, the rejection of the president's efforts was made easier by the fact that the program was scheduled for reauthorization at the end of fiscal 1976.

While Ford's efforts were thwarted in Congress, they set the stage for congressional reauthorization. The President was determined to push for increases in stamp prices and restrictions on eligibility, and he submitted legislation to that effect in late 1975. Agriculture committees in both chambers held extensive hearings on these bills as well as on numerous others focused on the reformation of the program. There was a significant congressional concern about the overall size of the program (which was running at about $6 billion a year) as well as with alleged fraud and abuse. On both scores, there appeared to be a general belief that many program benefits were going to those who were either not "really" poor or who had chosen voluntarily to receive low incomes.

The Senate Agriculture Committee, under its new chairman Herman Talmadge (Dem., Ga.), reported legislation in March of 1976 fairly close to the administration proposals. It would have restricted eligibility to those below the poverty line, tightened the assets test, removed students and the voluntarily unemployed, increased the purchase requirements, and imposed criminal penalties for fraud.

However, as in 1969, the committee lost its bill on the floor. McGovern and Dole (Rep., Kan.), proposed a substitute bill that weakened many of the stringent requirements of the committee bill. By incorporating a purchase requirement in their substitute, they persuaded Talmadge, who believed that the unamended committee bill would lose on the floor, to support their amendment. Having divided the conservative opposition, the substitute amendment passed on a 52 to 22 vote. Southern Democrats divided in favor of the substitute by a 12 to 4 margin, while the Republicans split on the proposal. The bill emerged from the Senate in April of 1976.

The House Committee had a much more difficult time with the administration's proposals. In August, after extensive hearings and markups, the committee, by a 21–19 vote, finally reported legislation. The committee report contained 141 pages of supplemental and dissenting views: some liberal members complained that the proposed bill was "punitive," while the Republicans generally regarded it as "lax" and a "nonreform." As reported, the committee bill contained somewhat more restrictive eligibility tests and higher purchase requirements than did the Senate legislation.

No doubt, because the committee was so divided, the Democratic leadership decided to keep the bill off the floor. It was clear that the legislation would be heavily rewritten through amendments during the debate and that it would require the newly elected members of the class of '74 to vote on a number of controversial provisions just before their first attempts for reelection. In the event, the leadership decided to wait until after the elections to act on the program.

While Congress wrestled with program reform proposals, the Ford Adminstration tried again to restructure the program through administrative action. In February 1976, it proposed regulations that would have cut over five million recipients from the rolls and reduced expenditures by $1.2 billion. This attempt at administrative reform was blocked in the courts by injunctions against the implementation of the proposed regulations. Thus, reauthorization and reform of the program had to await the outcome of the presidential election of 1976.

By the time President Carter took office, there was broad concern in both chambers over abuses of the program. In addition, liberal members of both chambers still wished to eliminate the purchase requirement, which they regarded as a barrier to participation in the program by the poorest people in society. In addition, the rapid growth of the program during the recession of 1974–75 continued to cause broad congressional concerns about its costs. Moreover, President Carter had pledged an overhauling of the welfare system that would, eventually, have eliminated the food stamps program altogether.

Congress had also undergone a significant demographic transformation in the first half of the decade. A substantial fraction of the members of both chambers had arrived since 1972. The turnover in the House was reflected strongly in the makeup of the House Agriculture Committee, where two-thirds of the members had arrived since 1973. While most of the committee members represented agricultural constituencies, only 12 of the 31 committee Democrats represented southern districts. Thus, the committee was markedly more liberal than it had ever been before and, under Foley's chairmanship, it could be expected to support the food stamps program.

If the prospects for favorable committee consideration of the food stamps program were better than they had ever been, the outlook for farm legislation in Congress was bleak. Recent surpluses had driven grain prices down. Thus, higher support prices promised to be extremely expensive and to face substantial opposition in Congress and from the President.

But the President had pledged to introduce legislation to reform and consolidate the welfare system, legislation that would eliminate the food stamps program altogether. Thus, the administration asked only for a two year open-ended reauthorization to carry food stamps through the period while Congress considered his welfare reform proposals. Administration proposals included eliminating the purchase requirement and tightening eligibility restrictions in various ways. The estimated impact of these reforms was to increase program participation by about one and half million people.

The Senate considered these proposals together with a number of other food stamps bills in the context of the general farm bill. The central issue in Senate consideration was the purchase requirement. Conservatives, led by Talmadge, argued that to eliminate the purchase requirement would complete the transformation of food stamps from a nutritional to a welfare program. In the end, the Agriculture Committee, over Talmadge's objections, eliminated the purchase requirement on an 11–6 vote. It also rejected proposals to remove strikers and students from the program, and turned down a proposal by McGovern, Dole, and Humphrey to extend the program authorization for five years (on a 9 to 9) vote.

When the bill reached the floor, Carl Curtis (Rep., Neb.), moved to reinstate the purchase requirement. His amendment lost by a vote of 31 to 64, with the northern Democrats providing 39 of their 40 votes against the motion and southerners splitting 8 to 10. McGovern, Dole, and Humphrey were also unable to persuade the Senate to extend the authorization for five years, losing 46 to 49, on a vote on which Southerners split 4 to 13, Republicans 13 to 25, and northern Democrats, 29 to 11. Finally, the Senate rejected Strom Thurmond's (Rep., S.C.) proposed restriction against the provision of stamps to strikers. Again, the majority of southern Democrats voted with a majority of Republicans for Thurmond's position.

While the administration's proposals on food stamps survived the Senate intact, the Senate passed a much more liberal farm subsidy bill than the administration had proposed and was threatened with a presidential veto. The price support level for wheat was raised to a level that promised to double the costs of the program. The crucial vote was on an amendment offered by Edmund Muskie (Dem., Me.) to reduce the target price for wheat to the level Carter had proposed. It lost by a 46 to 50 vote with wheat state Senators dividing 19 to 1 against. The Agriculture Committee split 15 to 3 against Muskie's motion.

The House Committee's bill provided for a four-year, open-ended authorization for food stamps. Under this proposal, both food stamps and the farm program would expire in 1981. Like the Senate bill, it eliminated the purchase requirement, tightened eligibility, and imposed new work requirements. A proposal to eliminate strikers lost by a 17 to 24 vote in committee, as did one that would have eliminated strikers and students (16–24). A Republican attempt to cash out the program and transfer it to HEW was also easily defeated. Finally, an amendment proposed by Dawson Mathis (Dem., Ga.), which limited the authorization to a level starting at $5.8 billion and increasing to $6.2 billion over the four years, lost 19 to 26.

In an action thought to be critical to enactment, Chairman Foley made a determined effort to hold wheat price supports to levels acceptable to the Carter administration. He narrowly prevailed, on a 23 to 22 vote in committee, to keep the wheat support level at the level of the administration's proposal.

When the farm bill was reported from committee it did not contain the complete food stamps title, because the committee had not yet completed markups on that section by the May 15 Budget Act deadline.[6] Thus, a special rule was required that allowed this title to be substituted for a "truncated" title of the bill. When Chairman Foley proposed this amendment, Robert Bauman (Rep., Md.) complained that "it was the height of cynicism to marry the food stamp program to the agricultural bill...it was done for purposes of political logrolling to gain votes for both bills" (*Congressional Record*, July 26, 1977, p. 24973).

The debate on the agriculture bill lasted more than two weeks, with twelve hours devoted to food stamps. Much of the debate centered on the commodity programs. Over the course of House consideration, it became clear that the House would accept an increase in the target price for wheat to the level the Senate had voted. When it also became clear that Carter would not veto the bill over this issue, Foley capitulated to wheat area representatives.

In the end, the House accepted the bill with only minor changes to the food stamps section. The principal modification was the acceptance (242–173) of the Mathis amendment, which had failed in committee, to limit progam authorization levels. The vote breakdown was familiar: Republicans voted 129 to 12 for the amendment, southern Democrats 65 to 23, and northern Democrats 48 to 138.

The conferees were able to reach accord on the food stamp provisions of the farm bill without difficulty. Both bills contained the major administration proposals, and the disagreements were largely insubstantial. The most significant disagreement was resolved when the Senate conferees agreed to the House's provision for a four-year "capped" authorization in place of its own recommended two-year open-ended extension. Thus, as had become the practice, the commodity and food stamp programs were extended for the same period and would both come up for reauthorization once again in 1981.

While the program had received a four-year lease on life, a number of congressional events touched the program in the following years. First, congressional support for the Carter administration's welfare proposals disintegrated in 1978 as the costs and divisiveness of such reforms became evident. Not the least of the reasons for this was the determination of the Agriculture committees to keep control of the food stamps program and not to allow it to disappear into the jurisdiction of the Ways and Means and Finance committees. Second, the spending caps imposed in the 1977 Act turned out to be unrealistically low, forcing Congress to enact emergency legislation in 1979 and 1980.

Omnibus consideration of the 1973 and 1977 agriculture bills had allowed the committees fuller use of their procedural advantages during floor consideration. Because both farm subsidy and food stamps legislation would go to the same conference, defections on floor votes were less damaging. Repairs could be made in the conference and returned to the House under a closed rule. Moreover, by retaining a hold on food stamps jurisdiction, the agriculture committees increased their chances of prevailing on increasingly controversial agricultural bills. Finally, it seemed that omnibus consideration actually helped the committees hold onto their nutritional jurisdiction in the face of assaults from House conservatives as well as from Presidents Nixon, Ford, and Carter. Chairman Foley, like Poage before him, successfully fought off proposals for welfare reform and rationalization, relying on the support of rural as well as urban members.

In retrospect, however, it seems that the political basis for the external assaults of the 1970s was really quite weak. The secure Democratic dominance of Congress did not allow conservative opponents sufficient strength to attempt to drive the programs apart. This situation changed in 1981.

The Conservative Attempt to Separate the Programs

The election of President Reagan and the substantial Republican gains in Congress that accompanied it presaged a major shift in the strategic setting for food stamps legislation. The President was pledged to remove the "undeserving poor" from the welfare rolls and was determined to tighten eligibility requirements and reduce benefit levels throughout the welfare system, including food stamps. There was broad support for these efforts in the newly conservative Senate; indeed, some Senators wished to go even further by reinstating the purchase requirement in the food stamps program.

The agricultural committees had also undergone important shifts. Most significantly, the new chairman of the Senate committee was Jesse Helms (Rep., N.C.), a long-time opponent of the program. In the House, Tom Foley gave up his agricultural committee chairmanship to become the Democratic Whip, leaving the leadership of the committee to E. de la Garza (Dem., Tex.), and the stewardship of the food stamps program to Fred Richmond (Dem., N.Y.). Moreover, long-term trends in committee assignments had produced a shift in the House committee favorable to nutrition programs. For the first time in its history, the House was more disposed toward the program than the Senate. The implications for the program were altogether unclear.

Leaving aside appropriations legislation, events conspired to offer the new administration three separate opportunities to affect the shape of the program. In addition to enacting a reauthorization for the program, the administration had decided on a bold use of a reconciliation procedure to force Congress to modify the authorizations of existing entitlements programs.[7] Finally, as in the previous fiscal years, emergency legislation was required to allow the program to provide full benefits during the current fiscal year.

Legislative action was most urgent on the matter of emergency funds for fiscal 1981. As everyone knew it would be, the 1981 authorization turned out to be insufficient to carry the program through that year. The authorized funding level had been set at $9.7 billion as a political convenience and with the general understanding that additional legislation would be required. Facing the prospect of administrative reductions in benefit levels, Congress agreed to a $1.7 billion increase in the authorized level of the program.

While Senator Helms stalled the bill for several weeks, hoping to use it as a vehicle for imposing cost reductions on the program, the administration indicated that it preferred rapid enactment of a simple increase in the authorization. Helms agreed, knowing he would have plenty of chances to modify the program when marking up his committee's authorization bill as well as in reconciliation legislation.

Both committees considered food stamps legislation in April and May. The principal issues centered on the authorization "caps," eligibility of those with relatively high incomes, the purchase requirement, what would count as income in determining eligibility, indexing of benefits, and stamps for strikers. Lying beyond these issues was a more fundamental one: would the program remain within the ambit of general agricultural legislation or would it be split off from the farm bill and considered by itself.

Though Senator Helms had introduced the food stamps authorization as a part of the farm bill, the committee ended up by reporting separate legislation. The committee bill tightened the income tests for eligibility, reduced the deduction that could be considered in calculating income, reduced benefit levels to most recipients by postponing indexing, prohibited food stamps for strikers, and imposed spending caps of $10.9 billion, $11.3 billion, $11.3 billion, and $11.8 billion in fiscal 1982 through 1985.

When Helms tried to move beyond the administration position and reimpose the purchase requirement, the committee, led by Dole and Leahey (Dem., Vt.), refused. Helms also failed in attempts to add further restrictions to the program in committee. Finally, after rejecting another attempt to reintroduce a purchase requirement, the Senate accepted the committee bill in early June.

While it finished its hearings in early May, the House committee chose not to report a separate food stamps bill but to wait until it could agree on general farm legislation. Consideration of that bill was controversial because of administration objections to many of the proposed farm subsidy programs. Richmond and de la Garza were determined to keep the farm program and food stamps together and not allow the administration to force separate congressional treatment.

In the meantime, many of the restrictions on the food stamps program in the Senate bill were written into the Reconciliation Act for fiscal 1982. When enacted, that measure reduced the maximum income permitted, reduced deductions in computing eligibility, eliminated food stamps for strikers, and increased the number of administrative regulations that would affect the states and recipients, but it did not determine the funding level of the program. The administration estimated that these changes would remove more than a million people from the program and reduce benefits for virtually all participants.

While the Reconciliation Act introduced restrictions on the program, they would apply only for a single year unless they were written into the reauthorization act. The Senate passed farm legislation in September, having already completed action on a food stamps reauthorization three months earlier. The Senate bill was close to the administration's recommendations and would result in substantial reductions in subsidies. The House did not begin general debate on its legislation until after the authorizations for the farm and food stamps bills had expired.

The debate on the bill took seven days and resulted in damaging amendments to almost all of the commodities programs.[8] The food stamps section authorized a four-year extension with funding levels of $11.3 billion, $11.2 billion, $11.1 billion, and $11.3 billion. After rejecting a Republican attempt to limit the authorization to two years, on a 180 to 193 vote, the bill finally passed.[9] The House bill provided higher support levels than the Senate bill for dairy products and for wheat and feed grains.

The conferees considered the two Senate bills and the omnibus House bill together. Most of the disagreements arose from the administration's determination to hold to fixed budgetary targets. This strategy made logrolling among the commodity programs difficult and resulted in substantial reductions in them. The conference report recommended deep cuts in the House recommendation and extended the food stamps program for only one year while the commodities programs were given a four-year extension. The food stamps authorization contained many of the Senate-passed restrictions. In particular, it tightened eligibility, reduced benefits, eliminated food stamps for strikers, and limited the authorization to $11.3 billion for fiscal 1982. The report did not emerge from Congress until the very end of the session. The House vote was 205 to 203 and reflected the opposition of farm Democrats.

By the end of the first session of the 97th Congress, it was clear that the Reagan administration had made a serious and partly successful assault on the farm-city alliance. It had forced a wedge between general farm legislation and the food stamps program so that food stamps had to come up separately for a new authorization in 1982. And, by imposing relatively tight funding limits on agricultural legislation, it had undermined the omnibus approach that characterized it. The fruits of this shift were found in the reduction of funding for commodity supports and a reduction in the size and scope of the food stamps program.

On the other hand, the administration did not succeed in getting Congress to give up on "target prices" in the commodity programs. Moreover, the reductions in the food stamps program, while serious to many of the recipients, represented a temporary halt in the growth of the program. Finally, as the events in the two committees illustrated, President Reagan had not succeeded in breaking up the agricultural "political economy." Senator Dole, chairman of the Nutrition Subcommittee of the Senate Agriculture, Nutrition and Forestry Committee, together with committee Democrats, successfully blocked Chairman Helms' attempts to make larger cuts in the program both in committee and on the floor.

In the House, the marriage of farm programs with food stamps seemed stronger than ever. Faced with a conservative Senate and a Republican President, farm state representatives recognized their dependence on urban Democratic votes if they were to have any hope of keeping their subsidies. Even if they failed to retain supports for all the crops they wanted, urban Democratic votes represented their only chance to keep subsidies on the basic commodities. The Agriculture Committee insisted on keeping the two programs together, voted to keep food stamps and farm programs on the same authorization schedule, and delegated leadership on food stamps issues to Richmond and de la Garza. The result was that committee recommendations were much more liberal than either the Senate or the President would accept.

The real test of the resilience of the food stamps program in the face of administration efforts to circumscribe it would come in 1982, when it again came before Congress for reauthorization. The administration, intent on keeping the program on a short leash, recommended a one-year authorization of $9.6 billion with new restrictions aimed at reducing eligibility of the working poor. These restrictions included reducing allowable deductions for computing income and increasing the "benefit reduction rate."[10]

The committee hearings in 1982 focused most attention on program administration. There was much concern over high "error rates" in determining eligibility compared to those of other programs such as AFDC.[11] Both committees agreed to require the states to reimburse the federal government for errors in excess of 5%. Moreover, conservatives argued that one reason for the laxness in administration is that the states, the administering units, had no stake in the program at all. Helms persuaded the Senate committee to provide block grants to the states, in place of funds for food stamps, to allow them to set up their own nutritional programs free of federal guidelines.

Both the House and Senate committees included their recommendations in the fiscal 1983 agriculture reconciliation bill, which included amendments to the dairy and wheat and feed grains programs. By tying the programs together, once again the committees had thwarted the administration's effort to force separate congressional consideration. In the Senate, Senator Dole again led the committee in moderating President Reagan's requests for program cuts. The committee bill included a three year authorization, which would put food stamps back on track with the farm programs, of $11.9 billion, $12.3 billion, and $13.2 billion. The principal savings in the committee's proposals were obtained by delaying the indexing of program benefits. When the Senate adopted the omnibus reconciliation bill, it accepted the committee recommendations without amendment.

The House committee bill was somewhat more generous than the one that emerged from the Senate. After rejecting increases in the expenditure levels proposed by Dan Glickman (Dem., Kan.), it provided for a three-year authorization ($12.6 billion, $12.9 billion, and $13.7 billion). When the reconciliation measure reached the floor, the Republicans made several attempts to force reductions on the food stamps program. After an attempt to prevent the adoption of an essentially closed rule for the bill[12] failed on a party line vote, the Republicans lost in two attempts to revise the food stamps section.[13] At that point, the bill passed with solid Democratic support.

Most of the disagreement in the conference centered on the agricultural provisions of the two bills. Over administration objections, the conferees recommended a number of changes in the wheat, and feed grains, and dairy programs. The food stamps provisions were more acceptable to the President. The conferees simply split the monetary differences between the two bills and dropped Helms' amendment to set up nutritional block grants. The two chambers rapidly accepted the conference report and sent it to the White House.

By the end of the 97th Congress, the political status of food stamps had become clear. The program had received a three-year authorization and would be brought up for reauthorization in 1985 along with the commodities program. While disagreements remained over its administration, size, and the incidence of benefits, representatives of agricultural constituencies in both chambers were determined to keep the programs together. Urban members seemed happy with this arrangement too, as long as the committees continued to report out favorable legislation and protect it in conference. Besides, both parties could appreciate more clearly than ever that the arrangement allowed both programs a substantial degree of insulation from electoral events outside their control.

DISCUSSION

We have argued that the history of food stamps legislation can be seen as the institutionalization of a committee-based logroll. In the 1950s, rural congressmen controlled the agricultural committees and faced the problem of securing support for commodity programs. At the same time, urban Democrats had been unable to force welfare legislation, for which they had majority support in both chambers, through the House Committees on Rules and Ways and Means. This configuration of powers and interests permitted the construction of a coalition that reached across the stages of the legislative process. It depended vitally on the agricultural committees reporting legislation acceptable to urban Democrats and eliminating restrictive amendments in conference. Had they failed to do so, the committees might have lost control of the program altogether. For their part, northern Democrats were obliged to provide some support for farm programs on the floor of the House of Representatives.

In the early years of the alliance (the events of 1964 and 1967 are good examples), this arrangement was carried out on an ad hoc basis. The exchange of support was based on a negotiated explicit logroll. The vote divisions reflect the successes and failures of the arrangement. The Republicans repeatedly tried to induce the southern Democrats to place restrictions on the food stamps program in the committee, and to persuade northern Democrats to limit their support of commodities programs. Occasionally they succeeded in the House, but leadership interventions prevented Republican strategies from prevailing. Moreover, on occasion frustrated urban members showed a willingness to retaliate against agricultural legislation when they thought the House committee was not sufficiently supportive.

Later as the program expanded and as resentments grew over the failure of one side or the other to keep up its part of the bargain, committee members moved to merge the programs in an omnibus bill. The merger of the programs permitted fuller use of the institutional features of committee consideration: the programs would automatically be considered together on the floors of the chambers, and the conference report could restore whatever damage might be done to the bills in either house. Explicit assistance from the leadership was no longer required. Republican tactics in this period remained the same as before, but now committee leaders had to make sure they had an attractive omnibus bill to bring to the floor. This consideration, together with the evolution of committee membership toward more liberalism, generally sufficed to ensure favorable consideration of food stamps legislation.

The election of Ronald Reagan and a Republican Senate in 1980 provided a fortuitous opportunity to see how well established the omnibus approach to farm and nutritional programs had become. Despite the persistent attempts of the administration to undermine the "political economy" of agriculture, members of the two committees—Republicans as well as Democrats—worked to keep the programs consolidated. The failure of the Reagan administration to separate the programs suggests that supporters of the two programs had become convinced that the legislative success of farm programs rested on the omnibus approach.

The evolution of the food stamps program over three decades illustrates some important features of the "logic" of coalition formation in American politics. To a greater degree than in other advanced democracies, administrative programs in this country are required to maintain substantial legislative popularity to survive and expand. While strong presidents or clever party leaders in Congress may be able to sustain a program without a substantial constituency for a while, eventually political tides will erode it and wash it away. Unless a popular basis can be built, the politics of the program will remain contentious and divided by ideological issues. This truth has faced the proponents of agricultural and welfare programs since the New Deal.

Moreover, this case study also suggests something about the evolution of political institutions in a legislative setting. The endemic instability of logrolls induces members to invent institutions that embody and stabilize agreements. Once these institutions appear, other social processes may come into play to reinforce them. For that reason, institutional change may be a largely irreversible process in which successive layers of institutions pile one upon the other, each layer formed in response to the strategic problems created, in part, by the deeper ones.

Acknowledgments. Thanks are due to David Fallek for assisting with some of the research reported here and to Matt McCubbins, Roger Noll and Ken Shepsle for helpful discussions.

NOTES

1. The seminal paper on logrolling is by Kadane (1966). See also Tullock (1970; 1981) and Schwartz (1981).
2. Such a configuration of preferences that seems to correspond more closely to the actual case.
3. The following account is drawn from public documents, such as the *Congressional Record*, committee hearings and reports, and from the *Congressional Quarterly Weekly Reports* and the *Congressional Quarterly Almanac*. Aside from specific quotations, repeated attributions to these sources are not made.
4. In 1969, Senator George McGovern (Dem., S.D.) and his Select Committee on Hunger managed to substitute their own legislation for the food stamps authorization proposed by the Agriculture Committee.
5. The program lost more than a million recipients to the SSI program when states were permitted to provide cash instead of food stamps to those who qualified for SSI benefits. These people were then prohibited from receiving stamps.
6. The Budget Act of 1974 requires that authorization committees report any legislation that will necessitate an increase in expenditures by May 15. If they fail to do so, their legislation may be modified on the floor by a simple "point of order." This requirement may be circumvented in the rule under which the legislation is considered.
7. The Budget Act provided for the use of reconciliation legislation to bring congressional statutes into line with the final Budget resolution. The President decided to use reconciliation to force the legislative committees to reshape legislation to fit with the first resolution.
8. For example, the House voted 250 to 159 to repeal the acreage allotment system for peanuts and 213 to 190 to reject sugar price supports. In both cases, majorities of Republicans and northern Democrats combined against most of the southern Democrats. The same fate would have befallen tobacco price supports, but for the intervention of the Democratic leadership in persuading a bare majority of northern Democrats to support their southern brethren.
9. The division on the motion to restrict the authorizations to two years was as follows: Republicans favored the motion 159 to 9, northern Democrats opposed it 12 to 127, and southern Democrats split 9 to 57. The final passage vote was by a 192 to 160 margin and was, again, along party lines.
10. The rate at which marginal benefits are taxed as income changes.

11. Testimony before the committees by the GAO established the error rate in the food stamps program at 13%. For AFDC the comparable rate was around 7%.
12. The rule permitted only two amendments to the bill: one directed at the farm provisions and the other at the food stamps sections.
13. The closest vote came on a substitute offered by Representative Wampler (Rep., Va.), aimed at revising the food stamps sections of the bill, which failed 181 to 210. The division pitted the Republicans (who voted for the provision 144 to 31) against the northern Democrats (8 to 136), while splitting the southern Democrats (29 to 43). The other vote was on a motion to recommit with instructions offered by Delbert Latta (Rep., Ohio); it too lost on a party vote.

REFERENCES

Ferejohn, John (1974). *Pork Barrel Politics*. Stanford: Stanford University Press.

House Committee on Agriculture (1967). Hearings to extend the Food Stamp Act of 1964 and amend the Child Nutrition Act of 1966, March 15 and 16, 1967, p. 77.

House Committee on Agriculture, (1968). Hearings to amend the Food Stamp Act of 1964, p. 13.

Kadane, J. B. (1966). On division of the question. *Public Choice* 13: 47–54.

Ripley, Randall B. (1969). Legislative bargaining and the Food Stamp Act, 1964. In Frederic N. Cleaveland et al. (eds.) *Congress and Urban Problems*. Washington, D.C.: The Brookings Institution, 279–310.

Schwartz, Thomas (1981). The universal instability theorem. *Public Choice* 37: 487–501.

Shepsle, Kenneth A. (1979). Institutional arrangements and equilibrium in multidimensional voting models. *American Journal of Political Science* 23: 27–59.

Shepsle, Kenneth A. and Weingast, Barry R. (1981). Structure induced equilibrium and legislative choice. *Public Choice* 37: 503–519.

Tullock, Gordon (1970). A simple algebraic logrolling model. *The American Economic Review* 60: 419–426.

Tullock, Gordon (1981). Why so much stability? *Public Choice* 37: 189–202.

Part

V

Conclusion: Pulling the Pieces Together

10

Congress and Policy Change: Issues, Answers, and Prospects

Leroy N. Rieselbach

The twentieth century may be, as some observers have claimed, the "age of the executive," but the message does not seem to have reached the United States Congress. The American national legislature can, when its members collectively determine to do so, act with dispatch. It may often defer to executive initiatives, but it may also move decisively to define and enact its own priorities. Congress' decisive passage of the Reagan administration budget and tax bills in 1981 and its insistence on its own tax and jobs legislation in 1982 and 1983 illustrate the broad range of policy actions it may undertake. Nor is this recent history atypical: Past public policies also bear the imprint of Congress (Chamberlain, 1946; Moe and Teel, 1970; but see Huntington, 1973). Policy change, for better or worse, can and has come *from* Congress.

The problem, then, is not whether Congress can make policy, but when, why, with what processes, and under what conditions it chooses to do so. The chapters in this volume address some aspects of this issue, and this essay attempts to weave these threads and a reading of some relevant literature into a broader tapestry. We want to specify the circumstances that induce Congress to alter the content of public policy. To set the stage, we need to define what we mean when we talk of policy and policy change; we need, that is, to be clear about what it is that we are attempting to explain, about our "dependent variable." Next, we would like to learn about the antecedent factors—in Congress and outside—that incline members to entertain policy innovations, the "independent variables" that relate to change in what the government does. This concern leads to a focus on the impact of the electoral process (nominations, campaigns, and voting), external forces (public opinion, pressure groups, and political executives), and internal structures (committees and subcommittees, parties, rules, and informal norms) on congressional policy making in general and on policy change in particular. Finally, we would benefit from an integration of our findings into a "model" of policy making—in reality a model of representation—that would both organize what we know and point out areas in need of further exploration.

A review of recent research pertinent to policy change in Congress suggests the obvious: Congressional scholarship has made enormous progress in unravelling some of these mysteries, but some aspects of these matters remain shrouded in uncertainty if not totally obscured by ignorance. What follows is an effort to indicate some problems in studying congressional policy formulation and alteration that we have solved and some that remain in need of resolution.[1]

POLICY AND POLICY CHANGE:
PROBLEMS OF DEFINITION AND MEASUREMENT

Policy, at the most elemental level, is what the government does (or does not do); more formally, it is the "allocation of value," in Easton's (1965) famous phrase. Such a definition, while perfectly plausible, does not prove particularly helpful in trying to picture precisely what the government does or in seeking to specify the players and processes that produce policy or policy change. Implicit in virtually all policy analysis, but explicit in only some of it, is the notion that there are different types of policy and that "different politics," diverging political patterns, characterize these varying species of decision making. If this is the case, students of policy need to be precise about the sorts of programs they seek to describe and explain. At present, the literature lacks definitional clarity.

This is not to deny that there exist some basic, and useful, distinctions, which serve as reasonable starting points for analysis. For example, Bachrach and Baratz (1970) separate policy decisions from "nondecisions"; they make clear that *not* to act, which preserves the status quo, has as profound implications for policy as any act of innovation. Unfortunately, it is often difficult to determine when inaction is conscious—the result of concerted efforts to keep some item off the political agenda—or inadvertent—the consequence of disinterest. Another dichotomy of policy types contrasts tangible programs, which allocate material benefits or impose costs, with "symbolic" rewards, which confer psychological gain (see, e.g., Edelman, 1964, 1971). Here, too, it may be hard to know whether (or when) policy, particularly of the symbolic variety, is intended to provide psychic satisfaction or, in reality, does so. A third pair of policy types—incremental and nonincremental—represent the poles of a continuum (cf. Lindblom, 1980 and Wildavsky, 1984, with Schulman, 1975, and Light, 1981–82). The polar extremes make easy cases: The space program, "putting a man on the moon," is surely a nonincremental program; adding a dime to the minimum wage is just as surely incremental. The problem comes, of course, in the intermediate ranges: In what category does a "major" increase in funding for an existing program belong?

The most influential effort to identify policy types—and the political patterns that accompany them—is Lowi's (1964, 1972) identification of distributive, regulatory, and redistributive "arenas of power." (For attempts to clarify and elaborate the Lowi typology, see Salisbury, 1968; Salisbury and Heinz, 1970; Ripley and Franklin, 1984; and Hayes, 1981). Different primary actors, divergent decision-making settings, and varying influence relationships characterize the separate arenas. For example, congressional committees and subcommittees are the chief architects of distributive policy, play a less dominant role with respect to regulation, and are minor participants in redistributive decisions, which are made on the House and Senate floors (Lowi, 1964). The intuitive logic of this schema has brought it much renown, but the lines between the categories are not always easy to draw. Quite the contrary, it is often difficult to assign a policy to a given type. The problem is compounded because policies may alter in character both in the short run and over the long term.[2]

The foregoing are all "content-free" definitions. Each points to a set of attributes that specifies a given policy type. None provides a set of objective measures that permits reliable assignment of particular programs to partic- ular categories; none distinguishes, conceptually or emprically, among specific issues—foreign, domestic, or subtypes of either. Each relies on the insights, often substantial, of individual scholars. In contrast, Clausen (1973) proceeds inductively to define content-specific issue domains. He scales roll call votes in five distinct "policy dimensions"—civil liberties, international involvement, agricultural assistance, social welfare, and government man- agement—that persist over six Congresses.[3] The problems here are, in a sense, the obverse of those encountered previously. If the more subjective definitions make precise classification problematic, an objective approach may eliminate some of the most interesting cases. Is the matter of grain sales to the Soviet Union an agricultural assistance or an international involve- ment item? It is, perhaps, both, or the former to some legislators and the latter to others. If it is *not* unidimensional, however, it may not fall in either domain, and the analyst may be deprived of the opportunity to investigate a particularly interesting sort of policy question, one that pits, in the abstract at least, constituency concerns against the broader "national interest."

Finally, these are not mutually exclusive typologies. Any policy can fit logically into more than one of these schemes. A redistributive policy can be either incremental (a modest increase in social security tax rates or retirees' benefits, for instance) or nonincremental (national health insurance). A civil liberties policy (mandatory busing for school desegregation) may be material or symbolic, depending on local conditions; it would be tangible where actual practices changed, but psychological in areas (without black residents) unaffected in any real sense. Decisions and nondecisions could, presumably, fall in any policy arena or issue domain.

None of this is to denigrate these typologies. Their widespread acceptance and use testifies eloquently to their value. The point, of course, is that if we seek a better understanding of the ways Congress makes policy, it is imperative that we have a solid grasp on what it is we want to explain. We should move beyond these broad categories, seeking more rigorous indicators that promote genuinely comparative analysis of policy formulation in the House and Senate, in the various committees within a single chamber, or over time. And what is the case for policy in general is also true for *policy change*, which is no more than a special case of policy making. Even more refined standards may be required to identify when a policy—of whatever type—is sufficiently different from a prior program to merit attention. In any case, we need to establish, as precisely as possible, what policy and policy change mean before we can assess the processes with which Congress makes and changes policy.

DETERMINANTS OF POLICY CHANGE

Fortunately, some instances of policy change—particularly nonincremental and redistributive types—are sufficiently obvious that observers can agree that a major departure from the status quo has occurred. Indeed, much research on Congress has, indirectly at least, sought to account for the policy-making activities of the legislature. From such work, there emerges the simple view that elected legislators make and alter policy in a political context defined both by forces outside Congress and by the structures and processes of the institution itself. We have learned much about the impact of elections, executives, lobbyists, and internal practices of Congress on law making, but in each general area we encounter major obstacles to developing a fuller understanding of congressional policy making and policy change.

Elections: Paradoxical Problems

Research on congressional elections has been a growth industry for political scientists (Hinckley, 1981, and Jacobson, 1983, summarize the findings). Here, it is sufficient to note that this scholarship presents a paradox: citizens, as individuals, seem curiously indifferent to policy (issues) in their voting (Kinder and Kiewiet, 1979; Mann and Wolfinger, 1980), responding more to local conditions than to national tides; at the same time, however, the aggregate election returns suggest a direct influence of national political trends, particularly the state of the economy and the standing of the president in the polls (Tufte, 1978; Kernell, 1977). Thus, modest levels of issue voting in the constituencies alter the probabilities for policy change in Washington to the extent that new members, with new programmatic goals, take seats in Congress.

Jacobson and Kernell (1983) provide the link, the strategic behavior of elites, that resolves the paradox. The important campaign figures—the candidates and those who support, especially fund, them—*assume* that voters react to national conditions. When those trends are favorable, attractive challengers choose to run and elicit strong support. Such challengers emerge disproportionately in the party that national conditions favor, but they tailor their campaigns to the constituencies in which they run.[4] Candidate and contributor decisions, thus, "so structure the vote choice that electoral results are consonant with national level forces even if individual decisions are not" (Jacobson and Kernell, 1983, p. 3). Though citizens choose in consequence of local conditions, the choice they confront reflects reality, and the set of verdicts they render in the country at large translates that reality into the aggregate congressional returns. Incumbents, of course, win most often, especially in House races, because the circumstances that encourage strong challengers occur so seldom.

If elections, in this fashion, bring those inclined toward policy change to Congress, they may also send more subtle signals to sitting members. Indeed, there is a modest controversy about the relative significance of various mechanisms that induce policy change. One line of argument suggests that "personnel turnover," the replacement of old by new members, especially when an incumbent of one party yields a seat to a member of the opposition, is the prime engine for new programs (Brady and Lynn, 1973; Brady, 1985; Asher and Weisberg, 1978, inter alia). Sinclair (1982), on other hand, finds evidence of "conversion," of a shift in policy preference on the part of incumbents; her data reveal few differences in floor voting between holdover and new members. Both processes—turnover and behavioral change—may occur simultaneously; the issue is the relative importance of the mechanisms.

Once again, a resolution is apparent. Sinclair (1982) suggests that "agenda change" creates the conditions for opinion change. Thus "when new problems are perceived, when new solutions to existing problems are proposed, or when the terms of the debate...change significantly" (Sinclair, 1981, p. 221), old bets are off and behavioral change in the form of new voting postures is likely. Clear public signals, such as an electoral realignment that leads to numerous switched party seats and/or communication of new agenda concerns that force incumbent legislators to reasses their issue positions, contribute directly to program innovation in Congress. Elections regularly provide the voters with policy relevant choices (Sullivan and O'Connor, 1972; Wright, this volume), even if the citizens do not always appreciate or seize their opportunity; when times are propitious, enough of the challengers are strong candidates who win, and in consequence, alter Congress' policy-making potential.

We could learn more about the electoral contribution to the conditions conducive to policy change if we paid renewed attention to an old, but often neglected topic—recruitment. If members come to Congress to pursue particular goals—reelection, influence in Washington, and public policy— and following Fenno (1973) most observers assume they do, then it may be informative to see in what ways, if any, the electoral process enhances or retards the success of candidates concerned with policy. Do policy-oriented candidates run more or less often than those motivated by other aims? Do they emerge more often in one party, region, or other locale? Are they found disproportionately among "self-starters" as opposed to those party or local leaders recruit to run? Do they appear more often in those years that Jacobson and Kernell identify as most promising for "out party" challengers? Answers to these, and related, questions would increase our understanding of the ways that elections winnow the field and contribute to the pool of policy-motivated legislators who wind up in Congress.

External Actors: Problems of Power and Influence

Elections, in short, both alter the cast of characters in the drama of policy change and give stage directions to some of the continuing performers. Whatever their inclinations toward policy making, the dramatis personae, the members of Congress, must relate to other participants with their own policy agendas. Those outside the legislature—executives, including the president, and lobbyists—will most certainly press their claims on Congress. Whether policy change occurs or is defeated may well reflect the complex interactions between legislators and those beyond the Capitol, and while speculation about such relationships is rife, hard data about them are scarce.

We know a good deal about the general contours of the problems of concern, but little about the precise forms of behavior that take place within these specific settings. With respect to the presidency, it seems clear that the chief executive has a substantial impact on Congress' agenda (Walker, 1977; Light, 1983; Kingdon, 1984; Fishel, 1985); what he wants discussed, the legislature is hard pressed to evade. The president has a broad battery of weapons, formal and informal, with which to seek victory for his preferred positions (Wayne, 1978; Edwards, 1980, 1984) but his success requires skillful persuasion because he cannot compel independent lawmakers. With the arsenal available to him, and the resistance Congress often offers, the president's policies will prevail only part of the time, at most.

Interest groups operate in similar circumstances and with similar results. They possess a range of resources—money, campaign aid, expertise—that they can bring to bear through direct access to legislators (Truman, 1971) or indirectly through "grass roots lobbying" in the states and districts (Ornstein and Elder, 1978). If journalistic accounts credit lobbyists with substantial influence over legislative outcomes, neither Washington lobbyists nor elected representatives are prepared to acknowledge that the relationships are more than cooperative and voluntary. The former insist that they employ mainly "soft-sell," persuasive techniques (Milbrath, 1963; Bauer et al., 1972); the latter claim that they can control their contacts with lobbyists without compromising their own independence (Matthews, 1960; Kingdon, 1981). Perhaps all we can say with confidence is that pressure groups are omnipresent but not necessarily omnipotent.[5]

The policy preferences of executives and lobbyists, on one hand, and legislators, on the other, raise complex problems of power, influence, and authority (for simplicity, used interchangeably here). Policy making and policy change seem clearly to reflect the ability of some participants (inside and outside the legislature) to get (using methods that range, in principle, from simple requests through complex bargaining to powerful pressure) others to accommodate their wishes. Influence is, of course, reciprocal: Executives and lobbyists want lawmakers' support, but the latter often solicit aid from the former (Bauer et al., 1972). Authority is also implicit: Building credits does not require written contracts; indeed, parties to power relationships are likely to be reticent about the exact nature of these arrangements. Finally, influence relationships appear to be partial and transitory, shifting from one issue to another, and altering with the passage of time.

Power, in short, is a basic but troublesome concept. Intuitively, we sense that some of those involved in policy making have more authority than others, that they can win acquiescence from other participants, and that on occasion they may be able to secure the policy results they desire. Yet we remain uncertain about the ways, if any, that power operates in the congressional setting, and some clarification of its use seems essential (see Dahl, 1957; Riker, 1964; Nagel, 1975; Oppenheim, 1978; and Baldwin, 1978). Despite our identification of the bases of authority, there are few studies which lead to generalizations about their use: who asserts influence, under what circumstances, and with what results. On the executive branch, there is little beyond anecdote (but see Jones, 1981). With regard to groups, Bacheller (1977) has shown how different interests systematically vary strategies according to the type of issue and the legislative circumstances in which the matter is treated. Hayes (1981) argues that conflict is central to assessing group influence: Where groups agree, they may often get their way; where they divide—where there are competing coalitions—legislators may gain considerable freedom by playing the sides off against one another.[6] Meier and von Lohuizen (1978) present data consistent with this view. Bureaus of the Agriculture Department that win "strong" group support, on whose behalf, for example, many groups testify at budget hearings, experience large budgetary growth rates. But congressional support—the number of members testifying in favor of bureau appropriations—is even more strongly associated with favorable decisions, and there is no way to assess the relative power of these two sets of adherents.

It will not be easy to extend the frontiers of knowledge here. There are numerous power holders—executives, lobbyists, and legislators—to consider, and, as noted, they have little incentive to be forthcoming about their mutual relationships. It is difficult to observe power in operation, much less to determine the direction in which influence flows. In most instances, we cannot accurately ascertain who initiated contacts, what these contacts exchanged, which party to them yielded, or what is the net policy effect of interaction over time. Moreover, participants may dissemble, acting "strategically" (professing positions contrary to their own in the hopes of exacting concessions for supporting programs they favor initially) rather than "sincerely." If they succeed, they may claim exaggerated credit for their accomplishments; if they fail, they may be loath to reveal that they succumbed to more powerful forces. Untangling these complicated and reciprocal influence processes will require more sensitive and sophisticated research than scholars have been able to produce to date.

Admittedly, it is far easier to call for a theory of congressional power and influence than to provide one, but the need remains real. Unless and until we can learn more about authority and its exercise, our understanding of the power relations among members of Congress and those who seek to influence them and our ability to cumulate our findings in comprehensive explanations of legislative policy making and policy change must inevitably remain incomplete and unsatisfying.

Internal Actors: Problems of Leadership

Each legislator, again regardless of policy predilection, must also adapt to, or confront, a variety of structures and processes internal to Congress. Committees (and subcommittees) and parties, operating within a set of formal procedures and informal norms, define the legislative context within which policy is formulated and altered. Moreover, committee chairpersons and party officials, as formal leaders, have policy positions of their own to advance. The programmatic postures of these leaders may constrain or enhance the ability of individual members to make and change policy; in any event, the rank-and-file must come to terms in some fashion with the preferences of the leaders. All this raises the issue of leadership—a problem that has been treated in the literature with modest success, at best.

Committees have, since Woodrow Wilson's time, appeared as a central feature of congressional policy making (Wilson, 1885). Until recently, most studies have focused on single committees (e.g., Fenno, 1966, and Horn, 1970, on the Appropriations Committees; Manley, 1970, on House Ways and Means; and Robinson, 1963, and Matsunaga and Chen, 1976, on House Rules). The early work (summarized in Morrow, 1969, and Goodwin, 1970) emphasized the general: Committees are autonomous, expert, and success-ful policy makers; their decisions most often become Congress' decisions.

More recent scholarship has moved beyond these sweeping generaliza-tions about "the congressional committee" and "the committee system." Comparative studies (Price, 1972, and Fenno, 1973; see also Price, 1985, and Smith and Deering, 1984) make clear that the conventional wisdom may conceal more than it reveals. Committees differ in predictable ways. Panel members' behavior reflects their motivations and their places in the larger congressional system. They struggle to obtain desirable committee assign-ments, some of which relate to their policy preferences (Shepsle, 1978; Bullock, 1979); they adapt, and contribute, to distinctive patterns of committee leadership, structure, and process (including partisanship and integration) (Fenno, 1973; Dodd, 1972; Parker and Parker, 1979); and they learn to cope with a host of resource management problems, especially staff (Kofmehl, 1977; Fox and Hammond, 1977; Malbin, 1980) and computer technologies (Frantzich, 1982).

In a pioneering book, Fenno (1973) has recognized these many facets of committee performance and reoriented the study of committees, proposing an analytic scheme that promotes truly comparative treatment of them. He stresses the differences rather than the similarities among committees: "Committees differ from one another. And...they differ systematical-ly...with respect to five variables: member goals, environmental constraints, strategic premises, decisionmaking premises, and decisions" (1973, xiv). Fenno posits that members' behavior reflects their *goals* (to seek reelection, power, or policy influence) and the particular *environmental constraints* (the chamber itself, the political party, the administration, and clientele groups) within which their committee operates. These variable antecedent condi-tions, in turn, shape distinctive committee *strategic premises* (or norms or decision rules) and specific *decision-making processes* (partisanship, special-ization, and leadership). All these committee attributes contribute to committee *decisions*, the result of panel deliberations.

Fenno's formulation has outstripped research on committees. The panels he studied (as well as those Price, 1972, examined) bear little resemblance, in composition and in performance, to their appearance a decade ago. His scheme has been applied comprehensively to few other committees (but see LeLoup, 1979, and Perkins, 1980) and not at all to specific subcommittees, despite their increasing importance. In addition, there may be intracommittee variations that reflect the policy issues that comprise any panel's jurisdiction (Price, 1978). Perhaps panels adopt different strategic premises or respond to different environmental actors when they deal with distinctive portions of their agendas. In short, there remain substantial gaps in our knowledge about the ways committees formulate and alter public policy.

The same conclusion applies to political parties in Congress, though a few studies have made distinctive contributions here. The standard generalization, of course, is that parties, and their formal leaders, possess limited resources that permit them to bargain for, but not to command, the loyalty of their fundamentally independent partisans. We have clear descriptions of party organization—offices and committees—and party resources—members' psychological commitment to party and leaders' bases of influence (Peabody, 1976, 1985; Davidson, 1985; Ripley, 1969; Jones, 1970; Dodd, 1979; Sinclair, 1983). We lack, however, full knowledge of the ways in which party shapes members' policy-related activities.

Importantly, some progress has been made. Access to party leaders, in the House at least, has permitted observers to begin to describe more fully and assess more precisely the techniques with which party officials seek to lead (Waldman, 1980; Sinclair, 1983, and this volume). Specifically, Froman and Ripley (1965) define the conditions that facilitate leadership success: Active, committed, and unified party leadership is most likely to generate party cohesion, especially on low visibility issues that arouse little controversy or at low visibility, often early, stages of the legislative process where opposition is unable to coalesce. Westefield (1974) indicates that leaders use the committee assignment process to accommodate rank-and-file members whose support they seek. Similarly, the House Democratic leadership has employed ad hoc committees (Vogler, 1981) and Speaker's task forces (Sinclair, 1983) to advance members' goals and thus to secure their backing for party positions. In the same vein, Dodd and Sullivan (1981) chart leaders' "vote gathering" strategies, and discover that efforts to generate party cohesion vary both with the nature of the issue and with the character of the partisans at whom particular appeals are aimed.

Such studies of committees and parties are promising but partial beginnings in the quest to comprehend leadership strategies, tactics, and effectiveness. They highlight the pervasive question of leadership and our general ignorance of the specific ways leaders deal with followers. Like power relations, leader-follower interactions are difficult to observe, much less to measure systematically.[7] Leadership is also a reciprocal, two-way relationship, and we seldom are able to specify with certainty the direction in which its influence flows. Leaders, in some settings and circumstances, probably do, in fact, lead—do steer their followers along desired paths. In other instances, leaders may simply share their followers' policy perspectives; their views naturally coincide with those of the rank-and-file. Finally, some leaders may, in reality, be followers simply conforming or adapting to on-going relationships within the party or committee.

Beyond this basic influence problem, other questions remain unanswered: Who are the leaders, those with formal positions or those who have simply acquired influence? What strategies and tactics do leaders employ? What do they offer (or their ostensible followers demand)? What responses do their initiatives engender? What conditions facilitate follower support? The answers to these puzzles, moreover, are likely to vary by party or committee, by chamber, and with the passage of time. Policy making and policy change, in sum, involve complex issues of leadership, which constitute a challenging research agenda for students of Congress.[8]

These leader-follower relations are channelled and constrained by Congress' formal procedures and informal customs and traditions. The rules, as is so often noted, are not neutral, but rather shape, often decisively, the policies that the legislature produces (Oleszek, 1984). They do so, first, by protecting the independence of committees; they define committee jurisdictions and they make it difficult for noncommittee forces to reverse the panels' decisions easily. The procedures also specify a policy process marked by multiple "veto points," at each of which a determined minority may be able to defeat a bill or to exact significant substantive concessions from its proponents. It follows that the rules, sustaining as they do a decentralization of authority, mandate an incremental mode of policy making that confers advantages on defenders of the status quo. Change, if and when it comes, is most often modest; leaders pushing major innovation, from party or committee bastions, find that the rules frequently compel compromise that leads to nonradical policy change at most.

Norms impose similar constraints. Unwritten but widely accepted expectations about appropriate behavior may foreclose legislators' policy and strategic options (Huitt, 1957, 1961; Matthews, 1960). Limited benefit norms—apprenticeship and specialization—that confer advantage on some but not all members may have declined in importance (Rohde, Ornstein, and Peabody, 1985; Asher, 1973; and Loomis and Fishel, 1981). General purpose norms—reciprocity and personal courtesy, for instance—continue to foster an individualism that spreads the opportunities for policy influence widely, if not altogether equally, among senators and representatives. Such understandings, like the written rules, complicate the lives of ordinary members, and those who would exercise leadership, in their efforts to enact and alter public policy.

TOWARD MODELS OF POLICY CHANGE: PROBLEMS OF POLICY REPRESENTATION

Members of Congress, then, whatever their motivations, act to achieve their aims in a context that requires them to adapt to external actors and adjust to internal leaders and processes. Such policy as they can make in these circumstances will reflect power and influence relationships among policy-oriented legislators and other policy participants with their own programmatic agendas. Attempting to account for the outcomes of these policy contests raises problems of policy representation: We want to know whose policy interests are represented in Congress, by whom, and with what ultimate consequences. Following Miller and Stokes' (1963) empirical and Pitkin's (1967) philosophical revival of interest in the age-old issue of representation, there has been a substantial increase in research on the topic. At root, matters of policy making and policy change pose the fundamental question of represention: Whose policy preferences prevail, when, and why?

Most generally, representation is a reciprocal, but asymmetric, relationship between citizens and lawmakers that involves several components (Eulau and Karps, 1977). The link is reciprocal because communication, and thus influence, can begin at either end of the chain. Citizens may request (demand) that elected officials enact particular programs (policy representation) or perform specific chores—"casework" for individuals, projects for the consitituency—that is, engage in service representation. The ultimate sanction for such performance, of course, lies in the voters' ability to turn lawmakers out of office at the ensuing election. Alternatively, legislators may initiate constituent contacts, directing a variety of messages to the voters (symbolic representation) in order to structure citizens' views of them—and of the assembly itself—and to secure for themselves the freedom to pursue their policy predilections on many matters (Fenno, 1978).

The representational link is asymmetric because any given communicative or influence effort does not automatically generate an "equal and opposite" effect. Residents of particular constituencies, and different classes of citizens within any district, may differ in the extent to which they make demands on their legislators. Members of Congress may vary widely—across issues and in terms of their electoral circumstances—in the degree to which they respond to citizen communications, policy-related and other varieties, and to which they undertake symbolic representational activities (Cover, 1980;

Johannes, 1984). Lawmakers must decide what representative stance to take toward their constituencies (as they define them); how to allocate their limited resources among policy and other types of representational activities; and, indeed, what commitment to make to representation generally.

Early work on policy representation adopted a "congruence" (or "concurrence") view that assessed the citizen-legislator link in terms of a match between preferences: Legislators were expected to act consistently with their own constituents' desires. Empirical work using this paradigm found representation to be far from perfect. Only on a few "hot" issues—where citizens feel strongly and communicate clearly—will legislators feel constrained to heed the "folks back home" (Miller and Stokes, 1963; Erikson, 1978; Kuklinski and McCrone, 1981). Subsequent research, however, suggests a second standard. Weissberg (1978) proposes a criterion of "collective representation" that transcends congruence; "good" representation requires only that Congress enact what the nation as a whole wants. There is some evidence that it does (Backstrom, 1977, and Monroe, 1979; but cf. Hurley, 1982a).

Representation, as a theoretical and empirical notion, thus subsumes the issues of concern in this volume: What are the causes and consequences of policy formulation and, especially, policy change in Congress? Although representation itself, and the concepts of power and leadership that constitute basic elements of the representative-represented relationship, raise complicated questions of causality,[9] the literature reviewed here and the chapters in this book provide some clarification of policy representation. At the very least, we can identify the basic components that, singly or in combination, contribute to policy change in Congress. Speculatively at least, this may move us in the general direction of explaining varying types of policy change.

In general, nonincremental (or "major," or "significant") policy change is both most interesting and most readily identifiable: It is likely to be redistributive (and controversial) and material (allocating real benefits). It is, thus, safest to speculate about the kinds of forces that incline Congress to adopt programs that constitute fundamental departures from the status quo. If the impetus for basic change can be specified, admittedly in the most dramatic instances, then perhaps subsequent analyses can isolate which, if any, of these same factors are pertinent to our understanding of other— incremental, symbolic, distributive—types of policy alteration. Nondecisions, cases where Congress declines to act, may be less tractable. At the very least, we may try to list those forces that stimulate new programs or adjustment of old ones; whether these forces are necessary and/or sufficient to induce such change is problematic.

The analytic problem will not be easy, for as Dodd's theory of policy change (chapter 1) makes abundantly clear, Congress' behavior reflects a multitude of forces internal and external to the legislature. Policy making is, in a sense, the end result both of members' needs to respond to their constitutents (the "external world") and of the necessity to cope with "organizational cycles" within Congress. Representatives bring obligations, which they propose, incur, and retain in pursuit of electoral security—as a means to power and policy goals—to their congressional service. They seek to promote these agendas in a legislature characterized at different times by varying degrees institutional fragmentation and rigidity. When congressmen and women share an agenda, when they constitute a political generation that is large and committed, with substantial public approval and a propitious political setting in Congress—low decentralization and reduced rigidity—they may innovate and enact major programs.

These conditions seldom appear in favorable conjunction. Rather, Dodd postulates, they operate in inconsistent, conflicting cycles. Inevitably, pursuit of "organizational mastery," to advance to influential policy-making positions, impels members to reform the legislature. They seek to acquire resources that permit them to work to implement their policy agendas. Paradoxically, their success in these individual endeavors reduces Congress' collective capacity to act, to produce satisfactory public policy. Moreover, over the interval required before members can attain decision-making power, the programs they wish to legislate may become increasingly irrelevant as social, economic, and political conditions in their constituencies change. Members, thus, may be simultaneously "out of touch" and impotent in policy terms. Only when a crisis of immobolism strikes—when the public is irate, Congress is inert, and the executive is impelled to intervene to promote policy progress—will the legislators undertake reform to restore congressional capacity. In the immediate aftermath of such structural change, Congress can enact policy change, but Dodd suggests the productive period is likely to be shortlived; the conflicting and contrasting cycles of organizational and electoral mastery recur.

In attempting to sort out the conditions that facilitate policy innovation and change, it appears that the "*national mood,*" the beliefs, values, and attitudes of the populace, conditions Congress' propensity to act decisively. If there is, or if lawmakers perceive there is, a public consensus—for a defense buildup or tax cuts or deficit reduction—Congress will be inclined to respond (Ornstein, 1981; Fenno, 1977). Congress remains the "people's branch," and when it hears the citizens "loud and clear," it will heed their voices. If the messages are clarion calls for policy innovation or change, as they were in the New Deal, the Great Society era, and briefly and perhaps to a lesser extent in the early days of the Reagan administration, the legislators will innovate, or retrench, consistently with citizen communication.

Elections, particularly realigning elections, constitute the chief channel through which citizens register their complaints and preferences about the course of public policy. Congressional elections can, and sometimes do, drastically change the composition of Congress; to the extent that voters send new members, with new and distinct programmatic goals, to Washington, Congress may find it possible to enact major departures from the status quo. Policy innovation is more probable if the newcomers are partisans of the "out-party," the most likely to challenge incumbents on substantive matters. Democrats, taking "switched seats" from Republicans, are most likely to favor new programs in response to the electorate that rewarded them with seats in Congress. Conversely, Republicans ousting Democrats will, on balance, have decidedly more conservative outlooks than the members they replaced.

Realigning elections provide the most dramatic instances of electoral impact on legislative policy making. Although, as Brady (chapter 2) demonstrates, realignments vary, each type does produce significant personnel turnover in Congress. Realigning eras are rare—there have been three, perhaps a fourth is underway—but when they occur "clusters of policy change" may well ensue. Citizen concerns bring national rather than local issues to the fore in realigning periods. The political parties, in response, take polar positions on these issues—slavery, coinage of silver, depression. Voter choice tips heavily to one or the other party: Republicans in the 1860s and 1890s, Democrats in the 1930s. Large contingents of the now-dominant party go to Washington and assume significant positions in Congress, including those on committees with important policy making responsibilities. The new, large majority retains control for a decade or more. Numerous new members, well situated in the legislature, in the wake of realignment, enact significant nonincremental policies. In each of the major realigning eras, Brady shows convincingly, this pattern was clearly visible.

Elections need not, however, be realignments to replace one set of legislators with a new generation oriented toward policy change. Carmines and Stimson (chapter 3) and Wright (chapter 4) indicate that member replacement, with obvious policy implications, may occur in "ordinary" congressional elections—like 1958, 1964, or 1974—not associated with realignments. Wright suggests that the electoral process often offers voters a clear choice: Democratic candidates for Congress are regularly less conservative than their Republican opponents, especially in the Midwest and West, and in races for open seats. If the electorate, for whatever reasons, votes overwhelmingly for the nominees of one party and turns out numerous incumbents, a new replacement generation, positioned to engage in policy initiation, will come to Capitol Hill. Seats may switch, in other words, in the absence of realignment, enhancing the possibilities for the winning party to change policy directions.[10] The incumbency effect, however, Wright warns, retards the number of switched seats. Sitting members of Congress, able to resist national tides or deter strong challengers through nonpolicy activities, regularly win reelection. To the extent that incumbents survive, the number of new members, with outlooks favorable to policy innovation, declines.

If electorally induced party changes in Congress can set the stage for new programs, Carmines and Stimson remind us that Congress can lead as well as follow public opinion. Their evidence suggests, that with respect to civil rights issues at least, Congress' policy change may precede, and influence directly, public preferences. Representation, that is, is a two-way street: Legislators are more than slavish adherents to citizen sentiment (or whim); they may get "out front" and enact programs that the public comes, sooner or later, to accept as legitimate if not altogether desirable. The underlying stimulus for such policy change is still the electoral process; new members with new perspectives produce new and significant programs. They do not do so, however, in response to policy mandates *from* the voters; rather their own preferences dictate policy departures that their constituents eventually endorse. The ideas they push, of course, may not originate in Congress—they may come from various elite or attentive publics who set the national policy agenda, but in any case Congress may, in these relatively rare instances, lead mass opinion.

At a broad, *aggregate* level, then, elections can, though they do not always, contribute to policy change in Congress by sending to Washington a large enough cohort of new members to permit the legislature to strike out in new programmatic directions. Elections may also have an impact at an *individual* level, on single members of the House and Senate. What lawmakers experience in their campaigns in their particular districts and states, what those electoral experiences teach them, may color what they do when they serve in Congress, including the ways they undertake their policy-making responsibilities. Hershey (chapter 6) explicitly conceives the campaign as a learning experience. In light of what they see and hear in the constituency, members construct an "interpretation" or "dominant explanation" of what their race meant that "affects the importance [they] place on various issues."

For one thing, the campaign may inculcate a sense of the national mood. If candidates, challengers or incumbents, perceive some issue sweeping the country—e.g., revulsion over the Watergate scandals, or distress about economic circumstances—they may place high priority on reforming the legislature, or regulating campaign finance, or cutting government spending. Similarly, if the voters at home seem more moved by local problems—deteriorating roads or unemployment at the district defense contractor's plant, for instance—their representatives may perceive where their policy-making energies can be most profitably spent. If policy is not particularly salient, the member may have considerable freedom to pursue personal policy preferences—to lead rather than follow opinion—or to pay attention to nonpolicy components of representation: providing service or conducting oversight.[11]

Members of Congress, in assessing constituent opinions, may look less to the entire electorate than to particular segments of it. Both Fenno (chapter 5) and Hershey (chapter 6) find that candidates often turn to, and learn from, political activists in the district. To the extent that these elite participants hold distinctive views on the issues, and there is every reason to expect that they do, the campaigners may perceive more concern with policy in general, or matters of local concern in particular, than the voting population (the geographical constituency) actually feels. In any case, member perceptions of constituent attitudes about policy questions may well shape and constrain their policy-making activities in Congress.

Fenno's analyis of members' "period of adjustment" underscores the impact of the campaign, among other things,[12] on subsequent behavior: "the dynamics of the campaign...can have a constraining effect on a newcomer's early adjustment to the Senate." Unless they can "get over" the campaign, in a sense put it behind them, senators may be unable or unwilling to move on to the process of governing. If they are captives of their own rhetoric or hostages to the needs of the next election, they may slight the serious business of making public policy: They may be unwilling to consider controversial new programs; they may devote too little effort, in the short run at least, to learning the legislative routines that will enable them to exert policy-making influence. The innovative capacity of the institution at any given time may reflect the number of newcomers and veterans with genuine commitments to Congress' lawmaking responsibilities.

Finally, the campaign—its lessons and its effects on members' process of adjustment—may contribute to the conversion of incumbent legislators. If member replacement is the prime source of policy change, on some issues sitting members do shift their stands (Brady and Sinclair, 1984). Lawmakers' interpretations of the most recent elections, theirs and those for other offices, may persuade them that there is a consensus, or a new mood, in the country to which they must respond. They may sense that their old views are no longer appropriate either for dealing with pressing policy problems or for protecting their own local electoral security. In either case, senators and representatives may conclude that acceptance of some new policy position (conversion) is required. The more members who come to such a realization, the greater the innovative capacity of Congress will be. In short, elections— in the aggregate through membership replacement and conversion and at the individual level through the impact of individual campaigns—contribute to the presence, or absence, in Congress of significant numbers inclined to consider novel policy initiatives.

Numbers and commitment, however, are insufficient to guarantee enactment of nonincremental policy. Members must work in a complex environment that extends well beyond their own constituencies; they must also adapt to Congress itself. Policy innovation will reflect the conditions current with respect to environment and Congress. The *president*, of course, is the central figure in the legislature's external world. The White House is a force to reckon with in any process of policy initiative. The president's policy agenda defines to a large extent the programs that Congress will take most seriously (Kingdon, 1984; Light, 1983; Fishel, 1985). A president who resists policy departures will dampen, if not wash away, any surge of policy innovation that may flood the legislature. Without presidential leadership, Brady notes, even a passionate legislative majority, swept into Congress on a full realignment tide, may see its policy initiatives flounder.

When the presidency and Congress are in the hands of different political parties, as has so often been the case under Republican administrations, the problem is compounded. Under such circumstances, Congress will encounter the executive veto. It will require extraordinary majority support to override presidential rejection of innovative programs; the threat to veto, announced in advance, may well deter passage of such laws. A president who, like Ronald Reagan, can claim a popular electoral mandate, will be even more difficult to overcome. Assuming that the public will side with the executive when the lines of policy conflict are drawn, legislators may be reluctant to take the offensive against the president. Overall, presidential leadership, support, or at the very least acquiescence seem necessary before congressional initiatives will succeed. Executive opposition, sustained by personal persuasion and White House lobbying and by skillful opinion leadership, may quash legislative policy-making experimentation.

Interest groups, like the president, are a constant presence on Capitol Hill. They, and their adjunct political action committees, complicate legislators' lives. They have much to offer legislators—campaign support, legislative backing, and information; but they can cause problems as well, such as backing a congressional challenger or opposing preferred bills. Most important, they often have vested interests in existing programs, and in consequence will mobilize against anything they see as likely to damage their present positions. Since major policy departures are almost inevitably redistributive, with visible winners and losers, legislators interested in policy innovation, such as national health insurance plans, or tax simplification, will almost always encounter antagonism from those groups that see themselves as potential losers—the health insurance industry or those who benefit from threatened tax "loopholes." To act at all, in these circumstances, is to offend, with obvious political consequences; some set of interests will take umbrage whatever stance the lawmaker adopts.

More generally, the pattern of interest group involvement seems critical to policy change. In the nonincremental, or redistributive, case, as noted, conflict will be rife. Legislators will be tempted to duck controversy, to avoid the risk of making enemies, by tempering or perhaps abandoning "radical" policy-making proposals. When groups agree, where conflict is low or minimal, policy departures may seem more promising. These conditions, however, seem most common with respect to incremental, or distributive (pork barrel), policy; "iron triangles," cooperative relations among interest organizations, legislators, and bureaucracts, or "issue networks" abound with regard to such matters (e. g., subsidies or public works projects; see Lowi, 1964; Heclo, 1978; Ripley and Franklin, 1984). Ironically, congressional policy making may be easiest—where groups agree—on those matters that provide the least opportunity to alter the status quo; major innovations, by contrast, may falter in the face of fierce group conflict.

Congress itself, its internal organization and procedures, also conditions policy change. Congress is a decentralized institution, dispersing the ability to influence policy widely, though not equally, among many, though not all, members. The process by which legislation passes is not neutral; standard operating procedures place the onus on those who want to innovate. They must overcome a series of obstacles, in subcommittee and full committee, on the floor, and in conference, before new programs are finally adopted. Policy change will come, if it comes, when its proponents are able to overcome the impediments that a fragmented, serial legislative process imposes.

The *political party*, of course, is the prime force in Congress for centralization. The majority party is in position at each stage of the lawmaking process to carry the legislative day if its members cohesively support its programmatic initiatives. The problem is that a party's power remains more psychological—members want to back their party, when and if they can—than tangible. Party leaders lack the sanctions to compel compliance with their views: They are required to entreat their members to vote for their policy preferences; they cannot in the last analysis force their followers to do so when personal commitment, constituency pressure, or presidential persuasion convinces the latter to do otherwise.

Nonetheless, there are conditions under which the party can, and does, overcome the tendency to immobilism that a decentralized legislative process creates (Hurley, 1979; 1982b). When its majority is big enough, the party can win even if it suffers some defections in the ranks; large numbers offset lowered unity. When the party's majority is small, however, it must act cohesively, for it cannot afford to lose even a few votes from its side of the aisle unless it can win backing from the minority. Conversely, the size and cohesion of the opposition affects the majority party's ability to pass the bills it proffers. If few minority members serve and if they are divided in their policy preferences, they will be hard put to prevail even against a relatively disunited majority.

Such circumstances—a large, cohesive majority confronting a small, divided opposition—occur infrequently. National moods, translated through elections in realigning eras or landslides, produce these conditions periodically. Most of the time, however, the majority party contingent in Congress is neither large nor cohesive enough to work its policy will readily. Rather, its leaders must seek, pragmatically and incrementally, through bargaining and persuasion, to take advantage of whatever potential for party unity exists. Sinclair (chapter 7) identifies the difficulties that party chiefs encounter in facing this task. In reality, she suggests, the party hierarchy has two broad, and often irreconcilable, obligations. It must assemble coalitions to pass party programs, but at the same time, it must maintain "peace in the family." The latter is an onerous chore given the diversity of members' ideological positions, constituency commitments, and vested interests. Leaders cannot readily induce their ostensible followers to "rally round" party positions when the rank-and-file face so many pressures to go their own ways.

While their prospects are often dim, party leaders are not without some resources to use in their efforts to produce winning coalitions. Though each policy battle is likely to require a separate alliance, party leaders follow some fundamental strategies. For one thing, Sinclair demonstrates, they pursue a "strategy of inclusion," seeking to involve as many members as possible in designing and enacting a program. Thus, recent Speakers of the House have used task forces and an enlarged whip system to give a maximum number of their followers a stake in supporting party positions. Second, leaders can use available authority to structure "the choice situation" members face. They can, for example, refer bills to friendly committees or impose time limits on committee consideration; they can use their control over the House Rules Committee to get the bill to the floor under conditions that make it relatively easy for members to vote for it.

Finally, leaders can engage in classic persuasion. They can offer individual members inducements to back party policies. They can supply tangibles, like information, or intangibles, such as the psychological satisfaction that accompainies consultation or flattery. They can make "deals," trading support on legislation members desire for votes on party priorities. Leaders can also, however reluctantly, compromise on their preferred items, accepting amendments that make the legislation satisfactory to a majority of members. Most often, party leaders lack the large, cohesive majorities that guarantee policy-making success; they will have to do their best, with limited resources, in the face of strong countervailing pressures, to induce members to give party positions a modicum of support. Needless to say, under these circumstances, they seldom assemble majorities for truly innovative, nonincremental policy.[13]

Perhaps the highest hurdles leaders face in their coalition-building efforts are the congressional *committees*. Legislative decentralization reflects, above all else, the existence of independent standing committees, divided into numerous subcommittees, with jurisdiction over various portions of the policy agenda. Committees are critical players in the legislative drama: bills they choose to report, Congress considers; those they ignore languish and die. Committees differ in character; they possess distinctive combinations of member goals, partisan propensities, ideological outlooks, and commitments to outside interests (Fenno, 1973; Smith and Deering, 1984; Unekis and Rieselbach, 1984). In policy making, committees are most often decisive. Without their cooperation and approval, new policies are unlikely to survive. To be sure, the full House or Senate can override a reluctant committee. Majorities on the floor can always prevail, but members are loath to overrule the resident experts, and most often consent, within broad limits, to the advice committee specialists proffer.[14] Policy initiatives with committee support may pass; those without are unlikely to do so.

Ferejohn's (chapter 9) case study of food stamp legislation clearly illustrates the centrality of committees in congressional policy making. House and Senate Agriculture Committee members, eager to protect the subsidies that farmers in their districts and states received, confronted declining support in the 1950s for farm programs. Simultaneously, urban, liberal Democrats found themselves unable to enact food stamp legislation; opposition in the Ways and Means and Rules Committees prevented them from passing this welfare program, which a majority on the floor supported. The solution was a committee-negotiated "logroll." Agriculture Committee Democrats claimed and won jurisdiction over the program, asserting that food stamps offered a way to reduce farm product surpluses. They reported a food stamp bill, and voted for it, in return for northern Democratic votes for commodity price supports. Neither party to the bargain had more than minimum high enthusiasm for the other's program, but each realized that it could not attain a desired goal without the alliance. Thus, the agriculture committees proposed, and protected on the floor and in conference, an explicitly linked pair of bills.

The commodity price support–food stamp coalition was shaky at best. While it survived through the 1960s, the agreement often seemed on the verge of collapsing as conservative opponents tempted one side or the other to defect, offering restrictive amendments or proposing reductions of funds.

To protect its interests, the Agriculture Committees altered their tactics; they merged what had hitherto been separate bills into a single, omnibus farm package. Combining the two programs in one bill shored up the coalition; farm and urban interests had a strong incentive to pass legislation that contained their favored policies. The omnibus scheme, Ferejohn reports, was successful so long as the Democratic majority in Congress endured.

In the 1980s, Democratic dominance on Capitol Hill declined dramatically. The G.O.P. sweep in 1980 gave the party the White House and a Senate majority, and vastly reduced the Democrats' strength in the House. The Reagan administration and its congressional allies determined to reduce the scope and the cost of the food stamp program. The Senate, where conservative Jesse Helms (N.C.) chaired the Agriculture Committee, in 1981 separated the two components of the package, and imposed substantial cuts on food stamps. The House committee, however, insisted on an omnibus bill and the full chamber deferred to its judgment. A year later, in 1982, a three-year authorization of both the commodity support and food stamp programs passed. Although the new law imposed some restrictions that the agriculture committees disliked, the panels succeeded in protecting the fundamental form of both.

The food stamp experience, as Ferejohn recounts it, indicates clearly that committee strategy and tactics shape both policy adoption and efforts to bring about policy change. The Agriculture Committees guided initial passage of food stamp legislation and found ways—moving from separate bills to an omnibus package—to keep the program alive. Subsequently, the committees used their expertise and strategic advantages to fend off the worst features of the post-1980 conservative assault on the programs. What the committees do, in short, shapes what Congress does. Where committees favor policy innovation, innovation may occur; where the panels oppose new initiatives, the prospects of those proposals dim appreciably.[15]

Both parties and committees operate under constraints that the formal *rules of procedure* impose on decision making. Herzberg (chapter 8) points out clearly that many of these rules confer "blocking power" on minorities strategically entrenched at numerous locations along the road legislation must traverse to become law. Advantageously situated minorities can use their "negative powers" to defeat or delay bills they find objectionable. As a price of removing the roadblocks, they may demand and extract concessions: lower funding or restrictive amendments. The rules, in short, are not neutral; they offer opportunities to opponents of policy change to overwhelm those seeking policy openings.

Blocking coalitions may appear at various points in the policy process. Legislative decentralization, of course, makes it possible for minorities to win in sub- or full committee. Norms protecting individualism, specialization, and reciprocity (see Fenno, chapter 5; Asher, 1973; Rohde et al., 1985) make members unwilling to overrule committees too frequently. Committees continue to control the agenda, and an interest in command there may subvert, or require concessions from, any majority that might exist on the chamber floor. The House Rules Committee, though it has been disciplined in recent years, poses a special problem; as a price for releasing legislation, the panel may insist on substantive concessions. The minority party may seek to obstruct the majority, using a variety of parliamentary procedures, in committee and on the floor. In the Senate, small groups, or even a single member, may use the filibuster to force the majority to abandon or modify pending bills.

To be sure, minorities may go too far. The majority, if large and committed enough, can work its will. In the House, it can discharge a recalcitrant committee; it can use the Calendar Wednesday or Suspension of the Rules devices to move legislation to the floor. Sixty senators can invoke cloture to end a filibuster. If judicious, however, given the disinclination of most members to intrude on the sanctity of committees or to impose on individual members' freedom of action, a minority can exploit its location, and procedural advantages, to weaken if not defeat policy proposals it deems undesirable.

Rules and procedures, thus, give shape to congressional policy making. Blocking power sustains the status quo: it enables minorities, ensconced at particular "veto points," to frustrate majorities, liberal or conservative, that promote new policies. In addition, and more generally, obstructionism may reduce the quality of congressional deliberation. Procedural snarls and dilatory tactics may consume time and effort that might be spent more productively on the substance of legislation. Policy, Herzberg concludes, if any is enacted, may be ill-conceived and, ultimately, ineffective. Finally, blocking possibilities may impose strategic requisites on majorities; to avert defeat, they may resort to new forms of legislating: omnibus bills or "backdoor" financing devices such as entitlements and multiyear authorizations and appropriations. Such tactics obviate the need to run the obstructionist gamut annually; rather, the policies, once adopted, become the status quo, and the burden of changing them falls on their opponents, who will have to take positive action—and face blocking power—to defeat them in subsequent years. In general, however, rules, and the strategies they entail, reduce the probability that Congress can adopt innovative programs.

Policy making and policy change take place in a complex setting that public sentiments (expressed through elections and other channels), the president, interest groups, and Congress itself define. While no conditions seem to be necessary and sufficient to induce policy change, innovation seems most likely when:

1. A national mood, or consensus, favors policy innovation (of some sort) to solve a perceived policy problem.
2. The electoral process, through realigning or decisively one-sided elections, produces a congressional majority committed to policy change.
3. The president, especially if he can claim a popular mandate and is of the same party as the congressional majority, submits and commits his resources to an innovative program.
4. The interest groups with a stake in the issue agree that policy departures are needed.
5. The congressional party leadership is unified, active, and has a large, cohesive majority favorable to policy initiatives.
6. The congressional committees with jurisdiction back programmatic departures from the status quo.
7. Congressional minorities are not strategically located in the policy process to exploit opportunities to block a majority favorable to policy change.

No one of these conditions occurs commonly; an effective combination of them is rare indeed. Thus, policy innovation is the exception, not the rule. Ordinarily, congressional decision makers are unwilling or unable to enact significant nonincremental policy. When they are, ironically, they may be the least critical element in the configuration of forces that generates innovation. Where the public overwhelmingly supports an active and dedicated president, Franklin Roosevelt in the 1930s, Lyndon Johnson in the Great Society era, or Ronald Reagan in 1981–82, Congress may have little choice except to go along with the tides of change. Legislation may receive only cursory committee consideration; bills may be passed with a minimum of deliberation and debate, virtually without amendment. To cite an extreme case, the House of Representatives, with a Democratic majority, in 1981 enacted a Reagan budget that was not even printed, was partially written in longhand, and contained the telephone number of a Congressional Budget Office aide. Congress, in these circumstances, acts more to legitimate or modify at the margins than to impose its own innovative preferences. The legislature may represent best, in other words, when it is least creative. If so, then the power of external influences—national mood, the electoral process, and presidential influence (conditions 1–3)—becomes readily apparent. When the major forces beyond Capitol Hill push in the same direction, they may alter internal, structural, and procedural constraints—party leadership, committee independence, and the availability of blocking power (conditions 5–7)—in ways that clearly increase the probability of congressional compliance with the policies they wish to enact or change. Outside influences, in these circumstances, may prove well-nigh irresistable.

Paradoxically, Congress' independent contributions may be most significant when redistributive policy change is least likely, when there is no compelling impetus to do more than adjust the status quo incrementally. Specifically, Congress seems most inclined to enact incremental, distributive policy when:

1. No national mood or consensus exists, and the public is divided, satisfied, or quiescent.
2. The electoral process promotes little or no member replacement or conversion in Congress.
3. The president is passive, lacks a popular mandate, has a small and/or divided majority, or faces a Congress in which the opposition controls one or both chambers.
4. The interest groups involved in any issue are in conflict and active on both sides of the question.
5. The congressional party leadership is divided, has only a small and/or divided majority, or stresses party maintenance over policy innovation.
6. The congressional committees with jurisdiction have reservations about policy change.
7. Congressional minorities, especially if large and cohesive, have blocking power to prevent or retard policy initiatives.

If the field of political forces is in balance or in conflict, Congress may be in position to impose its own views, assuming they are not extreme, and adjust policy modestly in one direction or another.

These same conditions, especially if conflict is high, may prevent action entirely. Some issues are simply "too hot to handle," and the legislature is unlikely to want to tackle them. Nondecisions may ensue as such items are shunted off the political agenda. Alternatively, if the matter requires some treatment, Congress may enact a symbolic policy, one that offers psychic rewards but that is not likely to alter the status quo substantially. Finally, when there is no consensus or obvious answer to some policy question, Congress may shift the conflict to the bureaucratic or state arenas. It may pass a broad delegation of authority to the administrative branch, letting the contending forces focus their policy aims on the executives who will write and implement the regulations that, in reality, define public policy. Similarly, Congress may divert policy controversy to the federal system by choosing to transfer programs and their implementation to the states. In these cases, it evades the responsibility to represent interests, including its own, directly through enacting statutes that embody clear policy choices.

Identifying the factors that influence congressional policy making and policy representation is, of course, only a small, first step in explaining congressional behavior. Much remains unknown. It would clarify matters if we could establish the relative weights of the various factors. For instance, the civil rights case (see chapter 4) suggests that a committed government can create a supportive national consensus—representation is a reciprocal relationship—if it takes the initiative. Thus institutional considerations may, on some occasions, have greater policy making significance than public opinion. Similarly, conditions conducive to policy change may vary across policy domains, or even within them. Governmental innovation in foreign affairs seems likely to win acceptance from the public, often indifferent, more readily than domestic initiatives that affect citizens more directly. Or the factors may impinge on the House and Senate differently: The two-year election cycle in the former may sensitize its members to the national mood to a greater degree than electoral needs energize senators. In addition, the correlates of policy innovation may change as time passes; what inspires new programs in one era may not have a similar impact in a later period. Wright (chapter 3), for example, suggests that public preferences will be less easily translated into policy departures when incumbents, less attuned to changing constituent opinion, can count on easy reelection.

Finally, to come full cycle, there remain basic problems in legislative research that impinge on the ability to understand and explain policy change. The precise contours of policy—conceptual and empirical—need clarification: What do we mean by policy? How do we identify and measure various categories of policy? The link between elections and policy requires clearer specification, especially with respect to the ways policy preferences affect the recruitment of legislative candidates. The problems of power and influence, though not easily solved, will not go away: What bases of authority do executives or lobbyists possess? How do they use them, and with what effect on congressional decision making? Leadership remains an elusive phenomenon: How do party and committee leaders use their resources to win support for policy initiatives from their followers? Under what circumstances are they most likely to succeed? In sum, political scientists have begun a long journey toward explanation of policy making and policy change, and the papers in this collection move us ahead. There remain many miles to travel, however, before we rest content that we understand the intricate processes by which Congress performs its critical role as policy representative of the nation.

Notes

1. I have explored some of these matters elsewhere, from a somewhat broader perspective (Rieselbach, 1983), and the present effort draws on this earlier paper. See also Oppenheimer (1983) for a far fuller and comparative treatment of the "outputs of legislatures." For a monumental bibliography, listing more than 5500 references, see Goehlert and Sayre (1982), esp. Parts II, VII, VIII, X–XIII.

2. For instance, Hayes (1981) suggests that the protective tariff was a redistributive item in the 1930s but became a regulatory issue when Congress enacted the reciprocal trade program and delegated rate setting to the Tariff Commission. Similarly, Lyndon Johnson's model cities program was introduced as redistributive—substantial sums were to go to a small set of cities—but over the course of the legislative process became a distributive policy— smaller amounts to many metropolitan areas—to win legislative approval (Ripley and Franklin, 1984, pp. 187–189).

3. A follow-up study (Clausen and Van Horn, 1977) found that the five dimensions were indeed "durable and dominant," but also that two new dimensions developed during the Nixon Administration. In the 91st and 92nd Congress, there emerged an "agricultural subsidy limitation" domain distinct from the more general agricultural assistance dimension, and a "national security commitment reorientation" narrower than the broader international involvement issues. These results indicate the changing character of issue areas as well as their more enduring qualities. See also Sinclair (1982).

4. This view is entirely consistent with what we know about contemporary congressional campaigns. Given the general weakness of national political party organizations, candidates take nearly complete responsibility for their own campaign organizations, strategies and tactics, and financial resources, and if they win feel few if any obligations (see Kingdon, 1966; Leuthold, 1968; Hershey, 1974; and Fishel, 1973). Such circumstances are presumed to reinforce congressional parochialism and to undercut the potential influence of the legislative parties.

5. Moreover, group involvement in legislative politics has changed of late: Changes in campaign finance, featuring the proliferation of political action committees, and the rapid rise to prominence of "single issue" groups that place a nearly exclusive emphasis on one topic may render what little we know about interest group influence obsolete. For a current review of these developments, see the papers in Cigler and Loomis (1983). Also see Schlozman and Tierney (1983) and Walker (1983).

6. For case studies that illustrate—perhaps typically, perhaps not—the problems of ascertaining groups' influence as distinct from their activities, see Gelb and Palley (1979) and Vogel and Nadel (1977).

7. Leadership, as used here, involves power and influence in additional settings. The research need is to specify the ways that party and committee leaders seek to influence, exert power with respect to, those who are their at least nominal followers.

8. Space considerations preclude treatment of similar questions involving member-staff interactions. We remain largely ignorant of the policy roles staff plays; the extent to which they influence, or are influenced by, their nominal principals; and the variations in member-staff relations between the chambers and among the committees in either House. Some excellent work has begun to explore these matters for committee staff; see Patterson (1970); Price (1971); Fox and Hammond (1977); Malbin (1980); and Salisbury and Shepsle (1981a,b).

9. The problems here resemble those that pertain to power and leadership. We simply do not know enough about whether, when, why, and how representatives and represented initiate communications, in which directions the messages flow, who responds to whom, and how faithfully they do so.

10. Note that policy change, reflecting party replacement, need not require "rational" voting by individual citizens. Whenever, for whatever reasons, they choose a relatively ideologically homogeneous set of new legislators, they may, however inadvertently, create the conditions for policy innovation. As noted, Jacobson and Kernell (1983) offer one convincing explanation of this possibility (but cf. Abramowitz, 1984).
11. Campaign learning, Hershey points out, can also influence the ways members allocate their staff—between service and legislative activities—the sorts of committee assignments they seek, and the nature of their commitments to president and political party.
12. Campaigns, obviously, are not the only influence on the adjustment process. Fenno assesses the impact of prior occupation; senators with previous legislative experience have a different, and relatively easier, adjustment to the upper house than those with different backgrounds.
13. Incrementalism, or even policy immobilism, may not always be undesirable. Gerald C. Wright has proposed to the author that some circumstances, for example, when the national mood is calm, suggest that the majority party may already have achieved its policy goals or that there may be a rough "fit" between policy and public preferences. The "failure" of party leaders to produce innovation in this context is not serious. The real problem occurs when, or if, Congress proves incapable of responding to popular preferences for major change, when congressional organization and procedures frustrate creative policy making. Given the frequent absence of popular policy mandates, it is perhaps unrealistic to expect regular policy innovation in Congress.
14. Recently, deference to committee proposals seems to have declined. The "new breed" of younger, more ideological, more activist members more often offers floor amendments to committee bills (Ornstein, 1981; Smith and Deering, 1984). Still, the onus is on such legislators to make a case for rejecting committee specialists' initiatives, and the committee continues to define the terms in which the debate most often is cast.
15. For his broader discussion of the role of committees in innovative policy making, see Ferejohn (1983).

References

Abramowitz, Alan I. (1984). National issues, strategic politicians, and voting behavior in the 1980 and 1982 congressional elections. *American Journal of Political Science* 28: 710–724.

Asher, Herbert B. (1973). The learning of legislative norms. *American Political Science Review* 67: 499–513.

Asher, Herbert B. and Weisberg, Herbert F. (1978). Voting change in Congress: some dynamic perspectives on an evolutionary process. *American Journal of Political Science* 22: 391–425.

Bacheller, John M. (1977). Lobbyists and the legislative process: the impact of environmental constraints. *American Political Science Review* 71: 252–263.

Bachrach, Peter and Baratz, Morton S. (1970). *Power and Poverty: Theory and Practice*. New York: Oxford University Press.

Backstrom, Charles H. (1977). Congress and the public: how representative is the one of the other? *American Politics Quarterly* 5: 411–435.

Baldwin, David A. (1978). Power and social exchange. *American Political Science Review* 72: 1229–1242.

Bauer, Raymond A., de Sola Pool, Ithiel, and Dexter, Lewis A. (1972). *American Business and Public Policy*, 2nd ed. Chicago: Aldine-Atherton.

Brady, David W. (1985). A reevaluation of realignments in American politics: evidence from the House of Representatives. *American Political Science Review* 79: 28–49.

Brady, David W., and Lynn, Naomi (1973). Switched-seat congressional districts: their effect on party voting and public policy. *American Journal of Political Science* 17: 528–543.

Brady, David, and Sinclair, Barbara (1984). Building majorities for policy changes in the House of Representatives. *Journal of Politics* 46: 1033–1060.

Bullock, Charles S. III (1979). House committee assignments. In Leroy N. Rieselbach (ed.), *The Congressional System: Notes and Readings*, 2nd ed., pp. 58–86. North Scituate, Mass.: Duxbury Press..

Chamberlain, Lawrence (1946). *The President, Congress and Legislation*. New York: Columbia University Press.

Cigler, Allan J. and Loomis, Burdett A., eds. (1983). *Interest Group Politics*. Washington, D.C.: CQ Press.

Clausen, Aage R. (1973). *How Congressmen Decide: A Policy Focus*. New York: St. Martin's.

Clausen, Aage R. and Van Horn, Carl E. (1977). The congressional response to a decade of change, 1963–1972. *Journal of Politics* 39: 624–666.

Cover, Albert D. (1980). Contacting congressional constituents: some patterns of perquisite use. *American Journal of Political Science* 24: 125–134.

Dahl, Robert A. (1957). The concept of power. *Behavioral Science.* 2: 201–215.

Davidson, Roger H. (1985). Senate leaders: janitors for an untidy Congress. In Lawrence C. Dodd and Bruce I. Oppenheimer (eds.), *Congress Reconsidered*, 3rd ed., pp. 225–252. Washington, D.C.: CQ Press.

Dodd, Lawrence C. (1972). Committee integration in the Senate: a comparative analysis. *Journal of Politics* 34: 1135–1171.

Dodd, Lawrence C. (1979). The expanded roles of the House Democratic Whip system. *Congressional Studies* 6: 27–56.

Dodd, Lawrence C. and Sullivan, Terry (1981). Majority party leadership and partisan vote gathering: the House Democratic Whip system." In Frank H. Mackaman (ed.), *Understanding Congressional Leadership*, pp. 227–260. Washington, D.C.: CQ Press.

Easton, David (1965). *A Systems Analysis of Political Life*. New York: Wiley.

Edelman, Murray (1964). *The Symbolic Uses of Politics*. Urbana, Ill.: University of Illinois Press.

Edelman, Murray (1971). *Politics as Symbolic Action: Mass Arousal and Quiescence*. Chicago: Markham.

Edwards, George C. III (1980). *Presidential Influence in Congress*. San Francisco: Freeman.

Edwards, George C. III. (1984). *The Public Presidency: The Pursuit of Popular Support*. New York: St. Martin's.

Erikson, Robert S. (1978). Constituency opinion and congressional behavior: a reexamination of the Miller-Stokes representational data. *American Journal of Political Science* 22: 511–535.

Eulau, Heinz, and Karps, Paul D. (1977). The puzzle of representation: specifying the components of representation. *Legislative Studies Quarterly* 2: 233–254.

Fenno, Richard F., Jr. (1966). *The Power of the Purse: Appropriations Politics in Congress*. Boston: Little, Brown.

Fenno, Richard F., Jr. (1973). *Congressmen in Committees*. Boston: Little Brown.

Fenno, Richard F., Jr. (1977). Strengthening a congressional strength. In Lawrence C. Dodd and Bruce I Oppenheimer (eds.), *Congress Reconsidered*, pp. 261–268. New York: Praeger.

Fenno Richard F., Jr. (1978). *Home Style: House Members in Their Districts*. Boston: Little Brown.

Ferejohn, John (1983). Congress and redistribution. In Allen Schick (ed.), *Making Economic Policy in Congress*, pp. 131–157. Washington, D. C.: American Enterprise Institute.

Fishel, Jeff (1973). *Party and Opposition: Congressional Challengers in American Politics*. New York: McKay.

Fishel, Jeff (1985). *Presidents and Promises*. Washington, D.C.: CQ Press.

Fox, Harrison W., Jr., and Hammond, Susan W. (1977). *Congressional Staffs: The Invisible Force in American Lawmaking*. New York: Free Press.

Frantzich, Stephen E. (1982). *Computers in Congress*. Beverly Hills, Cal.: Sage.

Froman, Lewis A, Jr., and Ripley, Randall B. (1965). Conditions for party leadership: the case of the House Democrats. *American Political Science Review* 59: 52–63.

Gelb, Joyce and Palley, Marian L. (1979). Women and interest group politics: a comparative analysis of federal decision-making. *Journal of Politics* 41: 362–392.

Goehlert, Robert U., and Sayre, John R. (1982). *The United States Congress: A Bibliography*. New York: Free Press.

Goodwin, George, Jr. (1970). *The Little Legislatures: Committees of Congress*. Amherst, Mass.: University of Massachusetts Press.

Hayes, Michael T. (1981). *Lobbyists and Legislators*. New Brunswick, N.J.: Rutgers University Press.

Heclo, Hugh (1978). Issue networks and the executive establishment. In Anthony King (ed.), *The New American Political System*, pp. 87–124. Washington, D.C.: American Enterprise Institute.

Hershey, Marjorie R. (1974). *The Making of Campaign Strategy*. Lexington, Mass.: Lexington Books.

Hinckley, Barbara (1981). *Congressional Elections*. Washington, D.C.: CQ Press.

Horn, Stephen (1970). *Unused Power: The Work of the Senate Committee on Appropriations*. Washington, D.C.: Brookings Institution.

Huitt, Ralph K. (1957). The Morse Committee assignment controversy: a study in Senate norms. *American Political Science Review* 51: 313–329.

Huitt, Ralph K. (1961). The outsider in the Senate: an alternative role. *American Political Science Review* 55: 566–575.

Huntington, Samuel P. (1973). Congressional responses to the twentieth century. In David B. Truman (ed.), *The Congress and America's Future*, 2nd ed., pp. 6–38. Englewood Cliffs, N.J.: Prentice-Hall.

Hurley, Patricia A. (1979). Assessing the potential for significant legislative output in the House of Representatives. *Western Political Quarterly* 32: 45–58.

Hurley, Patricia A. (1982a) Dyadic and collective representation in 1978. *Legislative Studies Quarterly* 7: 119–136.

Hurley, Patricia A. (1982b). Predicting policy change in the House: a longitudinal analysis. *British Journal of Political Science* 12: 374–384.

Jacobson, Gary C. (1983). *The Politics of Congressional Elections*. Boston: Little, Brown.

Jacobson, Gary C., and Kernell, Samuel (1983). *Strategy and Choice in Congressional Elections*, 2nd ed. New Haven Conn.: Yale University Press.

Johannes, John R. (1984). *To Serve the People: Congress and Constituency Service*. Lincoln, Neb.: University of Nebraska Press.

Jones, Charles O. (1970). *The Minority Party in Congress*. Boston: Little, Brown.

Jones, Charles O. (1981). Congress and the presidency. In Thomas E. Mann and Norman J. Ornstein (eds.), *The New Congress*, pp. 223–249. Washington, D.C.: American Enterprise Institute.

Kernell, Samuel (1977). Presidential popularity and negative voting: an alternative explanation of the midterm decline of the President's party. *American Political Science Review* 71: 44–66.

Kinder, Donald R., and Kiewiet, D. Roderick (1979). Economic discontent and political behavior: the role of personal grievances and collective economic judgments in congressional voting. *American Journal of Political Science* 23: 495–527.

Kingdon, John W. (1966). *Candidates for Office*. New York: Random House.

Kingdon, John W. (1981). *Congressmen's Voting Decisions*, 2nd ed. New York: Harper & Row.

Kingdon, John W. (1984). *Agendas, Alternatives, and Public Policies*. Boston: Little, Brown.

Kofmehl, Kenneth (1977). *Professional Staffs of Congress*, 3rd ed. Lafayette, Ind.: Purdue University Studies.

Kuklinski, James H., and McCrone, Donald J. (1981). Electoral accountability as a source of policy representation. In Norman R. Luttbeg (ed.), *Public Opinion and Public Policy*, 3rd ed., pp. 320–341. Itasca, Ill.: Peacock.

LeLoup, Lance (1979). Process vs. policy: the House Budget Committee. *Legislative Studies Quarterly* 4: 227–254.

Leuthold, David H. (1968). *Electioneering in a Democracy: Campaigns for Congress*. New York: Wiley.

Light, Paul C. (1981–82). Passing nonincremental policy in Congress, Kennedy to Carter. *Congress and the Presidency* 9: 61–82.

Light, Paul C. (1983). *The President's Agenda: Domestic Policy Choice from Kennedy to Carter (with Notes on Ronald Reagan)*. Baltimore, Md.: Johns Hopkins Press.

Lindblom, Charles E. (1980). *The Policy-making Process*, 2nd ed. Englewood Cliffs, N.J.: Prentice-Hall.

Loomis, Burdett A., and Fishel, Jeff (1981). New members in a changing Congress: norms, actions, and satisfaction. *Congressional Studies* 8: 81–94.

Lowi, Theodore J. (1964). American business, case studies, and political theory. *World Politics* 16: 677–715.

Lowi, Theodore J. (1972). Four systems of policy, politics, and choice. *Public Administration Review* 32: 298–310.

Malbin, Michael J. (1980). *Unelected Representatives: Congressional Staff and the Future of Representative Government*. New York: Basic Books.

Manley, John J. (1970). *The Politics of Finance: The House Committee on Ways and Means*. Boston: Little, Brown.

Mann, Thomas E., and Wolfinger, Raymond E. (1980). Candidates and parties in congressional elections. *American Political Science Review* 74: 617–632.

Matsunaga, Spark M. and Ping Chen (1976). *Rulemakers of the House*. Urbana, Ill.: University of Illinois Press.

Matthews, Donald R. (1960). *U. S. Senators and Their World*. Chapel Hill, N.C.: University of North Carolina Press.

Meier, Kenneth J., and von Lohuizen, J.R. (1978). Bureaus, clients, and Congress: the impact of interest group support on budgeting. *Administration and Society* 9: 447–466.

Milbrath, Lester W. (1963). *The Washington Lobbyists*. Chicago: Rand McNally.

Miller, Warren E., and Stokes, Donald E. (1963). Constituency influence in Congress. *American Political Science Review* 57: 45–56.

Moe, Ronald C., and Teel, Steven C. (1970). Congress as policy-maker: a necessary reappraisal. *Political Science Quarterly* 85: 443–470.

Monroe, Alan (1979). Consistency between public preferences and national policy decisions. *American Politics Quarterly* 7: 3–19.

Morrow, William L. (1969). *Congressional Committees*. New York: Scribner's.

Nagel, Jack H. (1975). *The Descriptive Analysis of Power*. New Haven, Conn.: Yale University Press.

Oleszek, Walter J. (1984). *Congressional Procedures and the Policy Process*, 2nd ed. Washington, D.C.: CQ Press.

Oppenheim, Felix E. (1978). "Power" revisited. *Journal of Politics* 40: 589–608.

Oppenheimer, Bruce I. (1983). How legislatures shape policy and budgets. *Legislative Studies Quarterly* 8: 551–597.

Ornstein, Norman J. (1981). The House and the Senate in a new Congress. In Thomas E. Mann and Norman J. Ornstein (eds.), *The New Congress*, pp. 363–383. Washington, D.C.: American Enterprise Institute.

Ornstein, Norman J., and Elder, Shirley (1978). *Interest Groups, Lobbying and Policymaking.* Washington, D.C.: CQ Press.

Parker, Glenn R. and Parker, Suzanne L. (1979). Factions in committees: The U.S. House of Representatives. *American Political Science Review* 73: 85–102.

Patterson, Samuel C. (1970). Congressional committee professional staffing: capabilities and constraints. In Allen Kornberg and Lloyd D. Musolf (eds.), *Legislatures in Developmental Perspective*, pp. 391–428. Durham, N.C.: Duke University Press.

Peabody, Robert L. (1976). *Leadership in Congress: Stability, Succession, and Change.* Boston: Little, Brown.

Peabody, Robert L. (1985). House party leadership: stability and change. In Lawrence C. Dodd and Bruce I. Oppenheimer (eds.), *Congress Reconsidered*, 3rd ed., pp. 253–271. Washington, D.C.: CQ Press.

Perkins, Lynette P. (1980). Influence of members' goals on their committee behavior: The U. S. House Judiciary Committee. *Legislative Studies Quarterly* 5: 373–392.

Pitkin, Hanna F. (1967). *The Concept of Representation.* Berkeley, Cal.: University of California Press.

Price, David E. (1971). Professionals and "entrepreneurs": staff orientations and policy making on three Senate committees. *Journal of Politics* 33: 316–336.

Price, David E. (1972). *Who Makes the Laws? Creativity and Power in Senate Committees.* Cambridge, Mass.: Schenckman.

Price, David E. (1978). Policy making in Senate committees: the impact of "environmental" factors. *American Political Science Review* 72: 548–574.

Price, David E. (1985). Congressional committees in the policy process. In Lawrence C. Dodd and Bruce I. Oppenheimer (eds.), *Congress Reconsidered*, 3rd ed., pp. 161–188. Washington, D.C.: CQ Press.

Rieselbach, Leroy N. (1983). The forest for the trees: blazing trails for congressional research. In Ada W. Finifter (ed.), *Political Science: The State of the Discipline*, pp. 155–188. Washington, D.C.: APSA.

Riker, William H. (1964). Some ambiguities in the notion of power. *American Political Science Review* 58: 341–349.

Ripley, Randall B. (1969). *Majority Party Leadership in Congress.* Boston: Little, Brown.

Ripley, Randall B., and Franklin, Grace A. (1984). *Congress, the Bureaucracy and Public Policy*, 3rd ed. Homewood, Ill.: Dorsey Press.

Robinson, James A. (1963). *The House Rules Committee.* Indianapolis: Bobbs-Merrill.

Rohde, David W., Ornstein, Norman J., and Peabody, Robert L. (1985). Political change and legislative norms in the U.S. Senate, 1957–1974. In Glenn R. Parker (ed.), *Studies of Congress*, pp. 147–188. Washington, D.C.: CQ Press.

Salisbury, Robert H. (1968). The analysis of public policy: a search for theories and rules. In Austin Ranney (ed.), *Political Science and Public Policy*, pp. 151–175. Chicago: Markham.

Salisbury, Robert H., and Heinz, John P. (1970). A theory of policy analysis and some preliminary applications. In Ira Sharkansky (ed.), *Policy Analysis in Political Science*, pp. 39–60. Chicago: Markham.

Salisbury, Robert H., and Shepsle, Kenneth A. (1981a). U.S. congressman as enterprise. *Legislative Studies Quarterly* 6: 559–576.

Salisbury, Robert H., and Shepsle, Kenneth A. (1981b). Congressional staff turnover and the ties-that-bind. *American Political Science Review* 75: 381–396.

Schlozman, Kay L., and Tierney, John T. (1983). More of the same: Washington pressure group activity in a decade of change. *Journal of Politics* 45: 351–377.

Schulman, Paul R. (1975). Nonincrimental policy making: notes toward an alternative paradigm. *American Political Science Review* 69: 1354–1370.

Shepsle, Kenneth A. (1978). *The Giant Jigsaw Puzzle: Democratic Committee Assignments in the Modern House*. Chicago: University of Chicago Press.

Sinclair, Barbara (1981). Agenda and alignment change: the House of Representatives, 1925–1978. In Lawrence C. Dodd and Bruce I. Oppenheimer (eds.), *Congress Reconsidered*, 2nd ed., pp. 221–245. Washington, D.C.: CQ Press.

Sinclair, Barbara (1982). *Congressional Realignment, 1925–1978*. Austin, Tex.: University of Texas Press.

Sinclair, Barbara (1983). *Majority Leadership in the U.S. House*. Baltimore, Md.: Johns Hopkins Press.

Smith, Stephen S., and Deering, Christopher J. (1984). *Committees in Congress*. Washington, D.C.: CQ Press.

Sullivan, John L., and O'Connor, Robert E. (1972). Electoral choice and popular control of public policy. *American Political Science Review* 66: 1256–1268.

Truman, David B. (1971). *The Governmental Process*, 2nd ed. New York: Knopf.

Tufte, Edward R. (1978). *Political Control of the Economy*. Princeton, N.J.: Princeton University Press.

Unekis, Joseph K., and Rieselbach, Leroy N. (1984). *Congressional Committee Politics: Continuity and Change*. New York: Praeger.

Vogel, David, and Nadel, Mark (1977). Who is a consumer? an analysis of the politics of consumer conflict. *American Politics Quarterly* 5: 27–56.

Vogler, David J. (1981). Ad hoc committees in the House of Representatives and purposive models of legislative behavior. *Polity* 14: 89–109.

Waldman, Sidney (1980). Majority party leadership in the House of Representatives. *Political Science Quarterly* 95: 373–393.

Walker, Jack L. (1977). Setting the agenda in the United States Senate: a theory of problem selection. *British Journal of Political Science* 7: 432–445.

Walker, Jack L. (1983). The origins and maintenance of interest groups in America. *American Political Science Review* 77: 390–406.

Wayne, Stephen J. (1978). *The Legislative Presidency*. New York: Harper & Row.

Weissberg, Robert (1978). Collective vs. dyadic representation in Congress. *American Political Science Review* 72: 535–546.

Westefield, Louis P. (1974). Majority party leadership and the committee system in the House of Representatives. *American Political Science Review* 68: 1593–1604.

Wildavsky, Aaron (1984). *The Politics of the Budgetary Process*, 4th ed. Boston: Little, Brown.

Wilson, Woodrow (1885). *Congressional Government*. Cleveland, Ohio: World Publishing.

Author Index

Aberbach, Joel D., 27
Abramowitz, Alan I., 284
Allen, Harris M., Jr., 148 (Sears)*
Althoff, P., 52
Anderson, James E., 49
Arnold, R. Douglas, 14, 37
Art, Robert J., 35
Asher, Herbert B., 11, 94, 261, 267, 279

Bacheller, John M., 263
Bachrach, Peter, 258
Backstrom, Charles H., 269
Baker, Ross, 135, 136, 144
Baldwin, David A., 263
Bandura, Albert, 150
Baratz, Morton S., 258
Bauer, Raymond A., 263
Bendiner, Robert, 201
Berkmann, Michael B., 15
Beth, Richard S., 117
Bibby, John F., 104, 180
Blondel, Jean, 38
Bolles, Blair, 193
Bolling, Richard, 19, 25
Bositis, David, 155
Brady, David W., 3, 6, 11, 24, 34, 47, 52, 57, 62, 63, 65, 94, 96, 190, 192, 261, 273
Broder, David S., 19, 160
Brown, Barbara Leavitt, 155
Brown, George Rothwell, 19, 24, 194
Bullock, Charles S., 11, 36, 265
Burnham, Walter Dean, 11, 47, 55
Burns, James MacGregor, 3
Burstein, Paul, 94, 102, 105
Busbey, L. White, 192
Butler, David, 58

Carmines, Edward G., 37, 84, 92
Chamberlain, Lawrence H., 30, 257
Champagne, Richard, 35, 207, 218
Cigler, Allan J., 283
Clausen, Aage R., 6, 18, 91, 92 (Converse), 96, 105, 259, 283
Clubb, J.M., 55, 59, 67
Cobb, Roger W., 25
Collie, Melissa P., 34, 117
Converse, Philip E., 92
Cooper, Joseph, 3, 6, 24, 25, 38, 48, 52, 54, 67, 96, 190, 192
Cover, Albert D., 110, 111, 112, 268
Crouse, Timothy, 156

Dahl, Robert A., 48, 263
Daniels, R. Steven, 96
Davidson, Roger H., 5, 19, 24, 36, 266
Deering, Christopher J., 14, 35, 208, 265, 277, 284
Dexter, Lewis Anthony, 5, 263 (Bauer)
de Sola Pool, Ithiel, 263 (Bauer)
Dodd, Lawrence C., 3, 4, 5, 7, 11, 23, 24, 25, 28, 35, 36, 37, 38, 187, 206, 209, 265, 266
Downs, Anthony, 114, 155

Easton, David, 258
Edelman, Murray, 258
Edwards, George C., III., 262
Ehrenhalt, Alan, 134
Elazar, Daniel, 59
Elder, Charles D., 25
Elder, Shirley, 263
Elwood, John W., 35
Erikson, Robert S., 15, 110, 111, 114, 116, 269
Eulau, Heinz, 268
Evans, Rowland, 5, 161

Fenno, Richard F., Jr., 5, 6, 14, 15, 16, 17, 37, 38, 53, 113, 142, 149, 153, 154, 163, 168, 169, 178, 181, 206, 262, 265, 268, 270, 277
Ferejohn, John A., 27, 35, 110, 224, 284
Fiorina, Morris P., 14, 17, 27, 29, 36, 114
Fishel, Jeff, 262, 267, 274, 283
Flanigan, W.H., 55, 58, 59 (Clubb), 67 (Clubb)
Foley, Michael, 144
Follett, Mary Parker, 189, 190
Fox, Harrison W., Jr., 24, 265, 283
Franklin, Daniel P., 14
Franklin, Grace A., 19, 37, 259, 275, 283
Frantzich, Stephen E., 265
Froman, Lewis A., Jr., 18, 266

Gallaher, Miriam, 191; 192, 193, 194 (Polsby)
Galloway, George B., 24
Gelb, Joyce, 283
Ginsberg, Benjamin, 57, 66
Goehlert, Robert U., 283
Goodwin, George, Jr., 265
Gwinn, William Rea, 194

Hammond, Susan Webb, 24, 265, 283

*Names in parentheses denote senior author for "et al." references.

Hardin, Garrett, 37
Hasbrouck, Paul Dewitt, 194
Hayes, Michael T., 259, 264, 283
Hechler, Kenneth W., 19, 24, 195
Heclo, Hugh, 275
Heifetz, Joan, 4
Heinz, John P., 259
Hershey, Marjorie Randon, 6, 19, 150, 154, 169, 283
Herzberg, Roberta, 207, 218
Hinckley, Barbara, 260
Horn, Stephen, 265
House Committee On Agriculture, 234, 236
Huitt, Ralph K., 5, 7, 53, 124, 267
Huntington, Samuel P., 3, 19, 14, 23, 25, 26, 36, 37, 38, 49, 257
Hurley, Patricia A., 96, 190, 269, 275

Iyengar, Shanto, 161

Jacobson, Gary C., 6, 14, 106, 117, 149, 181, 260, 261, 284
Jackson, John S., III, 155
Johannes, John R., 28, 269
Jones, Charles O., 7, 25, 179, 211, 263, 266
Jones, Rochelle, 4

Kadane, J.B., 252
Kaiser, Fred M., 35
Karps, Paul D., 268
Kayden, Xandra, 154
Keller, Bill, 165
Kelley, Stanley, Jr., 164
Kernell, Samuel, 106, 261, 284
Key, V.O., 53
Kiewiet, D. Roderick, 260
Kinder, Donald R., 161 (Iyengar), 260
Kingdon, John W., 6, 18, 25, 26, 38, 91, 149, 155, 170, 178, 181, 262, 263, 274, 283
Kofmehl, Kenneth, 265
Kritzer, H.M., 96
Kuklinski, James H., 15, 17, 148, 149, 168, 269

Lau, Richard R., 148 (Sears)
LeLoup, Lance, 266
Lenchner, Paul, 36
Leuthold, David H., 283
Light, Paul C., 258, 262, 274
Lindblom, Charles E., 258
Longley, Lawrence D., 37

Loomis, Burdette A., 9, 36, 267, 283
Lowi, Theodore, 19, 37, 50, 219, 259, 275
Lynn, Naomi, 94, 96, 261
Lyons, Michael, 35

Maass, Arthur, 37
Macrae, Duncan, Jr., 91
Maisel, Louis Sandy, 153
Malbin, Michael J., 35, 265, 283
Manley, John F., 5, 6, 11, 265
Mann, Thomas E., 9, 11 (Stevens), 14 (Stevens), 25 (Stevens), 49, 104, 108, 110, 111, 148, 180, 260
Markus, Gregory B., 148
Masters, Nicholas, 7
Matsunaga, Spark M., 265
Matthews, Donald R., 5, 134, 148, 170, 263, 267
Mayhew, David P., 5, 14, 38, 92, 110, 111, 112, 149
McCrone, Donald J., 269
Meier, Kenneth J., 264
Milbrath, Lester, W., 263
Miller, Arthur H., 9, 11, 14, 25 (Stevens)
Miller, Judith, 165
Miller, Warren E., 92 (Converse), 268, 269
Minns, Daniel, 114
Moe, Ronald C., 30, 257
Moe, Terry M., 37
Monroe, Alan, 269
Morrow, William L., 265
Moxley, Warden, 165, 167
Muir, William K., Jr., 5

Nadel, Mark, 283
Nagel, Jack H., 263
Nelson, Garrison, 7
Neustadt, Richard, 49
Nie, Norman H., 148, 155, 157
Novak, Robert, 5, 161

O'Connor, Robert E., 95, 97, 262
Oleszak, Walter J., 5, 19, 24, 36, 37, 207, 216, 267
Oppenheim, Felix, 263
Oppenheimer, Bruce I., 28, 35, 187, 204, 219, 283
Orfield, Gary, 35, 53, 96
Ornstein, Norman J., 11, 19, 37, 104, 144 (Rohde), 180, 263, 267, 270, 279, 284

Palley, Marian L., 283

Parker, Glenn R., 14, 35, 265
Parker, Suzanne L., 265
Patterson, James T., 11, 12, 19, 26
Patterson, Samuel C., 283
Peabody, Robert L., 5, 11, 144 (Rohde), 266, 267, 279
Perkins, Lynette P., 266
Peters, Mark D., 161 (Iyengar)
Petrocik, John R., 148
Ping Chen, 265
Pitkin, Hanna F., 268
Plattner, Andy, 162
Polsby, Nelson W., 3, 14, 23, 25, 28, 36, 134, 191, 192, 193, 194, 195
Pomper, Gerald M., 92
Poole, Keith T., 96
Price, David E., 5, 6, 265, 266, 283
Price, Douglas, 36, 265, 266, 283
Prindle, David T., 14

Redford, Emmette, 50
Rieselbach, Leroy, 25, 34, 38, 277, 283
Riker, William H., 263
Ripley, Randall B., 7, 19, 37, 195, 198, 211, 232, 259, 266, 275, 283
Robinson, James A., 218, 265
Robinson, William A., 189, 190, 191, 192, 193, 265
Rockman, Bert, 37
Rogers, Everett M., 170
Rohde, David W., 11, 19, 36, 144, 267, 279
Rundquist, Barry S., 3, 19, 191; 192, 193, 194 (Polsby)

Salisbury, Robert H., 138, 259, 283
Sayre, John R., 283
Schick, Allen, 35, 138
Schiff, Steven H., 19
Schlozman, Kay L., 283
Schneider, Jerrold E., 96
Schott, Richard L., 24, 35, 37, 206, 209
Schulman, Paul R., 258
Schwartz, Thomas, 252
Schwarz, John E., 4, 38
Scigliano, Robert, 37
Sears, David O., 148
Shaffer, William R., 96
Shaw, L. Earl, 4, 38
Shepsle, Kenneth A., 7, 138, 206, 224, 265, 283
Shoemaker, F. Floyd, 170

Sinclair, Barbara, 7, 34, 35, 47, 53, 94, 96, 179, 196, 198, 261, 266, 273, 283
Skowronek, Stephen, 37
Smith, Steven S., 14, 19, 34, 35, 96, 116, 208, 265, 277, 284
Sorauf, Frank, 48, 50
Stevens, Arthur G., 9, 11, 14, 25
Stewart, J., 47, 57, 63, 65
Stimson, James A., 84, 92, 170
Stokes, Donald E., 58, 92, 268, 269
Strom, Gerald, 3, 19
Sullivan, John L., 95, 97, 114, 262
Sullivan, Terry, 266
Sundquist, James, 3, 25, 26, 38, 96
Swenson, Peter, 14, 36

Tate, Dale, 162
Taylor, Marcia Whicker, 35
Teel, Steven C., 30, 257
Thurber, James A., 35
Tierney, John T., 283
Truman, David B., 263
Tufte, Edward R., 110, 261
Tullock, Gordon, 252
Tyler, Tom R., 148 (Sears)

Unekis, Joseph K., 277

Van Horn, Carl E., 283
Verba, Sidney, 148, 155, 157
Vogel, David J., 283
Vogler, David J., 266
Von Lohuizen, J.R., 264

Waldman, Sidney, 266
Walker, Jack L. 262, 283
Wayne, Stephen J., 262
Weingast, Barry R., 224
Weisberg, Herbert F., 94, 261, 279
Weissberg, Robert, 269
West, Darrell M., 15, 148
Westefield, Louis P., 7, 266
Wildavsky, Aaron 258
Wilson, Woodrow, 52, 265
Wissel, Peter, 36
Wolfinger, Raymond E., 4, 148, 260
Woll, Peter, 4
Wright, Gerald C., Jr., 15, 114, 116

Young, James S., 36

Zingale, N.H., 55, 58, 59 (Clubb), 67 (Clubb)